ENTANGLEMENTS OF EMPIRE

Entanglements of Empire

MISSIONARIES, MĀORI, AND THE QUESTION OF THE BODY

TONY BALLANTYNE

Duke University Press

Durham and London   2014

Designed by Heather Hensley
Typeset in Minion Pro by Westchester Publishing Services

Library of Congress Cataloging-in-Publication Data
Ballantyne, Tony, 1972–
Entanglements of empire : missionaries, Māori, and the question of the
body / Tony Ballantyne.
pages   cm
Includes bibliographical references and index.
ISBN 978-0-8223-5817-6 (hardcover : alk. paper)
ISBN 978-0-8223-5826-8 (pbk. : alk. paper)
ISBN978- 0-8223-7588-3(e-book)

1. New Zealand—History—To 1840.
2. Māori (New Zealand people)—Missions—History—19th century.
3. Great Britain—Colonies—History—19th century. I. Title.
DU420.12.B35 2015
993.02—dc23   2014023503

Duke University Press gratefully acknowledges the support of the University
of Otago, which provided funds toward the publication of this book.

Cover art: Detail of drawing by Cliff Whiting. Courtesy of the Waitangi Tribunal.
Digital image from Hocken Pictorial Collections.

— FOR CLARA

CONTENTS

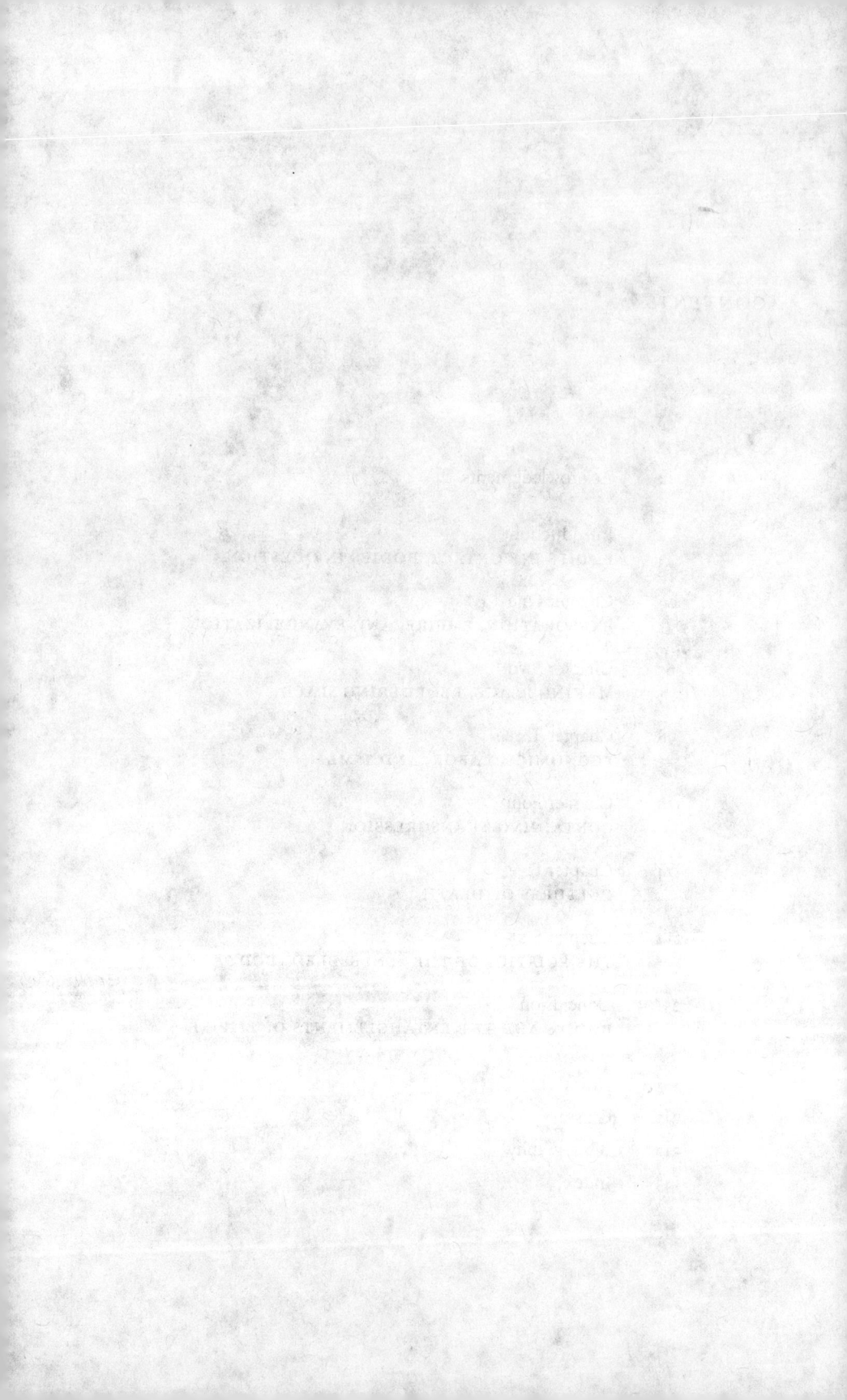

ACKNOWLEDGMENTS

This book has taken a long time. In fact, I began reading the archival material that this monograph is grounded in before I had ever contemplated becoming a professional historian. My first exposure to the encounters between missionaries and Māori in northern New Zealand came in a second-year honors history class taught at the University of Otago by Michael Reilly, who required his students to immerse themselves in missionary letters and journals. The excitement of that initial research experience, deciphering copies of missionary journals and, in some cases, handling their original letters, was profound, and it encouraged me to begin thinking differently about my own career path. In the fourth and final year of my honors degree I completed a dissertation on missionaries and sexuality in the Bay of Islands under the supervision of John Stenhouse. That year I worked through a range of early missionary sources and read widely in Māori anthropology and British religious history, an experience that convinced me to pursue a doctorate. To Michael and John I owe a great debt: as teachers they encouraged me and opened up new ways of thinking and writing.

I returned to those archives only after I had completed my doctorate in England and revised my dissertation for publication. A Millennium Fund research grant from the National University of Ireland, Galway, enabled me to extend my research on evangelicalism and empire, and after I took up a position at the University of Illinois, Urbana-Champaign, an Arthur Beckman

Distinguished Research Award kick-started my work on missionary sources and enabled me to return to New Zealand for research. In the later stages of the project, a Humanities Division Research Grant from the University of Otago helped me complete my archival work.

The manuscript bears the imprint of the work of many other scholars. In addition to Michael Reilly and John Stenhouse, my colleagues in the history department at Otago have shaped my work in a variety of ways: special thanks to Erik Olssen, Tom Brooking, Barbara Brookes, Brian Moloughney, Mark Seymour, and Angela Wanhalla. John Stenhouse remains a key early reader for all of my work that touches on religion. I am lucky to be a member of Otago's Centre for Research on Colonial Culture (CROCC), which has quickly developed into a dynamic group that nurtures new work on empire and colonialism. Lachy Paterson, a member of CROCC's steering group, has been a particularly generous colleague and helped me with some linguistic issues. I benefited as well from a couple of long conversations with Ryan Brown Haysom, an honors student at Otago, about my early work on William Yate. Ryan let me read his copies of the depositions relating to Yate and suggested that it was worth taking Yate's poetry seriously.

I am grateful to Damon Salesa for rekindling my desire to finish this book: he does not realize how much his encouragement, delivered as he drove me to the Detroit airport in 2010, is responsible for renewing my commitment to getting this book finished. Michael Stevens, Rachel Standfield, and David Haines all provided valuable responses to early parts of the manuscript, and it is my great good fortune to have Michael as a colleague now. Frances Steel and Lydia Wevers answered specific questions with grace, and, in quite different ways, their work has been important in spurring my commitment to placing questions of communication at the center of reflections on missionary work. Antoinette Burton continues to point me to new things to read and new analytical vantage points, which I greatly appreciate. For over a decade Alan Lester and I have explored similar research questions and methodological issues. I really appreciate Alan's engagement with my work and he remains an important scholarly fellow-traveller. I have also drawn encouragement and insights from the positive engagement of Penny Edmonds, Anna Johnston, Ann Curthoys, and Elizabeth Elbourne.

Portions of this project have been presented to a range of audiences at Griffith University (Brisbane); the University of Auckland; the Biennial Irish Historians Conference; the Anthropology Department at the University of Illinois, Urbana-Champaign; the Department of History and Art History at

Otago; and Otago's Te Tumu: the School of Māori, Pacific and Indigenous Studies.

I would also like to acknowledge the research assistance of Mary Stewart, Rachel Standfield, Elspeth Knewstubb, and, in the final stages, Katie Cooper: Katie painstakingly checked transcriptions and compiled the bibliography. In the winter of 2005 I received sterling assistance from New Zealand Historic Places Trust staff at their properties in the Bay of Islands and Hokianga, and Liz Bigwood was especially helpful. More recently, Rebecca Apperley from the trust has been generous in discussing the Church Missionary Society's New Zealand libraries. Les O'Neill, of the illustration unit in the Department of Anthropology and Archaeology at the University of Otago, did great service in producing the maps for the volume. Christine Rimene and Mark Brunton, successive Kaitakawaenga Rangahau Māori at Otago, advised me with regard to the research consultation process.

This work has drawn upon the knowledge and assistance of librarians and archivists in Britain, Ireland, the United States, Australia and New Zealand. I am particularly grateful to the staff of the Auckland War Memorial Museum and Library as well as the Alexander Turnbull Library, part of the National Library of New Zealand in Wellington. But my greatest research debts are to Hocken Collections at the University of Otago in Dunedin. The Hocken has an exceptional range of early New Zealand archives and printed works, with an incredibly rich collection of Church Missionary Society material, thanks to the intrepid endeavors of Dr T. M. Hocken himself. But it also has a wonderful team of archivists and librarians whose routine work makes publications like this possible and I would like to particularly acknowledge Anna Blackman, Katherine Milburn, the late David McDonald, Stuart Strachan, and Sharon Dell.

I was delighted to receive permission from the Waitangi Tribunal to use Cliff Whiting's striking depiction of the "imperial entanglements." I appreciate the approval of chief judge Wilson Isaac and the generous assistance of Jeff Abbott at the Tribunal. Whiting's response to my initial query was generous and supportive and his work speaks powerfully to many of the concerns that thread through the book.

I am especially grateful to my wonderful editor at Duke, Miriam Angress, not only for her expertise, but for her patience as well. As ever, the staff at Duke University Press have been a pleasure to work with. Danielle Szulczewski Houtz has overseen the production of the volume with great care and Patricia Mickelberry's assiduous copyediting helped to refine the final text.

This book owes a substantial debt to my wife, Sally Henderson. She was in Michael Reilly's history honors class where this project began: it is worth recording for posterity that her research essay on the mission was better than mine as she gained the top grade in the class. Although she took another academic path, her intelligent close reading over the years has greatly enriched this project. Our daughters, Evie and Clara, have encouraged me to finish this project, a book which I was supposed to complete soon after Evie was born, in late 2002. Clara's birth, in 2006, also slipped past with this book incomplete. I hope that they are all pleased to see it finally in the world. This book is for Clara, who will no longer have to ask for a volume dedicated to her.

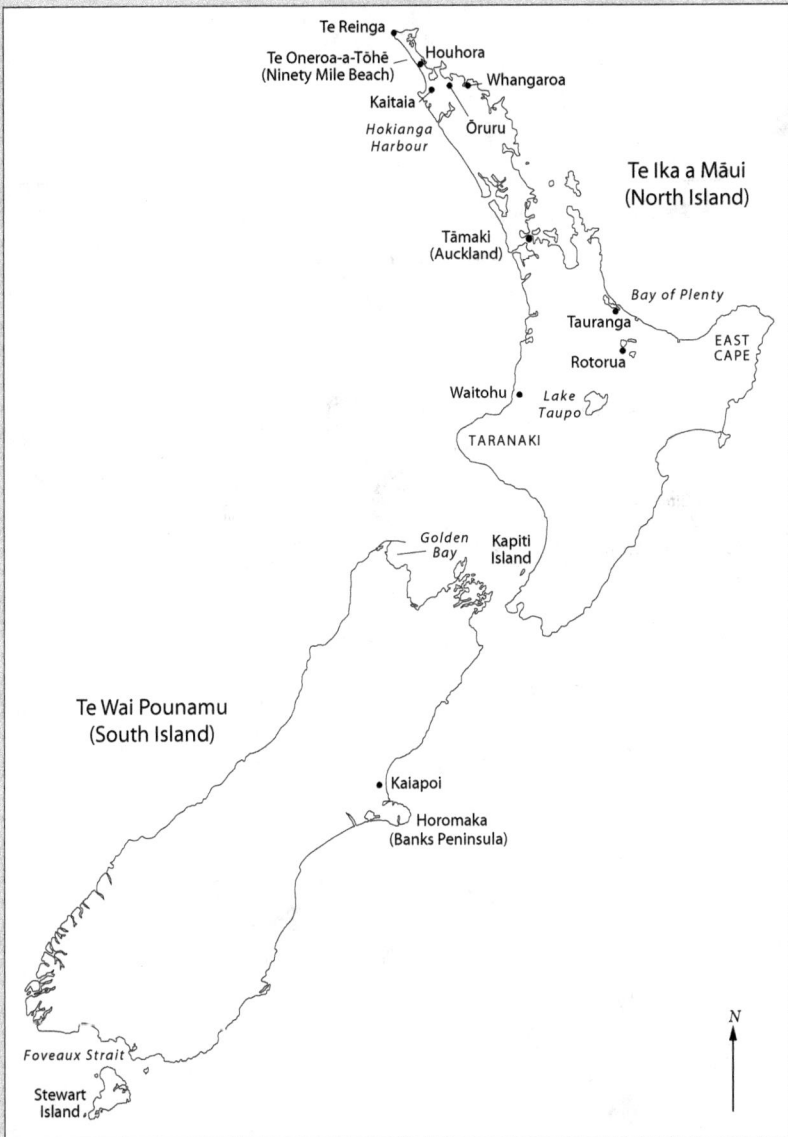

MAP 1 New Zealand

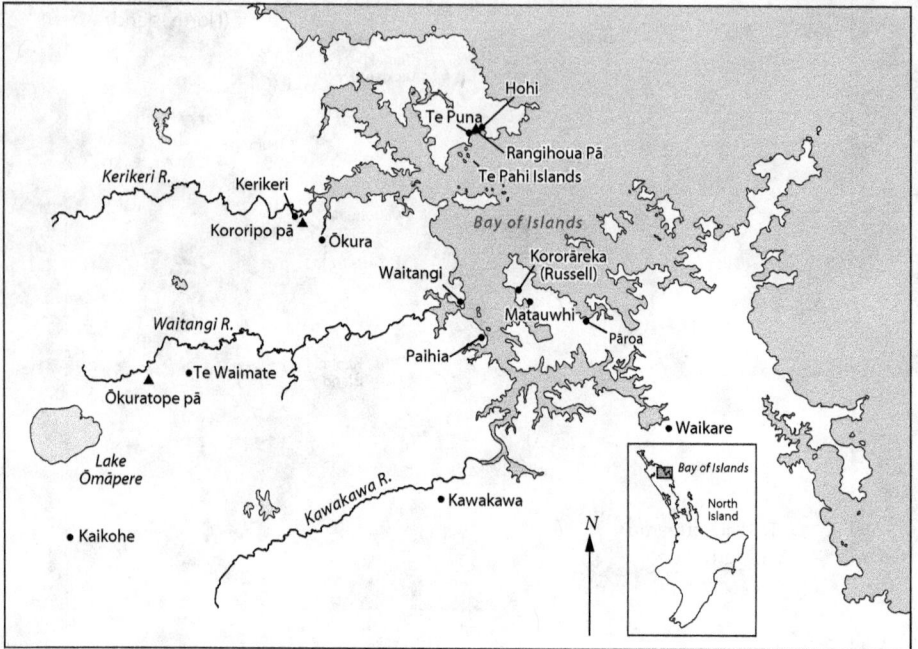

MAP 2 The Bay of Islands

Introduction BODIES IN CONTACT, BODIES IN QUESTION

Cross-cultural engagements have the power to initiate radical social change. Often fraught, rife with miscommunication, and marred by violence, encounters and entanglements between formerly unconnected peoples have frequently proven to be transformative moments in world history, occasions that have profound and often unexpected consequences, that are both material and cosmological. If we survey the last millennium of the global past, we see that such encounters have enabled the transfer of plants, animals, and germs, the diffusion of commodities and technologies, and the creation of a host of new trading relationships that created new forms of interdependence that linked previously disparate groups. These material exchanges have initiated far-reaching ecological modifications, as they have driven both tragic depopulation and sustained population growth, made fortunes and impoverished communities, and enabled the rise and fall of states and empires. Even though much historical work on cross-cultural encounters has documented their material consequences, both spectacular and horrific, we must not overlook the far-reaching but often elusive nature of the cosmological change that such meetings initiated. Meetings with newcomers, especially where those transitioned from brief encounters to lasting engagements, often undercut long-established pieties and created new spiritual orders. Encountering strangers has frequently called into question the power of "old" gods and their earthly representatives (from shaman to priests). This doubt created space for new gods, for new religious authorities, and for new visions of both the natural and supernatural worlds. Gods and their powers were the subject of crucial cross-cultural battles over meaning and frequently these struggles gave rise to particularly significant forms of innovation, as translation, appropriation, and reinterpretation produced new and unexpected forms of practice and belief.

In this book I examine the cross-cultural debates and entanglements set in motion by the establishment of Protestant missions in New Zealand in 1814, especially those arguments and engagements that turned on the ways in which the human body was understood and organized. Missionary work, which raised pressing questions about the body and its meaning as it tried to transform both the material and cosmological order of "native" life, developed in the wake of British imperial intrusion deep in the southern Pacific. The arrival of Lieutenant James Cook's *Endeavour* off Te Ika a Māui, New Zealand's North Island, in October 1769, punctured the long isolation that had conditioned the development of the Polynesian culture in New Zealand. In 1769, approximately 100,000 people lived in the islands that we now call New Zealand, a population that descended from the migrants who sailed south from the central Pacific around 1250 C.E. While this population shared common ancestors, spoke dialects of a common language, and had a common cosmology, they had developed a set of profoundly localized identities which were defined by the landscape, competition over valuable resources, and, above all else, *whakapapa* (genealogy). This cultural world was transformed by the arrival of Europeans, who appeared so strange and marvelous that they were initially called *tupua* (goblins), *pakepakehā* (fairy folk), or *atua* (supernatural beings). It was through the encounter with the overwhelming difference of Europeans—their unusual boats, their strange clothing, their unfamiliar languages, their unusual foods—that these Polynesian peoples who had long settled in New Zealand discovered the fundamental cultural commonalities that united them.[1] The new sense of their common way of life encouraged these communities to begin to define themselves by contrasting themselves with the strange outsiders who visited their world. They began to call themselves *tāngata māori*, the ordinary people, and with time, "Māori" became the term commonly used by both native and stranger to designate the first people who had made their home in the islands of New Zealand.[2]

Cook's arrival not only began to crystallize a new sense of "Māoriness," but also ushered in a new world, full of wonder, risks, and opportunities. In the wake of Cook, many European vessels visited New Zealand in search of timber and flax for shipbuilding or in search of seals and whales, which produced a range of commodities that were valued in industrializing Europe and that also might be used to pay for Europe's insatiable demand for Asian spices, tea, textiles, and porcelain. Through their engagements with these ships and their crews, most Māori communities learned about metal and the written word, and discovered a bewildering array of plants and animals (from potatoes to sheep, horses to cabbages). They also discovered the awesome power of European firearms and soon felt the terrible effects of the microbes, unseen and unknown, that were a largely uncontrollable part of the biological and cultural baggage that Europeans brought with them into the southern Pacific.

The Europeans who traveled to New Zealand before 1814 typically made only fleeting visits to a few regions: the far south of Te Wai Pounamu ("the Greenstone Waters," New Zealand's South Island); Cook's Strait between Te Ika a Māui and Te Wai Pounamu; the Thames area on the east coast of Te Ika a Māui; and the Bay of Islands in the far north of Te Ika a Māui (see map 1). Sailors and sealers had no intention of settling in New Zealand, and those who did briefly sojourn among Māori had no choice but to accept the power of Māori leaders and the authority of local lore and law. Conversely, the missionaries who arrived in the mid-1810s intended to remain in New Zealand, and their very motivation was the desire to effect cultural and religious change. They hoped that God would eventually allow them to "root out" those aspects of Māori life that did not fit with the injunctions of the Bible; they wanted to use the power of God's word to ultimately remake all Māori, to convert them into pious and God-fearing Christians. They understood that this was to be a difficult task, a great battle against both the weaknesses of the "heathen" and the power of Satan. In 1824, the wife of one leading missionary in New Zealand described this project as "Christian warfare with the great enemy of souls [Satan]!"[3] While they were confident that they would ultimately transform Māori society, as they entered the field missionaries expected to be tested, to be challenged by the "heathen," by immoral Europeans, by themselves, and by Satan himself.[4]

Progress was indeed slow for the missionaries, but even before large numbers of Māori began to convert in the 1830s, the missionary project began to effect significant change. Although Māori were initially wary about Christian teaching, they recognized that the presence of missionaries stimulated trade and made it possible for them to access valuable new technology. Metal tools were greatly valued as they allowed many traditional tasks to be completed more quickly and enabled land to be brought into cultivation with greater ease. But Māori also quickly realized that axes and hoes had further utility, that they could be deployed as potent weapons in hand-to-hand combat. Although the cross-cultural musket trade was a central point of contention in the mission, from the outset Māori associated these weapons with missionaries as Marsden had given the *rangatira* (chiefs) Korokoro, Ruatara, and Hongi Hika pistols and muskets, which quickly became key markers of the rangatira's *mana* (charisma, authority, power).[5] By establishing close relationships with missionaries, some chiefs, especially Hongi Hika, rapidly accumulated significant numbers of firearms, which they deployed in campaigns against local rivals and in a wave of long-distance raids to the south.

Most important, however, Māori were drawn to the missionaries because of their awareness of the power of literacy. Through their encounters with Samuel Marsden, at mission schools, through missionary itineration, and through the auspices of "native teachers," Māori learned how to read and write in their own language. The missionaries, of course, believed that these skills were essential for conversion and were the foundation for the construction of a "native church." For Māori, however, these skills not only allowed them to access the Bible, but also made possible an array of new forms of economic, social, and political activity. Some Māori used these skills to fashion their own understandings of scripture and developed distinct cosmologies and ritual practices: by the 1830s, the narratives of both the vernacular Old and New Testament had become an important store of metaphor, symbolism, and argument. Thus, even within the context of the increasing disparities of power that characterized frontier society, literacy and the Bible provided successive generations of Māori leaders with new skills and knowledge that could be turned against colonization. The radical potential of the Bible, particularly when wrenched free of missionary control, was clear; as one Māori bluntly stated in 1843, "This is my weapon, the white man's book."[6]

But vectors of cultural transformation did not flow only one way. Anglican and Methodist missionaries who lived with and among Māori while they worked on the frontier were also transformed by the experience. No matter how much they hoped to recreate British models of Christian faith, the Christian family, or civilized sociability, they made their new home in a land that would never be Britain. On the furthest frontier of the empire, the great bulk of their congregationalists and fellow Christians were Māori, not Britons. The missionaries initially lived in houses built on Māori models and constructed with local materials, and even after they were able to construct "civilized" British houses, their domestic arrangements never simply replicated British models. Māori were omnipresent in the mission station and in mission houses. Māori "girls" provided essential domestic labor for the mission, preparing food, cleaning and washing, and acting as nannies. Māori men accompanied missionaries on their expeditions, guiding them, providing physical labor, and teaching them about the history of the land, how they understood the workings of nature and the supernatural, and how indigenous social life was organized. On the mission stations, Māori men worked closely with missionaries as "native teachers," as increasingly skilled workers (sawyers, carpenters, and farmers), and as laborers, and were frequent visitors to mission houses. So even though propagandists imagined missionary stations as little models of England, the great weight of historical evidence suggests that Māori frequently dictated the rhythms of missionary life and were quite successful in indigenizing the mission station as a space.[7]

At the same time as the physical presence of Māori was an inescapable part of the missionary world, missionaries were also drawn into the mental world of Māori. In order to Christianize Māori society, missionaries first had to grasp the operation of essential social laws, develop a basic understanding of local politics and kin-group rivalries, and gain linguistic competence in spoken Māori. Te reo Māori (the Māori language) was the functional language of the mission. It was the language of native service, the language of educational and social instruction, and the primary idiom of cross-cultural communication. Most important, it was the language of scripture. Missionaries labored long and hard, individually and collectively, on the massive project of translating the Bible into te reo Māori with the aspiration of creating a clear and idiomatic rendering of God's word into the local vernacular. This vast undertaking, which took decades, not only reshaped the linguistic underpinnings of Māori mentalities and transformed Māori political idioms, but also changed the missionaries themselves. Listening, speaking, and writing te reo Māori modified the linguistic and mental worlds of the missionaries. Not only did many missionaries come to write a moderately creolized form of English that made routine use of Māori words and phrases, but the study of Māori language also suggested to some missionaries that deep affinities connected Britons and Māori, despite the manifold differences in the patterns of their everyday lives. Some leading missionaries even became convinced that the British and Māori peoples were long-lost cousins, members of an expansive racial family that was diffused across the face of the globe but who were ultimately connected by their common Indo-European or Aryan linguistic and racial heritage.[8]

Many advocates of colonization were critical of these missionary beliefs and argued that this immersion in the Māori world undercut the national and imperial allegiance of missionaries. They argued that missionaries, especially those who openly opposed the plans for the large-scale settlement of New Zealand formulated by the New Zealand Company, had become "philo-Māoris" ("Māori lovers") who were intent on preventing the extension of colonial authority and the effective "amalgamation" of settlers and Māori.[9] Even though British Protestant missionaries played a key role in the intensification of cross-cultural contact on the New Zealand frontier, boosters of imperialism saw the missionaries' commitment to the creation of a "native church" grounded in the Māori Bible as indicative of their betrayal of true British interests.

Bodies in Contact, Bodies in Question

My particular concern in this book is the place of the body in the exchanges between Protestant missionaries and Māori. At a fundamental level, this focus reflects the ubiquity of the body in the archival records of these encounters. The body is a recurrent concern in the early letters of Māori Christians, as well as in missionary journals, letters, travel narratives, and pamphlets. In this large and diverse archive, the body was mobile and polysemic. Early converts to Christianity blended indigenous metaphors with biblical imagery to explain their struggle to embrace Christianity. In a letter written in the early 1830s, a man named Wariki wove together the *ngārara*, the evil lizard of Māori mythology, with the New Testament's identification of the heart as the seat of the conscience and the core of an individual's character to explain that despite his best efforts, he had not yet been able to accept Christianity.[10] "My heart is all rock, all rock, and no good thing will grow upon it. The lizard and the snail run over the rocks, and all evil runs over my heart."[11]

For their part, missionaries constantly worried over the body. They believed that remaking Māori bodies was an essential part of the missionary project. Māori had to set aside practices, such as slavery, tattooing, and cannibalism, that some missionaries saw as evidence of Satan's continued power in New Zealand. Yet bitter experience taught the missionaries that effecting such changes would be very difficult, and they were forced to make a range of accommodations to these practices. In many ways, it was the less spectacular and more routine struggle to reshape Māori social arrangements that was at the center of the missionaries' drive to remake Māori culture. They worked very hard to encourage Māori to give up polygamy and to embrace Christian marriage as the basis for the sexual, social, and economic order. Missionaries also hoped to inculcate new models of work, hygiene, and comportment through mission schools and the exemplary model of the missionary family. In short, the reform of the indigenous body was an indicator of the spiritual advance of the mission. Missionaries were also concerned about the extent to which their calling imperiled their own bodies; they routinely reflected on the physical consequences of the heavy labor, constant walking, and poor diet that accompanied missionary work. Many dwelled at great length on the threat of illness and the dangers of childbirth, for even though the early missionaries in New Zealand ultimately produced large families, it seemed that death was never far from their door. Others worried about their ability to resist the physical temptations posed by the isolation of missionary life and the power of the culture that surrounded them.

Tā moko, or tattooing, demonstrates the ways in which cross-cultural engagements raised questions about the meaning and management of bodies. Missionary texts, especially those from the early years of the mission, dwelt on this custom and frequently suggest that tattooing had to be set aside if Māori were to truly embrace Christianity and if they were to progress toward "Civilization."[12] For example, Samuel Marsden in 1819 told the young but well-traveled rangatira Tuai that tā moko "was a very foolish and ridiculous custom; and, as he [Tuai] had seen so much of civilized life, he should now lay aside the barbarous customs of his country, and adopt those of civilized nations. Tooi [Tuai] replied, that he wished to do so himself; but his Brother urged him to be tattooed, as otherwise he could not support his rank and character as a gentleman among his countrymen, and they would consider him timid and effeminate."[13] Tuai's argument that tā moko was a crucial element of the projection of his chiefly authority confirmed the links between status and tattooing that many European observers had drawn by this time. Other rangatira went further than asserting the importance of the practice in representing rank and power, turning the mirror of cultural reflection to question British bodily practices. John Liddard Nicholas, a supporter of the foundation of the New Zealand mission, reported that when the rangatira Te Pahi was challenged about tā moko during a visit to New South Wales,

> he immediately censured some of our own [practices] as far more ridiculous, and many of his arguments were both rational and convincing. Like most of the New Zealand chiefs, he was highly tattooed, a mode of disfiguring the face which is generally practised by all the savage tribes in the Pacific

Ocean. The barbarous process consists in pricking on the face with a sharp instrument, a variety of semi-circular and other figures, and rubbing into the punctures a kind of blue paint, or sometimes charcoal, which gives the countenance a most disgusting appearance, and makes it truly hideous to the eye of an European. On being laughed at one day by a gentleman for having disfigured his face in so unnatural a manner, the sagacious chief immediately retorted with pointed sarcasm; telling him he was quite as much an object of derision himself for having put powder and grease in his hair, a practice which he thought was much more absurd than the tattooing.[14]

For Nicholas, this exchange confirmed Te Pahi's "shrewdness of remark" and "nicety of discrimination" and was suggestive of the abilities of Māori in general.[15] Nicholas's ambiguous response to tā moko, which suggested that it was simultaneously an uncivilized practice and incontrovertible proof of the dexterity and great skill of Māori, was echoed in the Church Missionary Society's *Missionary Papers* issued in September 1816. In its discussion of the rangatira Hongi Hika and Te Uri o Kanae, *Missionary Papers* recognized that tā moko was a key marker of chiefly status and went on to argue that its complexity and precision established that Māori were an "intelligent and skilful race of men."[16] Some later missionaries suggested to British audiences in the 1830s that the mission had "forbidden" the practice, but in reality missionaries generally had to accommodate themselves to the importance of tā moko: their school pupils and congregants would travel to be tattooed by tohunga tā moko (tattooing experts), and the practice continued to be strongly connected to rank and status in the 1830s.[17]

As these exchanges suggest, missionary sources from early New Zealand are punctuated by a deep and recurrent concern with the body, its meanings, and its regulation, and these reflections were frequently contradictory, ambivalent or ambiguous. Although the image of the repressive missionary is well established in New Zealand historiography and is firmly embedded in the nation's popular imagination, missionary archives themselves bear out the limitations of what Michel Foucault termed the "repressive hypothesis."[18] Foucault argued that contrary to popular stereotypes that imagine the nineteenth century as being characterized by a powerful impulse to repress everything to do with the body and sex, sexuality was in fact increasingly dwelt upon, spoken about "ad infinitum," albeit in terms that were carefully circumscribed and encoded.[19] There was, Foucault contends, a powerful new "institutional incitement" to discuss the body and sex, a desire to record and analyze behavior through "endlessly accumulated detail."[20]

Foucault's insistence on the ways in which power produced increasingly detailed forms of knowledge and new debates over the body is an important starting point for this study. In this work, however, my discussion is not restricted to the history of sexuality, a line of inquiry that is profoundly indebted to Foucault's pioneering work. Frequently the history of sexuality is seen as a rough equivalent of history of the body, a formulation that both reflects the flourishing historiography on the history of sexual practices and regimes and constrains the possibilities offered by historical readings of the body.[21] The body, of course, is the most fundamental and fluid of signifiers; the body can evoke birth and death, work and play, illness and health, as well as being mobilized as a metaphor of the abstract conceptualization of political relationships, national communities, and religious institutions.[22] And, of course, in addition to functioning as a potent signifier, the body is the most material of all "realities," providing communities with productive labor, reproductive capacity, and the ability to make war.

Kathleen Canning has observed that historical research has tended to focus on the body's operation as a signifier in processes of nation building and its operation as an "inscriptive surface" for the promulgation of morality, hygienic reform, and state power.[23] While this study remains alive to the symbolic power of the body, it is also framed against this tendency to dematerialize the body. At the heart of this book is a set of struggles over the materiality of the body, over its physicality, over its most basic operations in time and space, and its centrality to the experience of new models of work, faith, and cosmology. Rather than offering a narrow examination of the construction of sexuality on the New Zealand frontier or a deconstructive reading of European representations of the indigenous body, *Entanglements of Empire* examines a diverse array of *practices* surrounding the body as well as the many and variable ways that the body was *represented* and incorporated into discourse. This opens up the possibilities of writing a more mobile and flexible history of the body: in thinking through the body I pay close attention to the development of new commercial connections and work patterns, the spatial organization of mission stations, and the impact of "new" diseases on Māori, as well as reconstructing debates over the consequences of cross-cultural sexual relationships, the meaning of death, and the effects of empire on the native body.

But this book is not only trying to treat the material and discursive body with equal care; it is underpinned by a commitment to reconstructing the collision between two very different sets of understandings and practices relating to the body. Even though Foucault's arguments about the relationship between power and the body in *The History of Sexuality* are a starting point for this study, I am not offering a reading of imperial history through Foucault or formulating a rereading of Foucault through the prism of empire. Laura Ann Stoler's *Race and the Education of Desire* has both recovered the centrality of race in Foucault's late work and used Foucault's writings on sexuality to explicate the politics of intimacy at the margins of empire. Stoler's history of empire and sexuality, however, ultimately operates as an essentially European story of the production of the bourgeois self, where the production of eroticized Others in the colonies is refracted back to the metropole and plays a crucial role in the constitution of "internal frontiers" of European nations.[24]

My aim is quite different: rather than using the colony to illuminate European history, my central aim is to reconstruct the collision between two cultural regimes that were grounded in radically different understandings of the body, its social organization, and its cosmological significance. Thinking about "bodies in contact" requires the historian to explore how these engagements between radically different cultural orders raised fundamental questions about bodies, their management, and meaning.[25] Throughout this volume, I consistently emphasize the particularity of both Māori and British bodily systems, while remaining committed to tracking the uneven but very real transformation of both bodily systems on the New Zealand frontier. A more conventionally post-Foucauldian reading of the engagements between missionaries and Māori would struggle to deal with the profound cultural difference and social transformations that were the governing fact of life on early mission stations. The complex and mixed history of these sites—a central concern of this book—cannot be reconstructed by solely placing the mission within a genealogy of European religious history or by framing mission stations within a narrative that reconstructs the transformation of European epistemes. Such a project might have been viable had mission stations been institutions where British modes of life were largely re-created and where missionaries exercised hegemony over "native Christians." But despite the wishes of the missionaries themselves, mission stations in New Zealand were never sites where Europeans enjoyed unquestioned authority: missionary religious teaching, the mission's program of social reform, and the daily regimes of work and prayer were all open to contest and negotiation. Until a least the late 1830s, missionaries operated within a world where chiefly authority still held sway, where most Māori customs and laws were upheld, and where te reo Māori was the lingua franca.

Most important, missionaries largely worked within a Māori world defined by the workings of atua and the power of *tapu*. It is important to discuss these terms here not only because they are central to my analysis, but also because even a brief sketch of these concepts suggests the profound epistemic gap that initially divided Māori and Europeans. The term *atua* is frequently translated as "god"—it was applied to major deities like Tāne (god of the forests), Tū-mata-uenga (god of war), and Tāngaroa (god of the sea)—but its meaning was more expansive than this. Atua could take on many forms, ranging from deified ancestors to malevolent spirits. Unusual phenomena in the natural world (geysers, lightning, comets, rainbows, even unusually shaped or colored rocks and trees) were understood as atua or manifestations of the power of atua. The German traveler Ernst Dieffenbach pithily communicated the broad nature and function of these supernatural agents: "*Atuas* are the secret powers of the universe."[26] Atua were not distant entities sequestered in the supernatural realm, but rather were in constant contact with people and landscapes of *te ao mārama* (the world of light) across the thin and permeable boundary that separated the natural from the supernatural world.

Tapu describes the influence of atua over people, the natural world, and inanimate objects. This term, the root of the English concept of "taboo," is commonly translated as "sacred," and it designates those things that are set apart from daily life. Within the Polynesian world, tapu was one key physical manifestation of the work of atua in physical world. Many of the realities of human physicality—from the growth of hair and fingernails to headaches, the physical sensations accompanying fear to the male erection—were explained as the work of atua. The power and status of high-ranking chiefs was both a result of the constant influence of atua on their persons and a reflection of their tapu status.[27] This tapu was not simply restricted to the body of an individual, but rather "leaked" into their surrounding social world and was transferable. The dwellings, sleeping places, and clothes of the chiefs were highly tapu. The possessions of a rangatira—pendants, combs, treasured feathers—were very tapu and were frequently stored in *waka huia* (treasure boxes) that were hung off the rafters in a highly tapu position within the rangatira's whare (dwelling). Tapu could also be transferred through bodily fluids (especially blood) and contact with hair.[28] The superabundance of the tapu state of powerful rangatira and *tohunga* (ritual experts) meant that their shadows could wither trees or render food inedible.[29]

Tapu was balanced by its antonym, *noa*. Noa referred to things that were removed from supernatural influence, that were unrestricted, unclean, or profane. These states of being organized everyday life. They determined who was able to prepare food and the ways in which it was prepared. The operation of tapu and noa governed sleeping arrangements within whare (houses), dictated the rituals associated with tattooing and hair-cutting, and governed the spatial organization of settlements. Not surprisingly, these concepts also underpinned the ways in which Māori dealt with illness, death, and human remains. When Cook arrived in New Zealand, tapu and noa were absolutely fundamental in shaping understandings of the body in all its states and these concepts were at the heart of most important social and ritual practices.

Tapu and noa were also profoundly important in defining gender within the Māori world. Women were generally understood to be noa, and this meant that a certain set of particular social and ritual roles were appropriate for them. They were best suited to handling food and to carrying out any sort of labor that might expose a tapu male to any agent that might defile him. Because of their noa status, women could strip men of their tapu and their power. At times, this ability was harnessed for ritual purposes: visitors who entered *wharenui* (meeting houses) passed under carved female figures upon the *pare* (lintels), the noa status of these female figures removing the tapu qualities that were transmitted to individuals who had been inside the tapu-charged space of the house. The oppositions between male (tapu) and female (noa) were complicated because particular women could be tapu or a woman might be tapu for a particular period of time. A high-ranking daughter, for example, might be designated as a *puhi*, a tapu young woman whose chastity was strictly policed until the time of her marriage to an approved partner.[30] Ultimately, however, as the Māori feminist Ngahuia Te Awekotuku has argued, the operation of tapu meant that within precontact society typically "women were the negative and destructive element, the inferior, the passive."[31]

Māori understandings of the body were highly particular and supported a set of bodily practices that were very different from those carried to New Zealand by British evangelicals in the service of the Church Missionary Society (CMS) and the Wesleyan Missionary Society (WMS). A range of cultural influences shaped early nineteenth-century missionary understandings of the body. Strict control of the body and sexual desire was an essential element of the "world-mastery" that evangelicalism promoted. Evangelical sermons and pamphlets frequently dwelt on the need to master the self, to curb one's pride, and to reject (and repent for) sinful urges. Evangelicalism held that the individual must regulate worldly activity by disciplining the body through careful dress, the avoidance of excess alcohol, and hard work. The only legitimate outlet for sexual desire was within marriage, the structure ordained by God for the legitimate expression of sexuality. Evangelicals saw the sacrament of marriage as a safeguard against the indolence and chaos implicit in the indulgence of erotic desire.[32]

It has been commonplace to contrast the complex laws and strong regulation of sexuality that shaped missionary mentalities with the supposedly more "natural" place of sex within the Māori world, but it should be clear that Māori understandings of the body were just as highly enculturated as those of their missionary counterparts.[33] We must recognize that the Māori body does not belong only to the realm of culture, but is also amenable to historical analysis as well. Māori ways of organizing the body were not rigidly constrained by an unchanging culture, but rather were adaptable and dynamic. In this volume I offer an array of evidence that demonstrates that various Māori individuals and groups shaped and reshaped core practices and beliefs relating to the body as they actively engaged with missionaries, European traders, and early settlers. The outcomes of these engagements were manifold as a greater variety of bodily practices developed among Māori as contact progressed. Some *iwi* (tribes) remained largely isolated from contact and thus maintained old traditions, while other groups responded to the challenges of contact and missionization in a variety of ways. Some "went mihinare (missionary)" and reworked long-established bodily practices, especially those related to sexuality and death, as they embraced key elements of the Anglicanism, Wesleyanism, and, at a later stage, Catholicism. Other individuals and groups were drawn to the Bible, but rejected missionary authority and fashioned profoundly indigenized visions of Christian faith and practice. These new movements, which were a powerful force in *te ao Māori* (the Māori world) from the 1830s through to the early twentieth century, offered radical new interpretations of the place of the social and cosmological significance of body. These ranged from a distinctive brand of flagellant Christianity based on a very particular reading of 1 Corinthians 9:27 ("But I keep under my body and bring it into subjection") to an attempt to order village life around a strict interpretation of Mosaic law (where various transgressions were punished by stoning).[34]

I therefore offer a reading of the struggles over the body that developed as missionaries sought to transform Māori culture. Even though the missionaries were driven by a deep commitment to effect social and religious change, these encounters must not be understood through a simple challenge-response model wherein missionaries are imagined as active agents, while Māori stand as objects of historical processes. In the end it was Māori desire for contact with Europeans, their interest in agriculture, literacy, and muskets, and the support of powerful rangatira that enabled the foundation of the CMS mission in 1814. The early missionaries quickly found that they had at best a limited understanding of the communities they were ministering to and had even less ability to dictate the outcomes of their efforts to promote agriculture, to encourage commerce, and to foster the growth of Christianity. In fact, what emerges from early missionary texts is not a sense of mastery and confidence, but rather a persistent anxiety that conveys a very strong sense of what Ranajit Guha has termed the "rebel consciousness," the desire and power of various Māori individuals and groups to shape their own fortunes and to protect their own interests even as they were increasingly drawn into connection with the missionaries and mission stations.[35]

Archives and Historiography

Guha's argument is also an important starting point for my approach to the archives. Guha suggested that colonial writing, particularly what he termed the "prose of counter-insurgency," was imprinted by that "rebel conscious-ness" even if the aim of such texts was to justify imperial intervention or shore up colonial authority. In *Entanglements of Empire*, I take some cues from this approach, seeing missionary texts produced on the ground in the Bay of Islands as situated texts, inflected by their location and conditions of production. This means that missionary texts are not read as seamless projec-tions of a coherent and self-contained ideology, but rather as products of the interaction between evangelical worldviews, the sensibility and experience of individual missionaries, and their particular engagements with specific places, individuals, collectives, and events. By being seriously committed to recovering the porousness of missionary texts and how they were molded by local developments, historians can explore both the nature of Māori social action—even if this is accessed through thoroughly highly mediated texts—and the ways in which such action imprinted missionary understandings of events and the nature of Māori society. Reading missionary sources at the edge of the empire in this way allows the historian to break free from a nar-row focus on cross-cultural representation, where European or British texts come to read primarily as part of European ideological, intellectual, and tex-tual systems, which are typically understood to be in a position of cultural dominance over indigenous populations. Most important, when historians read Māori as active shapers of both missionary texts and real social forma-tions, they cannot write Māori themselves out of the history of these imperial entanglements or simply reduce them to being objects of Western discourse.

The value of such an approach has recently been demonstrated by Alison Jones and Kuni Jenkins's popular history of early Māori writing, *He Kōrero: Words between Us*, which has reframed our understanding of the first texts written and printed in te reo Māori. Jones and Jenkins recover the early history of Māori as creators of texts, language teachers, and cross-cultural commentators. In *Entanglements of Empire*, I not only make use of the limited but significant corpus of early Māori writing, but also draw on Jones and Jenkins's reassessment of the authorship and meaning of some key "missionary-produced" texts. Most notably, they suggest that *A Korao no New Zealand: Or, the New Zealander's First Book* (1815) was not a work simply produced by the missionary Thomas Kendall, as commonly suggested, but that this volume was "a remarkable product of Māori teaching" and that it was at the very least a kind of co-production between missionary and Māori.[36] I do not, however, extend this perspective to all missionary printed texts in general; in fact, *A Korao no New Zealand* and the 1820 grammar produced by Kendall and his Māori patrons, teachers, and translators are very particular products of cross-cultural collaboration. While other missionary texts were shaped by such engagements, a great deal of popular missionary print culture was highly processed. Letters and journals hastily written at the edge of empire were condensed, edited, and substantially reworked, as metropolitan editors prepared texts with the expectations and sensibilities of their British evangelical readers in mind; not surprisingly, the routine trials and anxieties of missionary life or the uncertain self-reflections that stud evangelical journals rarely made it into British publications designed to educate, entertain, and solicit funds. And, as I show in chapter 4, missionaries in New Zealand were well aware of the nature of those expectations, and some missionaries, such as William Yate, produced narratives about the mission and Māori that accorded too closely to those metropolitan conventions—at the expense of the particularities and messiness of life in the Bay of Islands—for the comfort of their peers.

In reading the mission archives, I have been committed to the value of Greg Dening's maxim that "*both* the native and the colonizing side of the encounter are owed *both* a history and an anthropology."[37] I have attempted to treat both evangelical missionaries and Māori equitably, imagining both of these collectives as complex agglomerations of individuals and interest groups whose actions and worldviews were conditioned by *both* culture and history. Following this strategy, I at times explore in detail particular aspects of both missionary and Māori cosmologies, offer lengthy readings of their different understandings of time, and reconstruct their very different attitudes toward death and the afterlife. Throughout, however, I also stress the dynamic and contingent nature of these engagements. Because *Entanglements of Empire* is framed by an insistence that engagements on imperial frontiers were acts of negotiation and translation, I stress the fluid and often mercurial nature of power relations in early New Zealand. The struggles over resources, space, and cultural meaning set in train by the establishment of mission stations were not structured by a simple opposition between Māori and missionary, but rather power flowed in a multiplicity of directions between an array of social actors who grounded their allegiances in a variety of concerns and interests.

Over the last fifteen years, a rich vein of work by New Zealand scholars on these cross-cultural histories has emerged. Much of this scholarship has been framed by a more rigid understanding of "encounters" than Dening offered, reconstructing the meetings between Māori and Britons as moments when relatively fixed and stable cultures came together. Anne Salmond imagined the earliest of these meetings as the collision of "two worlds," while she framed the 1773–1815 period as a set of exchanges "between worlds."[38] Beyond their rich rematerialization of the archives of these "meetings," these works by Salmond have been important because they have offered an elegantly crafted prehistory of the relationships between Māori and Pākehā that stand at the center of New Zealand's state ideology of biculturalism and which shape so much recent cultural and intellectual production. Other important recent studies of cross-cultural history have also worked within this analytical frame. Most notably, Vincent O'Malley's recent reassessment of early New Zealand's history, in *The Meeting Place*, imagined a kind of national prehistory of Māori and Pākehā leading up to the Treaty of Waitangi, the nation's "founding document." This is an approach that nationalizes messy and quite divergent localized pasts by imagining New Zealand as a "place" and that underplays the transformative consequences of imperial entanglements. Salmond and O'Malley are important, however, because they have pushed against the rather simple mission-centered models of social change that structured the earlier historiographical debates over the timing, extent, and meaning of Māori "conversion." Such interventions are important because a narrowly missionary-focused vision of social change continues to shapes some recent work on the place of gender in the mission, which simultaneously suggests that missionary women were silent or invisible and yet were key agents in establishing a hegemonic European moral and gendered order.[39]

This book is animated by a dissatisfaction with readings that stage the cross-cultural history of the Bay of Islands as a story of missionary cultural hegemony or which flatten out the dynamics of social engagement and trans-formation into a story of "meetings" or "encounters," analytical concepts which underplay the lasting consequences of being incorporated into empires. Throughout this volume, I suggest that imperial networks generated new entanglements, which wove previously disparate groups into new relationships of interdependence. As an analytical metaphor, "entanglement" alludes to my earlier work that has demonstrated that the British empire was a dynamic web-like formation, a complex and shifting assemblage of connections that ran directly between colonies.[40] "Entanglement" thus reminds us that empires were incorporationist regimes, which drew resources, land, skill, labor, and knowledge into expansive systems of extraction and exchange. Once communities were connected to these webs of interdependence, it was often hard for them to assert control over the direction and consequences of the cultural traffic that moved through these meshes of connection. And once incorporated into the reach of empire, however partially and fitfully, the consequences of cross-connection could not be erased: while thinking about empires through the metaphors of "meetings" and "encounters" allows us to imagine stable and discrete cultural formations existing *after* cross-cultural engagements, the metaphor of entanglement draws attention to the durable consequences that flowed from the integrative work of expansive imperial regimes. The image that adorns the cover of this volume was produced by the influential Māori artist and carver Cliff Whiting (Te Whānau-ā-Apanui) and it speaks directly to the ways in which imperial encounters and the formal colonization of New Zealand created new patterns of culture as te ao Māori (the Māori world) and the customs of the British were drawn together and interwoven in new and durable, if unpredictable, ways.[41]

Conceptualizing the operation of empires and the persistence of their cultural impact in such a manner echoes and parallels some significant South African work that has also mobilized metaphors of "entanglement."[42] Carolyn Hamilton's important work on Shaka Zulu mobilized entanglement as a way of making sense of the colonial order: rather than seeing colonial institutions and practices as a transplantation and imposition of European norms, she argued that they were instead the outcome of the "complex historical entanglement of indigenous and colonial concepts."[43] More recently, Sarah Nuttall has attempted to bring entanglement as a cultural state and as an analytical strategy from the wings to the center of scholarly practice: "Entanglement is a condition of being twisted together or entwined, involved with; it speaks of an intimacy gained, even if it was resisted, or ignored or uninvited. It is a term which may gesture towards a relationship or set of social relationships that is complicated, ensnaring, in a tangle."[44] Nuttall's project was to illuminate not only the entanglements that shaped South Africa's cultural landscape, but also those that conditioned its historical emergence, highlighting the "intricate overlaps," "seams," and connective membranes that generated contingent but powerful forms of connection which frequently remained unacknowledged and uninterrogated.[45]

Such work has resonated beyond South Africa. Lynn M. Thomas's examination of the politics of reproduction in Kenya, for example, has deployed Hamilton's arguments about the entangled nature of colonial formations as a way of foregrounding the continued uneven interplay and interdependence between "local and imperial" concerns and forces.[46] Thomas's stress on the unevenness of these forms of interdependence is useful. We can think of the entanglements that reshaped communities and places as knot-like structures which laced together various vectors of motion and different lines of cultural influence.[47] But, of course, knots are not necessarily symmetrical and stable: they can be messy and uneven; they can join threads of uneven thickness and strength together; they can exert differential pressures on different elements of the juncture; and they can ultimately slip and fail or, alternatively, cut hard into a particular cinch point. Given the inequalities that structured empires, the operation of these points of convergence and conjuncture often enriched and empowered the agents of empire in the long term and destabilized or undercut the indigenous formations that had been laced into the expansive world of imperial connections.[48]

Thinking through entanglement has powerful possibilities in the New Zealand context, where racial identities (Māori vs Pākehā) and the opposition between the "Crown" and Māori (or particular tribes) produce neat dichotomies that shape contemporary political debate and continue to undergird much historical writing. These oppositions reflect the ways in which ideologies impose clear meanings on messy cultural fields; any careful reading from the archive destabilizes such tidy pictures of the present or the past. As I argue, it is almost impossible to define any common set of "Māori interests" in the north of New Zealand that unified a large number of kin groups between 1814 and 1840, as complex and shifting connections and conflicts structured the life of the indigenous communities. Long-standing grievances and rivalries, new power blocs shaped by uneven access to European weapons, technologies, and food-plants, and the deep rifts between powerful chiefs and large populations of slaves molded the ways in which various Māori individuals and kin groups responded to evangelization. At the same time, the Europeans who settled on the frontier before New Zealand's formal annexation in 1840 were also riven by religious and class differences, and there were especially prominent conflicts between the men who came to New Zealand as sealers, whalers, sailors, and runaways and the "respectable" Europeans associated with missionary activity and, at a later stage, the British Residency. Tracing the lines of fracture and reconstructing the fragile ties of common interest that structured this social landscape are central concerns in my account of "bodies in contact." Throughout the text, I underscore the continual changes that shaped and reshaped these social formations, emphasizing the ways in which key events—from chance meetings to massacres, from unexpected deaths to the building of ships—could have a host of unforeseen outcomes and could seemingly speed up time itself, as important social processes and their outcomes accelerated.[49]

A Plan of the Book

This volume is not a traditional narrative history of the development of missionary work, even if there is a chronological progression from the first chapter, which deals with the period up to the middle of 1810s, to the last chapter, which focuses on the period between 1830 and 1840. I explore certain key problems that troubled missionaries and fundamental points of cross-cultural engagement: housing, work, trade, sexual transgressions, illness, and death. Therefore, I discuss certain important events at several points in the volume, as I analyze their meanings for different debates or social dynamics. In part because this is not a narrative history, I have not framed it as a prehistory of New Zealand as a nation, leading up to 1840, when those islands were finally formally absorbed into the British empire (even though my analysis does end around 1840). *Entanglements of Empire* is fundamentally a work of British imperial history, which examines the relationships and processes that incorporated the north of Te Ika a Māui and the Māori communities of that region into British commercial and imperial networks long before formal colonization began. At several points, I explore other parts of Te Ika a Māui and Te Wai Pounamu, where important developments elsewhere impacted on the north or broadly reshaped the ways in which Māori or New Zealand were understood. In a similar vein, my primary focus is on the CMS mission, but I do discuss the activities of the Wesleyans (whose mission was formally established in 1823) when they illuminate key aspects of missionary work or the dynamics of cross-cultural engagement. In keeping with my earlier work on the British empire, I reject a narrow analytical frame that prioritizes Britain and "Britishness" and, therefore, attach substantial analytical weight to indigenous social formations, cultural practices, and histories.[50] At the same time, however, I have not framed this volume as a history of *hapū* (subtribes; clans) and iwi: I do not use whakapapa (genealogy) as an organizing analytical tool, even though I stress the importance of genealogy at many points. My understandings of the development of cross-cultural engagements and the progress of missionary work in and around the Bay of Islands does draw heavily from works produced within a tribal frame, primarily Jeffrey Sissons, Wiremu Wi Hongi, and Pat Hohepa's landmark study of indigenous kinship and politics, *The Pūriri Trees Are Laughing*.

I begin *Entanglements of Empire* by offering an assessment of the ways in which both imperial ambition and the evangelical aspiration to remake the world shaped European, but especially British, visions of New Zealand, its resources and peoples, until around 1820. In chapter 1 I offer a brief sketch of European exploration of the southern Pacific and the early contacts between European expeditions and Māori. In addition to establishing the historical context for the remainder of the volume, I set out in this chapter two very important arguments. First, I suggest that during the later eighteenth century, Europeans developed a body of information and a set of arguments about "New Zealand" that were framed by an insistence on the islands' potential as a site for imperial extraction and colonization. This knowledge fed imperial interest in New Zealand, and from the 1770s on, various propagandists, including Benjamin Franklin, elaborated schemes to enable the incorporation of New Zealand into the British empire. Most important, this developing imperial discourse on New Zealand was central in shaping the plans of Samuel Marsden, who was initially appointed as assistant chaplain to the colony of New South Wales and who subsequently became an influential architect and manager of British missionary activity in the Pacific. I demonstrate how Marsden's assessments of both Māori and New Zealand drew on long-established discourses of "civilization" and "empire," as well as trace how Marsden's establishment of a CMS mission in 1814 was enabled by the commercial structures, institutions of governance, and bodies of knowledge established by British imperial endeavor in the Pacific from 1768 on. Second, I suggest that the genesis of the New Zealand mission must be also be understood within the framework of Māori history, especially the shifting political and cultural landscape of the far north of New Zealand's North Island. In particular, I reconstruct the relationships that influential rangatira such as Te Pahi and Ruatara established with Europeans as they attempted to harness the new technologies, skills, and commodities that they could access through cross-cultural trade, in order to cement and extend their chiefly influence within a fractious and highly competitive world of indigenous politics and warfare. I highlight the divergence between Marsden's aspirations and the motivations of these Māori leaders, but ultimately suggest it was willingness of these rangatira to extend their protection and patronage to Europeans that was absolutely foundational to the beginnings of Christianity in New Zealand.

Where in chapter 1 I highlight the place of the body in European arguments about the ability of Māori to embrace Christianity and "Civilization," in chapter 2 I turn to explore the development of mission stations in the Bay of Islands in the 1810s, 1820s, and early 1830s. In offering a reading of these institutions as distinctive spaces, I focus on the ways in which evangelicals envisaged mission stations as embodying Christian ideals of social relationships and religious practice. I show how these models reflected a powerful of set of evangelical ideas about space and the marked divisions they envisaged between sacred and mundane spaces, public and private realms, the domains of men and women, the worlds of children and adults. In chapter 2 I demonstrate, however, that the pressures exerted by both the limited resources of the mission and the persistence of Māori ideas about space meant that mission stations were never exemplary sites of Christian life or European civilization, but rather were culturally mixed spaces whose boundaries and meanings were always open to contestation.

In chapter 3 I offer a close reading of the failure of Marsden's plan to uplift and convert Māori through the introduction of the "civilized arts" to New Zealand. I highlight the absolute centrality of the body in Marsden's vision of socioeconomic transformation and reconstruct the ongoing battles over labor on the mission stations. My analysis places particular emphasis on the importance of time-discipline in Marsden's vision of the civilizing process and how the ability of Māori to dictate their terms of employment on mission stations until at least the mid-1820s undercut Marsden's plan. I conclude the chapter, however, with a discussion of the growing impact of missionary models of cosmological time in the late 1820s. Some Māori communities in the Bay of Islands and Whangaroa began to accept the authority of the Sabbath when missionaries were finally able to achieve a degree of economic independence and increasingly positioned themselves as agents of cultural change whose were no longer dependent on chiefly patronage.

In chapters 2 and 3 I really offer critical readings of the limited nature of the disciplinary regimes fashioned by missionaries and the accommodations that they were forced to make as they negotiated an often precarious series of cultural bridgeheads. In chapter 4 I extend this line of argument, revealing the moral precariousness of the mission and its deep anxieties around sexuality, status, and race through an analysis of missionary sexual transgressions, especially the contentious case of William Yate. Yate was alleged to formed an "unnatural" affection with one, or perhaps two, fellow male travelers sailing back to the Pacific from a visit to Britain. These allegations encouraged Yate's brethren in New Zealand to investigate the nature of his relationships with his Māori pupils and congregationalists. This investigation revealed substantial evidence that Yate had established ongoing sexual connections with a large number of Māori boys and men, relationships that had a commercial nature as Yate dispensed "gifts" of tobacco to his intimates. In chapter 4 I sketch the outlines of Yate's transgressions, before offering a sustained reading of the extended debates over intimacy, conjugality, and sexuality that his actions set in train. These anxious exchanges between British evangelicals, Marsden, and missionaries on the frontier reveal core moral values and deep-seated assumptions that structured evangelical understandings of family, faith, and sexuality. With regard to Yate, I place particular emphasis on how his former colleagues dwelt on Yate's betrayal of the particular moral responsibilities that were seen as a fundamental aspect of missionary work and how they sought to sever all of the mission's tangible connections with Yate, as they constructed Yate as a subhuman and unnatural figure. Most important, I demonstrate that while the transgressions of Yate were very real challenges to the theory and practice of missionary work, missionaries in New Zealand invested great effort in reinscribing the boundaries that he crossed, reaffirming the absolute centrality of the Christian family in the religious and social order.

In the final two chapters I shift from the questions of bodily discipline to consider the cosmological and political questions raised by illness and death on the frontier. In chapter 5 I focus on the contest over death on the frontier in the 1820s and 1830s. The question of death was crucially important to the missionary practice because it raised both profound cosmological questions about the nature of the body and a complex set of problems relating to the rituals surrounding death and the management of human remains. I begin the chapter by exploring the place of death within evangelical thought and the profound difficulties that the missionaries grappled with as they attempted to transplant their established deathways to New Zealand. In charting these compromises, I uncover significant new insights into the cultural dilemmas at the heart of evangelical work at the edge of empire, as well as into relationships between missionaries and Māori. I then turn to reconstructing the development of missionary knowledge about Māori death-ways, suggesting that the open and "public" nature of many of these practices were of particular value to the missionary project of conversion because they offered an important window into Māori cosmology when many other customs and beliefs relating to the supernatural were difficult for the missionaries to access. I conclude by exploring the ways in which missionary narratives around Māori illness and death were "composed" and ordered for metropolitan readers, revealing the very different ends of knowledge-making in the metropole and at the empire's edge.

I extend this line of argument in chapter 6, where I examine the imperial politics of death. My particular focus is the production and dissemination of images of suffering Māori and the growing political significance of this form of representation within metropolitan politics in the 1830s. By this time, the dominant image of Māori circulating in Britain was that of an "enfeebled" people, wracked by disease and conflict, and exposed to the "vices" of whalers, traders, and convicts. In addition to reading these "humanitarian narratives" against the backdrop of a particular evangelical form of the culture of sensibility, I highlight the political utility of these accounts by humanitarian reformers and evangelical propagandists. These narratives were initially used to oppose the extension of imperial activity in New Zealand, especially the plans of the "systematic colonizers" who hoped to plant substantial settlements of Britons in New Zealand. I emphasize the profound political outcomes of this form of representation, arguing that the insistence on the "enfeebled" nature of Māori ultimately provided a powerful rationale *for* colonization, as the extension of British law and the construction of supposedly highly ordered colonies were seen as important instruments that would "protect" Māori interests. The signing of the Treaty of Waitangi, in February 1840, reflected this understanding of colonization as a form of "protection," protection that came at a high price. New Zealand was finally formally incorporated into the British empire, and the sovereignty of Māori chiefs was highly circumscribed.

In traversing a wide array of themes and reconstructing a sequence of expansive cross-cultural debates over the body, I have written this book as an extended exercise in the type of "multiple contextualization" that George Stocking advocated.[51] Because I am committed to recovering the polysemic nature of the body, in this volume I think beyond sexuality, to grapple with the histories of space and time, faith and work, illness and death. Thus, *Entanglements of Empire* offers an expansive history of the body, traversing a wide range of thematic contexts in its attempt to recapture the manifold significance of the body in these meetings between Britons and Māori, but it is also framed by a desire to rematerialize the complexity and richness of these cross-cultural engagements. Each chapter is substantial and draws on a diverse array of archival and published material. Most important, each chapter is underpinned by a shifting and mobile analytical gaze that enables us to follow lines of communication and movement between New Zealand, Australia, and Britain, as well lingering on particular places (from Rangihoua to London, from Port Jackson to Paihia) and communities (from the evangelically inclined parishes of West Yorkshire to Te Hikutu hapū in the Bay of Islands).

Framing my analysis within these multiple thematic, geographical, and social contexts not only highlights the diverse range of actors and influences that shaped the social entanglements that began to knit Britons and Māori together on New Zealand's frontiers, but it also recognizes the distinctiveness of each of these sites. The "new imperial history" has emphasized the manifold connections between the metropole and the colonies, as well as emphasizing the hybrid nature of imperial social formations. *Entanglements of Empire* works within this tradition, yet at the same time it places a very strong emphasis on the particularity of each of these sites and communities. The dense webs of exchange fashioned by imperial activity connected disparate points across the globe into new and highly uneven systems of interdependence, entangling previously disparate communities in new and often fraught relationships. As I demonstrate repeatedly in *Entanglements of Empire*, the work of these integrative networks did not produce a homogenizing "global overlay."[52] The engagements and entanglements generated by these connections shaped and reshaped the particularities of each locale within the empire. At the same time, new forms of difference were generated out of the frictions that were attendant to the routine forms of cultural mobility, conversation, and translation that underwrote life in a global empire.[53] The impact of such imperial networks and exchanges on British culture has been much debated over the last twenty years by historians of empire, but even as it is an important intellectual and political endeavor to rediscover the diverse imperial linkages that shaped Britain, that project must not overshadow our commitment to understanding the cultural impact of missionary work and colonization at the edge of empire, nor the costs and consequences of empire-building for colonized peoples. In writing the history of the British empire, we must not privilege the metropole or British perspectives and lose sight of the weight, complexity, and specificity of the history of non-European locations and colonized communities. This book is animated by a desire to rematerialize the local histories as well as global connections that shaped the engagements between Britons and Māori and to recover both the accommodations and conflicts that arose when two radically different bodily cultures came into contact at the most distant frontier of the British empire.

One EXPLORATION, EMPIRE, AND EVANGELIZATION

I n order to understand the debates and transformations enacted by the meeting and entanglement of the very different bodily cultures of British evangelical missionaries and Māori, we need to locate these engagements within the broader framework of the cross-cultural relationships produced out of the European intrusion into the southern Pacific. In this chapter I sketch the encounters and entanglements that brought Māori and Europeans into connection and New Zealand's incorporation into the discourses and economic networks of the British empire during the late eighteenth century and early nineteenth. The four decades of imperial endeavor in this region that predated the establishment of the CMS mission in 1814 set the key parameters that shaped the ways in which Britons imagined both New Zealand's place within the empire and the nature of Māori society. Most important, this history of imperial exploration and commerce encoded Samuel Marsden's plan for the New Zealand mission and his vision of the types of social change that missionaries could enact. Thus, rather than follow historians, such as Andrew Porter and Brian Stanley, who have suggested that the evangelical ethos placed missionaries outside the mainstream of British imperial culture, I highlight Marsden's significant debt to an imperial set of discourses on the nature of "civilization" and his very real reliance on imperial commercial networks and the instruments of the colonial state in New South Wales.

In rejecting a simple "religion versus empire" formulation, I return missionary institutions to the broader field of empire, to what Mrinalini Sinha has termed the "imperial social formation."[1] This is not to argue for an undifferentiated reading of empire—which would see missionaries, merchants, and military men as part of an unified imperial project—for we must not conflate the aims and outcomes of missionary activity with the imperial visions of the Admiralty, Colonial Office, London merchants, or the colonial state in New South Wales simply because they share a common "British heritage." Rather, seeing missionary activity *within* an imperial framework allows us to strike a balance between an awareness of the particularity of the cultural vision underpinning the foundation of the CMS mission in New Zealand and acknowledgment of the ways in which Marsden's project drew on an earlier history of British activity in the Pacific and utilized the knowledge, institutions, and commercial structures produced by this activity.

With these aims in mind, I first examine the European "discovery" of "New Zealand," arguing that European understandings of this large archipelago of islands and its inhabitants were underpinned by interest in the Pacific as a sphere for empire-building. Much of the recent work on encounters between Māori and Europeans in the late eighteenth century and earlier nineteenth has seen these cross-cultural engagements as anticipating the bicultural social formations that have become central to state policy and national identity in New Zealand.[2] Rather than using the dominant ideology of the late twentieth-century nation state as an analytical lens, I place greater emphasis on the significance of imperial desire—for knowledge, land, resources, and strategic advantage—in bringing Europeans to New Zealand's shores and on the role of this quest for power in framing both New Zealand and Māori within a discourse of "imperial potentiality." Building on this argument, I examine the importance of the region in British evangelical thought and the ways in which missionary activity in New Zealand shaped imperial discourses and structures. After briefly sketching the place of the Pacific in the writings of influential English evangelicals in the late eighteenth century, I focus on Samuel Marsden's development of a plan for a mission to Māori. My reading of Marsden shows his dependence on imperial commercial networks, political structures, and discourses on cultural difference. I place particular stress on the importance of both labor and consumption in shaping the very divergent readings he developed of Māori and Aboriginal cultural capacity. As well as locating Marsden's thought within these discourses on civilization and improvement, I suggest that the personal relationships that leading Māori rangatira (chiefs)—such as Te Pahi and Ruatara—established with Marsden were crucial in convincing him of Māori potential and of the viability of a mission to New Zealand.

So while viewing missionary endeavor within the "imperial social formation" allows us to trace what Stoler and Cooper termed the "tensions of empire" or what Jeffrey Cox has seen as "imperial faultlines"—the fractures, points of tension, and competing visions of empire articulated from within the colonizing culture—the history of missionary activity in New Zealand also has to be seen as standing at the juncture of imperial history and Māori history.[3] Although it was Marsden's debt to post-Enlightenment and evangelical thought that encouraged him to believe that Māori were capable of embracing the "Gospel of Civilization," the genesis of the mission must be also read within the trajectories of Māori history.[4]

Not only was Māori patronage and protection essential to the establishment of the mission, but rangatira initially drove the development of these cross-cultural engagements. The efforts of Bay of Islands' rangatira to foster missionary activity occurred within two main contexts. First, by the early nineteenth century, Māori leaders in the far north were aware of the opportunities for enhancing their wealth and mana (status, power, authority) that contact with Europeans presented. The plants, animals, and tools introduced by Europeans were highly valued, not simply because they were "new," but because they aided the chiefs in discharging two of the essential responsibilities of chieftainship more effectively: the production of food and conducting war. Second, the very specific configuration of indigenous political power in the early nineteenth century encouraged these chiefs to place particular value on relationships with Europeans, including missionaries. From the late eighteenth century, two competing alliances of kin-groups were struggling to establish their economic and political hegemony over the Bay of Islands's fertile fields, rich estuaries, and sheltered bays.[5] A complex series of military campaigns and reprisal raids were a central feature of this political contest, and within this context, Europeans—with their access to metal, new weapons, and food items—became a potent new factor within the complex and tense terrain of indigenous politics.

Exploration and Empire

The rivalries in the Bay of Islands were the outcome of long histories of migration, settlement, intermarriage, and competition over valued resources. These processes were driven by entirely local forces: for the six or seven centuries that had passed since the north of Te Ika a Māui (New Zealand's North Island) was settled by Pacific peoples from the region that we now describe as East Polynesia, these communities had been isolated from the rest of the Pacific and the rest of the world. Their life and identity were invested in the local land- and seascapes, and their possession of this new homeland was undisturbed by outsiders.

Most important, Te Ika a Māui remained a mystery to Europeans. That is not to say that Europeans did not contemplate the southern oceans, but rather that their actual knowledge of the Pacific Ocean remained negligible. At least since the time of Ptolemy (around 150 A.D.), the geographers, historians, and theologians of the Mediterranean world and Europe speculated on what might lie to the south of the known world. Ptolemy himself suggested that an "unknown land" existed to the south of Eurasia, and he believed that this landmass was large enough to "enclose the Indian sea." This vision of a large and undiscovered continent persisted in European geographical thought during the medieval period and was elaborated during the Renaissance. The extension of Europe's commercial and imperial reach into the Atlantic and its discovery of direct maritime routes around the Cape of Good Hope and into the Indian Ocean expanded European knowledge of the world. Within this context of exploration, the growth of cartography, and European empire building, the notion of an unknown southern continent was consolidated within European thought. It was believed to be large; it had to match the northern landmasses of Europe, Asia, and the recently "discovered" North America in order to produce the symmetry and order that were discernible in the physical world.[6]

The southern continent—Terra Australis Incognita, as it was widely known—was both an integral element in early modern European geography and a potent imperial fantasy. As the value of long-distance trade in spices and Asian finished goods (such as silk and porcelain), the profits made from slave-trading, and the economic importance of new world plantations and mines transformed European states and their economies, European powers were increasingly alive to the commercial and strategic benefits of empire-building. The fevered imperial imaginations of geographers, merchants, and royal advisors imagined Terra Australis as an untapped treasure house, overflowing with precious stones, gold and silver, spices, and as yet undiscovered commodities of value. This imperial fantasy was fed by the first expedition of Alvaro de Mendaña (which discovered the Solomon Islands, in 1568) and his second expedition with Pedro de Quirós (which discovered the Marquesas and the Santa Cruz Islands, in 1595). These discoveries were tantalizing, convincing the Spanish explorers that they had discovered the edges and outliers of a substantial landmass roughly equivalent to Europe and Asia in size.[7]

While Quirós pursued this phantom again in a 1605–6 expedition that discovered the New Hebrides, other European powers were also drawn to this quest. In fact, from the middle of the sixteenth century, English proponents of empire had advocated expeditions to search for the southern continent and enthusiastically imagined an empire greatly enriched by the wealth of Terra Australis.[8] But it was the Dutch who took the lead in this project. Where the Iberian powers and Britain's East India Company had well-established commercial enclaves in the Asia-Pacific region at the start of the seventeenth century, the Dutch were keen to establish a secure presence in the "East Indies" and its adjoining territories. In 1606 officials of the Vereenigde Oostindische Compagnie (the VOC, or Dutch East India Company) in Bantam sent the *Duyfken*, under the command of Willem Janszoon, to search for "east and south lands," initiating a sequence of voyages that revealed much new detail of the islands of southeast Asia and the coastline of northern and western Australia.[9]

Eager to expand their commercial domain, the council of the VOC in Batavia sponsored another voyage in search of the "Unknown South-land" in 1642. In their instructions, the council emphasized their hope that the voyage would result in a discovery equivalent to that of the Americas, which had allowed the "kings of Castile and Portugal" to possess "inestimable riches, profitable tradings, useful exchanges, fine dominions, great might and powers."[10] The VOC dispatched the *Heemskerck* and the *Zeehaen*, under the command of Abel Janszoon Tasman, to explore the southern latitudes of the Indian and Pacific Oceans, advising him to chart in detail any newly discovered lands and to ascertain what valuable commodities and resources were to be found there.[11] The expedition set out from Batavia, paused in Mauritius, and from there, after the vessels had been refitted, sailed southeast. In late November 1642, the explorers "discovered" the landmass now known as Tasmania, which they named "Anthonij Van Diemens Landt," after the governor of Batavia. After making brief forays ashore and skirting the coast of Tasmania for several days, the *Heemskerck* and the *Zeehaen* sailed eastward in search of further evidence of the "South-land."

On 13 December 1642, this Dutch expedition sighted "a large high elevated land" as they approached the west coast of the landmass that Māori knew as Te Wai Pounamu (the home of Pounamu), what is now known as New Zealand's South Island.[12] The *Heemskerck* and the *Zeehaen* sailed north-

FIGURE 1.1 Gilsemans, Isaac, fl 1630s–1645?. A view of the Murderers' Bay, as you are at anchor here in 15 fathom (1642). *Abel Janszoon Tasman's Journal.* Amsterdam, Friedrich Muller & Co, 1898. Ref: PUBL-0086-021, Alexander Turnbull Library, Wellington, New Zealand.

east along the coastline, on 18 December 1642 rounding the large twenty-mile-long sandspit at the northern tip of the island, a spit which guarded the entrance to a wide open bay. This bay, which is now named Golden Bay, was known as Taitapu (the Tapu Coast) by the Ngāti Tūmatakōkiri people, who had migrated to the northwest of Te Wai Pounamu from their original tribal home in the central part of Te Ika a Māui (the North Island).[13]

The encounter between Ngāti Tūmatakōkiri and the Dutch was tense and full of miscommunication: the *haka* (action dance) and ritual challenges that Ngāti Tūmatakōkiri issued to the Europeans were met with warning cannon fire. Violence erupted when a large *waka* (war canoe) rammed the cockboat of the *Zeehaen*, knocking one sailor overboard, and the warriors swiftly killed three of the sailors and fatally wounded another (see figure 1.1). After hauling one of their victims onto the waka, the warriors quickly paddled to shore, avoiding the gunfire from the *Heemskerck*. Both ships subsequently opened fire on the eleven waka that had set out toward the Dutch vessels and then set sail.[14] The *Zeehaen* and the *Heemskerck* skirted up the west coast of the North Island, only pausing briefly in the Three Kings group, off the northern tip of the North Island. The crew of the cockboat that was sent ashore on "Great Island" in this group encountered people who resembled those they had met in Golden Bay, but these northern people were distinguished by their great height and extremely long stride. These giant men were well-armed and pelted the Dutch sailors with stones (see figure 1.2).[15] The Dutch beat a hasty retreat and *Heemskerck* and the *Zeehaen* sailed off into the Pacific.

On the basis of this initial engagement, this chain of islands, which Tasman named Zeelandia Nova, seemed to have little imperial potential. In clinging to the west coast, the *Heemskerck* and the *Zeehaen* got only a partial view of the islands' true geography: they saw abruptly rising mountains, few harbors, and beaches pounded by heavy surf, while the sheltered anchorages, coastal plains, and rich estuaries of the east coast remained out of view. Nor were there any signs of the great wealth that they hoped to find on the "Southland." Most important, the local population appeared aggressive, intractable, and eager to defend their land. Establishing trading relationships appeared to be an unlikely prospect, and gaining access to any valuable commodities— especially the gold and silver that the voc were so keen to discover—seemed even more improbable. The death of four sailors at the hands of Ngāti Tūmatakōkiri and the hostile reception given to the landing party in the Three Kings meant that Māori entered European imperial archives as a warrior race, a fearsome people who were, as Tasman observed, the "enemies" of Europeans.[16] Zeelandia Nova left only a faint impression of those archives. Tasman's journal suggested that at Taitapu the Dutch "could not expect to make here any friendship with this people, nor Would water and supplies be obtained."[17] Only a fragment of New Zealand's coastline was inscribed on European maps, and what was known was hardly inviting: Taitapu, the home of Ngāti Tūmatakōkiri, was named Moordenaers Baij (Murderer's Bay) by Tasman.

Thus, although it was imperial ambition that brought the Dutch to Te Ika a Māui and Te Wai Pounamu, Zeelandia Nova seemed ill-suited for imperial endeavor, and it was over 125 years before the next European visited the islands. On 6 October 1769, the hms *Endeavour*, under the command of Lieutenant James Cook, sighted the east coast of Te Ika a Māui. The *Endeavour* was ostensibly dispatched to the Pacific as part of the global effort to take observations of the transit of Venus, an exercise in international scientific cooperation that was coordinated by Britain's Royal Society.[18] But Cook received two sets of instructions from the Admiralty in July 1768: the first informed Cook that he was to sail to Tahiti—which had recently been "discovered" by Captain Samuel Wallis—to undertake the observation of the transit. The second additional set of secret instructions entrusted Cook with an important imperial mission.

Staten Landt Bezvlt en Ontdekt met de Scheepen Heemskerk en de Zeehaen onder het Commando van den E. Abel Tasman. in den Iaare 1642. Den 13 December.

Aldus vertoont zich het Drie Koningen Eyland, als gy het aen de Noort West Zyde op 40. Vademen van uw heeft.

FIGURE 1.2 The *Zeehaen* and the *Heemskerck* encounter Māori at Three Kings Islands. Gilsemans, Isaac, fl 1630s–1645?. Aldus vertoont zich het Drie Koningen Eyland, als gy het aen de Noort west Zyde op 40 Vaedemen van uw heeft. F. Ottens fec. direxit. (Amsterdam, 1726). Valentyn, Francois. Oud en nieu Oost-Indien. Amsterdam, 1726. Volume 3. Ref: PUBL-0105-004, Alexander Turnbull Library, Wellington, New Zealand.

Whereas the making Discoverys of Countries hitherto unknown, and the Attaining a Knowledge of distant Parts which though formerly discover'd have yet been but imperfectly explored, will redound greatly to the Honour of the Nation as a Maritime Power, as well as to the Dignity of the Crown of Great Britain, and may tend greatly to the advancement of the

Trade and Navigation thereof; and Whereas there is reason to imagine that a Continent or Land of great extent, may be found to the Southward of the Tract lately made by Captn Wallis . . . [y]ou are to proceed to the southward in order to make discovery of the Continent above-mentioned until you arrive in the Latitude of 40° unless you sooner fall in with it. But not having discover'd it or any Evident signs of it in that Run, you are to proceed in search of it to the Westward between the Latitude before mentioned and the Latitude of 35° until you discover it, or fall in with the Eastern side of the Land discover'd by Tasman and now called New Zeland.[19]

The Admiralty directed Cook to build up an archive of materials relating to the lands he explored: to produce detailed coastal charts; to record the soil, mineral resources, flora and fauna; and to assess the character of the local peoples they encountered.[20] Cook and his officers assiduously discharged this brief during their six-month visit to New Zealand. Cook's detailed coastal charts, Richard Pickersgill's plans of various bays and anchorages, Herman Spöring's detailed coastal views and his sketches of material culture (waka [canoe] prows and *hei tiki* [amulets in the shape of humans]), and Sydney Parkinson's portraits of tattooed warriors and drawings of haka, waka crews, and fishing practices provided a rich and textured visual archive. These images produced a detailed record of the islands' coastal geography, emphasized the sophistication of Māori gardening and material culture, and represented Māori as a warrior race (see figure 1.3).[21] And the work of the voyage's naturalists—Banks, Spöring, and Daniel Solander—in collecting and classifying a massive array of plants, birds, insects, and marine life was a potent manifestation of the spirit of the Enlightenment and underscored the value that such knowledge had for imperial commerce. Tupaia, an *arioi* (ritual expert) from Ra'iatea, mediated some of this knowledge, as he functioned as a valuable source of navigational expertise, an effective translator, and an at times critical cultural commentator on Māori for the *Endeavour*'s officers.[22]

Imperial Potentiality

But Cook and his crew were not only drawing on Tupaia's expertise and their own observations to generate a new archive of knowledge about these previously "unknown" people and lands in the spirit of enlightened inquiry. The close empiricism that suffused the ethnographic, linguistic, botanical, zoological, and cartographic knowledge produced by the *Endeavour* voyage was intimately connected to the question of empire. Cook, Banks, and their

Plate XV

J. Parkinson del.   *T. Chambers Sc.*

A New Zealand Warrior in his Proper Dress, & Compleatly Armed, according to their Manner.

FIGURE 1.3 Parkinson, Sydney, 1745?–1771. A New Zealand warrior in his proper dress & compleatly armed according to their manner. Parkinson del. T. Chambers sc. (London, 1773). From *A Journal of a Voyage to the South Seas, in his Majesty's ship, "The Endeavour." Faithfully transcribed from the papers of the late Sydney Parkinson* (London: Printed for Stanfield Parkinson, the editor, 1773). Ref: PUBL-0179-15, Alexander Turnbull Library, Wellington, New Zealand.

fellow travelers actively assessed New Zealand's potential both as a source of naval stores and as a colony. Banks emphasized the fine quality of New Zealand's timber supplies, particularly in the Thames region, which he described as "the straightest, the cleanest, and may I say the largest I have ever seen."[23] In a similar vein, Banks was keenly aware of the value of New Zealand's abundant and high quality flax for Britain's navy and industrial producers, stressing that because it was "so useful," it was "a plant [that] would doubtless be a great acquisition to England."[24] More broadly still, Cook himself was clear on the utility of the islands to Britain and imagined the establishment of a British colony in the islands: "It was the opinion of every body on board that all sorts of European grain fruits Plants &c would thrive here. In short was this Country settled by an Industrus people they would soon be supply'd not only with the necessarys but many of the luxuries of life."[25]

In light of the strong trading relationships that Cook and his crew established at many of their ports of call, he formed an optimistic vision of the ease with which a colony might be established if Britain exploited the tribal structure of Māori society: "So far as I have been able to judge of the genius of these people it doth not appear to me to be atall difficult for Strangers to form a settlement in this Country. They seem to be too much divided among themselves to unite in opposing, by which means and kind and gentle usuage the Colonists would be able to form strong parties among them."[26] Cook himself acted to lay the foundation for any such future colonization. On 15 November 1769, at Mercury Bay, Cook cut the name of the *Endeavour* into a tree, displayed "the English colours" and "took formal Possession of the Place in the Name of His Majesty."[27] Two and a half months later, on 31 January 1770, Cook claimed the South Island for Britain. At Queen Charlotte Sound, Cook took a flag post to the summit of a high hill and "hoisted thereon the Union Flag and I dignified this Inlet with the name of Queen Charlotte Sound. At the same time I took formal Possession of this and the adjacent Country in the Name and for the use of His Majesty. We then drank her Majesty's health in a Bottle of wine."[28] While these claims to New Zealand were not officially recognized by the British government, these rituals of possession were a potent dramatization of New Zealand's incorporation into the imperial vision of Britain.

The image of New Zealand as a potential colony produced by the records of the *Endeavour* voyage was widely disseminated through John Hawkesworth's popular compilation of travel narratives. He quoted Banks's estimation of the value of New Zealand's timber and suggested that New Zealand was blessed with "light but fertile soil." His narrative framed New Zealand as a rich and abundant land awaiting exploitation: its islands were "swarming" with "wholesome" fish, the hills were heavily wooded, and the land was blessed with plentiful supplies of fresh water.[29] Hawkesworth quoted Cook's opinion that European plants would flourish in New Zealand with "the utmost luxuriance" and that a colony of Europeans would ultimately enjoy "the luxuries of life in great abundance."[30] Hawkesworth's text was not only immensely popular, but was also widely abstracted and reprinted in the periodical press.[31] If we follow Damon Salesa in recognizing the "thin ribbons of text" produced by the officers and crew of the *Endeavour* as powerful instruments of connection that tugged the Pacific firmly into Britain's imperial ambit, it is important also to recognize that the extension of British and imperial print culture networks meant that such textual threads multiplied and thickened as a result of the operation of printing presses, libraries, and the book market.[32]

Cook's second voyage to the Pacific, between 1772 and 1775, further extended and enriched this archive, creating new textual connections. The work of the artist William Hodges, the observations of the astronomer William Wales, the botanizing of the Swedish naturalist Andres Sparrmann and the surgeon's mate William Anderson, and the detailed discussions of people and landscape that were produced by Johann Reinhold Forster and Georg Forster deepened British knowledge of the islands, especially Dusky Sound and Queen Charlotte Sound.[33] Again the journals and published accounts of the second voyage dwelt on the possibilities of colonization. When, for example, the *Resolution* passed Palliser Bay in November 1773, Johann Forster noted in his journal that the bay would be ideally suited for colonization: "It is certainly one of the most convenient spots for forming an European Settlement on, as it will afford flat Land enough for Cultivation, is on the mouth of the Streights & in all appearances has a navigable River." Forster thought that if the natives could be "taught to manufacture Canvas & Rope with their Flax," a profitable trade could be established between any fledgling colony or commercial settlement and India, which could, in turn, provide textiles, finished goods, and machinery.[34]

More immediately, New Zealand's value as a site for refueling ships, an important imperial concern, was reaffirmed on the second voyage. Charles Clerke, second lieutenant on the *Resolution*, extolled the virtues of Dusky Sound: "You Wood and Water here with the utmost facility; the Wood may be cut down close alongside your Ship, and the Water may be fill'd by a fine running Brook about a 100 yards from the Stern—in the next place it abounds most plentifully in Fish—principally Cold Fish with some Cavally's—Gurnets and Mackarel all large, firm and exceedingly well tasted: there are likewise great abundance of very large and very good Crawfish." The sound was blessed with abundant bird life as well as seals, "whose Haslets," Clerke observed, "make steaks very little inferior (some of our Gentry sware, far superior) to Beefsteak, and the Blubber renders very good Oil for lamps."[35] A decade and a half later, George Vancouver affirmed the value of Dusky Sound as an imperial way station. After collecting firewood and timber for planks and spars, as well as catching and salting large amounts of fish, Vancouver noted in his journal that he was "greatly indebted to its most refreshments, and the salubrity of its air."[36] He particularly recommended Facile Harbour, at the southwest corner of Resolution Island (Māui-katau), as an outstanding site for restocking: "a safe, commodious, and convenient station; capable of supplying every article that can be expected from this country, without going out of sight of the vessel."[37]

From the time of Cook's first voyage, New Zealand was quickly incorporated into a range of British visions of the future shape of the empire. The Greenock surgeon Godfrey McCalman, for example, identified New Zealand as a vital source of a greatly valued commodity: tea. Cook's experiments with anti-scorbutic agents on the first voyage included using mānuka (*Leptosermum scoparium*) to produce "tea" for his sailors. On the basis of these experiments, McCalman's treatise on the medicinal and commercial value of tea listed New Zealand as first among the "tea-countries" outside of China and Japan. "In New Zealand . . . where the soil is immensely fine, the tea-tree grows to a considerable size in the thick forests, sometimes to the height of 30 or 40 feet, and one foot in diameter."[38] Others saw New Zealand's value as a convict colony. In the wake of the American Declaration of Independence, the British government was looking for a new destination to which it might send its convicts. William Hussey, Member of Parliament for Salisbury, suggested that New Zealand might be a suitable destination, and he thought that the convicts "might form a useful colony."[39] Others still imagined the establishment of a regular colony in New Zealand. In 1792 one John Thomson set out a plan for colonization in a letter to Henry Dundas, the secretary of state. Thomson suggested that New Zealand could be colonized from British India, with the seeds of the colony being a party of "fifty sober men; one hundred sepoys, & 100 convicts." Thomson imagined that the colony would function as a crucial center for a developing Pacific empire, "from whence he [the king of England] would enjoy a fine Country, from whence he might conquer the greatest part of the South Seas Islands, & conquest would bring peace, hence improvement & civilisation &c. A work worthy of so great a King."[40]

But the most striking proposal relating to New Zealand was produced during the crisis that shook Britain's North American empire. In 1771 Benjamin Franklin, who held British law in high esteem and clung to a vision of a British empire of self-governing nations unified by a common cultural bond, and Alexander Dalrymple, the leading geographer and future chief hydrographer for the East India Company, formulated a scheme to expand British influence in the Pacific. They noted that the islands of New Zealand were "inhabited by a brave and generous race, who are destitute of *corn, fowls,* and *all quadrupeds,* except *dogs.*" In light of this material want, "it seemed *incumbent* on such a country as *this* [Britain], to communicate to *all others* the conveniences of life which we enjoy." Franklin offered to subscribe to a new voyage that would "communicate *in general* those benefits which we enjoy, to countries destitute of them in remote parts of the globe."[41] He argued, "Britain is said to have produced nothing but *sloes.* What vast advantages have been communicated to her by the fruits, seeds, roots, herbage, animals, and arts of other countries! We are by their means become a wealthy and a mighty nation, abounding in all good things; Does not some *duty* hence arise from us towards other countries still remaining in our former state?"[42] Here Franklin argued that Britain had a moral responsibility to uplift and improve the lot of Māori and other "uncivilized" peoples. In this vision empire-building was a powerful and potent force for good, a vector for civilization, and an instrument that could equalize relationships between peoples. But it would be a mistake to follow Anne Salmond and to read this plan simply as a "philanthropic scheme."[43] Dalrymple and Franklin stressed that by implanting "civilization," Britain would enlarge its imperial reach and enhance the prospects of benefiting from commerce: "It seems a laudable wish that all the nations of the earth were connected by a knowledge of each other, and a mutual exchange of benefits: but a commercial nation particularly should wish for a general civilization of mankind, since trade is always carried on to much greater extent with people who have the arts and conveniences of life, than it can be with naked savages."[44]

It was the dense body of information collated on Cook's first and second voyage that fed the imaginations of these imperial visionaries within the "British world." They were excited by the potential role that New Zealand might play within the empire in the future—whether as a site for refitting and resupplying, a source of "naval stores," a site of colonization, a destination for convicts or even as a purveyor of tea.[45] Of course, the islands were not formally colonized by Britain until 1840, but by the 1790s the islands were integrated into the increasingly extensive commercial networks and lines of communication that British imperial agents fashioned in the southern Pacific. Cook, Banks, Johann Reinhold Forster, and the other "experimental gentlemen" who graced Cook's first and second voyage not only suggested that New Zealand was of considerable value to Britain, but also that these agents of empire were crucial in enabling the imperial endeavor. Their maps, coastal views, sketches, journals, and published narratives indicated safe anchorages and the location of seal rookeries and stands of timber and flax, and provided valuable information on the location, size, and disposition of local populations, information that proved to be of tremendous value to British merchants, imperial strategists, and ships' captains.

New Zealand and Imperial Extraction

The establishment of the colony of New South Wales in 1788 provided an important base for British attempts to exploit the resources identified by Cook, Banks, and other explorers. Of course, Banks himself, along with James Matra, who sailed with Cook on the *Endeavour*, were pivotal in proposing eastern Australia as a site for colonization. Matra not only suggested that a colony in New South Wales might begin to offset the loss of the American colonies and give Britain a strategic advantage over its European imperial competitors, but also argued that such a settlement would enable Britain to exploit New Zealand's valuable flax and timber.[46] Matra accommodated his plan to a political climate where the transportation of convicts was a pressing issue and found support in the former East India Company officer Sir George Young. Young also stressed that a settlement in New South Wales would provide access to New Zealand flax, which was more useful than "any Vegetable hitherto known," a commodity that was of particular value within a climate of international conflict.[47] Although the decision to establish a colony in Botany Bay was ostensibly driven by the need to find a home for Britain's convicts, whom contractors could no longer transport to the newly independent United States of America, it is clear that the establishment of a British colony in New South Wales was also seen as an important strategic move. It forestalled French imperial ambitions, provided an important base for ships following the eastern path into the Pacific, and allowed Britain access to important naval stores.[48]

By the beginning of the nineteenth century, Port Jackson had developed as a crucial sub-imperial center that directed British activity in the southern

Pacific. The colonial establishment in Port Jackson was dependent on a legal and administrative system that was ultimately subservient to London and economically dependent on food, livestock, tools, and material culture from both Bengal and the Pacific. At the same time, however, it also functioned as the central hub in a complex series of maritime networks. These webs of connection, fashioned by "ocean-minded" officials, merchants, and financiers, encompassed other early Australian ports (including Norfolk Island [1790], Hobart [1803], and Launceston [1806]); extended to Java, Jakarta, Calcutta, Cape Town, and distant London; and reached north and east into the Pacific, including New Zealand.[49] Indeed, there is evidence to suggest that until the mid-1810s some colonial officials and moneymen in New South Wales understood New Zealand as having been incorporated into the territorial authority of their governor based in Port Jackson.[50]

The rich natural resources available on New Zealand's coasts were an important element in developing regional (the colony of New South Wales) and global (Britain's empire in Asia and the Pacific) economic structures. Sealing was pioneered by the *Britannia*, under the command of Captain William Raven, which deposited a sealing gang at Luncheon Cove in 1792.[51] This vessel was owned by Messrs Enderby of London, who were given a license to trade from the East India Company (EIC). While this sealing gang was not especially successful—gathering only 4,500 sealskins in ten months—it suggested that New Zealand could supply commodities that would earn good prices in China, confirmed the islands' reputation as a good source of naval stores (including timber for ship-building and flax for the manufacture of cordage), and underscored the abundant supplies of fish and birdlife that could be used to restock passing ships.[52] From this point, sealing developed rapidly, working through the Antipodes, Snares, Bounty, Auckland, and Stewart (Rakiura) Islands in the first decade of the nineteenth century.[53] Joseph Banks noted in 1806 that southern New Zealand "produce[s] seals of all kinds in quantities at present almost innumerable. Their stations on rocks or in bays have remain'd unmolested since the Creation. The beach is incumber'd with their quantities, and those who visit their haunts have less trouble in killing them than the servants of the victualling office have who kill hogs in a pen with mallets."[54]

Just as sealing developed under license from EIC, so did whaling. In 1801, on behalf of British merchants interested in whaling in the southern Pacific within the old monopoly of the EIC, Messrs Enderby and Messrs Champion won the right to operate anywhere in the Pacific so long as their journals were delivered to the EIC on return to England.[55] Over the next four decades, large numbers of whaling ships plied New Zealand's coastal waters, and in the 1830s a string of important shore whaling stations was established along New Zealand's south and east coasts: massive numbers of whales were taken, providing an array of products that were of great value in both Europe and Asia.

New Zealand also served as an important site for the extraction of naval stores. At the direction of the Bombay Marine (the EIC's navy), Edgar Thomas Dell oversaw the voyage of the *Fancy* to the Waihou River in the Hauraki. During its three-month visit in 1794–95, the crew collected 213 spars and a large quantity of *muka* (dressed flax). This precious cargo was carried back to Port Jackson, then on to India, where naval supplies were desperately needed to repair British ships damaged in the global conflict with France.[56] The success of this experiment initiated a string of regular voyages aimed at extracting timber and flax: at least five ships visited Waihou between 1799 and 1801.[57] Flax was of particular value to a maritime empire embroiled in a series of wars, and the East India Company had been forced to reduce the size of its navy in the 1780s because of a shortage of cordage and rope.[58] While New Zealand was valued in part because it could furnish a large supply of flax, the settlement of Norfolk Island opened up an immediate supply of the plant, which grew vigorously there. Despite this new convenient source of flax, however, New Zealand remained instrumental to the efficient exploitation of the plant. The fibers of New Zealand flax were much stronger than were those of its European counterpart, and the convict flax-dressers were unable to find a method by which to efficiently dress the New Zealand flax. In January 1791 Lieutenant Governor Philip Gidley King suggested that "a Native of New Zealand" should be "carried to Norfolk Island" in order to unlock the secret of its preparation, a plan that ultimately received official sanction.[59]

Early in 1793, two Māori men, Tuki Tahua and Ngāhuruhuru (now commonly referred to as Tuki and Huru), were kidnapped from the Cavalli Islands, north of the Bay of Islands, by the HMS *Daedalus*. They were conveyed to Port Jackson, then to Norfolk Island, where they established close relationships with King and his family. While Tuki and Huru, high-ranking rangatira from Ōruru and Whangaroa respectively, knew little of weaving, their sojourn on Norfolk Island was of tremendous significance. At King's request, Tuki—who was deeply anxious about his ability to return home—produced a detailed map of New Zealand, especially the northern part of the North Island (see figure 1.4). This map conveyed much information about the sacred geography of the land (showing the path that wairua [the spirits] took after death), the operation of political power in Māori society, and the geography of the main kin-groups (hapū and iwi) in the northern North Island.[60] This,

Tettua-Woodoo *4000 Inhabitants*

Moodoo Whenua

Wongaroon, *2000 Fighting Men*

Chief Inimical to Hododo *and* Teer-a-witte *in Amity with* T'Souduck-ey, Moodoo-When-ua *&* Tettua Woodoo.

Ho-do do *about* 2000 *Men fighting*

Terry-inga

Tewy-te-wi *Chief*

Moodoo Whenua

Toogee's *Habitation*

Hododo's *Habitation*

Motu-a-ca-ete *not inhabited*

Residence *of the Chief*

Motu-a-ca-nue *not inhabited*

Here Toogee & Hoodoo *left the* Britannia

Modey-Mootoo *on which is an* Hippah

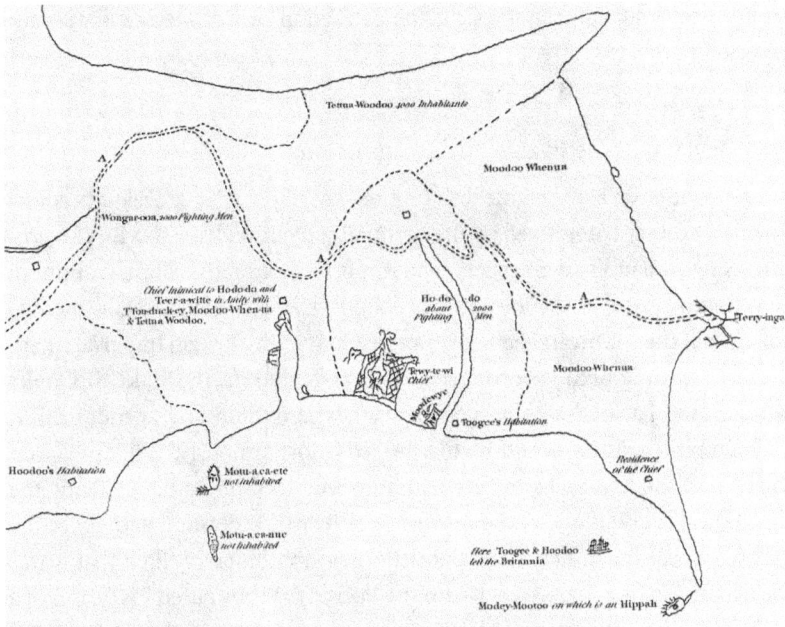

FIGURE 1.4 Tuki's Map. "Chart of New Zealand drawn by Tooke-Titter-a-nui Wari-pedo" (London: Cadell and Davies, 1804). From David Collins, *An Account of the English Colony in New South Wales from Its first settlement in January 1788 to August 1801*, 2d edn. (London, 1804). Ref.: MapColl 830ap [1793], Alexander Turnbull Library, Wellington, New Zealand.

together with the new understandings of the vocabulary and structure of te reo Māori, meant the colonial government in New South Wales and the Colonial Office had access to a much more detailed body of knowledge about the operation of Māori society. This knowledge was of great value given Britain's desire to develop commercial relationships with Māori and its interest in the possibility of colonizing New Zealand in the future.[61]

King formulated a very positive reading of Māori capacity on the basis of Tuki and Huru's enforced residence in Norfolk Island. And there is no doubt that Tuki and Huru appreciated the gifts that King gave them—axes, carpentry tools, scissors, hoes, spades, ten sows and two boars, and wheat, maize, and pea seeds—since food items and technology were important markers of mana in the Māori world. Tuki and Huru did not forget the hara (offense) of their kidnapping, but these gifts affirmed their mana and were a material demonstration of the connections that had developed between the two rangatira and the lieutenant governor.[62] After their return to New Zealand, in November 1793, Tuki and Huru functioned as important cross-cultural brokers, serving as facilitators for the extraction of various raw materials, especially timber.

New Zealand in the Evangelical Imagination

Thus, by the close of the eighteenth century, key parts of New Zealand's coastline had been encompassed by the commercial networks of the British empire. New Zealand had emerged as an important extractive site: a frontier of New South Wales, with commodities of both strategic value and commercial worth. But the southern Pacific was prominent in the British imperial imagination not only because of its economic potential. In the wake of Cook's voyages, the Pacific had emerged as a site where the moral agenda of English empire-building could be discharged. Most famously, William Carey, the Baptist shoemaker from Northampton who was influential in laying the theological foundations of the new wave of British Protestant activity in the 1790s and was the father of the Baptist mission to India, recalled that it was the expansion of Britain's reach into the Pacific that prompted his vision of a global mission: "Reading Cook's voyages was the first thing that engaged my mind to think of missions."[63]

The accounts of the Pacific produced by Cook's voyages stimulated the missionary enthusiasms of other British evangelicals. In October 1779 John Whitcombe delivered a sermon at the parish church of Walesby, in Lincolnshire, in which he advocated overseas missionary work. He took as his starting point Mark 15:16: "Go ye into all the world, and preach the gospel to every creature." Whitcombe argued against the tendency to interpret this injunction as applying only to Europeans, insisting that the "benevolent being [God] would have the rays of his heavenly truth shed, without distinction, on the souls of all mankind."[64] Whitcombe reminded his audience that their ancient British ancestors had originally lived far from the Holy Land and that if the "apostles and their successors" had applied a narrow definition of this teaching, Britons would "have remained in darkness and ignorance;— little superior, in the great concern of religious knowledge, to the people of Otaheite, or New Zealand."[65] Where Whitcombe argued that Māori and Tahitians deserved the opportunity to the hear the gospel, an opportunity that ultimately reflected Britain's greatness, the Church of England minister Thomas Haweis suggested that the Pacific was a key missionary field. In 1795 Haweis, chaplain to the Countess of Huntingdon, influential evangelical preacher and hymn-writer, and founding member of the LMS, argued in *Evangelical Maga-*

zine: "On frequent reflection upon all the circumstances of these islands, ever since their discovery, I have been persuaded, that no other part of the heathen world affords so promising a field for a Christian mission: Where the temper of the people, the climate, the abundance of food, and early collection of a number together for instruction, bespeak the fields ripe for harvest."[66]

This new commitment to the evangelization of non-European peoples and Haweis's vision of the Pacific as a ground for English missionary activity was transplanted to New South Wales with the appointment of Samuel Marsden as assistant colonial chaplain. Marsden was born on 25 June 1765, at Farsley in the parish of Calverley, near Leeds. The Marsden family had experienced some downward mobility during the eighteenth century due to the impact of enclosure and their failure to grasp the new economic gospel of "improvement," but Samuel reversed this trend. Where his grandfather was described as a "yeoman," Samuel's father Thomas was a simple butcher. Samuel Marsden was initially apprenticed as a blacksmith to his uncle at Horsforth. There Reverend Samuel Stones, of the Elland Society—an evangelical group that financed the training of young men intent on becoming minsters—noted the young Marsden's piety and arranged for the society to sponsor his education. After two years of tuition under Stones' direction at Rawdon, Marsden progressed to Hull Grammar, then to Magdalene College, Cambridge, in 1790. After two years at Magdalene, the center of the university town's evangelical and abolitionist circles, Marsden accepted the position of assistant chaplain to the colony of New South Wales, in January 1793, an appointment supported by the evangelical luminaries William Wilberforce, Charles Simeon, and John Newton.[67]

Marsden sailed to New South Wales after his marriage to Elizabeth Fristan and his ordination, arriving at Sydney Cove on 10 March 1794. Marsden quickly became an influential, if controversial, figure in the colony. His commitment to espousing the religious and social vision of evangelicalism was widely resisted by convicts, by leading colonial officials, and, later, by an emergent group of free settlers and emancipated convicts. Marsden's efforts were not restricted to the uplift and disciplining of convicts, especially the female convicts under his care at Parramatta, but he also became an important figure in the colonial state's administrative machinery, functioning as both a magistrate and superintendent of government affairs. Marsden, who became the colony's principal chaplain in 1800, also built up a substantial landholding and emerged as a catalyst in driving the expansion of pastoralism and the "improvement" of the colony's economy.

In March 1808, Marsden wrote to the Reverend Josiah Pratt, secretary of the CMS, suggesting the establishment of a mission to New Zealand. Marsden suggested that Māori were capable of "improvement" and appealed to Pratt's sympathy for the "heathen" waiting to hear the gospel: "Every benevolent Mind acquainted with the ignorant State of these Islanders, must feel a wish that some small attempt may be made towards their Civilization and general Improvement in the simple Arts, and Christian Knowledge."[68] Two weeks later Marsden presented a more comprehensive plan to the society. He proposed the establishment of a small mission, initially made up of three "Mechanics": "a Carpenter. Another a Smith and a third a Twine Spinner." These lay missionaries would teach Māori practical skills—making edged tools, boat making, the manufacture of twine and fishing nets—while introducing them to the rudiments of Christianity. (Ironically, with the exception of making metal tools, Māori were already highly adept at all of the production processes Marsden identified.) Marsden believed that these "trades would apply to their immediate wants, and tend to conciliate their minds and gain their Confidence." Instruction in these "useful arts" would provide the missionaries with the opportunity of religious teaching, and while undertaking "manual labour," the missionaries could "instruct the Natives in the great Doctrines of the Gospel, and fully discharge the Duties of Catechists."[69] Marsden hoped that this blueprint would allow the civilizing forces of the plough and the gospel to remake Māori and the New Zealand landscape in ways similar to those in which he had been able to "improve" and "civilize" the landscape of his vicarage at Parramatta and his extensive farms in New South Wales.

Marsden's plan for New Zealand was quickly supported by the CMS. By June 1808, he had identified and met the first of the missionaries destined for New Zealand, the carpenter William Hall.[70] Marsden also recruited John King, a rope- and shoemaker, and King joined Marsden, Hall, and Hall's wife, on board the convict ship *Ann*, which sailed for New South Wales in August 1809. Onboard the *Ann* was Ruatara, a high-ranking rangatira from the Bay of Islands, who had worked for several years as a sailor and had met Marsden in Port Jackson in 1806. Ruatara had arrived in England on the sealing ship the *Santa Anna* with the hope of visiting King George III, but the crew of the *Santa Anna* told Ruatara that he would be unable to see the king, and the captain had required him to work without pay before eventually discharging him, battered and sick. Ruatara made his way to Portsmouth and there boarded the *Ann*. The reunion between Ruatara and Marsden was fortuitous. Ruatara not only acted as a language instructor for the missionaries during the voyage, but also ultimately served as the key broker for the establishment of the mission in the Bay of Islands. Alison Jones and Kuni Jenkins have suggested that Marsden's solicitous care for Ruatara meant, from a Māori perspective, that Marsden's and Ruatara's *hau* (life breath) mingled, creating a strong reciprocal bond between the men.[71]

Marsden had expected that, soon after the arrival of the *Ann* in Port Jackson, Ruatara, the Kings, and the Halls would embark for Ruatara's home and establish the New Zealand mission. These hopes were dashed as news of the massacre of the *Boyd* at Whangaroa reached New South Wales. Underlying the sensational narratives that circulated widely about the attack was the reality that Whangaroa Māori destroyed the vessel and killed the crew in *utu* (retribution, seeking balance) for the mistreatment of their rangatira Te Āra. The missionaries were especially alarmed as the initial intelligence from New Zealand suggested that Te Pahi, the influential rangatira who had visited Australia in 1805–6 and become Marsden's friend, instigated the attack. In his letter to the CMS, John King recorded the dismay of the missionaries: "I am greatly disappointed that the Chief of the Bay of Islands [Te Pahi] who was to protect us and we was to put our selves under him as our temporal Refuge but alas he is the Chief of the Murderers he hath no pity he him self was at the head of this shocking scene."[72] An ad hoc retribution party had been assembled by five whaling vessels in the Bay of Islands and launched a retaliatory attack on Te Pahi and his people on 26 March 1810. About sixty inhabitants of Te Pahi's island, near Te Puna, were killed, and Te Pahi himself was wounded. Not until October 1810 did it become clear that the attack on the *Boyd* was instigated by Te Puhi of Whangaroa (alongside his brother Te Āra), not Te Pahi of Te Puna (who was Te Puhi's son-in-law). There is strong evidence that Te Pahi's rivals, including Matengaro and Tara, the leading rangatira of Kororāreka, had actively disseminated this misidentification.[73]

After fleeing his island, Te Pahi was quickly drawn into conflict with the people of Whangaroa over the destruction of the *Boyd*, and he died in April 1810 from the wound he received in this skirmish. With plans for the mission on hold, Ruatara remained with Marsden at Parramatta. During his residence Ruatara deepened his knowledge of European agricultural techniques and grew his own wheat, peas, and beans on the plot of land that Marsden had set aside for his use. Ruatara was keen to assume the mantle of the mission's patron and protector: he had developed a bold vision of establishing wheat cultivation in the Bay of Islands on a large scale to enable him to both supply his own people with a new staple food crop and to have a valuable crop to export to Port Jackson. He returned to the Bay of Islands and assumed Te Pahi's mantle as the senior rangatira in the Bay's northeast.[74] In 1814 Ruatara finally facilitated the foundation of the CMS's New Zealand mission. He provided a small plot of land at Hohi (frequently rendered as Oihi or Ōihi), under the shadow of his Rangihoua pā, for King, Hall, and the mission teacher Thomas Kendall (who had been recruited to the mission in 1813).[75] On Christmas Day 1814 Marsden conducted the first full service on land in New Zealand, preaching to large congregation of local Māori on Luke 2:10: "Behold, I bring you good tidings of great joy."

Capacity, Civilization, and Christianity

The establishment of the New Zealand mission was heralded as a major success for the CMS. However, the early years of the mission were turbulent, and the early mechanic missionaries made little progress in their efforts to convert Māori. The remainder of this chapter examines the cultural underpinnings of Marsden's plan for the New Zealand mission and reconstructs some of the factors that encouraged Ruatara and other leading rangatira to act as protectors of the mission. Marsden's vision of missionary work in the Pacific was restricted to the peoples who we would now designate as Polynesian, including Māori and the people of Tonga, Tahiti, and the Marquesas. Marsden was opposed to the extension of missionary work to the indigenous peoples of Australia. He told the LMS that missionary efforts to Aborigines were in vain: "Nothing can be done." "I am convinced we cannot do more for them than to give them a Loaf of Bread when hungry and a Blanket when cold—more they will not let us do—This is my full conviction."[76] Marsden explained the basis of this theory to Lachlan Macquarie, suggesting that "commerce promotes industry—industry civilisation and civilisation opens up the way for the Gospel." Because Aborigines had no interest in trade, the Gospel was beyond their reach.[77] Later Marsden suggested to Archdeacon Scott that the evangelization of Aborigines was "almost an hopeless task" as "they have no wants, nor is it in our power to create any which will benefit them."[78] The Scottish enlightenment's "conjectural history" tradition, which plotted the development of society through a sequence of stages (from hunter-gathering to pastoralism to agriculture to commerce), was almost certainly one influence on Marsden's understanding of Pacific peoples. But his deep commitment to "improvement" was also probably imprinted by the beginnings of the economic transformation of the North Riding of Yorkshire during his boyhood and youth, and also reflected his own ability to reverse his father's downward social mobility.[79] This blend of life experience and intellectual understanding encouraged his deep reservations about whether Aborigines were capable of progressing toward civilization. In his letter to Scott, Marsden speculated that Aborigines "have never been higher in the scale of human beings than their present state."[80]

While this skeptical reading of Aboriginal capacity reflected the dominant assessment of the intelligence and sophistication of the indigenous people of Australia articulated in both New South Wales and in Britain, it is important to recognize that other evangelicals were supporters of the evangelization of Aborigines. The Reverend Robert Cartwright was critical of Marsden's fixation with New Zealand and the Pacific, and felt that the energy of the church and colonial establishment energy should directed at the Aborigines.[81] In 1817 Hawkesbury settlers had requested that the Missionary Society provide a minister who might also evangelize Aborigines, and in 1819 a "Society for Promoting Christian Knowledge amongst the Aborigines of New South Wales and its Dependencies" was established.[82] Anna Johnston has also stressed Marsden's key role in the "paper war" that played out over the possibility of evangelizing Australian Aborigines, when Marsden repeatedly clashed with the London Missionary Society's Lancelot Threlkeld, the most prominent advocate for taking the gospel to Australia's indigenous communities.[83]

Marsden's reluctance was informed by the failure of his attempts to reform the Aborigines attached to his own household. From the mid-1790s, several Aborigines had been connected to the Marsden household in Parramatta. But where the letters and journals of Marsden and his family—including his wife, Elizabeth, and daughter, Ann—dwelt at length on the Māori visitors to New South Wales and the prospects of the New Zealand mission, they rarely reflected on the family's relationships with the indigenous people they lived with. But it is clear that the Marsdens were hopeful that they could transform an Aboriginal boy named "Tristan," who was attached to their household from around 1794 as an adopted son and domestic servant. Tristan accompanied the Marsdens on their voyage to England in 1807, but fled the family during their stopover in Rio de Janiero. Tristan had developed a taste for alcohol, and he left the family after "his master," as Elizabeth Marsden described her husband, disciplined him for his drunkenness.[84] Before he left, however, Tristan stole a "considerable sum of money" from the Marsdens. Tristan eventually returned to New South Wales, where he rejected the society of Europeans and returned to the bush, setting aside a "dislike to others of his own complexion" that he reportedly developed while under Marsden's care.[85]

Henry Reynolds has suggested that Tristan's flight from the Marsdens fits within a clear pattern, as the first generation of Aborigines who lived with Europeans exhibited a "strong tendency to rebel violently in their early teens—to run away, steal, drink, engage in promiscuous sex and be generally destructive and disruptive."[86] It is clear that Tristan's resistance to Marsden's desire to "improve" him was influential in molding Marsden's reading of Aboriginal capacity. Marsden reflected that Tristan never developed "that attachment to me and my family that we had just reason to look for. He always seemed deficient in those feelings of social affection which are the very bonds of social life."[87] This supposedly inadequate sensibility and lack of Aboriginal interest in the "civilized arts" meant Marsden emphasized the fundamental difference of the indigenous peoples of New South Wales, a difference that he understood as being of such an order that they were incapable of change and, as such, were beyond help. In a letter to Dandeson Coates, in 1836, Marsden argued that his experience with Aborigines had convinced him that "they have no Attachments, and they have no wants. . . . They are totally different from every Race of men that I have known. Many natives belonging to the different islands in the South Seas have lived with me; but all were full of wants, and capable of Improvements."[88] Marsden not only drew a stark contrast between Aborigines, with their resistance to "improvement," and Māori, but also suggested that Māori themselves were disdainful of Australia's indigenous population.

> When they attain the Age of 13 or 14 years [Aborigines] always take to the woods. They cannot be induced to live in any regular way. And as they increase in years they increase in every vice, and particularly drunkenness, both men and women, and still go naked about the Streets. They are the most degraded of the human Race. . . . The New Zealanders would never be induced to live with them if it were possible to confine them—They cannot bear their degraded Appearance; their Conduct is so disgusting altogether as well as their Persons.[89]

The contrast between Marsden's reading of the capacity of Aborigines and Māori is striking.[90] He consistently emphasized Māori acuity, their "natural" ability, and—in keeping with a long line of texts dating back to Cook—the strength of the Māori interest in trade and technology. In 1819 Marsden explained the genesis of his commitment to Commissioner Bigge, saying that he learned of the intellectual ability of Māori when he heard detailed reports of Tuki and Huru during a lengthy sojourn on Norfolk Island in 1795, and this initial impression was confirmed when high-ranking

Māori from the Bay of Islands began to voyage to New South Wales. These visitors convinced him that "that the New Zealanders were capable of any instructions that the civilized world would impart to them."[91] The visit of Te Pahi to New South Wales in 1805–6 was of particular importance in molding Marsden's reading of Māori character. Marsden echoed the judgments of Governor King and John Liddiard Nicholas in proclaiming the talents of Te Pahi: "He possessed a clear, strong, and comprehensive mind, and was anxious to gain what knowledge he could of our laws and customs. He was wont to converse much with me about our God, and was very regular in his attendance at church on the Sabbath; and, when at public worship, behaved with great decorum."[92] On the basis of Te Pahi's interest in British law, religion, and agriculture, Marsden argued in his April 1808 plan for the establishment of the New Zealand mission that the "New Zealanders appear to be a very superior People in point of mental Endowments."[93] Marsden later reflected that that he planned the mission because the mind of Māori "appeared like a rich soil that had never been cultivated, and only wanted the proper means of improvement to render them fit to rank with civilized nations."[94]

Marsden's vision of the New Zealand mission was grounded in the "improvement" of Māori through the introduction of the "civilized arts." In his April 1808 plan Marsden argued,

> The attention of the Heathens, can only be gained and their vagrant Habits corrected, by the Arts. Till their attention be gained and the moral and industrious habits are induced, little or no progress can be made in teaching them the Gospel. I do not mean that a native should learn to build a Hut or make an Axe before he should be told any thing of Man's Fall and Redemption, but that these grand Subjects should be introduced at every favourable opportunity while the Natives are learning any of the simple Arts.—To preach the Gospel without the aid of the Arts will never succeed amongst the Heathens for any time.[95]

Marsden reaffirmed this vision in a letter in 1811.

> My friend one of the chiefs [Ruatara] who has lived with me and acquired a knowledge of agriculture will introduce cultivation among his countrymen. This will add greatly to their civilization and comfort and prepare the way for greater blessings. I may be too fond perhaps of the garden, the field and the fleece. These would be the first object of my attention was I placed among a savage nation. The man who introduced the potato into

Ireland and England merited more from those nations than any General who may have slain thousands of their enemies.[96]

Here it is clear that Marsden was aware that his emphasis on the "civilized arts" was controversial and that some evangelicals might feel that he placed "the garden, field and fleece" ahead of religious instruction. This vision was a response to the failure of the first attempts of the Missionary Society (later, from 1818, the LMS) to evangelize in the Pacific, as well as the product of Marsden's early years as a blacksmith and farmer in industrializing Yorkshire. The Missionary Society mission in the Marquesas was terminated in 1799, the Tongatapu mission was disbanded in 1800, and the Tahitian mission was temporarily abandoned in 1808. Although the pioneering British missionaries seen out to the Pacific on the *Duff* were primarily "mechanics" of the type that Marsden wanted for New Zealand, Neil Gunson reminds us that this first Protestant experiment in the Pacific prioritized evangelization over civilization: "These men were sent to preach the gospel before all else."[97] The disintegration of these missions convinced an influential cohort of evangelicals connected to the Pacific that civilization should precede the drive to convert the local people to Christianity. The Reverend J. F. Cover, who was among the first group of missionaries on Tahiti, told the Missionary Society in 1800 that civilization had to precede Christianization, an opinion shared by his fellow Missionary Society missionary William Henry, who served with Cover on Tahiti and subsequently worked on Huahine and Moorea. The balance between Christian teaching and the inculcation of the "civilized arts" remained a constant concern for the Missionary Society in the years during which Marsden was working on his plan for the New Zealand mission. In 1812, for example, the directors of the Missionary society were critical of the "small degree of Improvement made among the natives in respect of Industry and civilization.[98]

Empire and Mission: Mission as Colony

Thus while the prioritization of "civilization" in Marsden's plan reflected his own deep faith in the "improving" power of agriculture and trade, it was also in keeping with the main current of missionary strategy for the Pacific in the 1810s. In realizing his plan to introduce the "civilized arts" and Christianity to New Zealand, Marsden was very reliant on the economic institutions and networks that Britain had developed in the Pacific. From the outset, the New Zealand mission was not to separate itself from the world of trade and empire, but was rather deeply implicated in that world. As the Pacific agent of the Missionary Society and as a patriarch of the New Zealand mission, Marsden utilized long-established imperial networks and commercial agents who had made their name within the empire. The most notable of these was Robert Campbell, a Scottish Presbyterian merchant of the Calcutta agency Campbell, Clarke and Company. He arrived in New South Wales in 1798 and soon became the colony's most important merchant. Campbell was the chief economic backer of the Missionary Society mission in the Pacific, acting variously as its merchant, warehouseman, and banker, and in 1807 he became the mission's Pacific agent.[99] He quickly became a key player in the importation of pork from Tahiti to bolster New South Wales's patchy meat supply, a lucrative trade that had far-reaching consequences for Tahiti's ecology, economy, and social formations.[100]

From 1815, Campbell acted as a chief supplier of goods to the New Zealand mission and provided the missionaries based in New Zealand with various items for their private consumption.[101] Campbell was pivotal in the development of the extractive industries that harnessed the resources of New Zealand's coastline—especially seals and timber—to the wider economy of the British empire, and he provided Marsden with advice on the economics of the New Zealand mission, suggesting that the *Active* should be fitted out as a whaler in order to use whale oil as a commodity that could generate income for the CMS and help defray the costs of the New Zealand mission.[102] Marsden, in turn, worked hard to use his connections to protect Campbell's interests, acting as a significant sponsor of the trade with Tahiti, as well writing to William Wilberforce to request the great evangelical politician to protect Campbell and other colonial merchants from the East India Company's efforts to control Pacific commerce.[103] The close bond between Marsden and Campbell—Campbell named one of his sons Frederick Marsden Campbell—undoubtedly shaped Marsden's vision of the Pacific as a valuable imperial resource and Marsden's insistence that "New Zealand must be always considered as the great emporium of the South Seas, from its local situation, its safe harbours, its navigable rivers, its fine timber for ship-building, its rosin, its native flax."[104]

For Marsden, the extension of commercial networks of the type fashioned by Campbell into the Pacific was an important instrument for civilization (as long as the trade with "natives" was strictly governed). Ideally, Marsden believed, there was no opposition between religion and empire: the two should go hand in hand, a view that grew out of his wider belief that the "Throne and the Altar generally fall together"—that civil and religious authority should be mutually supportive.[105] In the early years of the New Zealand mission, Marsden consistently used Britain's imperial interests as an important instrument in his arguments for supporting the CMS mission. When he suggested the establishment of the mission to Māori in 1808, he told Pratt that "New Zealand & it's natural Productions are little known to the civilized world" and that the commerce conducted in New Zealand to date had the support of local chiefs, especially Te Pahi, who had "shewn every Attention to the South Sea whalers." Marsden went on to suggest that New Zealand's proximity to both Norfolk Island and Australia was of value as "it's local Situation would open an easy Communication with either of these Settlements."[106] While these arguments were addressing key concerns of the CMS—the affordability of the mission and the safety of the missionaries—they were framed in an idiom that owed as much to imperial strategy as to evangelical aspiration.

As the mission matured, Marsden repeatedly fell back on arguments that invoked British national interest and the strategic value of New Zealand to secure economic and political support. In 1820, for example, Marsden wrote to Pratt suggesting that the spars that might be manufactured from New Zealand timber meant that "New Zealand will be of great national Importance." He suggested that the missionary settlement allowed Britain to "derive all the advantages they may wish for from New Zealand, without the Expenses of forming a Colony." The prospects, Marsden suggested, were even brighter because of the untapped timber supplies that could be found on the river "Gambier" (Hokianga). Ruatara had informed Marsden of the significance of the Hokianga, and Marsden explained to the CMS that the "River [would] form a very fine Settlement for the Mission" as well as a valuable extraction point for "the lofty Pine" that graced the Hokianga's long estuary.[107] Later in the same year, Marsden looked forward to the arrival of the HMS *Coromandel* and the HMS *Dromedary* to harvest timber. He suggested that "there would have been difficulties in the way of the Ships getting their Cargo if the mission had not paved the way for them—I think these Ships will lay the foundation of a permanent Intercourse between the British Govt. and these Islands."[108]

As these quotes suggest, Marsden argued that the mission was an important element in Britain's imperial presence in the Pacific. Marsden not only believed that the mission would foster the growth of trade and forward Britain's strategic interests in the region, but that it should enjoy the protection of both the metropolitan government and the colonial state in New South Wales. When he proposed the mission, Marsden noted that the fact that the Anglican CMS might sponsor the work in New Zealand gave the

mission access to political power. "A Governor of New South Wales, however profane he may be [a reference to Governor Bligh], and however great
an Enemy to real Godliness, will avoid for his own Sake, all open war with
the Ministers of the Establishment. . . . They will at all times have a Claim
upon the Governor for his Protection and Support in the due Performance
of every moral and religious duty."[109] During his visit to Britain, Marsden
encouraged Josiah Pratt of the CMS to meet Lachlan Macquarie, who had
been appointed governor of New South Wales, in order to shore up the
governor's support for the mission to New Zealand, and Marsden himself
visited Macquarie to inform him of the details of the proposed mission.[110]
While Marsden's relationship with Governor Macquarie proved to be tense,
he consistently encouraged the governor to use his authority to pass regu-
lations that protected the interests of both the indigenous peoples of the
Pacific and missionary activity. Marsden wrote to Macquarie in November
1813, requesting that he provide some protection for "the much-injured New
Zealanders. . . . [S]ome measures should be adopted to prevent, as far as
may be, a repetition of those acts of oppression, rapine, and murder, which
they from time to time suffered from our people, to the eternal disgrace of
our name and nation."[111]

In December 1813, in response to concerns over the impact of British shipping in the Pacific, Macquarie stipulated that no ships—whether registered
to the East India Company or of "plantation registry"—be allowed to leave
New South Wales for the Pacific Islands or New Zealand without signing a
bond that regulated their operation. This bond, which was to come into effect on 1 January 1814, prohibited trespassing on lands, plantations, and burial
grounds of Pacific peoples, prevented officers and crews from interfering in
local politics or religious rites, specifically banned the carrying of women
without the explicit approval of the governor, and stated that all crimes against
Pacific peoples would be punished "with the utmost rigour of the law" in addition to the imposition of a £1,000 fine.[112] This was followed by a second regulation, issued by Macquarie in November 1814, that specifically attempted to
control shipping in the Bay of Islands and the movement of people within
the Pacific. This regulation was precipitated by reports, collected by Marsden,
that detailed the mistreatment of Māori sailors and documented the violence
directed against coastal communities. In the regulation Macquarie articulated his concern that British ships had "been in the habit of offering gross
insult and injury to the natives of those places, by violently siezing [sic] on
and carrying off several of them, both males and females, and treating them
in other respects with injudicious and unwarrantable severity."[113]

Thus, Marsden imagined the CMS mission to Māori developing with the strong support of British imperial power, even though New Zealand remained formally outside the boundaries of the British empire as Cook's territorial claims had never been activated. While Marsden, like all evangelicals, was critical of what he saw as the irreligious aspects of British society and frequently attacked the immorality of British sailors in the Pacific, he did not articulate the kind of generalized critiques of colonization that a later generation of CMS leaders and missionaries would offer in the mid-1830s. Indeed, it is clear that in the 1810s and 1820s Marsden used the language of empire when he imagined and described the mission to Māori: he routinely spoke of "settlers," the "missionary settlement," and the mission as a "colony." These terms were also frequently used by London-based CMS officials and the New Zealand-based missionaries in their discussions of the mission.[114]

Moreover, in 1817, Marsden supported the establishment of a "small Colony at New Zealand," a proposal crafted by a vocal supporter of the CMS in Britain, the Reverend Andrew Cheap and endorsed by Marsden and the Reverends Robert Cartwright (chaplain of the Hawkesbury district of New South Wales) and John Youl (a pioneering Missionary Society missionary to Tahiti). This plan suggested that the establishment of such a colony would aid the work of the missionaries already settled in New Zealand: "To introduce the Arts of Civilization at New Zealand by the Establishment of a small Colony is a very desirable object, and we think there would be little difficulty in doing this as far as the New Zealanders would be concerned since they are so anxious for Europeans to reside amongst them." New Zealand was eminently suitable for colonization: "They would have a good soil, a fine Climate, a well Watered Country, plenty of Timber, and would command what Laborers they might require as a small expense from the Inhabitants, to carry on all their various operations of Agriculture &c." The establishment of the colony would present a particularly important opportunity for the CMS. Cheap's plan involved stationing a vessel at the colony, and the three reverends suggested that the *Active*, a ship purchased by Marsden to supply the Pacific and New Zealand missions, was ideally suited to the task. The *Active* would be able to access valuable imperial commodities—timber, flax, whale oil—allowing the CMS to recoup some of the costs it had incurred in New Zealand. The reverends argued that if the CMS sponsored this plan, the colonization of New Zealand would proceed under the auspices of the "real Friends of Religion" and the society would protect the interests of both Māori and the existing missionary settlement.[115]

"Improvement" and Māori Interest in Christianity

Although this 1817 colonization scheme was not supported by the CMS, Marsden's plan for the mission to Māori was formulated within a cultural context that emphasized New Zealand's potential value to the British empire, and he believed the success of the mission was in many ways dependent on that empire: on its political institutions, its commercial networks, and a particular evangelical vision of a moral and spiritual responsibility. But at a very concrete level, Marsden's scheme for the establishment of a mission in New Zealand emerged out of the relationships he developed with Māori, with Te Pahi in the first instance, and subsequently with Ruatara and Hongi Hika. On the basis of the character of these rangatira—especially their interests in agriculture, technology, and British ways of life—Marsden formulated both his positive estimation of the cultural capacity of Māori as a whole and his extremely optimistic reading of the future of the mission.

Most important, it was the mana—the authority and charisma—of these high-ranking leaders that made the mission possible: the establishment of the mission was entirely dependent on Māori patronage, material support, and protection. The history of European exploration prior to 1814 and the physical vulnerability of missionaries post-1814 remind us of the ability of Māori to ultimately control contact situations in the late eighteenth century and early nineteenth. The killing and eating of the French explorer Marion du Fresne in October 1772, the destruction of the *Boyd*, the attacks on sealers at Stewart Island in 1810, the sacking of the Wesleyan mission station at Whangaroa in 1827, and the frequent acts of *muru* (ritualistic plunder) directed at missionaries' property in the 1810s through the late 1830s all testify to the ability of Māori communities to exert control and authority over the Europeans who ventured to New Zealand's shores. Until at least the late 1830s, Europeans who sought to make New Zealand their home, whether temporarily (like sealers) or permanently (like missionaries), either required the protection of high-ranking rangatira or had to possess skills or technology that were highly valued by Māori. In this early period, Māori proved highly adept at incorporating Europeans into their communities, whether through intermarriage, chiefly patronage, or, in a few cases, slavery.

Marsden himself was woven into the Māori world. Known as Te Matenga, Marsden welcomed the rangatira who traveled to Poihākena (Port Jackson or Sydney), providing for their material needs, introducing them to new technologies, practices, and ideas, and drawing them into the life of his family. The rangatira appreciated the attention and hospitality offered by Marsden and his family. Kawiti Tiitua, the son of the "southern alliance" rangatira Tara, was greatly impressed by Marsden on his visit to New South Wales in 1811, especially given that no other person in the colony recognized Kawiti's status as a "king." Marsden respected Kawiti's mana and even offered Kawiti "as much land as he liked" from his holdings at Parramatta. In turn, Kawiti suggested that he himself would travel back to the Bay of Islands and then return to Parramatta with a hundred of his men to work on Marsden's property.[116] This manākitanga (hospitality that recognizes and enhances mana), which Marsden freely dispensed, was a key component of the mana he came to wield in te ao Māori (the Māori world). It underwrote his connection to Ruatara from 1806. When, in March 1814, Marsden wrote a letter to Ruatara that Thomas Kendall and William Hall would carry on the *Active* during their exploratory trip in June 1814, Marsden framed his relationship with the chief primarily in the idiom of reciprocity. In fact, the letter began with clear deference to Rautara's mana, being addressed to "Duaterra King." But the body of the letter stressed their common interests: Marsden had sent Ruatara wheat seed and a teacher for Ruatara's "Tamoneekes [*tamariki* (boys)] and Kocteedo's [*kotiro* (girls)]"; his son, Charles, had provided Ruatara with a cockerel as a present; and his wife, Elizabeth, had gifted Ruatara a shirt and jacket. Marsden promised to send Ruatara anything else that he desired. In return, Marsden asked Ruatara to protect the missionaries and to load the *Active* with muka (dressed flax), potatoes, fishing lines and nets, mats, and other trade goods. The *Active* also carried the present of a jacket for Kawiti. Marsden ended the letter by informing Ruatara of the well-being of Marsden's family and intimate circle, naming each individual with whom the rangatira had become well acquainted during his time in Parramatta.[117] Familial connections between the Marsden family and Ruatara's *whānau* [family] were also consolidated by Elizabeth Marsden's gift to Ruatara's wife, Rahu: a red gown, red being a color prized by Māori and associated with chiefly status.[118]

Such connections meant that the languages of kinship and friendship did frame the foundation of the mission, even if such relationships would become strained after the mission community was "planted' at Hohi.[119] Alison Jones and Kuni Jenkins have noted that these intimate languages clearly present in the first book produced by the Mission, *A Korao no New Zealand: or, the New Zealander's First* Book, which was printed in Sydney in 1815. In that work Kendall used the word "wanhoungha"—*whanaunga* (relative)—to describe being "friends." Jones and Jenkins convincingly argue that here Kendall had absorbed the language of kinship that his Māori language teachers had used to explain Kendall's relationship to them.[120] Despite the fraught development of the mission, the language of kinship persisted in *A Grammar and Vocabulary of the Language of New Zealand* (produced in 1820 by Kendall with the assistance of rangatira from the Bay of Islands), which described missionary school pupils as "wanau," "whānau," or "family," a lexical choice far removed from the implications of subordinate status implicit in the words "pupil" or "student."[121]

These personal connections and forms of reciprocity enabled the establishment of the mission, and they provide an often-neglected social context for understanding the mission's foundation. Of course, these ties were strong in part because the rangatira were consistently interested in Marsden's passions for agriculture and trade. Te Pahi's and Ruatara's enthusiastic engagement with European agriculture and their support for Marsden's plan for a mission were integral to what James Belich has termed the "Maori discovery of Europe."[122] Marsden was convinced of the cultural capacity of Māori and of New Zealand's suitability as a mission field because of the desire of rangatira like Te Pahi and Ruatara to seek "improvement." In 1808 Marsden told the CMS that Te Pahi was not only a "very extraordinary man" who possessed "the greatest natural Abilities," but that he also "expressed the most ardent desire to improve his Subjects."[123] Marsden also found these same qualities in Ruatara: "The grand object of all his toils—an object which was the constant topic of his conversation—[was] namely, the means of civilizing his countrymen."[124] John Liddiard Nicholas, a close friend who accompanied Marsden to New Zealand in 1814–15, also suggested that Te Pahi and Ruatara were united in their desire for "improvement."

> The same ardent desire for acquiring knowledge, which was so strongly displayed by his predecessor [Te Pahi], could also be perceived in this young man [Ruatara], who, from the advantage of a longer residence among our people, and a tolerable acquaintance with our language, was better enabled to judge of the abject condition of his own countrymen, while he promised to exert all his influence in order to improve it. He not only readily acquiesced in the proposal of Mr. Marsden to form a Missionary Establishment among his people, for the purpose of disseminating the great truths of Divine Revelation, but expressed an anxious solicitude to have it commenced as soon as possible; and guaranteed to all persons engaged in it, hospitality and kindness from his own tribe, and safe protection from the attacks of any other.[125]

Nicholas continued, framing Ruatara as the Pacific's counterpart to the great "civilizer" of Russia: "Duaterra [Ruatara], like Peter the Great, if I may be allowed in this instance to compare the obscure chief of a savage tribe, with the mighty Emperor of a comparatively savage nation, laboured with indefatigable industry at all sorts of employments; but particularly agriculture, which he wished to introduce among his people, and spared no pains that he might be enabled to instruct them in it on his return."[126]

But Marsden did not inquire as to Māori motivations for seeking improvement; rather, he read their efforts as a manifestation of their "natural disposition," a feature of their "national character." There is no doubt that Māori were eager to engage with many aspects of European material culture and intellectual life, but we must guard against seeing this as a natural, unchanging, and essential element of Māori mentalities. The flexibility and adaptability of Māori culture was the product of history. The profound changes that accompanied migration from the tropical islands of the Pacific to the very large temperate islands of New Zealand meant that the Polynesian communities that settled in New Zealand had a history of radical cultural adaptation. Moreover, the sustained history of long-distance trade among Māori communities—which involved valuable items such as tītī (muttonbirds) from Kā Moutere Tītī (the Muttonbird Islands, in Foveaux Strait), pounamu from the west coast of Te Wai Pounamu, argillite from the Nelson region, and obsidian from Tuhua (Mayor Island, north of Tauranga)—reflected the economic and social value Māori attached to items that were not available locally.[127] Due to these broad forces, Māori had by the late eighteenth century developed a strong interest in the opportunities that might be presented by cross-cultural contact, as well as in the novel technologies and ideas that they might access from strangers.

It is clear that Te Pahi and Ruatara were particularly alive to the economic and social advantages that might arise from engaging with Europeans and from their friendship with Marsden.[128] Te Pahi had witnessed the benefits that Tuki and Huru had enjoyed as a result of their sojourn in Norfolk Island. He was particularly aware of the advantages bestowed on these northern rangatira by the seed potatoes—which produced larger, more reliable, and more frequent crops than the delicate Polynesian kūmara (sweet potato)—that they had received from Lieutenant Governor King. Therefore, although traveling to Norfolk Island "was much against the wishes of his dependants," Te Pahi sought out King because he was convinced that his family's discomfort would be "outweighed by probable advantages they would derive from his visit." Te Pahi also personally benefited from his visit to King, as he received a box of seedling fruit trees, iron utensils and tools, a prefabricated house, and a special silver medal affirming their friendship.[129] On his return to New Zealand, Te Pahi allowed visiting ships to anchor off his island at Te Puna, providing them with food (including potatoes), and in turn he used the ships to convey seed potatoes and prepared flax to Port Jackson, thus initiating the long involvement of Māori in trans-Tasman trade.[130] After Te Pahi's death, in 1810, Ruatara, too, was acutely aware of the material benefits of cross-cultural contact. Marsden noted that Ruatara had "made arrangements with his people for a very extensive cultivation of the land, and formed a plan for building a new town, with regular streets, after the European mode, to be erected on a beautiful situation, which commanded a view of the harbour's mouth, and the adjacent country round. We, together, inspected the ground fixed on for the township, and the situation of the intended church."[131]

Marsden presumed a congruence between his motivations and those of Te Pahi and Ruatara. But as time progressed, the missionaries stationed in New Zealand warned Marsden that there was in fact considerable divergence between the motivation of the rangatira who "protected" the mission and Marsden's dream of using the "civilized arts" as an instrument that would ultimately effect the conversion of Māori. In 1817 Thomas Kendall, the missionary school teacher, explained to Marsden,

> The Natives approve of Europeans settling amongst them through mo-
> tives of self-interest. . . . We must not try them beyond their strength, and
> it becomes us, as it will do any others who may settle with us, or near us,
> for the sake of the natives as well as our own, to be watchful, and not to
> injure them by placing too much confidence in them. . . . The Natives are
> eager after trade. . . . Felling axes, large and small chopping axes, hoes,
> spades, shovels, large and small fish-hooks, &c, please them well.[132]

Early nineteenth-century rangatira may well have been drawn to Mars-den's gospel of improvement, but not because they wanted to radically re-fashion the ideological basis of their own society. Te Pahi and Ruatara were certainly interested in Christian practice and cosmology, but their initial in-terest in their respective connections with Marsden were very much focused on European technology and farming.[133] The processes of "improvement"— especially the promotion of trade and the application of technology to cultivation—and the outcomes of these processes—the extension and inten-sification of agricultural production—resonated with the central responsibili-ties of *rangatiratanga* (chieftainship). One fundamental aspect of traditional leadership was overseeing the production, storage, and dissemination of food for routine distribution to whānau and hapū.[134] Accumulating large surpluses of food, especially highly prized food items, was also a potent display of a chief's mana: surpluses could be distributed through trading relationships or at *hākari*, ritual feasts that accompanied *hui* (meetings; forums). Within the context of traditional leadership, food items introduced by Europeans were of great significance. Pigs—which King had gifted to Te Pahi—and potatoes came to serve as key items of trade with visiting European ships and functioned as basic units of currency in cross-cultural commerce. Potatoes had a particularly wide-reaching social impact. They were much hardier than kūmara, allowing new regions and colder soils to be cultivated and greatly increasing the per-acre output of Māori agriculture. At the same time, however, the large-scale production of potatoes for trade with Europeans required a much larger labor force, providing a significant spur to the extension of slavery in Māori society.[135] Potatoes also assumed new significance as the introduction of Eurasian mammals depleted certain traditional food sources—especially native birds—and in this context potatoes were particularly significant in providing a new material base for the long-range military campaigns conducted by Bay of Islands Māori during 1820s and 1830s.[136]

Thus the new food plants, animals, and technologies that Te Pahi and Ruatara accessed were of substantial economic and social importance: they both extended and displayed the mana of these rangatira. This brings us to the other, very specific, context for understanding the enthusiasm of these chiefs for the establishment of the mission. In the early nineteenth century, the Bay of Islands was a site of significant conflict, as the social boundaries and political balance of the region was contested. The genealogical connections, social alliances, and political rivalries that shaped life in the Bay of Islands and its surroundings were dynamic and complicated. The work of Jeffrey Sissons, Wiremu Wi Hongi, and Pat Hohepa has demonstrated that the politics of the region in this period were roughly organized around two key "alliances" of hapū. The "northern alliance" was a grouping of hapū based at the settlements of Kaikohe, Te Waimate, Kerikeri, Waitangi, Te Puna, and Rangihoua. These groups were linked by a tight web of genealogical connections, and the major rangatira of this group included Te Pahi, Ruatara, and Hongi Hika (who emerged as the missions's chief patron in the mid-1810s). The people at Rangihoua pā, Ruatara's power base, were primarily members of Te Hikutu hapū, a group that retained strong connections to the Hokianga region as well.[137] This broad grouping of kingroups was competing for political and economic dominance with the "southern alliance," which counted the settlements at Ōkura, Kawakawa, Paihia, Waikare, Matauwhi, and Kororāreka as its main seats of power (see map 2).

Trade and contact with Europeans became an important new element in the long-standing conflicts between these two groups. These clashes were primarily driven by various *take* (actions that were basis of disputes) and tensions produced by the particularly complex skein of genealogical connections that shaped the region's social formations; but the differential impact of trade with Europeans and missionary activity added a new layer of rivalries to the Bay of Islands's geopolitics.[138] By the mid-1810s, the "northern alliance" was ascendant, a position that was secured in part by Te Pahi's accessing of new food plants and his ability to attract European ships to his anchorage. Te Pahi used the potatoes he was producing to access iron, a commodity that had great practical and military utility.[139] By the time the Hall and Kendall first visited New Zealand, in June 1814, the northern alliance had also used these trading relationships to procure European muskets.[140]

The leading chiefs of the southern alliance were jealous of the economic and military advantage flowing to their rivals. By the late 1810s, Marsden was painfully aware of the extent to which missionaries had been embedded in indigenous political and economic rivalries. During his second visit to New Zealand, Te Morenga and Waitara, rangatira from the inland Taiamai district, complained to Marsden that Ruatara and Hongi Hika had dominated trade with Europeans because of their connections with the CMS. They informed Marsden that "by this means, the power and wealth of Shunghee [Hongi] were greatly increased." Hongi effectively monopolized trade because he would not allow his rivals to trade with Europeans who anchored near his settlements or visited his pā. The southern chiefs protested that they "had not been treated with that respect and attention, which their rank and power in New Zealand entitled them to." They explained that what they "wanted was an equal advantage of Trade, which they could not enjoy without the residence of a Missionary amongst them."[141] Two weeks after Marsden left the Bay of Islands, war erupted between Te Morenga's and Hongi's people over the theft of some shellfish and a *taua* (war party) from Taiamai plundered the new mission station that the CMS had established at Kerikeri, under the shadow of Hongi's Kororipo pā.[142]

Conclusion

By the time this conflict erupted, it was clear that translating Marsden's vision of the mission into reality was much more difficult that he had initially hoped. In the next two chapters I assess the development of the mission stations and the ways in which the CMS mission and the fledgling Wesleyan mission, which was established in 1821, were forced to accommodate themselves to the reality of their economic dependence on Māori and to the strength of fundamental Māori ideas about social organization and cultural meaning. Marsden's belief that the introduction of the "civilized arts" would enable the "improvement" and Christianization of Māori society foundered as the mission was wracked by internal disputes and the ability of Māori, at least initially, to dictate the terms of their engagement with missionaries. Marsden's optimism owed much to a set of imperial discourses about the Pacific to which he was heir. Cook, Banks, and other British reporters on the Pacific in the second half of the eighteenth century consistently emphasized New Zealand's potential as a future colony and stressed the islands' value to the empire. Marsden echoed these sentiments, demonstrating his willingness to use national interest and the language of empire in formulating his plans for New Zealand: indeed, he regularly described the missionaries to New Zealand as "settlers" and understood the missionaries establishing a "colony" themselves. Marsden was dependent on imperial structures—from business houses (like Campbell, Clarke and Co) to the powers of the governor of New South Wales—in realizing his desire, and the desire of Te Pahi and Ruatara, for the mission in the Bay of Islands. While Marsden was a vocal opponent of some of the consequences of imperial activity—especially the mistreatment of indigenous crewmen on European ships and British sailors' sexual exploitation of indigenous women in the Pacific—he considered the empire to be a potent vehicle for the dissemination of Christianity and Christian missionaries to be agents for the extension of commerce around the globe. In the 1810s Marsden understood Christianity, commerce, and colonization as a tightly bound cultural package, but the trials of the missionaries in New Zealand over the next decade encouraged Marsden to eventually recognize the tensions between these elements of British culture.

W hen Charles Darwin visited the Bay of Islands on board HMS *Beagle* in December 1835, he was struck by the transformations that the Anglican missionaries of the CMS had affected. His diary offered lengthy and passionate reflections on the improving power of the missionary project, detailing the environmental, economic, moral, and spiritual impact of missionary work. The progress of the mission was thrown into relief by the persistence of unimproved lands and communities, which had not been touched by the "enchanter's wand" that Darwin imagined the missionaries wielding. Darwin suggested that the large tracts of fern-covered country between Paihia and Waimate had a "desolate aspect" which gave an impression of "useless sterility," but he also noted that the "land by tillage becomes productive." In its current state, however, Darwin suggested that it was "uninhabited useless country," a reading of the landscape that was oblivious to the centrality of fern root as a key foodstuff and of fern as a flexible material for Māori.[1] Conversely, Darwin imagined the Waimate mission station, where human labor and skill was consistently applied to nature, in ways that were immediately legible to Britons. To him it appeared as if it were "an English farm house" with "its well dressed fields." He described the scene.

On an adjoining slope fine crops of barley & wheat in full ear, & others of potatoes & of clover, were standing; but I cannot attempt to describe all I saw; there were large gardens, with every fruit & vegetable which England produces, & many belonging to a warmer clime. I may instance asparagus, kidney bean, cucumbers, rhubarb, apples & pears, figs, peaches, apricots, grapes, olives, gooseberries, currants, hops, gorse for fences & English oaks! & many different kinds of flowers.

These transformations of the landscape echoed deep shifts in the material base of indigenous society. Darwin's narrative underscored the role of new patterns of labor, of introduced technology, and of new tools in driving forward these changes. The mission's yard featured a "threshing barn with a winnowing machine, a blacksmith's forge, & on the ground, ploughshares & other tools," and it also boasted a "a large & substantial water mill." These were potent agents of improvement. Because of the transformations these modernizing instruments enabled, Darwin imagined New Zealand as if it were England at several points in his narrative. Waimate looked, sounded, and felt like Darwin's "Home." These parallels were underscored by Darwin's observation that "at the mill the New Zealander may be seen powdered white like flour, like his brother miller in England."[2]

This image of the deracinated Māori miller hinted at the depth of the social changes that Darwin cataloged. At Waimate, Darwin observed several young Māori men, former slaves who had "been redeemed" by the missionaries and who were dressed "in a shirt & jacket & had a respectable appearance." These young men worked hard and were honest, but they were also "very merry & good-humoured," and in the evening they played a game of cricket with the son of a missionary. But the transformation of Māori women on the station was even more marked. As a result of the "decided & pleasing change" affected by missionaries and their wives, their Māori female charges had been remade. Darwin suggested that they now appeared like "dairy maids in England" and as such "formed a wonderful contrast to the women of the filthy hovels of Kororarika [Kororāreka]."[3]

On the evening of 23 December 1835, Darwin dined with the CMS missionary William Williams. The Williams family and Māori connected to the station gathered in the Williams's home. In his account of this house, Darwin mobilized cannibalism as a way of indexing the success of the mission. He recorded that he found "a very large party of children . . . who were sitting around a table at tea. I never saw a nicer or more merry group: & to think that this was in the centre of the land of cannibalism, murder & all atrocious crimes!" This gathering was characterized by "cordiality" and "happiness"; the mission formed a unified family, an impression confirmed the next morning when Darwin joined "the whole family"—which included those Māori attached to the household—for "morning prayers [which] were read in the native tongue."[4]

Darwin's narrative was optimistic and he did not dwell on the vast amounts of labor and many struggles that were needed to produce these performances of Christian respectability.[5] Its positive assessment of missionary work, as Mark Graham has suggested, was shaped by Darwin's reading of the "mission controversy" in England, a debate that was partially energized by the criticisms of missionaries in New Zealand made by the traveling artist Augustus Earle, who was aboard the *Beagle* in the early stages on its voyage.[6] Darwin's diary of his time in the Bay of Islands offered a vivid catalog of environmental and social change. Yet due to the brevity of Darwin's visit to the Bay of Islands, he did not recognize the difficulties that beset missionary work, nor did he fully apprehend the struggles and conflicts that swirled around mission stations. He was an astute enough observer, however, to understand that even though the missionaries had affected significant change, there were real limits to missionary influence. He observed, for example, that some of those "clean tidy & healthy" native women attached to the mission resisted the arguments of missionary wives against tattooing, seeking out moko on their lips when a renowned tohunga (ritual expert) from the south visited the Bay of Islands.[7] He also recognized that the authority of rangatira remained potent, that Māori continued to maintain many of their own deathways, and that slavery persisted within some Māori communities. Even Darwin could see that there were limits to the reach of "enchanter's wand."[8]

In advancing a critical reevaluation of these "enchanter's wands," in this chapter I offer a spatially inflected history as I explore the mission station as a site of cross-cultural engagement, struggle, and transformation. In tracing the developing relationships between missionaries and various Māori communities from the late 1810s to the late 1830s, I lay some foundations for a discussion of labor and time I offer in the next chapter. Where in that chapter I demonstrate the persistence of established Māori understandings of work and the ability of Māori workers to negotiate their place within the mission's economic order, in this chapter I examine both the symbolic and social importance of the mission station.

In many ways, in this chapter I address a central concern of the last three decades of feminist historical inquiry: the articulation of gendered "separate spheres" under modernity, which identified men with the "public" realm of paid work, the professions, and political life, and women with the "private" world of unpaid domestic work, child-rearing, and nurturing. Here I try to move beyond the rather abstract and superficial treatment of space that has characterized some of this work, by carefully connecting the production of gendered identities to the architecture of mission houses, to the organization of fields, gardens, buildings, and boundaries of mission stations, and to the inescapable physicality of cross-cultural contact on the mission stations. My treatment of these cross-cultural contests over gender is framed by a firm conviction that the ways in which any given community organizes space both reflects its central cultural concerns—understandings of the relationships between the natural and supernatural, men and women, children and adults—and in turn structures social interaction. The ordering of space guided sleeping arrangements, defined the locations of socially sanctioned intimacy, specified where labor was to be carried out, and determined where food was to be prepared, served, and consumed.[9]

Mission stations were produced out of and shaped by a range of forces. They were symbols of the missionary project, making manifest the missionaries' vision of their role in the world and the power of houses, schools, chapels, gardens, and workshops to educate and transform Māori. But they were never simply symbolic: they were real places, too. As such they were molded by the constraints imposed by the topography and climate, the influence of the shifting political geographies of hapū and iwi, and the demands and interests of Māori individuals and families who developed an association with the missions. We can also think of them as being produced by the trajectories of people, animals, tools and implements, books and things, commodities and trade goods that moved in and out of the stations. These movements were not smooth flows, but rather produced various forms of friction.[10] While friction could occasionally spark open conflict, the movements of and encounters between the different elements that were integral to mission stations were fundamental to the making of these places and the production of new visions of community.

Foundations and Locations

Missionary stations were a fundamental element in the practice of Protestant evangelization in New Zealand. Where the Catholic Marist mission, after its establishment in 1838, pursued a strategy that depended on itinerant teaching rather than on the establishment of permanent settlements, mission stations were pivotal to the work of the CMS and WMS from the outset

No. LXVI. Midsummer, 1832.

R. Watts, Printer, Crown Court, Temple Bar.

CHURCH MISSIONARY SOCIETY.

CHURCH MISSIONARY SETTLEMENT OF RANGIHOUA, NEW ZEALAND.

FIGURE 2.1 "Church Missionary Settlement of Rangihoua, New Zealand." *Church Missionary Quarterly Papers* 66 (Midsummer 1832). Ref.: PUBL-0031-1832-66, Alexander Turnbull Library, Wellington, New Zealand.

of their missions in New Zealand.[11] These substantial settlements were designed to provide security for missionaries and their families, to establish a sound economic base for evangelization and a seat from which itineration could be organized, and to provide a site where local peoples could be introduced to Christianity and a range of new technologies and skills. At the same time, they were imagined to be ideal communities that exemplified the models of spiritual discipline and social comportment that were expected of the Christian who had embraced the "seriousness" of evangelicalism.

In their celebration of mission stations as "enchanter's wands," both missionary propaganda, like William Yate's hyperbolic *An Account of New Zealand*, and the narratives of European travelers in the 1830s offered very partial readings of the development of mission stations. These narratives tended to underplay the uneven progress of missionary settlements and marginalized the role of Māori in the genesis of mission stations. In a similar vein, the visual archive of the mission emphasized the order, symmetry, and "Englishness" of the settlements in order to underline the transformative power of the missionary enterprise. The *Church Missionary Quarterly Papers*, for example, published an image of Rangihoua and Hohi (Ōihi) in 1832, after the Hohi settlement had actually been abandoned (see figure 2.1). This image simultaneously anglicized the Rangihoua pā, with neatly linear streets and fences, and transformed the landscape at Hohi, depicting the small missionary settlement as immediately adjacent to the shoreline in a relatively flat and cultivated landscape.

Thus, both written texts and visual representations have encouraged scholars to see mission stations in early New Zealand as fundamentally European, English, or "white" spaces and as centers for a project of Europeanization. In such work, the picket fence stands as the central symbolic marker of the missionary project, which itself is primarily understood as a form of cultural imperialism.[12] A close spatial reading of the development of mission stations reveals the limits of such arguments.

The location and foundation of mission stations reveals that these complexes were not simply imposed by missionaries, but rather were borne out of complex negotiations between missionaries and Māori, with Māori leaders generally in a position of power.[13] This can clearly be seen in the dynamics that led to the siting of the first mission established at Hohi in late 1814. This choice of location emerged out of the relationships that had initially developed between Samuel Marsden and Te Pahi, an influential chief in the north of the Bay of Islands in the first decade of the nineteenth century. Te Pahi traveled to New South Wales in 1805, forming close relationships with Marsden and Governor King. Te Pahi sought to establish reciprocal relationships, gifting King with fine mats and a mere, and explaining that he was motivated by the benefits, including potatoes, that had followed from Tuki and Huru's visit.[14] On his return to New Zealand, Te Pahi carried with him new seeds, livestock, a silver medallion from the governor, and other gifts. Under his leadership, Te Puna emerged as an important center for cultivation and trade with Europeans. John Savage's 1807 account described Te Puna as the "capital" of the north, which had become a central location for cross-cultural trade as Te Pahi's people grew and traded excellent potatoes for iron.[15]

But this productive engagement did not last long, as the growing influence of Te Pahi and Te Puna precipitated conflict. Visiting Europeans plundered the potato cultivations at Te Puna, and cross-cultural trade was disrupted by the willingness of European captains and crew to use violence and to kidnap Māori, including Te Pahi's daughter Atahoe.[16] Te Pahi found that his complaints about these raids and the mistreatment of Māori sailors roused little interest among Governor King's successors, including Lieutenant Governor Joseph Foveaux and his secretary, James Finucane, who produced a mocking portrait of Te Pahi in 1808.[17] Within the Bay of Islands, Te Pahi's prominence and the influence of Te Puna had destabilized the existing balance of political and commercial power, and the resulting disruptions ultimately lead to Te Pahi's death. In 1809 Te Pahi was in Whangaroa when the *Boyd* was destroyed. As we have seen, Tara, Te Pahi's rival who controlled the anchorage and trade at Kororāreka on the south side of the Bay of Islands, encouraged Europeans and the colonial authorities in New South Wales to believe that Te Pahi was responsible for the destruction of the *Boyd*.[18]

By this time, Marsden was working on plans for the mission to the Bay of Islands. Marsden, who had developed a "particular intimacy" with Te Pahi, was skeptical of the allegations that the rangatira played an active role in the attack on the *Boyd*.[19] He had established another close connection with Te Pahi's people after nursing Ruatara, who Marsden understood to be Te Pahi's nephew, on board the convict ship *Ann*, which transported both men from London to Port Jackson in 1809. Ruatara had failed in his effort to see George III, having been denied permission to land in England, and had been beaten by his crewmates. Ruatara and Marsden forged a close relationship, and Marsden was delighted with Ruatara's commitment to the small farm gifted to him by Marsden at Parramatta while he subsequently lived in New South Wales.[20] After returning to the Bay of Islands, around 1812, Ruatara assumed the mantle of leadership around Te Puna, in part because of the genealogical connections of his wife, Rahu, the daughter of Rākau, an influential rangatira at Rangihoua. Like Te Pahi, Ruatara sought a close connection with the authorities in New South Wales, and he received livestock and a military uniform from Governor Macquarie and a hand-powered flourmill from Samuel Marsden. He also promised to his people that he would bring Europeans, teachers who could introduce the arts of writing and reading, and horses. Ruatara thus functioned as the key patron of the mission that was planted in 1814.[21]

Ruatara extended his protection over the missionary party that arrived on 22 December 1814. Ruatara's own mana was fragile, given that his long absence had limited his ability to participate in warfare or to be a provider for his people. Acting as a patron for the missionaries and championing new forms of agricultural production were important ways of enhancing his standing and importance. Where possible, Ruatara helped broker amicable relationships with other the kin-groups, including the people of Whangaroa. He guided Marsden on his travels and, most important, facilitated the construction of the first mission houses at Hohi under the pā at Rangihoua. Rangihoua was also associated with the great rangatira Hongi Hika, whom Marsden understood as Ruatara's older kinsman, and who wielded considerable influence as the most powerful chief of the northern alliance of hapū (subtribal groups), which dominated the northern Bay of Islands and the interior.[22] By 1814, Hongi had emerged as a key military leader driving the consolidation of Ngāpuhi and the extension of that iwi's power. Acting as patron to the mission and cultivating cross-cultural trade were key to Hongi's strategy. Marsden's summary of the foundation of the mission stressed how important such connections were to the rangatira: "Tippahee being dead, and Shunghee [Hongi] promising, with Duaterra [Ruatara], that he would take care of the missionaries, they came, and were placed under their protection by me."[23]

Ruatara and Hongi, who had cultivations and a temporary settlement near Te Puna, exercised considerable control over the initial development of the mission. This was clear from the construction of the first cluster of mission houses and buildings to the east of the Rangihoua pā at Hohi. The buildings were constructed on terraces overlooking the beach at Hohi and in the shadow of the Rangihoua pā. This was a position that meant that the missionaries' activities could be easily observed from the pā. More important, these terraces were effectively narrow platforms within a steeply sloping landscape that offered limited productive land for cultivation in the immediate vicinity and no space for any significant expansion. Thus, in effect, Ruatara had located the Hohi settlement near important sites of power and commerce, Rangihoua pā and Te Puna, while imposing heavy constraints on the mission's operation and placing missionaries in a position of dependence. This was ameliorated, to some extent, by Marsden's purchase of two hundred acres adjacent to Rangihoua from Te Uri o Kanae, another of Ruatara's kin, in February 1815.[24]

But the missionaries were unable to occupy this land and remained hemmed in by the steep terrain at Hohi. Kendall and King were extremely unhappy about the lack of space for cultivation. In 1815 Kendall complained, "We have now resided nearly two years at this place, and to all appearance there is no probability of our obtaining the necessaries of life in any other way than at the expense of the Society. The spot on which we live is barren, and as you will observe from the view [it] is so mountainous that it is quite unsuitable for the purposes of cultivation, or for cattle."[25] William Hall and his wife, Dinah, decamped in 1815 to flat land at Waitangi, but they had barely established their house when a plundering party attacked, stripping them of their possessions and knocking Dinah unconscious.[26] The Halls immediately returned to Hohi, revealing the extent of their reliance on their chiefly protectors at Rangihoua. With his deep investment in his relationships with the people of Rangihoua and Te Puna, Marsden was slow to recognize the unenviable situation in which the missionaries had been placed. But in 1823, in a letter to Hongi Hika, he finally suggested that "I never liked Rangeehoo [Rangihoua] because the land was very bad."[27]

Due to its marginal economic basis, the mission continued to be dependent on the patronage and protection of powerful rangatira like Hongi. From the outset of the mission, Hongi worked hard to get Marsden to establish a missionary settlement at Kerikeri, where the Kerikeri River flowed into a basin-like inlet in the northwest corner of the Bay of Islands. Hongi exercised his mana over this area: in the 1790s his father, Te Hōtete, occupied the Kororipo pā, which had commanding views of the basin and stood strategically at the junction of the Wairoa and Kerikeri Rivers.[28] This site effectively controlled the primary pathway from the ocean to the significant centers of settlement and cultivation inland, including Hongi's great pā Ōkuratope. As Hongi's dominance rose, Kerikeri became the heart of his power. From there, Hongi launched his raiding campaigns to the south, and it was to Kerikeri that his men returned with their war captives. It was a rich place as the *kāinga* (village) by the pā had good *kirikiri* (gravel-rich) soils and provided access to excellent fishing.[29]

In 1815 Marsden and Hongi agreed that the missionaries based at Hohi could plant wheat at Kerikeri in the coming spring.[30] During Marsden's visit in 1819, Hongi guided Marsden and a party of missionaries up the Kerikeri River, offering the mission any lands they wished to use. This was an exciting prospect as Marsden observed that the soil was "rich, the land pretty level, free from timber, easy to work with the plough and bounded by a fine freshwater river, and the communication by water free and open to any part of the Bay of Islands." [31] For Hongi, the missionaries' presence enhanced his mana, providing an important opportunity for accessing European goods and giving him greater control over trade within the region. Such commercial advantage was integral to Hongi's ability to continue sending taua (war parties) to the south, which had substantially enlarged his power. Korokoro, a Ngāre Raumati chief whose authority focused on the eastern islands of the Bay and the coastal lands on the south side of the Bay, protested that this new establishment would disrupt the relationships between chiefs in the region by marginalizing his people and enhancing Hongi's strategic position. Marsden observed that Korokoro felt that "it was too great an affliction for him for all the Europeans to reside with Shunghee." Marsden placated Korokoro by visiting the lands of his people, near Pāroa, on the south side of the Bay of Islands, promising to establish a mission there, an undertaking that he never delivered on.[32] Marsden did, however, place the mission gardener James Shepherd at Ōkura, on an inlet to the southeast of Kerikeri, where he established a garden and a plant nursery under the patronage of the rangatira Te Morenga and Perehiko of the Ngāti Hauta hapū, part of the southern alliance of kin-groups. This initiative served not only as an attempt to mollify the chiefs and maintain connection with Hongi's rivals, but also as utu (recompense, restoring the balance) for the death of Perehiko's son in New South Wales.[33]

A missionary settlement at Kerikeri was quickly conjured into being. In August 1819 Marsden and the missionaries laid out the plan for the settlement at the site agreed to by Hongi, and the chief also allowed a shelter to be constructed at the site for the builders. In the following month, sites for the storehouse, school, smith's house, and shop were all cleared and the fledgling mission's garden was planted and sown.[34] In November Hongi affixed a copy of his moko to mark his assent to the transfer of land to the missionaries.[35] Relationships between the missionaries and Hongi later became fraught—in part because of Hongi's close relationship to the difficult Thomas Kendall and in part because Hongi was angered by the reluctance of some of the missionaries to trade muskets, powder, and repair guns—but a strongly symbiotic relationship existed between the mission and the great chief until his death, in 1828, even if Hongi was less enthusiastic about Christian teaching than about the benefits of trading with missionaries.[36]

By that time both Kerikeri and, especially, Hohi had been eclipsed as centers of Māori population and locations for trade, although Kerikeri remained strategically significant because of its schools and the substance of the missionary presence.[37] Eventually, missionary unhappiness with the constraints of the Hohi site were such that the CMS allowed the mission to be relocated a short distance to the west, in Te Puna. The flatter, more open land at Te Puna had long been appealing; in 1815 Kendall observed in his complaint, "I objected to landing here [Hohi] at first very strongly to Mr. Marsden, because there was on the other side of the village and in sight of it a more even tract of land with a more fertile soil."[38] By the 1820s, the missionaries at Hohi were not only frustrated by their limited agricultural capacity, but also marginalized within the shifting economic and social geography of the Bay of Islands. Changing patterns of trade had rendered Te Puna and Hohi relatively isolated; due to the downturn in commercial opportunities and cultivation for passing ships, Te Puna was no longer the "capital" of the Bay of Islands.[39] Furthermore, given the oscillations of Māori politics, Rangihoua was no longer a key seat of power, in part because the primary bases of Hongi, the dominant force in the region, were at Kerikeri and Ōkuratope.

In May 1828 John King purchased ten acres of land at Te Puna, on the western side of the Rangihoua pā, the tract that Kendall had admired from the start of the mission. This was purchased with a significant consignment of blankets, metal tools, and implements to the rangatira Wharepoaka, Manuwiri, Waikato, Marupainga, and Pani.[40] King and Shepherd agreed that Te Puna would allow the mission to cultivate a secure food supply and to limit their dependence on trade. It would also allow them to maintain their connections to the people of Rangihoua. The progress of this new settlement was hesitant, as King and Shepherd clashed over the details of its development, but finally both the King and Shepherd families moved to Te Puna, in September 1832.[41]

By the late 1820s, the dependence of missionaries on their chiefly patrons had been diluted. The illness of Hongi Hika, the CMS's key protector, had caused great anxiety, and the missionaries prepared themselves for violent disturbances in the advent of his death, burying their valuables and preparing to evacuate.[42] But no such attacks occurred when he finally died, in March 1828, suggesting that under Henry Williams's leadership the mission by this time had accumulated its own mana.[43]

The success of the Paihia mission station was central to this greater confidence. From his arrival in New Zealand, Henry Williams was concerned by what he understood as the missionaries' dependence on and subordination to Māori power brokers. The station established at Paihia, in the southwest of the Bay of Islands, was designed to put the mission on a firmer footing, as Williams became the settlement's leader. Williams and Marsden explored the west and southwestern portions of the Bay of Islands, including Waitangi, but eventually fixed on Paihia on the banks of the Kawakawa River. Although imagined as marking a fresh start for the mission, the site at Paihia was at least in part selected because of webs of personal connection with its chiefly patron and protector, Te Koki. Te Koki seems to have been an ally of the rangatira Tara, Pōmare, and Te Morenga, key figures in the southern alliance of hapū that controlled the southern and southwestern sections of the Bay of Islands. When Marsden visited Paihia in August 1823, he recorded that Te Koki had spent time with him at Parramatta and was a "very worthy man."[44] Marsden had promised Te Koki that a missionary would be sent to his people after his son, Te Ahara, died at the Parramatta Native Institution, echoing the arrangement that Marsden had made with Perehiko at Ōkura.[45] In September 1819, when the decision to found a settlement at Kerikeri had been taken, Marsden himself had been implored by Te Uri o Kanae of Rangihoua, who had connections to Te Koki, to consider establishing a mission at Paihia, to the north of where the Kawakawa River entered the southwest corner of the Bay of Islands.[46] Even as he wished to break free of dependence on Māori, Henry Williams noted in his discussion of the selection of Paihia as a site, "The missionary becomes one with the tribe with which he is connected."[47] Ultimately, however, the Paihia site was extremely advantageous and gave the mission a heightened sense of material confidence. Henry Williams was quickly aware of the great value of this location: it had flat and good ground, a garden that was quickly planted with vegetables, an orchard, access to excellent fisheries, a sheltered beach, and a clear view of the Bay of Islands out to the heads.[48]

Connections by sea underpinned a new stage in the mission's development. In 1824 Henry Williams initiated the building of a schooner of about fifty tons, which was constructed on Paihia beach. This vessel, the *Herald*, enabled the New Zealand missionaries to control communications with Sydney. It also allowed Henry Williams and other missionaries to travel along the east coast south to Tauranga and around the North Cape to the west coast.[49] This fundamentally reconfigured the economics of the mission, allowing trade to be undertaken with hapū and iwi who accepted fishhooks as a medium of exchange for meat rather than demanding muskets.[50] Thus, the *Herald* enabled the missionaries to exercise a greater degree of control over the movement of food, tools, livestock, and trading goods that sustained the mission. This gave them a new degree of material independence. Henry Williams observed in 1825 that this meant they would not longer be at "their wits' end for common necessaries," which had been the frightening reality for the mission and which had sapped morale.[51] The particular importance of this economic freedom was underscored by Williams when, on the same day, he observed that the mission was still deeply embedded in Māori politics and that Te Koki was the "liege lord" for the missionaries at Paihia.[52]

The establishment of a mission station inland at Waimate diluted that political dependence and reflected the greater material stability of the mission. The missionaries at Waimate had no "liege lord," although the mission there again grew out of long-standing relationships with key chiefs. In 1815 Marsden traveled with Hongi Hika inland to Ōkuratope pā, which was protected by a complex of three palisades. The Europeans were impressed by the regularity of the plantations of potatoes and kūmara that covered more than thirty acres around the pā.[53] Developing Waimate's agricultural capacity was an important part of the conversations that linked Hongi and Marsden. In November 1823 Marsden wrote to Hongi stressing the rangatira's importance to the mission's success, promising him seeds and tools for new cultivations at Waimate, and explaining that agriculture, rather than war, should be his priority: "Then you will become a very great man and will be able to feed and clothe many people." This was a canny argument that recognized the importance of food as a currency for a rangatira's mana.[54] The following year, Marsden wrote to Hongi explaining that he was sending him "a gentleman who would be able to make a farm at Wymatte." This was the CMS missionary Richard Davis, a successful tenant farmer from Dorset, who was to teach Hongi's people how to plough, grow wheat, use bullocks, and produce flour.[55]

Davis played a key role in the foundation of the Waimate settlement, even if William Yate was the only ordained minister who took up residence in 1831. Davis attempted to develop Waimate as a mixed English farm on the 250 acres that the CMS had purchased, although this project ultimately proved challenging. Darwin's visit coincided with a time of relative abundance and calm, but Davis had difficulty sourcing adequate labor, livestock were vulnerable to attacks by dogs owned by local Māori, and the development of the farm along English lines was hampered by a lack of adequate tools. Nevertheless, before the Waimate station's conversion into a primarily educational establishment in the early 1840s, the wheat fields and flourmill certainly produced significant supplies of flour that mitigated the pressures that the mission had previously routinely experienced.[56] In the end, Waimate was most important in that it signified the ability of missionaries to pursue an economic model that they themselves dictated. Through the middle and later 1830s, the mission expanded to the south and the north. While the construction of new stations always entailed local negotiations and the missionaries were dependent on key chiefly brokers, such as Panakareao of Te Rarawa at Kaitaia, the CMS operated with a degree of autonomy that had been unknown to the first generation of missionaries.[57]

Housing

Thus mission stations were never simply planted by the missionaries at locations they deemed desirable; the fundamental contours of the CMS mission to New Zealand were dictated by the mission's deep implication in kin-group politics and rivalries. If compromise and accommodation were central to the foundation and placement of mission stations, the actual physical construction of these complexes was also dependent on local materials, skills, labor, and cultural negotiations. Translating the ideal of the mission station as an orderly and civilized Christian settlement into a reality on the ground in

New Zealand proved very difficult. Between the 1810s and 1830s, of course, the missionaries in New Zealand were operating a long way beyond the frontiers of formal British authority within the empire. And the mission operated under considerable economic pressure, with the missionaries struggling to source and process sufficient timber locally to construct large and elaborate dwellings.

These material challenges meant that the early missionaries initially occupied houses built on Māori models, using local materials (a practice that echoed the use of Xhosa huts by the early generations of missionaries in southern Africa).[58] At Hohi, the two sawyers who had sailed to New Zealand with Marsden on the *Active*, the ship's blacksmith, Thomas Hansen (the son of the *Active*'s captain), and Rangihoua Māori worked together to construct a sixty-foot long hut, which they divided into four sections, one each for the missionary families (Kendall, King, Hall), and the fourth, presumably, for Marsden's own use.[59] Many subsequent missionary families, especially those establishing new settlements, would spend significant amounts of time in single-room dwellings primarily clad in *raupo* (bulrush). When the Williams family settled at Paihia, in 1823, they lodged in a raupo hut in the shape of a beehive; this dwelling had two rooms, originally with packed dirt floors.[60] Even when the mission was more securely established, the early mission houses were not "European." At Waimate, in 1831, missionary families initially lived in temporary cottages built by Māori workers out of pūriri trees and locally made bricks.[61]

Some missionaries found such temporary dwellings trying. In early 1815, for example, John King complained about the communal hut at Hohi.

> It [the house] has no Chimney in it it will neither keep wind nor Rain out, we have no window in it Mr. M[arsden] gave orders to have it made he says it is very comfortable indeed it will do very well, This is a very wet Day it has been so for this three Days.
>
> On Sunday last Feb 12 it rained very much the watter came through upon our wheat rice bed clothing &c the watter was half over my shoes in our bed room. From the wetness of the durt floor as our hut is on low flat ground our clothing is dampt tho we do all we can to keep them dry we have no fire to dry them when it rains, as our fire is out of doors.[62]

King's letter reveals a series of expectations about the structure and function of houses: not only should dwellings be weather-tight, but they should have a hearth and chimney, separate bedrooms for sleeping, and secure, dry space for storing food. While Māori whare were traditionally constructed to withstand heavy rain and winds, they were not designed as repositories for food (which would traditionally be stored on elevated storage platforms [*whata*] or in specialized storehouses [*pātaka*]), they never included chimneys, and they were designed to be a unitary social space.

This reminds us that in the early stages of each mission station's development, the missionary family was unable to call on the European house as a pedagogic model, and the material base of missionary work remained both localized and hybridized. At Kerikeri, for example, the mission dwellings were very rudimentary. William Bean and William Fairburn, the mission carpenters, initially occupied a raupo whare as they built the seven-by-five-meter blacksmith's shop, which they then used as sleeping quarters. Next, they constructed a small wooden house of ten meters by two-and-a-half meters for the Māori laborers working on the mission site and a twenty-by-five-meter mission store. This store was quickly partitioned into six small units for the mission families: the Fairburn family, the Bean family, and the Puckey family each inhabited one unlined and earth-floored section, while the Butler family and their servant took two sections, leaving the final section as a communal storeroom. The Kemp family took up residence with the missionary Francis Hall in the blacksmith shop; this was an undesirable arrangement in a poorly sealed building, and Kemp was soon complaining about having to sleep on a rotting bed.[63] When Ensign McCrae visited Kerikeri in March 1820 he noted that the mission houses were "far from being either clean or comfortable in fact not much as those of the natives who tho' not boasting the advantages of civilization are superior to the missionaries in those respects."[64] This rather attenuated material condition really was the normative state in the mission until at least 1823. In this context, mission workers were critical of their brethren, such as John Butler at Kerikeri in the early 1820s, who were too wedded to the comforts and pretenses of a complex timber house constructed on European lines and who thus placed their own worldly comfort ahead of the more urgent priorities of evangelization, teaching, peacemaking, and helping the sick.[65]

Nevertheless, the construction of mission houses was considered central as a marker of the progress of the mission. The rules of the mission stipulated that each mission family should ultimately expect its own house, with a garden and a yard which would be used to support the family beyond the quarterly rations provided by the CMS.[66] The construction of houses for mission families was not only a demonstration of the growing capacity of the mission itself, but also as an integral element in the improvement of Māori society, as Māori were exposed to novel tools and skills and new ways of organizing work in addition to the educative model of the mission house itself. When Dandeson Coates, the secretary of the CMS, was called before the Parliamentary Select Committee on Aborigines in 1836, he provided samples of evidence to underscore the importance of mission houses to the project of evangelization and social transformation.

The missionaries employ the natives who reside with them in those kinds of labour which render them at once useful to the mission, and impart knowledge and form habits calculated to promote their civilization and social welfare. The following passages illustrate this branch of the operations of the mission.

"Kerikeri, 4 July 1831.—The natives under my care have been employed in shingling, fencing, burning lime, carpentering and landing stores."—(Mr. J. Kemp.). . . .

"With the assistance of natives, I have erected a weather-board building, 40 feet by 20, with a skilling at the back, which we intend using for our chapel and school."—(Mr. G. Clarke.)

"As to our mechanical labour, we do it all with the assistance of our natives; such as carpentering, blacksmith's work, &c. We have just finished making 50,000 bricks for our chimneys, and are now employed getting timber and other materials for building our permanent dwellings, barns, &c."—(Mr. R. Davis.)

"With my natives I have been employed upon my house in putting up fences, &c. I have also, assisted by the settlement natives, burnt a quantity of lime for the purpose of the European school."—(Mr. C. Baker.)

"Employed in attending to native sawyers, to natives digging a well, and to natives clearing land."—(Mr. J. Hamlin.)[67]

Space: Mission Houses

Coates's testimony underscored that mission houses, schools, and barns were integral to the project of evangelization. Their construction introduced Māori to new technologies, skills, and disciplines. But once constructed, they were even more potent as pedagogical instruments that modeled and inculcated a new social order. As each mission station transitioned out of its foundation phase, its buildings became more permanent, more sophisticated, and loaded with greater symbolic significance. One- and two-room huts were

FIGURE 2.2 Gardiner, Thomas, fl 1830s–1850s. View of the Missionary House, Waimate, New Zealand (1835 or later). Note the additions at the back left of the house, as well as several outbuildings, including a dovecote, on the right. Ref: A-049-020, Alexander Turnbull Library, Wellington, New Zealand.

replaced with houses that had a complex social and spatial order, where different tasks and functions were, at least in theory, separated from each other. For example, the house that Thomas Kendall and his son, Thomas Surfleet Kendall, were working on at Hohi in 1822 was much more sophisticated than the first communal hut. It had a complex internal order, featuring a sitting room, study, and parlor, as well as bedrooms, multiple chimneys, and glazed windows, and it used at least four thousand feet of boards and featured a painted timber roof (see figure 2.2).[68]

The well-constructed mission house built for the Butlers at Kerikeri, which drew critical comment from fellow missionaries like William Hall, was more substantial still. A solidly and neatly symmetrical two-storied timber construction with an enclosed verandah, it became the center of the Kerikeri station from its completion, and several missionary families cycled through the dwelling. Missionary wives, especially Martha Clarke and Charlotte Kemp, introduced the daughters of leading rangatira, including Hongi, to the domestic arts and literacy within the house. In the 1830s the house was extended by the carpenter Ben Nesbit with the addition of skillings (lean-tos) at the rear of the house, one designed to accommodate young Māori women and the other an enclosed kitchen. The latter was a novel addition and gave the house a more strongly "European" feel, as many early missionary dwellings, like Māori whare, separated food preparation and cooking areas from the main house.[69]

The three permanent homes constructed over some fourteen months to replace the temporary huts at Waimate adhered closely to the Kerikeri model, perhaps because George Clarke, who probably took the lead in planning the Waimate homes, had lived in the mission house at Kerikeri from 1823 to 1830. These again were two storied, hipped-roof houses. A central entrance hall, a common form found in British colonies, divided the houses and separated the two public rooms at the front of the constructions.[70] Smaller rooms were at the back of house, and these included internal kitchens, which brought most food-related practices into the dwelling. The small rooms upstairs were typically used as bedrooms.[71] Over time, these dwellings were modified and added to; such changes—as when George Clarke added a small dressing room to the main bedroom on his family home—marked further specialization. In this case, the dressing room was a mechanism that further enhanced privacy, a key desire that propelled the growing size and complexity of mission houses.

We must recognize the novelty of these forms of architecture and their attendant order in the New Zealand context and the profound challenge that they posed to long-established patterns of settlement and social organization. Over the many centuries of Polynesian settlement in New Zealand, the reasonably uniform organization of communities and dwellings was key to cultural cohesion: although the size of, building materials used in, and forms of decoration that adorned whare took on distinctive regional features, their basic structure was common. Both the archaeological and textual record suggest that whare did vary in size. A "typical" whare would be a rectangular construction of about three meters by four, but these dimensions could vary: some small dwellings were only two meters by three, while larger dwellings might be six meters by seven. The front of the whare, which often faced the sun in the north, had a small porch, which functioned as an important social space for the greeting of visitors and for eating. The whare's entrance was a very small door positioned on the right-hand side of the structure, looking out. The front wall of the whare also contained a pihanga (small rectangular window). The floor of the dwelling consisted of hard packed earth covered with rauaruhe (fern), raupo, and finally whāriki (mats); the soil removed from the interior was heaped at the sides of the whare in order to provide insulation. The central portion of the chimneyless interior was dominated by a stone hearth, on which a fire would be lit to provide heat and light during the evenings. The hearth itself was typically lined by *pāuruhanga* (lengths of timber) or stones, which in effect created a central corridor within the dwelling.[72]

The structure of the whare both reflected and reinforced the centrality of tapu in daily life. Food would never be consumed within the sleeping areas of the whare because the noa quality of cooked food would defile the whare and the tapu of the ancestor who the whare embodied.[73] Sleeping arrangements also reflected the need to protect tapu. Highly tapu men of rank and *kaumātua* (elders) slept on the left side (looking out) of the whare, with the place of honor being closest to the pihanga. Women and slaves slept on the opposite side of the whare. Bodies were not only arranged by rank, but also carefully positioned during sleep: individuals slept with their heads next to the external wall of the whare, and this, together with the demarcation of a corridor to direct movement down the center of the dwelling, protected the most tapu part of the human body: the head. This spatial organization was very important within the cramped confines of the whare, where a large number of people would sleep in close proximity, and, in particular, this division made sure that the whakanoa (to make common; to remove tapu) power of women was contained.[74] While it was not unusual for a nuclear family of parents and children to occupy a whare, often dwellings were occupied by whānau (family) groups that were extended "horizontally," with several siblings, their spouses, and children sharing a dwelling, or "vertically," with grandparents, uncles and aunts, parents and children living together. In some cases, a complex mix of both vertical and horizontal connections coexisted within a dwelling group.[75]

The social and spatial configuration of mission houses did offer a significant departure from this Māori order. The ideal was that a single family should inhabit that mission house and that this kinship grouping was a cohesive affective, spiritual, and economic unit. In reality, however, mission houses were frequently home to a rather more complex social configuration, blending in single missionaries, such as William Yate, who shared the Clarke's house at Waimate, or joining two missionary families together. Most important, the "dwelling group" was also extended as some "native Christians," typically Māori girls and young women, moved in with missionary families, a practice that began with Ewhora, Ruatara's daughter, who lived with the King family.[76] Missionaries and their wives also had to oversee the welfare of various Māori sawyers, farm laborers, timber workers, brick makers, and gardeners under their charge. John Butler complained in 1820

FIGURE 2.3 A stylized image of whare (dwellings) and whata (food-storage platforms) inside a Māori kāinga. From Joel Polack's *New Zealand: Being a Narrative of Travels and Adventures* (1838). Read, W, fl 1901–1902. Polack, Joel Samuel 1807–1882: Interior of a native village in New Zealand. J. S. Polack del. W. Read, sc. London, Richard Bentley, 1838. Ref: A-259-006, Alexander Turnbull Library, Wellington, New Zealand.

that his wife had become a "complete slave" in her efforts to sustain their extended household.[77]

Space, Families, Domesticity

If there were some interesting resemblances between the reality of these extended missionary dwelling groups and Māori social organization, the actual structure of mission houses did produce novel sets of social relationships. They certainly offered a different way of ordering the key routines of daily life: preparing food, eating, and sleeping. Māori whare had a single sleeping area. This was not a shapeless common space, as it was ordered by various practices designed to maintain tapu, but within it individuals of different ages and genders mingled in very close physical proximity. Conversely, the chief social aim of missionary architecture was to produce a differentiation between public areas of social engagement—sitting rooms, studies, and parlors—and bedrooms, those "private" spaces associated with sleep and sexual intimacy. Male missionaries frequently slept in whare and shared tents with various Māori traveling companions when they were visiting distant communities, exploring new frontiers, and itinerating. Missionary wives did not mingle in such a fashion, and within established missionary homes, the master bedroom not only separated the missionary couple from Māori, but from their own children as well, enabling the complete privatization of sexual relationships and the clear production of generational distinctions. If the intimacy of sexual relations were privatized, foodstuffs moved much more freely within a mission house than they did in the Māori world, where certain foods—especially kūmara—were highly tapu when raw and could strip tapu away (whakanoa) when cooked. The trajectories of such foods was carefully monitored and controlled within the Māori world, and while missionaries largely disregarded these injunctions within their houses, they remained important topics of cross-cultural discussion and contestation.[78]

At a broader level, mission stations also tended to produce a clear division between some spaces that were delineated as male and those designated as female. Male spaces tended to be associated with manual labor, including blacksmith shops, fields of crops, plant nurseries, paddocks, sawyers' pits, and timber yards. Missionaries worked closely with Māori men, but this work was primarily outside the house. Conversely, domestic spaces were under the control of the missionary wife. These included the kitchen, dining room, laundry, and parlors or sitting rooms, where missionary wives worked closely with Māori women, introducing them to complex rules of housekeeping, domestic management, and child-rearing that were integral to the mission. Bedrooms were strictly ordered on gendered lines for Māori children attached to the CMS mission, a practice followed by the Wesleyans as well.[79] But the male and female spheres were never entirely separate: the mission family would gather, often with a range of Māori workers and guests, for mealtimes, prayer, and to hear scripture being read aloud. Of course, entire missionary communities—adults and children, men and women, Māori and European—came together for public worship.

Schooling was a more difficult question. There certainly were persistent anxieties over the easy mixing of Māori boys and girls, concerns that fixated on the looser regulation of premarital sexuality in Māori society. But the foundational project of missionary education, the extension of literacy and facilitation of Māori access to scripture in the vernacular, was targeted at both genders. Boys and girls mixed together in the first formal school established at Hohi, by Thomas Kendall, with the assistance of Towai (Te Pahi's son), in 1816.[80] This school failed by the end of 1818 largely because the mission's inadequate supplies of food and trade goods could not sustain an institution where clothing, food, and gifts of scissors, fishhooks, beads, and earrings were key inducements to gain Māori support.[81] Kendall also faced great challenges in the classroom, as he was unable to use established schemes of discipline without angering local Māori. This left him in a trying position: "When a teacher amongst the heathen . . . is surrounded by a number of children, and perhaps while one is repeating his lesson, another will be playing with his feet, another taking away his hat, and another his book, and all this in a friendly manner, he cannot be angry at them, yet it requires some study how to introduce salutary discipline."[82]

One solution to the question of discipline within the mission was the growing division between boys and girls. This developed as the pedagogical drive of the mission was relaunched under Henry Williams's leadership. After the failure of Kendall's school, missionary teaching was fairly sporadic, relying on ad hoc arrangements as the missionaries toured local settlements and the more regular instruction of Māori "girls" by missionary wives. From the early 1820s, schooling was increasingly ordered along gendered lines, in part because of the different temporal rhythms of male missionary work and that of their wives. Men preferred to teach reading and the "practical arts" in the early morning, the busiest part of day for missionary wives (and daughters). Thus, at Paihia, boys would be taught in the mornings, while Jane or Marianne Williams would instruct Māori girls and young women later in the day. A similar pattern developed at Kerikeri, where Martha Clarke, Elizabeth Hamlin, Charlotte Kemp, and Hannah Baker shared responsibility for teaching the "girls' school." Additional focused teaching along gendered lines was routinely provided on Sundays at established stations like Paihia and Kerikeri.[83]

Anxieties about the delineation of clear gender roles were not restricted to Māori children. Marianne Williams noted that her five-year-old son, Henry Jr., was "fond of playing with the little girls, and such an admirer of everything they do." As a response to this interest in feminine play, Henry and Marianne transplanted their son into the boys' school in 1828 and "decreed that boys and girls must play separately."[84] An additional fence was erected in 1830 at Paihia to separate boys and girls when playing.[85] At that point, it was common for children and youths attached to the mission to dine separately on gendered lines. On 25 May 1830, for example, the seven boys under missionary care dined at Marianne Williams's, while the girls ate with the family of her sister-in-law Jane.[86]

Missionaries tried to police such boundaries more generally within the mission community. At Paihia in the late 1820s, the missions used a bell to demarcate separate swimming and bathing times for men and women attached to the mission.[87] In November 1832 Henry Williams held a "court" at Paihia after discovering that a mixed party of Māori attached to the mission went to gather shellfish together. Williams warned them against such improprieties and designated "respective places" for men and women to gather shellfish so that there would be no "interfering" with the other gender. Williams noted that this elicited "some few expressions of displeasure."[88]

Thus, missionary education, work, and discipline not only prepared local children for different gender roles in adulthood—with boys being equipped for work as farmers, traders, and artisans, and girls being groomed for their role as mothers and wives—but actually produced these forms of difference from the moment children entered the mission stations. Although both boys and girls received a common core of instruction based around literacy and knowledge of scripture, their "practical arts" were seen as fundamentally different: ploughing, agricultural work, animal husbandry, and carpentry for men; sewing, cooking, cleaning, and childrearing for women. Many scholars have highlighted this divergence, and recent work has stressed the disciplinary nature of the missionary regime. A key marker of this was the physical transformation of Māori entering the mission. Young children and youths would frequently have their hair cut as an initial marker of their connection with the mission. At another level this was a hygienic measure, as missionaries were concerned by the prevalence of *kutu* (lice) among Māori, and kutu appeared to become even more common as Māori embraced blankets as a key medium for trade and as an item of apparel. [89] Hair—as something that grew and thus was understood to be in connection with the animating spirit of atua (supernatural agents)—was highly tapu, and missionaries were aware that the head and hair were rarely touched by Māori.[90] While the missionaries persisted with the washing and trimming of the hair of those Māori who were drawn to the mission, it was common, however, for missionaries to burn the cut hair. This was a significant accommodation to Māori practices, where hair and nails were typically burned as a protection against those tapu body parts being utilized in malevolent magic.[91]

Regular routines of washing and the dispensing of soap, sometimes from the supplies of missionary families, to the Māori living and working on the mission suggest that the remaking of the Māori body was a key marker of the transformative project of evangelization. Long-established Māori bodily practices—including the use of *kokowai* (ochre) and fish oil to dress the body—could challenge the sensibilities of missionaries who worked in close quarters with Māori, especially when travel necessitated that missionaries share sleeping quarters with local guides, chiefs, and hosts.[92] Although Samuel Marsden was known for his ability to tolerate these practices, from the genesis of the mission Māori were encouraged to regularly wash themselves and their clothes using soap.[93] By the mid-1820s, Māori connected to the mission were frequently requesting soap, which was also a medium in cross-cultural trade.[94] Missionaries also used cloth and clothing as important inducements to connect Māori to the mission. In the early years of the mission, gifts of scarlet cloth—a color with chiefly associations— were made to influential chiefs, and in the 1820s blankets became a key medium of exchange.[95]

Even as their presence shifted the material base of local communities, the ability of missionaries to discipline and control Māori bodies remained limited. This was a particular problem at the outset of the mission. In 1815 King complained about one local boy who paid little heed to the hygienic regime supported by the mission and reverted to his preferred forms of bodily comportment: "After cutting his hair cleaning him from filth and lice, makeing him clothing, washing & mending keeping him clean feeding & learning him, for him to go back into filth and dirt with half a belly full is as surprising as it is distressing to me."[96] This was a recurring challenge for the King family, as two Māori girls explained to Hannah King in January 1816. After working at sewing for two wet days, they left the mission, explaining, "Mother when it comes plenty more rain, I will do plenty more sewing for you, when it is fine weather, I will dance and play this is very good at N.Zealand." King noted that most of the children attached to the mission remained deeply connected to their kin: "They are under but little restraint from their parents therefore we cannot expect to have them at present under our controle altogether, but we are still striving to instruct them and to leade them on by degrees as they will bear it."[97] Nor could missionaries always direct or control the use of the cloth and clothing they dispensed. In the 1810s and early 1820s scarlet cloth became a significant currency in the rivalries between rangatira.[98] Even as some Māori attached to mission stations saved their European clothes for Sunday worship, Māori also displayed a persistent ability to mix mission-dispensed or mission-sewn clothes with blankets and traditional flax-fiber clothing as well as making the most of these new materials as trade items.[99]

By the 1820s, the connections between the local Māori attached to the mission stations and missionaries were stronger, but they were not always entirely secure. Missionaries worried about backsliding and the powerful lure of old customs. In some cases this led them to cut connections with some Māori individuals who had been actively involved in the life of the mission.

In December 1821, for example, the Kerikeri families shunned "Koshaddei," who had helped to raise young Henry Tacy Kemp, after James Kemp saw her kill two Ngāti Maru war captives when Hongi's taua returned from a raid to the south.[100] At a more routine level, within the mission stations it was often difficult to ensure that Māori internalized the new regimes that the missionaries were teaching. The precisely calibrated and carefully structured routines of domestic work eluded some Māori women, or they rejected the mission expectations of consistency and accuracy. Marianne Williams noted with frustration that the "best of the Native Girls, if not well-watched, would strain the milk with the duster, wash the tea-things with the knife cloth, or wipe the tables with the flannel for scouring the floor."[101]

Struggles over time discipline recurred as many mission-connected Māori continued to heed established seasonal and ceremonial cycles as well as to exert their autonomy by coming and going as they pleased. Others brought their kin and friends into the mission to keep them company while they worked, forcing the missionaries to accommodate themselves to the new-comers who were not necessarily interested in heeding the evangelicals' call to seriousness.[102] These struggles continued to play out into the late 1830s, es-pecially in new stations. Susan Maunsell wrote to a correspondent in England from Manukau in 1838.

> You may complain much in England of the badness of servants; but can have little idea of the awkwardness, idleness, and perversity of our native domestics. When we take them in they are ignorant of everything—even so simple thing as sweeping out a room—They generally learn quickly; but every fresh bit of knowledge they pick up puffs up their pride, and by the time they know enough to be useful, lose all heart for their work, and so that things are got through, care not how. We have constantly to be looking after, teaching and scolding. Washing, scrubbing, cleaning dishes and every other kind of rough work must, in turn take our attention.[103]

Lines of pedagogical authority were difficult to maintain and hard to con-trol. Missionaries might have aimed to construct a disciplinary regime to in-culcate a new way of understanding the world, new models of comportment, and new practical skills, but they could not necessarily control the ends to which such novelties were turned. By the middle of the 1820s, vernacular literacy had become a key Māori cultural technology used for a range of purposes.[104] And in the following decade, native teachers, Christian con-verts, new Māori readers, and prophetic leaders produced a range of distinc-tive Māori Christianities that missionaries struggled to channel and direct.

With regard to the "practical arts," the close observation of missionaries by Māori enabled them to turn the new skills and technologies introduced by the mission to new ends. Perhaps most telling here was the interest that Māori showed in the work of the mission blacksmiths Walter Hall and James Kemp. These men were directed to produce articles of trade and useful tools for Māori, but they were explicitly enjoined against repairing guns or other weapons. Nevertheless Māori quickly learned how to cast bullets, a valuable skill as Hongi and other chiefs worked hard to build up stores of muskets and ammunition to use in their military campaigns. When Hongi Hika returned from his voyage to England with Thomas Kendall in 1821, one of the ways in which his people exerted their dominance over the Kerikeri mission was by ejecting Kemp from his smithy and using his furnace and tools to cast musket balls and to repair muskets.[105]

Fences and Boundaries

The seizure of Kemp's smithy is an important reminder of the vulnerability of the mission. The construction of fences was an important priority in the establishment of mission stations, and fences figure quite prominently in the visual archive of cross-cultural engagement and evangelization, such as Antoine Chazal's 1826 aquatint of Kerikeri (see figure 2.4). Tanya Fitzgerald has highlighted the symbolic significance of the fences that surrounded the mission stations in the Bay of Islands. For Fitzgerald, these fences are a clear indication of the power wielded by missionaries and their ability to Anglicize the landscape and to Christianize Māori. Fitzgerald has suggested that fences "created a physical barrier between the mission station and the world beyond these fences," consolidating an opposition between "Englishness, progress, Christianity and civilisation" and "the heathen, uncivilised and backward."[106]

While there is no doubt that the fences built around mission stations were designed in part to clearly demarcate a distinct cultural space, it would be a mistake to see these boundaries as either entirely novel or authoritative. Fences, walls, and boundary markers were important components of Māori social landscapes: walls were central to delineating both units of cultivation and usage rights in Maori horticultural traditions, social boundaries could be inscribed within settlements by fences, and palisades were used to demarcate and fortify community boundaries.[107] Viewed against such a backdrop, mission fences should not be read as marking a radical cultural rupture. In the 1810s, in particular, fences were regularly breached and destroyed. At Hohi, building fences was an ongoing challenge, and the

FIGURE 2.4 Antoine Chazal, "Etablissement des missionnaires anglais a Kidikidi. Nouvelle-Zelande" (1826). This aquatint, which shows a red ensign flying over the fenced mission buildings at Kerikeri, was based on an 1824 drawing by Jules Louis LeJeune. Ref.: C-082-094, Alexander Turnbull Library, Wellington, New Zealand.

mission attempted to build eight-foot fences around missionary houses to provide some security for their homes, property, and livestock.[108] But these fences provided limited protection, and they were frequently broken by Māori curious to explore the strange newcomers, by individuals or groups who were searching for tools, iron, or livestock, or by *taua muru* (plundering parties) who raided the mission because of slights to custom or political infractions. It is telling in that in one of the first books printed for the mission, it recorded the te reo phrase "the fence is broken" [Ka kore te taihepa].[109]

Almost a decade after the foundation of the mission, John King and his family were still dependent on the basic security that their fences offered at Hohi. In February 1823 the King family was anxious about the safety of their livestock, and of themselves as well, as "the natives" were "very teaseing." King noted that "Te [the] natives troublesome—gets upon our fences—thieves our peaches before they are ripe & other things that are outside—very teaseing untill late at night—and begin at break of day—not regarding what we say—whether we laugh or cry."[110] For the missionaries at Hohi that was a turbulent year, as Thomas Kendall's difficult connection with the mission finally broke down, relationships between the other missionaries and Māori were frequently unsettled, and intertribal conflicts continued to play out. In December 1823 John King noted in his journal that he was effectively a prisoner within his fences.

> The natives being in such a wild state—bakeing and eating th[e] flesh of men just outside our fence & c & c—did not feel inclined to go to Kaiheke to Day—my Family receiving such a fright yesterday—the native coming naked, in such a formidable manner with his weapon in his hand—unexpectedly without the least notice or alarm—and without the least provocation—even his own people did not know what he was going to do and had not time to think before he had broke the House—[111]

It was only in 1825 that William Hall was finally able to report that Rangihoua Māori "left off breaking our fences and robbing our gardens," a shift that he attributed to the removal of Thomas Kendall from the mission, which allowed more stable relationships to develop between missionaries and local Māori.[112] When the missionary settlers finally relocated from Hohi to Te Puna, fencing was much less a priority, and the King family home was unfenced, reflecting a new confidence and security.[113]

Fencing the Kerikeri mission was a top priority, especially given its close relationship with Kororipo pā and the staging grounds for Hongi's great taua. In December 1819 John Butler worked hard on building split-pale perimeter fences: "We have hundreds about us all the day, and from their natural curiosity they throng the doors so that we are scarcely able to get out or in. Their noise, singing, talking, laughing, ochre, lice, and other filth is exceedingly disagreeable, especially to the [missionary] women and children, indeed it is impossible for them to go out of doors."[114] While this passage suggests that fences helped produce social distance, they were also a significant source of psychological and real security. Their importance was made clear after the attacks on the mission sawyer Conroy and then on William and Dinah Hall as they attempted to established an unprotected new settlement at Waitangi.[115] At the new Paihia station, fences also provided some security; during the 1820s, various individuals and groups did breach the fences when the mission's gates were closed, but the fences themselves slowed intruders and, on occasions, seem to have become a proxy target for attacks on the mission. In the early years at Kerikeri, the fences were broken down and taken by local Māori, both as an assertion of their power and to be used as firewood.[116]

The repurposing of mission fences as kindling reminds us that fences were never simply cultural boundaries, but also material objects with multiple uses. Tanya Fitzgerald's symbolic reading of mission fences as enacting a rigid divide between the missionary and Māori "worlds" neglects their important economic function: they enclosed units of economic production and restricted movement of animals, a very valuable resource for the mission.[117] In fact, from their arrival missionaries were unable to erect sufficient fences to contain their animals. This was a source of considerable cross-cultural friction and, in some cases, open conflict. In March 1816 William Hall recorded that Māori had speared the settlement's pigs "that had been trespassing upon their Cumera [kūmara] grounds." Kendall was enraged, and, according to Hall, he "abused the Natives" and hoped "to shoot them with a gun." Kendall's desire for revenge was thwarted, however, because he had lent his gun to a local man a few days before. The people of Rangihoua saw Kendall's abuse and angry demands for the return of his weapon as an insult. Hall reported that "a great number of Natives came down and were very angry brandishing their spears and War instruments about." This reaction underlined the precariousness of the mission, and that evening Kendall "gave them a pig besides the one they had speared, for a reconciliation."[118] This token, however, proved insufficient, as on the evening of 23 March Hall recorded that "the Rangehoo Natives have killed more of Mr Kendall's pigs this evening," and further pigs were killed on the 25th of that same month.[119]

Unrestrained animals continued to be a difficult issue for the mission through the 1820s and 1830s. At Kerikeri, the initial perimeter fences enclosed the mission buildings and about an acre of land that had been broken up for gardening and the planting of an orchard. This was insufficient for the mission's livestock, which were turned out to graze around the mission, and in 1820 these wandering livestock ate the mission's first wheat crop, which was grown on an unfenced six-acre field.[120] At Waimate, which had the largest complement of domesticated animals, it was impossible for the missionaries to produce enough pasture or enough post-and-rail fences to have the mission's animals grazing in enclosed fields. As a result, the mission's sheep, pigs, and cattle wandered freely, becoming difficult to manage and vulnerable to attacks by the dogs associated with Māori communities. This lack of fencing not only rendered the farm inefficient, but also produced significant conflict as the mission's animals strayed onto the tapu cultivations maintained by Māori in the district.[121]

Fences were designed to be impediments to movement, constraining livestock and acting as a barrier to human access to the mission station. But gates that were designed to facilitate and channel movement into the missionary settlements punctuated them. The opening of the gates allowed the routine movements of missionary life to unfold: the coming into the mission household, workshops, and schools of the Māori attached to the mission; the movement in and out of chiefly patrons, visiting Māori, missionaries, British officials, European travelers, and Euroamerican captains; and the itinerant movement of missionaries and native teachers who visited various communities, local and distant, to preach, to distribute printed texts, and to discuss Christianity. Things moved through the gates, too: significant amounts of fish and shellfish were brought into stations like Te Puna by Māori, and this was an important source of sustenance for the mission communities as a whole.[122] Poultry, livestock, and horses moved in and out of the missions, as did seeds, seedlings, and new foodplants. While iron and building materials (timber, raupo, and fern) were brought into the stations, nails, *toki* (adzes), and simple tools moved out of the smithy, as did sawn timber from the sawyers' pits and furniture from William Hall's workshop.[123] Fishhooks, beads, cloth, clothes and hats, soap, and food all served as portable inducements and rewards dispensed by missionaries. Most important, from 1830, and especially after the arrival of William Colenso, in 1834, printed texts also moved out of the missions in growing numbers. These were highly valued and potent inducements, as Māori were interested not only in the skills of literacy that the missionaries could teach, but also, strongly, in the events and ideas within these texts.

Some of the mission's earliest printed texts themselves remind us of the social and physical intimacy that underwrote evangelization. These texts were used as teaching tools in mission schools and as templates for printed cards that served as pedagogical tools.[124] Alison Jones and Kuni Jenkins have noted that *A Grammar and Vocabulary of the Language of New Zealand* (1820)—a collaborative work between Kendall, Hongi Hika, and the rangatira Waikato, completed while they were visiting England in 1820—contained many phrases relating to meeting, building relationships, traveling together, conversation, and argument, all of which were fundamental to mission work. *A Grammar* also stressed the importance of bodily management.

E aire kau ána: A walking naked. . . .
O'ro hĩa: Wash (thou). . . .
Kakahua dia ki ou kakahu: Put on thy clothes. . . .
E kúpa ána ra óki koe: Thou art belching . . .

This text did not avoid fundamental physical processes as it offered useful phrases relating to blood as well as to excreta. Excreta were carefully managed in Māori society because such materials were potent agents that could strip away tapu.

Ka póka i te tóto: Besmeared with blood . . .
Nóu áno te úere: That saliva is thine. . . .
Ki a no e tíko nóa?: Has he not eased himself?[125]

A Grammar is shot through with movement: people come and go, meet, return, and depart. One dialogue discusses Hongi's departure for England and his planned return, and Māori were introduced to new vocabulary related to European transportation technologies, such as "a cabin of the ship" [E páre-máta no te kaipúke].[126] This mobility echoes the constant movement and motion that is produced by a sustained reading of the archives associated with any particular missionary site: Hohi, Kerikeri, Paihia, Waimate, Te Puna, or any of the later stations. The stations themselves were firmly linked together by the frequent traffic of missionaries, local chiefs, Māori workers, and, from the 1830s, converts and native teachers. Samuel Marsden's seven visits to New Zealand were a series of peripatetic circuits between these sites, as well as expeditions to distant timber grounds, trading sites, and potential locations for new stations.

Some pathways were particularly important. The Māori route within Hongi's domain from Kerikeri, for example, was the starting point for the first "road" established by the mission, which was surveyed in May 1830 and completed in November that year, with substantial labor inputs from local Māori. This was a considerable achievement as the twenty-four-kilometer road allowed heavy loads to be moved by cart, and a bridge designed by George Clarke enabled the Waitangi River to be traversed.[127] Most mission stations were littoral communities supported by Māori waka, mission ships, and other vessels that called at the Bay of Islands, carrying materials, tools, people, seeds, animals, and commodities. These maritime networks in turn articulated with trans-Tasman shipping focused on Port Jackson, trans-Pacific trading networks, and the global commercial linkages fashioned by the British empire. These connections not only underwrote the governance of the mission through correspondence and allowed missionaries to maintain their own familial networks, but also brought into the Bay of Islands a range of key materials, including muskets, clay pipes, Staffordshire ceramics, paper, slates, pencils, and ink.[128] If we recognize the simultaneous operation of these linkages over both short and long distances, it is necessary to imagine mission stations as complex assemblages made up of many moving parts. They were constantly reshaped by transport, communication, and shifting but seemingly ceaseless patterns of motion.

Conclusion

For Samuel Marsden and the Protestant missionaries who labored in New Zealand from 1814, the quest to civilize and Christianize Māori communities depended on the construction of missionary stations. These building complexes (houses, chapels, schools, storehouses, and "huts" for "native" Christians), enclosed fields, and gardens were imagined as both symbols and agents of missionary "improvement." Ideally, at least, the mission house, the disciplines of the mission school, the station's carefully maintained gardens and its fences were embodiments of the evangelicals' "godly order," a vision of social organization which prioritized the economic, social, and religious significance of the Christian conjugal family. These structures were not simply symbolic manifestations of evangelical ideology, but were also central to the actual processes of conversion and civilization. Mission stations were sites where old practices were contested, where novel modes of action were demonstrated, and where new patterns of behavior were both explicitly taught and tacitly reproduced through constant reiteration. In the mission house, the missionaries' chiefly patrons shared meals with "their" missionaries and participated in family prayers led by missionary patriarchs. At the same time, local women and girls learned complicated routines relating to hygiene, cooking, and housekeeping, and carried out domestic work under the supervision of missionary wives. In the mission schools, boys and girls of various social ranks encountered the routine regimens of schooling and were introduced to the core skills of literacy as well as biblical teachings. And in the mission garden and in the various fields, sawpits, mills, and smithies attached to mission stations, Māori men learned European agricultural methods, mastered new tools and technologies, and became familiar with the bewildering array of domesticated animals, trees, cereals, fruit, and vegetables that the missionaries introduced to New Zealand.

Where optimistic evangelicals hoped that mission stations would be sites from which radical cultural change could be effected—with the ultimate aim of fashioning an independent "native" church of Māori Christians—the change the missionaries were actually able to implement was limited by the reality and persistence of cultural difference. Despite their European-style houses, their gardens full of potatoes, and their ever-busy smithies, mission stations were never essentially European spaces. Rather, they were culturally mixed sites of translation, contestation, and conflict. They were, to borrow from the geographer Doreen Massey, "meeting-up" places, sites where a multiplicity of cultural trajectories intersected, collided, and coexisted. Mission stations were not simply empty sites that European culture "expanded" into and took over, as demonstrated by the ways in which the very locations of these stations were shaped by the indigenous geopolitics of the Bay of Islands. Stations developed at sites that had a prior history and social associations, and these places could not be simply "emptied out" and entirely remade. Mission stations remained embedded in local spatial and cultural configurations, even as they helped transform those arrangements.[129] And that change was often initiated and driven by Māori themselves; missionaries struggled to control and channel social change, even when it ran in their favor. Thus, contrary to some cultural readings of the mission, the missionaries did not carve out little Englands where mission fences created a self-contained cultural space in opposition to the Māori world that surrounded them.[130] Instead, they were sites of translation, compromise, and struggle that stood at the center of new cultural circuits. The constant motion within these networks carried new ideas, technologies, skills, words, and ways of thinking and acting beyond the fences of the mission. Neither fully British nor purely Māori, mission stations were pivotal in the emergence of the new, mixed, and messy cultural order that had emerged in the north of New Zealand by the middle of the 1830s.

Three ECONOMICS, LABOR, AND TIME

W here in chapter 2 I offered a critical historical geography of mission stations, here my focus shifts from space and place to time. In this chapter I explore missionary attempts to transform Māori economic behavior by stimulating their interest in commerce and encouraging new models of work to "improve" their moral and spiritual character. In particular, I examine the place of "industriousness" in Marsden's civilizing scheme and the struggles over labor and the organization of time on mission stations in the 1810s and 1820s. The realization of Marsden's sketchy program for effecting social change in New Zealand depended on establishing the mission's economy on a sound basis. Productive gardens, effective farming practices, and successful trading activity would not only make the mission self-supporting, but would also enable the incorporation of Māori into the mission.

Marsden hoped that the Māori desire to acquire new tools and technology through the mission would enable the creation of an important set of economic, social, and cultural relationships. The missionaries would not only be the vector through which instruments of civilization—such as axes, spades, and ploughs—would be introduced, but they would also function as the masters and employers of Māori, who would have to work on the mission stations in order to be able to pay for these novel items. This economic cycle, Marsden believed, would be self-sustaining: the more Māori "wants" were stimulated, the more they would have to work for the missionaries. This missionary-directed labor would not only help "improve" the settlement, through the extension of cultivation and the construction of buildings, but it would also provide the opportunity for introducing Māori to Christian thought. In short, Marsden saw the absorption of Māori into the mission's economy as central to the effective inculcation of work discipline and the production of industrious and pious native Christians.

In the discussion that follows I explore the unfolding of this plan and its ultimate failure. I begin by returning to Marsden's plan for "civilization," placing it in multiple contexts: the cultural changes that accompanied the "industrious" revolution identified by recent work on eighteenth-century British economic history, Marsden's understandings of improvement, and Marsden's particular rendering of a strong evangelical tradition of thought relating to work. I then examine the profound difficulties that the missionaries faced in translating this vision into reality in New Zealand and their inability to significantly transform Māori society. In-fighting, conflicts over resources, struggles over status between convict laborers and "mechanic missionaries," and clashes over goods and authority seriously hampered the progress of the mission. More fundamentally, I highlight the failure of early missionary attempts to break free from their economic dependence on Māori. Into the 1820s, Māori dictated the ways in which they engaged with the economy of the mission, effectively controlling the terms of labor and trade. Because of these various pressures, missionaries were unable to undercut the authority of leading rangatira, such as the great warrior-chief Hongi Hika, or to effectively challenge the centrality of slavery in Māori social formations.

I conclude this chapter by offering a more-detailed analysis of one key aspect of "industriousness": time-discipline. Missionaries struggled to dislodge traditional rhythms of work, underlining both the persistence of the long-established indigenous temporal schema and open Māori resistance to the missionary emphasis on the social and spiritual importance of sustained and regular labor. By the mid-1820s, however, some Māori, particularly those connected to the CMS station at Paihia and to the fledgling WMS station at Whangaroa, began to recognize the significance of the Sabbath. This significant transition was a product of the greater economic self-sufficiency and cultural authority (mana) of the missionaries. I contrast this acceptance of one key element of missionary teaching with the rejection of the Sabbath that was fundamental to the radical reworking of biblical teachings offered by the first significant Māori prophet, Papahurihia of Rangihoua.

Given its stress on the inability of the missionaries to transform Māori economic patterns and the greater interest of Māori in the Bible than in the missionary ideal of "industriousness," this chapter can be read as a contribution to a long-running debate over the connections between Protestant missionary activity and the globalization of capitalism. While the work of Brian Stanley and Andrew Porter in the 1980s responded to Marxist and nationalist critics of missionaries by highlighting the shifting relationships between "Christianity, Commerce, and Civilization," more recent anthropologically inflected work has reinstantiated a strong link between the expansion of missionary activity and the growing global power of capitalist forms of economic relations.[1] Most notably, Jean Comaroff has suggested that the "great British revival of the late eighteenth century . . . was one of the most pervasively successful vehicles for extending what is often called the European world system." Even prior to the fully fledged development of industrial capitalism, Comaroff contends, the evangelical "civilizing mission served to hitch African communities to commodities, money, and the market."[2] Historians and cultural critics have forwarded similar interpretations in New Zealand, arguing that evangelical missionaries eroded Māori cultural norms by transplanting capitalism as well as Christianity to New Zealand.[3]

In challenging this interpretative tradition, I take some inspiration from Elizabeth Elbourne's reappraisal of the LMS mission in southern Africa, which has highlighted both the limits and complexities of the economic changes enacted by missionaries and the extent to which missionaries were operating in an indigenous socioeconomic context which was already being reshaped by both local vectors of change and globalizing imperial forces.[4] I identify similar dynamics on the New Zealand frontier, suggesting that the impact of missionaries on established economic and social structures in the Bay of Islands was initially highly circumscribed and stressing the strength and persistence of indigenous understandings of work and time. Following in the wake of Frederick Cooper and Keletso Atkins's demonstrations of the ways in which colonized groups retained long-standing social attachments and temporal sensibilities, I argue that indigenous mentalities were central in determining the terms of the economic engagements between missionaries and the peoples of the Bay of Islands for at least the first decade of the mission.[5] In the New Zealand case, it was only in the mid-1820s, once the missionaries at the newly established Paihia and Whangaroa stations were able to break free of their economic dependence on local people and began to position themselves "outside" Māori culture, that indigenous communities exhibited their first sustained interest in Christian teaching.

Work as a Civilizing Agent

Commerce and agriculture were central to Marsden's understanding of civilization and his vision for the mission to Māori. During his visit to New Zealand to oversee the foundation of the mission in late 1814 and early 1815, Marsden paid particular attention to the question of agriculture and assessed the landscape's capacity for "improvement." As his party traveled inland from Wainiwaniwa (the "Rainbow Falls" near Kerikeri) toward Te Waimate on 9 January 1815, Marsden noted that the "whole tract of this tract of country, taken collectively, would form a good agricultural settlement."[6] Marsden stayed at Hongi Hika's Ōkuratope pā, which stood on the summit of a steep-sided hill that dominated the landscape around Te Waimate, and although he was very impressed by Hongi's embrace of agriculture (noting that he "had never seen finer potatoes under the best culture"), he bemoaned the rudimentary technological basis of Māori cultivation. "Axes, hoes, and spades are much wanted. If these could be obtained their country would soon put on a different appearance. No labour of man without iron can clear and subdue uncultivated land to any extent."[7]

Marsden was not only convinced that the improvement of agriculture would help Māori become civilized by feeding their hunger for commerce, but also believed that work itself had intrinsic value. He believed that work was a crucial element in moral and spiritual reform: long and regular hours of intense physical labor strengthened the body, promoted moral discipline, and quelled any inclination toward rebellion. Marsden's understandings of work must be anthropologized carefully, rather than being seen simply as an unproblematic statement of the ethos of European capitalism or simply a justification for cultural imperialism. We need to read these beliefs as the outcome of values attached to work in the specific cultural milieu in which his worldview took shape, his understandings of how societies should be "improved," and his particular theological proclivities.

The most immediate context for understanding Marsden's insistence on the value of work as an instrument for improvement was his multifaceted role as a pioneering pastoralist, a wielder of religious and judicial authority, and a social reformer in New South Wales. As the colony developed, Marsden was an influential architect of a coercive disciplinary regime that aimed to implant a new moral sensibility in both male and female convicts, while simultaneously deploying convict labor as an instrument of economic "improvement" through the extension of cultivation and the basic infrastructure for the colony. In 1790 Governor Phillip had observed that the colonial state struggled to "make men industrious," suggesting that this desire to reform the moral character of convicts was thwarted because many of the transportees "dread punishment less than they fear labour."[8] Throughout his career in Australia, Marsden attempted to overcome this reluctance to work, which he read as the product of sloth and moral indolence, rather than as a strategy of resistance. He regularly deployed convict labor on his farm in the hope that the workers would ultimately internalize the need for hard work and self-discipline, a project that Marsden believed was successful by 1810.[9]

More infamously, Marsden used his power as a magistrate to implement a harsh regime of physical punishment. Marsden authorized torture to extract confessions from convicts who were suspected of plotting rebellion, argued all convicts should be compelled to attend church on the Sabbath (forcing Catholics to attend Protestant services), used physical punishment to suppress "vice" among his convict congregationalists, and used heavy sentences of flogging as a favored instrument to enforce public order.[10] While these measures won Marsden the sobriquet of the "flogging parson," he remained steadfast in his belief that work that was the most powerful tool for social improvement. He argued that the most recalcitrant convicts should be disciplined through sustained physical work on isolated government farms or through the back-breaking work of bringing "virgin" territory into cultivation.[11] Reading Māori society against the backdrop of his experiences with convicts and Aborigines, Marsden believed that Māori were capable of sustained work—noting at Ōkuratope, for example, that "Shunghee's [Hongi's] people . . . appeared very industrious"—but believed that the missionaries had to "improve" this undeveloped proclivity for industriousness by systematically inculcating the habits of work discipline.[12]

Marsden's faith in the redeeming power of work was not simply the product of his Australian experiences; this vision of work discipline was both the outcome of broad-based cultural change within England and, more narrowly, a manifestation of a specific tradition of evangelical theology and social thought. Recent work on the onset of industrialization in Britain has suggested that the shifts that historians have denoted as the "industrial revolution" were not the product of rapid technological change, but rather the outcomes of a longer shift in economic behavior and social attitudes. These transformations are styled as the "industrious revolution," and Jan de Vries has argued that these reorientations occurred at the household level. Households reallocated their resources, increasing the time that household members devoted to work in order to purchase from the growing range and number of consumer goods and valued commodities. In other words, households increased their inputs into labor, amplifying production and fueling a burgeoning market for consumables.[13]

Where de Vries located this "industrious revolution" in the seventeenth century, Hans-Jaochim Voth has identified the late eighteenth century as its main locus.[14] Either way, these shifts profoundly reshaped the economic relationships and social values imbibed by the young Samuel Marsden, who was born in 1765. He was raised in Yorkshire's West Riding, which Pat Hudson identified as a, if not the, key site in Britain where the economic and cultural shifts underpinning the transition to industrial textile production played out.[15] These broad modifications in economic behavior were powerfully expressed in Marsden's insistence on the connection between labor and consumption as levers of civilization. In his reflections on his visit to New Zealand in 1814–15, Marsden argued that

> The want of iron is at present, however a great obstacle to their further improvement, and without it I fear these people could scarcely rise much above their present situation; but if means be adopted to supply them with that essential article their country will soon produce to them all the necessaries and conveniences enjoyed in civil society, and as such comforts increase to reward their labour so will their wants increase to stimulate them to greater industry, and thus lay a solid foundation for their progressive, social, and mental improvement in the arts of civilization and in that which is the grand and most important object of all, a saving knowledge of Christianity.[16]

While Marsden's stress on the connections between labor, consumption, and civilization can be fruitfully read as articulating the social vision of the "industrious revolution," we also need to embed his work within a more specific theological context: evangelical understandings of the spiritual value of work. A long and influential line of sociological and historical work—running from Ernst Troeltsch and Max Weber through to R. H. Tawney and E. P. Thompson—has explored the ways in which evangelicalism, as a form of ascetic Protestantism, sought to rationalize worldly life by emphasizing self-restraint and discipline and thereby provided a powerful set of ideas that supported capitalism and helped shore up the political status quo.[17] The basis of these evangelical—both dissenting and Anglican—understandings of economics are often traced back to John Wesley's influential sermon "The Use of Money" (1760). Here Wesley reconsidered Protestant social thought in light of the economic opportunities presented by the growth of commerce, the onset of industrial production, and the emergence of a range of new consumable goods and forms of leisure. In Wesley's positive reevaluation of worldly activity, work was not to be understood as the outcome of the Fall (as some commentators had interpreted Genesis 3:17–20) or as a remedy for sin, but rather as an integral part of Christian spiritual and social duty.[18] Wesley exhorted his congregationalists to follow a basic set of rules that he identified as providing a matrix that should govern Christian worldly behavior: "Gain all you can," "Save all you can," and "Give all you can."[19]

For Wesley, an individual's economic conduct was a clear marker of their spiritual concerns. The true Christian understood that work advanced God's plan for the world and was central in upholding a pious social order. Workers were to labor as hard as possible in honest toil, accumulating money to look after their families. This work was to be discharged promptly ("Do it as *soon* as possible"), with skill ("And do it as *well* as possible"), and with energy ("let nothing be done by halves, or in a slight and careless manner"). Work undertaken according to these principles would enhance one's spiritual well-being, giving workers and their families' security while forwarding national interest.[20] But the fruits of labor had to be treated with care. Wesley reminded his followers that they were not the proprietors of their worldly existence, but stewards of the gifts bestowed by God.[21] In encouraging charity ("Give all you can"), Wesley was exhorting Christians to discharge their moral duties to their utmost, but he also saw this as a way of forestalling the temptations of excessive accumulation, a theme that he frequently warned against in later writings, especially his sermon on "The Danger of Riches" (1780).[22]

If E. P. Thompson ignored the importance of Wesley's warnings against excessive accumulation and his emphasis on charity, he was undoubtedly correct in identifying Wesley's teaching as providing what Thompson termed the "inner compulsion" for the organization of labor in the new industrial order.[23] Samuel Marsden's career gave material expression to this "inner compulsion"—an imperative that he was exposed to during his youth in Yorkshire, under the influence of his parents, who had strong Methodist connections and named their sons after the Wesley brothers. Although Marsden remained attached to the established church after the Methodists formally separated themselves form the Church of England in 1795, and although he remained a staunch believer in Anglican evangelical understandings of predestination, his biographer A. T. Yarwood has argued that Marsden's "thoughts on morality, personal deportment, education and family government were in essential harmony with Wesley's teaching."[24]

Daniel Bradshaw and Suzanne Ozment have observed that in the wake of Wesley, evangelicals did not shun worldly life, but rather embraced it, as "true work is the activity of stewardship, of caring for, developing, and perfecting things in order that they might better serve the higher purposes that God wills."[25] Marsden was motivated by this notion of stewardship and this teaching, at least as much he was by the Enlightenment's application of observation and experimentation to the natural world, which drove his attempts to transform the landscapes of New South Wales, to increase the yield of his extensive landholding, to refine animal breeds, and to "improve" the indigenous peoples of the Pacific. In pursuing this earthly stewardship, Marsden exhibited the restless energy that was celebrated by evangelicals. Hannah More argued that "action is the life of virtue," while John Wesley, who David Bebbington has described as "a typhoon of energy," railed against sloth and "excessive sleep."[26] The former governor Lachlan Macquarie argued that the colonial chaplain was exceptionally energetic and enthusiastic in his worldly engagements, but suggested that this tended to lead Marsden away from spiritual matters. Macquarie characterized Marsden as "a man for ever engaged in some active, animated pursuit;—no man travels more from town to town, or house to house. . . . [T]he variety of his pursuits, both in his own concerns and in those of others, is so extensive, in farming, grazing, manufactories, public and private agencies, and bartering transactions."[27]

It is clear from this discussion that evangelicals were convinced of the importance of worldly action and saw labor as a crucial element in "improvement"; indeed, one of the chief markers of conversion was a new dedication to work. Nonevangelical social commentators repeatedly highlighted the social transformations enacted by evangelical teaching. In 1791 the journalist, editor, and publisher William Woodfall contended that the rise of evangelicalism among the urban poor initiated a profound moral revolution, elevating and civilizing the "savages" who lived within Britain. He suggested that Wesley had "penetrated the abodes of wretchedness and ignorance, to rescue the profligate from perdition; and he communicated the light of life to those who sat in darkness and the shadow death. He changed the outcasts of society into useful members; civilized even savages, and filled those lips with prayer and praise that had been accustomed to oaths and imprecation."[28] This argument was reaffirmed by the renowned engraver Thomas Bewick who argued that Wesley and the Methodists did "a great deal of good" in Bewick's native Tyneside. Bewick suggested that Wesley crushed heathenism at "home," as he "greatly civilised a numerous host of semi-barbarian[s], the pitmen and others employed in the pit-works. These seemed like Cherokees and Mohawks, but they were more wicked."[29] Marsden went even further than this. He did not contend simply that spiritual rebirth of conversion would remake "savages" into workers, but that work itself was a crucial instrument in precipitating civilization and spiritual rebirth.

Conflicts and Constraints

Transplanting this vision to New Zealand following the establishment of the mission at Hohi (Ōihi) in 1814 proved extremely difficult.[30] The three missionaries that Marsden left in New Zealand had been instructed to "introduce amongst the Natives the knowledge of Christ; and, in order to do this, the Arts of Civilized Life." They were warned by the CMS to "spend no time in idleness," but rather to "occupy every moment set apart for labour in agriculture, building houses or boats, spinning twine or some other useful occupation." This labor had a double significance. It would provide an opportunity for religious instruction, as the mechanics were exhorted to teach the rudiments of Christianity "when employed in planting potatoes, sowing corn, or in any other occupation." It was also designed to make the mission financially independent, providing sufficient grains, vegetables, and meat to support the community. The mechanics were expressly forbidden from giving and receiving presents and were encouraged to foster Māori handicrafts, such as weaving, so that finished goods could be exported for sale at Port Jackson, introducing Māori to the true value of commerce.[31] As Marsden and his party prepared to return to New South Wales, it seemed that the project had started well. Marsden's traveling companion, John Liddiard Nicholas, described the industry of the fledgling settlement at Hohi in January 1815.

> Going on shore in the afternoon, we found Mr. Kendall and Mr. Hall tolerably comfortable in their new dwellings: they had got a number of the natives busily employed in securing the roof against the rain; the sawyer was at work in cutting up the timber, and the smith in preparing a further supply of charcoal; nor was there a single individual on the premises who was not employed: so that the whole presented a scene of activity and cheerful exertion. Mrs. Hall had set Gunnah's [Te Uri o Kanae's] wife to the wash-tub, where the lady was rubbing away the linen at a great rate; and for the first time in her life, enjoyed the luxury of soap and water. Though the wife of a rungateeda [rangatira], she felt herself highly honoured by this employment; and imagined it, very probably, the most suitable of any that the packaha [Pākehā] could assign to her. Many inter-

esting ideas occurred to me while I beheld the missionaries thus seated in their new residence, and preparing for the work of civilization in a land where never before was the least gleam of knowledge, except what nature instinctively supplied; and where man, roving about as a lawless denizen, acknowledged no authority except that of an individual barbarous as himself, who constantly led him on to deeds of carnage against his fellows, and taught him not only to satisfy his revenge with their destruction, but to crown it with a bloody banquet. In such a land it was that a few civilized beings were now going to reclaim a whole race to subdued and regular habits; and afford, at the same time, another proof of the immense superiority of mind over matter.[32]

The three missionaries—William Hall, John King, and Thomas Kendall—who remained in New Zealand soon doubted the efficacy of the civilized arts as instruments for reform. Until the mid-1820s, the missionaries faced serious challenges in establishing the kind of regime that Marsden had envisioned and in achieving Nicholas's vision of a swift transition to civilization.

Missionary letters and journals catalogued their inability to put the mission on a confident footing and to make significant progress in introducing the "civilized arts." By mid-1815, two profound problems faced the mission. First, Marsden's friend and the mission's protector, Ruatara, died just four days after Marsden sailed for New South Wales. While Marsden remained convinced of Ruatara's abilities and his commitment to the mission, the mechanic missionaries were skeptical of the depth of the rangatira's commitment to the mission. John King, for example, observed that Ruatara's mind was "much prejudiced" against the mechanics.[33] Although Ruatara facilitated the sale of around two hundred acres of land at Hohi from two of Te Pahi's nephews to Marsden (on the behalf of the CMS), he had developed suspicions about the mission's connection to empire before the *Active* sailed for New Zealand in late 1814. It seems likely that while Ruatara hoped to enjoy the material benefits that might flow from his relationship to Marsden and his protection of the settlement at Hohi, he remained concerned that the mission might initiate the large-scale European settlement of New Zealand and reduce Māori to a position akin to that of the Aborigines in Australia.[34] While Ruatara had been pivotal in facilitating the foundation of the mission at Hohi, his death left the missionaries in a very exposed position. In July 1815, John King noted: "Ever since the Death of Duaterra we have been left exposed to the mercy of all parties both far and near." He reported that the mission stations had been regularly raided: ten chickens and eighteen turkeys were taken from his family, and the local people had broken into his house and subjected his family to "ruff and indecent treatment."[35]

Second, the mechanics were increasingly aware of just how economically dependent they were on Māori. From their point of view, their location at Hohi was poor. The strip of steeply banking land that ran up from the beach at Hohi was too small to effectively support the settlement, and the remainder of the land that Marsden had purchased—an unpromising mixture of rugged hills and swampy land—was ill-suited to agriculture. While the proximity to Rangihoua pā meant that the mechanics were able to access a significant semi-permanent population of around 200, they were also under the close surveillance of the local people. Kendall had objected to Hohi as a possible site for the mission, arguing instead that the flatter open ground at Te Puna, to the west of the Rangihoua pā, or at Waitangi, some eight miles across the Bay of Islands, would be superior locations. But Marsden insisted that Hohi was the best site, as it placed the missionaries firmly under Ruatara's protection.[36] By May 1815, Kendall and Hall had resolved to ignore Marsden's instructions and relocate to Waitangi. But in September 1815 Hall moved alone, as Kendall felt that recent death of Waraki, an influential rangatira at Waitangi, had destabilized politics in that part of the Bay of Islands. Hall was forced to abandon his settlement at Waitangi, which he believed was the "garden of New Zealand," after a party of visiting Māori attacked his "fledgling" station at Waitangi in January 1816.[37]

But some of the most profound obstacles to the introduction of the "civilized arts" came from within the missionary community itself. Isolated, without protection, and eking out a precarious subsistence from the land at Hohi, the settlers and their families were quickly riven by a host of rivalries and antipathies. Despite evangelical theology's suspicion of earthly status, sharp social distinctions operated even among the mechanic missionaries. The King family were seen as the least respectable of the families, and Hannah King, in particular, was marginalized as a result of her strong connections to maritime culture (she was the daughter of Thomas Hansen, captain of the *Active*). Her inferior social status in the eyes of the missionary families was confirmed by Samuel Marsden's allegation that her brother Thomas Hansen Jr. had established a sexual relationship with a chief's daughter from Rangihoua and then by her brother's subsequent decision to marry Elizabeth Tollis, the illegitimate daughter of a female convict in Port Jackson.[38] Angela Middleton's excavation of the Te Puna mission station (where the Kings settled in 1832) has suggested that even though the CMS mission as a whole operated on a secure economic basis in the 1840s and beyond, the

Kings remained a "subsistence household" marked by their "frugality" into the 1850s.[39]

Both King and William Hall resented Thomas Kendall's attempts to wield power over the settlement. Kendall had been invested with the powers of a magistrate for the Europeans in the Bay of Islands before he left New South Wales and he believed that this position meant that he was responsible for upholding the Sabbath, policing the morality of the settlers and overseeing the community's material progress.[40] King complained to the CMS, accusing Kendall of drunkenness. More important, he recorded Kendall's claim that "he is the same here as the Governor is at Portjackson."[41] By the middle of 1815, the politics of the small community had become even more fraught as a deep personal animosity had developed between Kendall and William Hall. While Hall was at Waitangi, Kendall encouraged the sawyers from Rangihoua who had traveled with Hall to abandon the new settlement: an action that Hall saw as contributing to the ultimate failure of this attempt to relocate the mission.[42] Kendall for his part told the CMS that Hall's absence at Waitangi was good for the mission, as the two men "were better friends by being placed at a distance from each other."[43]

There were also marked fault lines between the mechanics and the convict workers sent with the mission. John King noted that the "mechanic" missionaries were not only vulnerable to Māori but to the convict workers as well, reporting in January 1816 that the convicts "abuse us [the mechanics] . . . strike us and ill use us."[44] Kendall was at the heart of most of these conflicts. King suggested that Kendall had encouraged his family's convict servant, Richard Stockwell, to abuse the other missionaries.[45] But Kendall and Stockwell were themselves soon at odds. In December 1816 the two men were involved in a spectacular fist-fight at Rangihoua pā. While this fight was occasioned by Stockwell denying the accusations of Rangihoua Māori that he had been having "imprudent connections" with the local "girls," deeper tensions were also certainly involved, as Stockwell had established a relationship with Kendall's wife Jane, a liaison that resulted in a son, Samuel.[46] And Kendall was also embroiled in standing conflict with the convict blacksmith Walter Hall and his wife. Just six months before Kendall's fight at Rangihoua, the tension between him and Walter Hall also erupted into violence. In late May or early June 1816, Kendall had lent his flour sieve to the Halls. On the afternoon of Monday, 3 June 1816, Kendall requested the return of the sieve, but Mrs. Hall denied any knowledge of it.[47] Kendall stormed into Hall's smithy, throwing the door off its hinges. Kendall then attacked Hall, pushing him into the smithy's trough of water before stabbing him in the face, head, and chest with a chisel he had borrowed from William Hall. Walter Hall, who had armed himself with two horse pistols, fired two shots at Kendall from close range: the first set Kendall's jacket on fire, and the second missed its intended target, grazing his wife instead.[48]

These serious conflicts forestalled the progress of the mission and profoundly shaped the economic relationships that developed at the fledgling mission station. Marsden's vision of a pious and industrious community had dissolved within six months. Marsden had insisted that the mechanics should work together and run the mission out of a communal store, but the economic as well as the social relationships between the Kings, Halls, and the Kendalls broke down quickly. In early 1816, for example, William Hall and Kendall clashed, as Hall accused Kendall of monopolizing the labor of the convict sawyers Conroy and Campbell, requiring them to dress the timber for his house instead of preparing timber for the visiting missionary ship *Active*. Kendall also told Thomas Hansen that he could have no timber for his house, asserting that the "timber at the Settlement was his own, and that he meant to apply it to his own purposes."[49] In turn, John King refused to manufacture shoes for Kendall, and after William Hall completed the construction of his own house, he refused to assist the other missionary settlers in building their own permanent dwellings.[50]

The conflicts between the mechanics and the convicts also had profound economic consequences. Kendall's wounding of Walter Hall placed missionaries in a precarious situation. The products of Hall's smithy were key mediums of exchange and thus were crucial to the future of the mission.[51] Walter Hall was unable to work for six weeks because of the wounds inflicted by Kendall's chisel. This limited trade, forcing King and William Hall to use their scant reserves of axes to pay for the limited commerce they engaged in, while the large amount of timber that had been prepared by native sawyers went unpaid for.[52]

Kendall's biographer Judith Binney has observed that these conflicts over status and authority inhibited the operation of the mission. While she suggests that William Hall's and John King's "insistence on equality" made the "organization and distribution of labour and trade" impossible, one could equally argue that it was Kendall's will to power and his desire to exercise his authority over his fellow mechanics that crippled the mission's economy. But Binney is undoubtedly correct in arguing that it was the economic domain—specifically labor and trade—that was the key social terrain on which the conflicts in the mission played out.[53] Questions related to economics were vitally important to the mechanics, for not only did they entail access to resources to support each mechanic's family, the projection of social authority, and the maintenance of respectability, but work and consumption were also crucial markers of piety within the evangelical imagination.

The outcome of these conflicts was that Marsden's vision of a communitarian spirit uniting the economic and spiritual life of the community was soon set aside. Each missionary family effectively operated as an independent economic unit, with the male "heads" of the households attempting to put each family on a secure financial footing and to enhance their standing with local Māori by being able to supply valued trade goods. And in light of both the poor supply of goods from New South Wales and the limited productivity of the environs at Hohi, this local trade became crucial to the survival of the missionaries. This trade, as Binney has argued, was conducted "essentially on Maori terms."[54] Initially the main items for trade were the goods supplied to the mechanics from the CMS's agent in Port Jackson— nails, axes, spades, and hoes. These were bartered for food, primarily the potatoes and pork that communities throughout the Bay of Islands had begun to cultivate to sell to missionaries and visiting ships. Very quickly, however, local rangatira were not satisfied with these goods from Port Jackson. They retained some interest in the axes and chisels produced by Walter Hall, items that made labor more efficient while also doubling as effective arms in close quarters conflict, but increasingly local leaders were seeking more powerful weapons in return for their goods.[55] Muskets and gunpowder were highly valued: these acquisitions were both powerful markers of the mana of their owners, but were also of considerable strategic value within a context of local conflicts and the long-range military ambitions of northern alliance rangatira, especially Hongi Hika.[56]

By the middle of 1815, all the mechanics were involved in private trade, and soon the mission station became an important vector through which muskets, fowling pieces, and gunpowder were diffused through the Bay of Islands. Kendall acted as a broker, facilitating Hongi Hika's purchases of muskets from visiting ships, as well as effectively enabling Hongi Hika to source a large consignment of muskets at Port Jackson during their voyage to England and Australia in 1820–21.[57] Although Samuel Marsden learned about the growth of the musket trade and reproached the mechanics, he was blind to the economic realities underlying this shift, believing that Māori would willingly accept the rates of return that were established in his early visit; the twelve axes that Marsden paid for the land at Hohi apparently led him to believe that Europeans in New Zealand could exact low prices in all transactions with Māori.[58] Marsden's attempts to rein in private trade and to prevent missionaries from trading in guns were repeatedly foiled. Although the missionaries—with the exception of Hall—promised Marsden that they would curtail private trade in March 1819 and collectively signed an agreement repudiating the musket trade in May 1819 (which was soon broken), the reality was that missionaries had become profoundly enmeshed in the Māori economy of the Bay of Islands. They were unable to establish the kind of financial independence that would allow them to sever the economic and social relationships established with their local trading partners and protectors.

This was most evident in Kendall's voyage to England with Hongi and Waikato, the young rangatira from Rangihoua. While this journey allowed Kendall to shore up his relationship with Hongi, who had emerged as the most powerful of the leaders in the Bay of Islands, the two rangatira made their motivations for this trip clear. Soon after their arrival in England, Kendall recorded their demands. Kendall was to aid them in putting together a party of men to "dig up the ground" in search for iron ore, to gather more "preachers," and one hundred settlers to be taken to New Zealand. The missionary was also to furnish the chiefs with a large dog each, as a marker of their mana, and to recruit a contingent of twenty soldiers accompanied by three officers.[59] During their sojourn in England, Hongi and Waikato did not recruit their army or their settlers, but they were received by King George, who presented these "Kings" of New Zealand with gifts in recognition of their status. Waikato received a helmet and an engraved gun, while Hongi received a coat of chain mail and two guns.[60] King George did not envisage the ultimate use that these gifts would be put to. On their arrival in Port Jackson, the rangatira dispensed with these valuable products of the royal armory—with the exception of Hongi's coat of mail and Waikato's muskets—and other gifts they collected in England, exchanging them for a large consignment of muskets (perhaps over three hundred) and powder, a cache of arms that was quickly put to use in Hongi's raids, in 1821, against Te Hinaki of Ngāti Paoa at Tāmaki and Ngāti Maru near present-day Thames.[61]

Labor and Slavery on the Early Mission Stations

Kendall's memorandum on the "Objects of Shunghee and Whykato in Visiting England" reveals the extent to which these rangatira believed that they were capable of dictating the pattern of cross-cultural relationships.[62] In 1820 this belief was far from misplaced. Europeans visiting or living in the Bay of Islands entered a world that remained governed by Māori *ritenga* (customs, practices) and *tikanga* (rules, protocols). The authority of the major rangatira such as Hongi Hika or Korokoro, the influential chief of the southern alliance, remained untrammeled by the missionary presence. These great leaders were able to administer justice through traditional methods, make war, trade with European vessels for weapons, procure, and, if they wished, kill slaves in open defiance of the missionaries. At the same time, they enjoyed the benefits of close association with Europeans, gaining access to new skills (like reading and writing), as well as tools, seeds, livestock, and weapons. The precarious CMS mission had increasingly come under the ambit of Hongi Hika's power. The dependence of the mission on Hongi was confirmed in 1819, when the second CMS mission was established at Kerikeri on land purchased from Hongi in the shadow of his Kororipo pā.[63] After his return from Britain, Hongi's confidence was unbounded. In 1821 a missionary reported that Hongi was telling his people that the missionaries were "only a set of poor Cooks—that King George knew nothing about [the missionaries] nor Mr. Marsden either—In consequence of this [the missionaries] have had many hard speeches and cruel mockings."[64] At this point, Kendall himself recognized "the absolute power which the natives have over us," and he stressed that this dominance was the product of their "having it in their power very considerably to increase or diminish our supplies."[65]

Thus, the rangatira's belief in their dominance over the missionaries reflected the economic relationships that had developed during the first five years of the mission. By 1820, the missionaries were not only profoundly dependent on the ability of the people and chiefs of the northern alliance to furnish them with basic foodstuffs, but also dependent on them for labor. Marsden had imagined his missionaries as working hard at the civilized arts, acting simultaneously as models and teachers, training Māori in the skills that he believed to be essential to civilization: tending stock, cultivating wheat, erecting fences, dressing timber, rope making, making and repairing simple iron agricultural tools. Māori were, he imagined, to embrace these skills and learn to deploy them on a regular basis through daily labor, a disciplined regime that would "civilize" them and inculcate Christian models of social interaction and morality.[66] These goals were not achieved; both the rangatira and common folk were aware that they and not the missionaries dictated labor relations on the early mission stations.

One way in which the nature of these relationships can be accessed is through changing patterns of payment for Māori on the missions. In the first two or three years of the mission, Māori workers expected to be furnished with food by the missionaries and to be paid in iron tools, especially "tokees" (toki, or axes). William Hall recorded, for example, that the group of Rangi-houa Māori who worked for a week in mid-1816 breaking up two acres of ground for wheat received "nine large Tommahawks—besides all their vict-uals."[67] These tools were valued for their great utility and for their ability to be deployed as weapons; in some cases, they were modified and personalized, with their wooden handles being replaced by bone hafts.[68] With time, many workers only grudgingly accepted toki, and they were adept judges of the quality of different brands of axes, refusing to accept implements that they believed were of inferior quality.[69]

By 1820, many Māori workers were demanding fowling-pieces, muskets, or gunpowder for payment, not only reflecting a desire for those potent weapons, but also pointing to the widespread distribution of toki as well. In February 1820 John Butler recorded the mission's dependence on local people, noting that the fledgling Kerikeri station was in jeopardy because the mission had depleted its timber supplies. Suitable timber could only be procured from Kawakawa, but Butler knew that this would be difficult as "the natives of Kawa Kawa are very saucy, and full of trade; and they will not look at us, except we have a new musket in our hands."[70] In December that same year, Hall also reported that that he was unable to get his workers to transport wood the twenty miles from the timber grounds to the settlement: "The natives will not bring it for our mode of payment, neither will they sell us any pork scarcely. They save it all up for the shipping that gives them muskets and powder. We are apprehensive that we will have to be supplied with animal food from New South Wales."[71]

Hongi's visit to England was also the vector for introducing new ideas about work to Māori, as soon after his return one missionary reported that the "Na-tive Sawyers immediately struck work, and demanded payment for their labour in Money, as was the Case in England, or else in Gun powder."[72] The ability of those Māori who undertook work on the early mission stations to determine the medium and rates of their payment had profound conse-quences. The mechanics struggled to access workers on a regular basis, and when they were able to find workers, the mission's limited finances placed severe restraints on the length of time that they could be retained. As a result, the missionaries undertook more of the physical labor entailed in establish-ing the mission—preparing land for cultivation, cutting and dressing timber, erecting houses, storehouses, and fences, and attending to cultivation—than they had envisaged. In effect, this meant that both the "improvement" of the mission stations and the teaching of the "civilized arts" progressed much more slowly than Marsden had expected.

The mission's dependence on local patterns of economic organization and the inability of the mechanics to effectively transform this economic order (and its attendant social formations) are clearly attested to by the persistence of slavery in Māori society. Early European explorers were struck by the prominence of unfree people in Māori social organization and economic life. They recorded various names for these people: *kuki* (cook), *taurekareka* (captive, scoundrel), or *tūtūā* (mean, low-born), although this last term could apply to low-ranking free people as well as to those who were captured during war. Because the labor and very lives of these individuals were under the discretion of rangatira, Europeans understood these unfree individuals as "slaves," even though some subsequent commentators have disputed these acts of cultural translation.[73] Typically these slaves were captured by *taua* (war parties), and it seems that in some cases the sourcing of slaves may have been a significant motivation for the campaigns of taua.[74] Once captured, the slaves played a crucial role in the economic lives of precontact communities, carrying out routine and heavy labor, especially tasks that might endanger the tapu status of high-ranking people.[75] While the slaves were of economic value to their masters, they had very limited mana: they were considered to be noa, their masters could kill or hurt them with no fear of social sanction, and slaves were often ritually killed when their masters were sick or died.[76] Some enslaved women were allowed to marry into their new communities as the secondary or junior wives of rangatira who had enslaved them. While the offspring of such a union would be free members of the hapū, the wives themselves retained their unfree status and always remained junior to the free and high-ranking wives of a rangatira.[77] Even if some women were incorporated into their new hapū, being enslaved nevertheless radically and irrevocably transformed an individual's social being. Typically, the social bonds that had previously defined the slaves' standing within their own community were extinguished. Dislocated from both the mesh of genealogically defined relationships and the ancestral lands which defined their identity, slaves effectively forfeited their life at the point of capture. Although there is some evidence that in exceptional circumstances individual captives might be ransomed or returned, usually captives lost all standing in their former tribe as they effectively became *mate*—damaged, ill, dead—morally and socially dead.[78]

Given the strong connections between evangelicalism and abolitionism, it is not surprising that the missionaries were very critical of the treatment of captives in Māori society. But despite their connections and alignments with the antislavery evangelical activists in Britain, missionaries in New Zealand tended not to draw direct parallels between the fate of war captives in Māori communities and the enslavement of Africans. This seems to have reflected an understanding that slavery in te ao Māori was propelled and shaped by kinship rivalries and intertribal warfare. Perhaps the missionaries were also reluctant to see the operation of slavery in Māori society as a clear equivalent of race slavery in the Atlantic because Europeans were not directly involved in the trade and, as such, there was no direct moral taint on Britain of the type produced by the prominence of Britons in African slavery and plantation production. Nevertheless missionaries and those connected to both the CMS and WMS missions in Te Ika a Māui were persistently troubled by these Māori practices.[79] Samuel Marsden, who had strong personal connections to William Wilberforce (the leading parliamentary advocate of abolition), was painfully aware of the vulnerability of Māori slaves: "A slave has no security for his life. His master kills him whenever he pleases, and treats him in any way his passions may dictate."[80]

Despite Marsden's concern, the missionaries who settled in New Zealand generally had to accommodate themselves to the social importance of slavery in the Māori world. They lacked the economic means and social authority to "reform" existing practices or to impose new models of socioeconomic organization. Well into the 1830s, slaves were a ubiquitous feature of the social landscape of the mission. When missionaries traveled with rangatira as guides, the slaves of these high-ranking men often provided much of the labor for the traveling party.[81] When missionaries visited rangatira who ruled over their local districts or more distant communities, they frequently accepted food that was prepared by the chief's enslaved "servants."[82] As the mission grew, the missionaries attempted to "redeem" some slaves by paying their masters with axes or blankets for their freedom (see figure 3.1).

But even in the mid-1830s, when Christianity began to gain ground among some Bay of Islands communities, the missionaries were often unable to entirely sever the connections between former slaves and their masters. Even though they were supposedly free, many of the former slaves who worked on mission stations and embraced Christianity enjoyed their new status only as long as they continued to give a portion of the income they earned working for missionaries to their old masters.[83] Missionaries were also ineffective in protecting their redeemed slaves, who were occasionally "reclaimed" by rangatira and remained vulnerable to violence.[84] Nor were missionaries particularly successful in ridding their "mission natives" of their belief in slaves' lack of social value; in the mid-1820s "mission natives" actually killed slaves for various social infringements.[85] Most important, the missionaries were also

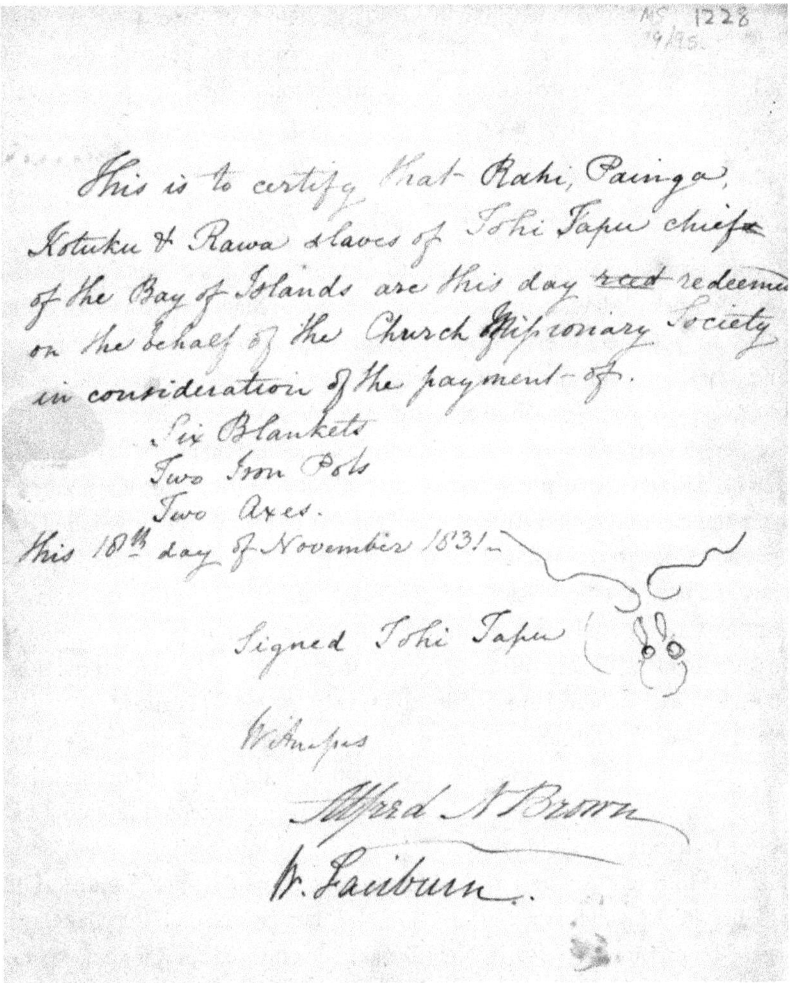

This is to certify that Rahi, Painga, Kotuku & Rawa slaves of Tohi Tapu chief of the Bay of Islands are this day ~~red~~ redeemed on the behalf of the Church Missionary Society in consideration of the payment of.

Six Blankets
Two Iron Pots
Two Axes.

This 18th day of November 1831.

Signed Tohi Tapu

Witnesses

Alfred N Brown
W. Fairburn.

FIGURE 3.1 This 1831 signed agreement redeemed four of the slaves of the rangatira Tohi Tapu, who signed the document with a rendering of his moko. Reproduced with permission from Auckland War Memorial Museum, MS-1228.

unable to convince their high-ranking patrons of the evils of slavery in the 1810s, 1820s, and early 1830s.[86] Slavery remained integral to material wealth and the projection of status for rangatira. Slaves were an indispensable labor force that could be deployed to produce the agricultural surplus that sustained warfare and facilitated commerce with Europeans. Great chiefs like Hongi were both intimates of the missionaries and large slaveholders. Acting as a patron of the mission allowed Hongi to project his mana through his mastery of the new world, while his large retinue of slaves were a potent demonstration of his mana within the long-established cultural idioms of Māori leadership, which valued the accumulation of food, weapons, prized ornaments, and captives as expressions of power.

Cultural Difference and Work in the Māori World

Thus, the missionaries were unable to dictate the terms of labor to Māori, and the work of slaves remained significant in the Māori world well into the 1830s. In fact, there is evidence to suggest that the presence of missionaries and other Europeans in the Bay of Islands may have prompted the extension of slavery. For some communities, especially those eager to access new military technology, slaves became the most valued items that a *teretere* (trading party) could bring to ports and coastal villages. During the 1820s, parties from the Hauraki region, Waikato, and the Bay of Plenty regularly visited the Bay of Islands to trade slaves and traditional finished goods (including *korowai* [cloaks] and *mere* [clubs]) for muskets and powder.[87] The use of slaves captured during raids to the south was undoubtedly an important facilitator of the expansion of agriculture, especially the extension of potato cultivation, to meet the demands of cross-cultural trade in the Bay of Islands.

Moreover, the missionaries found that when Māori did undertake work on or around their stations, they resisted the rhythms and disciplines that the missionaries upheld as ideals. In 1815 John King accepted "a young lad about fourteen years old" named "Terra" [Tara] into his household. King planned to teach him how to "read & to spin twine &c upon condition he will not steal & will folow my derection." He then reflected on the challenges posed by missionary work in New Zealand as opposed to Marsden's vision of "civilization," which was generated out of the sojourns at Parramatta of visiting rangatira: "He [Tara] is a promising youth very active & quick in learning, but so wild and unsettled, The natives when at port jackson are redey to learn, they are not so here upon their own ground, they are as capable of learning a trade or any thing else as we are if they had a taste for it, but confinement they cannot bear, therefore much patience is required to let them come & go almost as they please."[88] Here King was not forwarding a skeptical assessment of Māori cultural capacity on the basis of race; rather, he was grappling with the very real challenges that cultural difference posed. Marsden had been optimistic that "civilization" would bite quickly, effecting rapid change in New Zealand. But where Marsden's visits to New Zealand were temporary, King was already aware in mid-1815 that transforming local culture was a profoundly difficult project. Needless to say, King did not abandon this project, for the transformation of "heathen" cultures was the raison d'être of the missionary, but he clearly recognized that attitudes to work were, in fact, culturally contingent. "Industriousness" was not a transcendent value, but a habitual form of action, a discipline that was inculcated through teaching, routine, and perseverance.

A year later, in August 1816, William Hall also wrote to the CMS in London, informing them of the challenges of realizing Marsden's vision.

> I find it is almost impracticable to make Mechanics of them or to teach them the Arts at N. Zealand, they are not arrived at that state yet, I cannot work amongst them they pilfer the Tools so much, They have at different times stolen my working Axes so that I have not had one left to do anything with. . . . They are so inclined to ramble that they will not be confined to learn a trade, and although I were supplied with Tools, Victuals, payment, and Cloathing for them so as to enable me to keep them in employment, they are so fond of fighting and plundering that nothing will divert them from it or prevent their going away at certain times. Parties keep coming and going and if we employ any that will work, by that means we can get land cultivated rough fences made and such work as requires no time to learn it, but they would never learn a trade at that rate.[89]

Hall placed greater emphasis on cultural capacity than did his colleague King. Hall was frustrated by what he understood as Māori "thievery" and was skeptical of Marsden's assessment of the ease of "civilizing" Māori. But Hall recognized that some of the actions he was so frustrated by had meaning in the local culture, and he believed that the strength of these habits were such that it was beyond the mechanics to simply use instruction in the "civilized arts" to transform Māori. By outlining those areas in which he was actually able to actively engage with Māori, Hall sketched an alternative vision of how the mission might function. "I can spend my time very beneficially amongst them by conversing and bartering with them, visiting their sick and relieving them, by giving them suitable food and medicine which they are frequently in great need of."[90] Hall's vision anticipated some of the key elements in a new missionary strategy that would be adopted in the 1820s, when Marsden's "civilization" policy was finally abandoned.

What is striking about Hall's and King's responses to their failures in instructing the "civilized arts" is their relatively neutral rendering of cultural difference. Later missionaries and CMS officials would not be so generous. In the early 1830s, for example, the CMS missionary Richard Davis, who oversaw the mission's trial farm at Te Waimate, repeatedly fulminated against Māori "laziness."[91] Davis's opinions were influential as the CMS secretary Dandeson Coates wielded them to argue against the colonization of New Zealand when he gave evidence to the 1838 Select Committee on New Zealand. Coates argued that Māori "have never been accustomed to pursue any Object with Steadiness and Perseverance," and he asserted that even after two decades of missionary work, the "Habit[s] of steady Industry" remained unknown to Māori. Coates used this supposed lack of industriousness to insist on the need for prolonged missionary tutelage and to underscore the unsuitability of Māori for absorption into the kind of colonial market economy that advocates of the large-scale settlement of New Zealand envisaged.[92] Coates was convinced that "the idea of obtaining native labor at present, to any extent, or with any degree of steadiness, is perfectly chimerical."[93]

The arguments of Coates and Davis are early examples of the ways in which Europeans in New Zealand have used attitudes to work to delineate cultural difference and to order that difference into hierarchies.[94] They stand at the head of a long intergenerational discourse, which was first examined by Raymond Firth in his classic study of "traditional" Māori economics. Firth noted that this discourse emphasized Māori inferiority by emphasizing the "spasmodic nature of his [Māori] industrial life, his idleness, his volatile mind, his care-free attitude towards work, his lack of ability to concentrate upon his task, and his failure to complete the business in hand before turning to fresh fields of adventure." Arrayed against this position, Firth noted a range of commentators, including Cook, Marsden, J. L. Nicholas, and the CMS missionary William Yate, who had identified the "industrious character of the Māori, and his patience in accomplishing work." Firth himself favored this second position and suggested that many of the commentators who criticized Māori for a lack of industry were not discussing the "true" nature of Māori culture, but rather commenting on changes produced once Māori came under the "influence of European culture."[95]

There is limited archival evidence to support Firth's suggestion that contact resulted in a decline in Māori industriousness. In many ways it is more important to highlight the coexistence of traditional ways of organizing work and the introduction of the new ideals of discipline by missionaries and later colonists. It seems likely that long-established forms of organizing work within the Māori world were only mildly disrupted before the late 1840s. When the alienation of tribal lands accelerated, more Māori began cultivating agricultural produce on a large scale for both the colonial and trans-Tasman trades, and the first significant numbers of Māori were incorporated into the cash economy. However, even these transformations played out unevenly; some iwi, such as Ngāi Tahu Whānui in the South Island and those clustered around Auckland and Wellington were significantly affected, while the economic and cultural foundations of iwi in the central North Island remained largely unchanged.

It is clear that these long-standing patterns of labor organization were neither "natural" nor a generalized manifestation of the basic principles that link supposedly "primitive" societies. Rather, Māori forms of organizing labor, like their Pacific antecedents, were highly enculturated; they were carefully ordered, governed by various rules, required careful discipline, and necessitated considerable bodily effort. This is very clear, for example, if we examine the cultivation of kūmara (Polynesian sweet potato), a chief food crop for Māori in the Bay of Islands and most of New Zealand prior to the arrival of Cook. The sowing of the crop was initiated by the recitation of a karakia (incantations, "prayers") to the god Rongo-marae-roa by a tohunga (ritual expert). Planting was led by kiake (men who wielded kō [digging sticks]), who were followed by ngā tāngata tūāhu (men who broke up the soil and formed the puke [mounds] in which the tubers were planted), who were in turn followed by the rōpū (the company of men responsible for placing tubers in the puke).[96]

This type of endeavor suggests the sophistication, coordination, and careful management of people and processes that could order production within Māori culture. The agricultural basis of many Māori communities and this type of coordinated economic activity suggest that accuracy and persistence in work were valued in the precontact world. Although Davis and Coates were critical of Māori laziness and their want of "steady industry," a wealth of evidence suggests that those who labored hard within these traditional forms of labor were respected for their significant contributions to the material base of the community. Elsdon Best recorded the ancestral saying that inculcated these values: "Anei nga mea i whakataukitia ai e nga tupuna, ko te taha, ko te uaua, ko te pakari" [Here are the things valued by the ancestors: it is the strength, the vigor and the sturdiness].[97] The material effects of hard work on the body were also deemed attractive and socially important. One famous pēpeha (saying) was the injunction "E moe i te tangata ringa raupa" [Marry a man with blistered hands]. Hirini Moko Mead and Neil Grove note that "calloused hands were the trademark of an industrious person" and that within the context of a society grounded in gardening and fishing, "girls were advised to marry such men."[98] Conversely, numerous whakatauki (proverbs) reprimanded those reluctant to undertake work, who complained during labor, or with lazy dispositions. The pēpeha "He kai, ko tau e pahure; ko te mahi, e kore e pahure" [Eating is your accomplishment, work is not] and, even more pointedly, "Kei nui a Mahi, ka noho toretore a Mangere" [Work has plenty while Laziness sits complaining] indicated the disapproval directed at those who were keen to share the fruits of work, but were unwilling to labor themselves.[99]

Time-Discipline and Cultural Difference

In an important 1911 work the prominent Ngāi Tahu Anglican Hoani Parata observed that work in this "traditional" Māori world was harnessed to very different ends than it was within European culture. Parata suggested that labor was typically geared toward meeting a set of relatively simple wants; neither was Māori labor driven by a hunger for expensive luxuries, nor was it valued as an end in itself.[100] Although one element of Parata's formulation does not recognize a key feature of Māori society in an age of cross-cultural contact—as some early nineteenth-century Māori worked for Europeans precisely as a means of gaining access to highly valued "luxuries" in the form of firearms—he was correct in stressing the divergence between Māori and European attitudes to "industriousness." Established Māori patterns of labor were task-specific; they focused on completing a single act of labor or a sequence of acts of labor in order to facilitate a particular outcome, whether that was the production of a successful kūmara crop, snaring a large number of kererū (pigeon) or kiore (Polynesian rat), or completing an intricate korowai. Within this economic system, patterns of labor were shaped by the maturation of key food plants, the reproductive and migratory cycles of fish and birds, and the need to maintain and police socioeconomic relationships through journeys to conduct trade or wage war. As these broad seasonal rhythms dictated the tasks that needed to be completed, sustained periods of intense labor might be followed by periods where relatively little work was carried out.

Equally particular understandings of time- and work-discipline were central to Marsden's emphasis on "industriousness" as an engine for the "civilization" of Māori. Where Māori placed great value on the outcomes of work—in having full pātaka (store houses), valued foods that could be dispensed in hākari, or renowned taonga (treasured goods)—Marsden and the mechanics valued the labor process itself. Disciplined acts of physical work that were repeated day after day, week after week, month after month, year after year were seen as essential to the material well-being of the family unit and as inculcating good moral and spiritual values. E. P. Thompson's pathbreaking essay on temporal sensibilities and the new forms of work discipline that were essential to the Industrial Revolution sketched the broad shift in British understandings of time in the early modern period, a shift that Marsden and his mechanics were heirs to.[101] The relationship between work and time had, of course, concerned both Marx and Engels. Engels observed that production in the new industrial order of northern England during the 1840s was governed by an "iron discipline" typical of the military, which regulated the rhythms and responsibilities of British workers. In Engel's eyes, this regime meant that British workers experienced a "slavery" which was "more abject than that of the Negroes in America because they are more strictly supervised."[102] Enlarging on this tradition of criticism, Thompson mapped the broad changes that imposed a new awareness of time and a new rigidity in the organization of labor during the transition to capitalism: time was measured by the clocks that became common in workshops and the first factories; the speed and accuracy of laborers were increasingly scrutinized by their overseers; slow workers were penalized by fines, while those who worked quickly enjoyed financial incentives; and new models of work-discipline were extolled by teachers and preachers.[103]

Thompson's argument is a very useful starting point for considering the mechanics' efforts to "civilize" Māori, and it directs attention to the extent to which the missionaries were able to establish the disciplined values of capitalism among the Māori communities they were evangelizing. Although various "primitive peoples" appear fleetingly in Thompson's essay, his focus was firmly fixed on Britain, specifically, England.[104] The transplantation of this very particular way of thinking about the relationship between work and time—which was contested in England itself—to New Zealand's radically different demographic and cultural context was not easy. Missionaries struggled to harness Māori labor to the project of improvement; King and Hall were unable to get Māori to work when they wanted them to and were frustrated by their inability to get the workers they did secure to work in a regular and sustained manner; Hall expressed frustration at the ceaseless "coming and going"; and King complained that "one day with us, or a part of it the next or part of it playing and dancing about, per[h]ap[s] if I go out & ask them to come in to read or work they will begin dancing & shouting & laughing saying by and by."[105]

The failure to regularize Māori labor reflected the dominance that local people were able to exercise over missionaries in their economic relationships, but Hall and King were also responding to the strength and persistence of the very different temporal sensibility that had long ordered Māori life. Within this framework, periods of heavy labor were balanced by spells of relative inactivity. For most North Island iwi, the start of the year, with the first new moon after Matariki (the rising of Pleiades), signaled the beginning of the rat-trapping and bird-snaring seasons (which ran through to the summer for some species). Spring planting began around October, depending on the appearance of various *tohu* (signs, such as the flowering of particular shrubs). After planting, gardens required constant tending. This often fell to women, as summer was the season for war-making. In late February to March preparations were made for the harvesting of the key crop of kūmara, which was harvested in March and April.[106]

Around this core agricultural cycle, other seasonal patterns directed the rhythms of work, especially the harvesting of particular fish stocks. While these patterns varied significantly between iwi—depending on climate as well the seasonal movements and fluctuations of various food items—what is clear is that precontact Māori communities possessed clearly defined cycles of labor, cycles that were closely related to the production and harvesting of core food supplies.[107] This was a temporal system shaped by seasonally defined and task-based economic activity and as such allowed for a sustained period during the eleventh and twelfth months of the traditional twelve-month calendar (corresponding roughly to the mid-April to mid-June period) when little labor was carried out and when important social obligations were discharged through visiting, feasting, and the holding of hui (assemblies, meetings). This model diverged sharply from the mechanic missionaries' belief that work should be constant and carefully regularized by daily and weekly routines, and from their inherited work patterns, which were only moderately influenced by seasonality.[108]

Given the persistence of this model into the 1830s and well beyond, missionaries learned that Māori workers were likely to refuse to work during periods of traditionally heavy agricultural labor. During the planting and harvest times for key crops, especially kūmara, missionaries were not able to access local workers or interest people in hearing religious teachings.[109] Work would also be abandoned on occasions when a chance economic windfall presented itself. In October 1819, for example, a group of "native sawyers" joined the people of Rangihoua in abandoning their routines because of the excitement and opportunities presented when a dead whale floated into the entrance of the Bay of Islands.[110] In the 1810s and 1820s, when only a small number of Māori attached themselves to the mission stations on any regular or ongoing basis, any tasks that missionaries hoped to execute with the help of Māori labor were undertaken on Māori terms and on Māori time.

The persistence of Māori patterns of organizing work in time reflected the weakness of the temporal regimes constructed by the missionaries as well as the robust state of Māori cultural sensibilities. Where the lives of factory, domestic, and agricultural workers in Britain were increasingly tied to the disciplinary power afforded by the precision of clock-time, life on the early mission stations in New Zealand lacked the technology to be able to impose any such regulation. Despite the improved diffusion and affordability of timepieces in Britain in the late eighteenth century and early nineteenth, and despite the strong connections between Protestantism and the clock and watch trade, the New Zealand mission stations lacked the means of imposing any regular order of mechanical time.[111] Rest, work, and worship were initially subject to very loose regulation. Without clocks and reliable watches, the missionaries ordered their days according a rough reckoning of the time based on the movement of the sun across the sky. This lack of structure did not pose too many difficulties when the missionaries were concentrated together at Rangihoua, but after the establishment of the Kerikeri and Paihia mission stations, the inability to measure time accurately became more problematic, as coordinating meetings, expeditions to survey natural resources, or preaching tours proved difficult.

More broadly, it meant that the mission did not project the clearly ordered social and spiritual system that many of the missionaries desired. In 1827 Henry Williams complained from Paihia that there was still "no watch or timepiece in the Settlement, but one old, rickety thing, upon which no dependence could be placed." As a result, activities on the mission were more shapeless than Williams, a former naval officer, desired, and he complained that the "natives" and Europeans could not be gathered together for morning worship until "near noon."[112] At Kerikeri, a clock was eventually mounted on the gable of the station's chapel, but this was eventually moved to the bell tower that was added to the "stone store" at Kerikeri in 1834. The clock was removed within a decade: even in the mid-1840s, clock time did not rule supreme.[113] These problems also plagued the fledgling Wesleyan mission. After bemoaning that he "never had the use of a clock since we came to New Zealand," John Hobbs noted in October 1825 that he and the visiting CMS missionary James Kemp spent a day mounting a "cuckoo" clock—hardly the embodiment of evangelical seriousness or post-Enlightenment rationality—as the mission's public timepiece.[114] Hobbs himself became central to the uncertain upkeep of the European temporal order in the north of New

Zealand during the 1830s (and beyond) as he maintained and repaired the few timepieces owned by Europeans.[115]

Giordano Nanni has suggested that bells played a key role as "amplifiers" and transmitters of the rigid temporal orders that missionaries sought to impose in colonial spaces like South Africa and Australia.[116] On the New Zealand frontier, missionaries did use bells, and they were vital to the ordering of life on each station, marking prayers and the beginning and end of school, and even signaling particular times for specific leisure activities. But on new missionary frontiers (like Kaitaia in 1834), missionaries were without bells and used improvised materials (such as banging together two pieces of iron) to signal services and the divisions of the day.[117] More generally, mission bells were not especially effective in stitching these communities into a unified temporal scheme, given the scattered nature of both mission stations and Māori communities and without the support of synchronized timepieces at each mission station.[118] In this regard, the situation in the Bay of Islands echoes Elizabeth Elbourne's characterization of missionary attempts to cultivate time-discipline in colonial South Africa as only "ambiguously successful."[119]

Sabbath-Keeping and Māori Engagement with Christianity

If the measurement and coordination of activities on a daily basis proved difficult for the missionaries, they had less difficulty in maintaining the central and most distinctive feature of their temporal order: the sanctity of the Sabbath. Sabbath-keeping was a fundamental aspect of evangelical teaching and a key marker of evangelical identity. Sundays were a day to be set aside for spiritual concerns, where good Christians would devote themselves to what William Wilberforce termed "the exercises of humble admiration and grateful homage" to God.[120] The Sabbath was not only a day dedicated to spiritual contemplation and the performance of religious duties, but a day during which "the benevolent and domestic, and social feelings" were cultivated, especially through acts of family worship. As Catherine Hall reminds us, Sabbath-keeping was one of the key instruments through which evangelicals connected religion and domesticity and in so doing they invested the day with great spiritual and social purpose.[121] Missionaries were very aware that the maintenance of the Sabbath was a fundamental aspect of their duty as evangelists. In 1810 the CMS stated, "The duty of resting on this day, according to the commandment, is of utmost importance for the promotion of individual and national piety. Without this there can be no religion even in the most remote corner of the earth."[122]

The preservation of the Sabbath as a day of rest and religious observation was emphasized in the instructions issued to the mechanics by the CMS. In fact, the society's first injunction was that the settlers were to be diligent in their observance of the Sabbath. Sabbath-keeping was to be not only an act of true piety, by also a form of spiritual and moral performance: the CMS believed that it was crucial that the mechanics perform all of their major acts of devotion, including family prayer, as "publicly as possible," and thus enjoined the mechanics to make sure that they sang "loud enough to be heard by a passing native."[123] Most important, the Sabbath provided an important entry point for Christian teaching. The "mechanics" used it to teach Māori about the social discipline that evangelicals cherished, but also as an opportunity to introduce the larger cosmological and temporal scheme of Christianity. The Sabbath was sacred because it was God's gift to humanity, a time to be devoted to the remembrance of Him (Exodus 16:29). The day of rest reenacted the pattern of Creation itself: humans were to rest on the seventh day, just as God had rested after completing the creation of the Cosmos (Genesis 2:2). These were core teachings of the Bible and were more easily communicated to Māori than some of the more elusive concepts that Christianity presented, such as, for example, the Trinity or transubstantiation. Even when Thomas Kendall made his exploratory voyage to New Zealand, in 1814, with William Hall, he was able to communicate the rudiments of the Sabbath's origins and meaning to some of the leading chiefs in the Bay of Islands.[124] The 1820 grammar that Kendall helped prepare at Cambridge with Hongi Hika and Waikato, under the direction of the linguist Samuel Lee, reveals the theological centrality of the Sabbath. The first of the volume's "Familiar Dialogues between a Christian Missionary and His Pupil" explained the significance of the Bible, describing God and his role as the Creator of "all things." The English version of the dialogue proceeds.

> P[upil]: Who made all things, both in heaven above, and in the earth beneath?
> M[issionary]: God made them.
> P[upil]: In how many days did he complete his work?
> M[issionary]: In six days.
> P[upil]: Is the seventh day a sacred day?
> M[issionary]: It is a sacred day; a day appointed for calling upon God.
> P[upil]: Will not the good work on this day?
> M[issionary]: No: this is the day for praising his God.[125]

The early missionaries found that their conversations with Māori rarely followed this kind of script. A sequence of entries from John King's journal during 1822 and 1823 reveal the centrality of the Sabbath in King's efforts to communicate the rudiments of Christian thought and the ensuing cultural struggles over the meaning of time. After having dinner with his family on Sunday, 8 September 1822, King walked up the steep path from Hohi to Rangihoua pā. On arriving, he "explained to a Chief and other natives the origin of the Sabbath, our duty to observe it, how sin misery & Death entired [entered] into the world."[126] Two weeks later, he walked past Rangihoua to Te Puna in the next bay. There he spoke

> to the Chief, but he was so full of the world that he had no room for the Sabbath nor religion, came back to Rangiua [Rangihoua], proposed to a chief that a change might be effected with regard to the Sabbath Day among them—by their attending regular to instruction—If a few do, & all of you should rest from Labour on this Day, out of respect to the white man's Religion, this is, & would be but little satisfaction to me, but that you may not only rest from labour, but that ye may know how [to] worship Jehovah in Spirit & in Truth & spend the Sabbath according to his commandment is the Object of my visits to you on the Sabbath Day—[127]

This teaching had little immediate effect. Three weeks later, on Sunday, 13 October, King complained that his preaching had been impeded because the children from Rangihoua were "scattered abroad" and he "had to seek for them." His teaching was restricted to the children because the adults were "away seeking food & at work planting their sweet Potatoes, fishing & they are bad of food at this season."[128] In order to circumvent this problem, on Saturday, 26 October, King visited Rangihoua "to caution the natives against going to work on the Sabbath Day and to request the Children to be at Home tomorrow." This strategy failed. When he went back to the pā the following afternoon, he found that "the people was all scattered."

> I had to seek for the children, a few very young colected together, I began, but soon after a woman came from Hoshi [Hohi], & began talking & makeing so much noise bying [buying] fish, that I & the children was obliged to move further of[f] & make another begining, but soon after came the same subject & makeing so much noise we could not keep our own words we was obliged to leave of[f]. two canoes came [to] our settlement to sell fish & c—it set all the natives in a bustle & noise—& it had more of the appearance of a market Day than of a Sabbath, at Rangiua [Rangihoua].[129]

Here we not only have the missionary failing to overlay his vision of the Sabbath over a strong Māori temporal sensibility, but we also have open resistance to his teaching, as the enthusiastic sociability that accompanied trading relationships in the Māori world drowned out King's words. This resistance to his teaching continued into 1823, when he was told by two men at Rangihoua that the idea of the Sabbath and "all these good things" King taught were intended for "white people alone."[130] Meanwhile the people at Te Puna suggested "that if I will pay them—they will sit still on the Sabbath or come to receive instruction—some food or fishhooks they ask—they often remark to me that our own country people do not observe the Sabbath—the sailors work on board ships or do worse &c."[131]

This argument forwarded at Te Puna anticipated later Māori Christian critiques of the moral laxity of European culture. But what is striking is that the kind of resistance that King had encountered to his teaching regarding the Sabbath began to weaken elsewhere in the mid-1820s. In 1822 Samuel Leigh, who oversaw the establishment of the WMS mission in 1823, recorded that he had convinced a party of Bay of Islands Māori that "they and their slaves should rest on Sundays."[132] In April 1824 Te Koki, the principal chief of Paihia, invited the recently arrived Marianne Williams (wife of Henry Williams), to witness his people harvesting kūmara. As Marianne Williams related, Te Koki "told me, without my asking, that none of the people would work on the morrow, nor did they."[133] By this time, a group of Māori from the Kawakawa-Paihia region under the leadership of Te Koki began to regularly engage with missionary teaching. Henry Williams noted that the recognition of the Sabbath was a key marker of this new interest: "They know when it arrives as well as we do, and distinguish the day by wearing their European clothes and abstaining from work; our Settlement on that day is perfectly quiet. The head Chief, with his wife and many others, generally attend our services, and frequently family prayer."[134]

Just as Te Koki's people began to recognize the importance of the Sabbath, Whangaroa Māori seemed receptive to the Wesleyan missionaries who also used the Sabbath as the cornerstone of their teaching. In September 1824 William White wrote optimistically to his brother about the state of the mission.

It is a pleasing circumstance to us that the Sabbath of the Lord is in general observed by the Natives in our "immediate vicinity" and those who do work on that Blessed Day are ashamed to be seen by us and avoid as much as possible our observation. In going to and from the Native Villages for the purpose of instructing this People we have to cross and recross a River over which the Natives carry us on their Shoulders, for this we give each of them a fish hook or Button; On the week Days they will not give us a Moments credit, but on the Lords Day they do not as much as ask us for payment—Last Sunday whilst one of my Brethren and I were instructing one of the Schools a strange Female came in and sat down close by me and began to beg for something, when she was stopped short by one of our Scholars a fine little Girl who said to her Kaua inoa tani [tenei] te ra tapue [tapu] Do not beg this is the sacred Day. On the same occasion the Father of this Girl told me that some of the New Zealand Men say that this sacred day of ours is nothing to them and is therefore spent in vain when they do not work but as for himself he would not work on that Day for fear our God should be angry with him and spoil his crops of Potatoes and Coomaros [kūmara].[135]

Two months later, Nathaniel Turner recorded,

James [Stack, another WMS missionary] and I went over the hills to Pupuke, and found TEPERRY [Te Pere] the Chief, at home, who was glad to see us. Finding it was not Sabbath, he wished to have some conversation with us on temporal subjects before we commenced talking on divine things; "For," said he, "you will not talk about these things on the ra tabo, (sacred day,) but we may talk about them on a ra noa (common day.)" We complied with his wishes, and agreed to go round in a few days to trade with him for some potatoes. We spent about an hour talking to them about their souls as well as we were able, and the people, from forty to fifty in number, behaved very well.[136]

How do we explain this interest, especially when we compare the receptivity of the communities at Paihia and Whangaroa to the resistance that King found at Te Puna and Rangihoua? This divergence seems to be closely related to the broader nature of the relationships that were established between missionaries and their "host" communities. At Rangihoua and Te Puna, King was preaching to communities that had missionaries living in their midst for nearly a decade. These people, primarily of Te Hikutu hapū, had a long knowledge of the importance of the Sabbath. As early as 1811, Ruatara declared that it was his intention to institute the Sabbath at Rangihoua, and he requested a flag from Marsden, "a Colour that he might hoist on the Sunday morning for the information of his Subjects, and assured [Marsden] that none of his men should ever work again upon the Sabbath."[137] Despite Ruatara's professed enthusiasm, the Te Hikutu people exhibited little interest in either the Sabbath or Christian teaching more generally after the death of their rangatira in early 1815. The mechanics remained socially and economically marginal in the northeast corner of the Bay of Islands. They were dependent on local Māori for labor, food, and protection. Beyond their ability to act as commercial go-betweens, the mechanics had very limited mana; Hongi, confident of his authority over the missionaries, described them as kuki (cooks) and slaves.

Across the Bay of Islands, at Paihia, and farther north, at Whangaroa, the situation was very different. The willingness of Māori to recognize the Sabbath at these sites was produced out of very different social configurations, which emerged at the recently formed mission stations. At Whangaroa, where the Wesleyans evangelized both Ngāti Pou and Ngāti Uru, the mission was quickly established on a sound material basis. Certainly, the missionaries were at times apprehensive about their position in these early years, but by the end of 1824, the economic base of the mission was quite secure. Nathaniel Turner had overseen the establishment of a large garden planted with beans, peas, turnips, cabbages, and onions, as well as the planting of an orchard, and had successfully planted two acres of wheat and barley. The mission also had a good stock of chickens, turkeys, and cows.[138] This gave the mission settlement a degree of self-sufficiency that the CMS settlement at Hohi never enjoyed and allowed the Wesleyans to be less dependent economically on their "hosts." The ability of the Wesleyans to protect their economic standing certainly would have helped to secure their status in the eyes of the local rangatira, and both Te Pere of Ngāti Pou and Te Puhi of Ngāti Uru exhibited significant initial interest in the Christian message.[139] The progress made by Wesleyans would be erased in 1827, with the sacking of the mission station at Whangaroa, but this was more a product of inter-iwi politics and rivalries over European trade than a rejection of missionary teaching.[140]

The mission station at Paihia enjoyed two significant benefits that placed the missionaries of the late 1820s in a stronger position than the mechanics had enjoyed in the 1810s at Hohi. First, they had a resolute protector in Te Koki, an influential rangatira who had an existing personal connection to Marsden and whose patronage allowed Marsden and Williams to build links to the influential chiefs who controlled the southern portions of the Bay of Islands (the southern alliance identified by Sissons, Hohepa, and Wi Hongi).[141] Eager to secure his influence in the face of his northern alliance rivals Hongi Hika and Tohitapu, Te Koki engaged enthusiastically with the mission. He joined the Williams family in family prayers, encouraged his people to attend services, and offered to protect the mission in the turbulent days following the sacking of the Whangaroa mission.[142] He was, for a time, a supporter of a proposal to establish a Māori colony in New South Wales, a plan supported by some members of the southern alliance who were fearful of the consequences of Hongi's death.[143] Te Koki also functioned as an important guardian of Hongi's enemies, and this in turn helped strengthen the mission's position. During 1827, he had offered protection to a teretere (trading party) from Rotorua, which had been fired on by Moka of Hongi's Ngāi Tāwake people.[144] This was an extension of an established pattern of chiefly action, as significant numbers of people from Whangaroa, the southern parts of the Bay of Islands, and other outlying districts had settled at Paihia and Kawakawa by 1826, seeking protection from the aggression the of northern alliance.[145] The missionaries at Paihia were able to access this growing population, and it seems likely that the ill effects of war and the social dislocation that followed the abandonment of established homelands made this population more receptive to Christianity. Second, the Paihia mission projected an air of wealth and confidence. At the end of 1823, it had a sounder economic footing than any other mission settlement, with an extensive garden stocked with a diverse array of fruits and vegetables, oats and barley in cultivation, goats, chickens, and a horse.[146] And under the careful supervision of Marianne Williams, who worked indefatigably to project an ordered and civilized home, the mission's domestic arrangements came to exhibit a degree of affluence and comfort that was unknown in the earlier days at Hohi.

These economic and social relationships help to explain why the communities associated with the new mission stations engaged more readily with Christian teaching than did the people of Rangihoua and Te Puna. But why was the Sabbath the first element of Christian teaching that Māori showed consistent interest in? The answer to this lies in Māori ways of organizing space and time in the precontact period. Tapu was fundamental to the organization of the Māori world. Tapu applied not just to people (especially those of high status) or objects (particularly those of high quality or associated with people of high status), but also to places (such as kūmara fields or burial grounds) and times (in terms of seasons, the human life cycle, and the life cycles of valuable natural resources). Certain resources would be protected by the proclamation of *rāhui*, a ban, which rendered them tapu for a period of time, during which they could not be accessed in the normal manner. Violation of rāhui was understood as hara, a serious breach of tapu, an infraction which could have terrible consequences. Both missionaries and Māori mapped this indigenous regulatory language onto Christian teaching. Where the names of the other days of the week were simply transliterated into Māori, the missionaries used the notion of tapu to communicate the special status of the Sabbath. For missionaries and Māori who began to attach themselves to missionary teaching, Sunday became known as "rā tapu"—the day that is set apart or the sacred day—and working on the Sabbath was seen as a "hara," a violation of tapu, or in the language of the missionaries, a "sin."[147]

The incorporation of this novel temporal division was no mere superficial change. Through their acceptance of the Sabbath, Māori communities were beginning to fashion a new set of cosmological discourses that reassessed the old ways of thinking about the relationships between atua and men. Recognizing the Sabbath marked an emergent recognition of the power of the new atua that the missionaries were presenting to Māori. This was made clear to the Wesleyan missionary James Stack in 1825, when one old chief explained that he was now observing the Sabbath. He believed the Christian atua was responsible for the loss of his kūmara crop because he had refused to recognize the sanctity of rā tapu.[148]

And strikingly, when the first indigenized form of Christianity took shape, the Sabbath occupied a central place in its distinctive teaching. In 1833 a new prophet emerged: he was known as Penetana or Papahurihia, and he also took the name Te Atua Wera (the burned God). Papahurihia claimed that he had been inspired by a vision of the spirit named Nākahi: the transliteration used for "Nahash," the serpent of the Old Testament, in the missionary translation of Genesis 1–3 in 1827. In effect, Papahurihia was reclaiming biblical teaching from the missionaries, a point that was made clear when the prophet told the CMS missionary Charles Baker that while the Bible was true, the missionaries had corrupted it. The prophet accepted the existence of Heaven, but taught that the missionaries would spend the afterlife in Hell. He saw his message as one of religious restoration; the practices of true Christianity and the true teachings of the Bible, especially the Old Testament, were his guide. Papahurihia's followers positioned themselves in opposition to the missionaries, both in their self-designation as Hurai (Jews) and in their insistence that the true Sabbath should be observed on Saturday.[149]

Given the geography of Māori engagement with Christianity, it is revealing that Papahurihia was educated at the mission school at Rangihoua, was a member of the dominant Te Hikutu hapū of that locale, and counted influential chiefs of Te Hikutu (Waikato and possibly Wharepoaka) and the northern alliance (including Tītore and Tāreha of Ngāti Rehia) among his followers.[150] The prophet thus encountered Christianity at a site where missionaries were in a marginal position and where there was not only a long familiarity with missionary teaching, but also a strong tradition of resistance to substantial Christianization. When Māori did begin to form an interest in missionary teaching at Rangihoua, they quickly wrested it free of European control, reworking its temporal scheme and reinterpreting biblical eschatology to dismiss the missionaries as corrupters of God's word and as unnecessary intermediaries between the atua and humanity.

Conclusion

These engagements—from the acceptance of rā tapu's status by many Māori to Papahurihia's radical appropriation of the Old Testament—with the new temporal schemes introduced by the missionaries, marked a major turning point in the development of Protestant missions to Māori. By the early 1830s, the Bible increasingly shaped the ways in which the people of the Bay of Islands understood the relationship between the natural and the supernatural, provided a new stock of explanations for their world, and transformed their perceptions of time. A range of new Māori traditions of thought were emerging, many of which saw value in the Bible and accepted the interpretative authority of missionaries, while others, like that of Papahurihia, creatively reworked both Biblical teaching and Māori cosmology to new and often radical ends.

But contrary to both John M. MacKenzie's and Giordano Nanni's recent arguments about the authority of evangelicals' temporal schema and cultural vision within the empire, there were profound limits to the missionaries' ability to remake Māori beliefs and practices.[151] Missionaries in the Bay of Islands were keen to cultivate a new sense of time discipline, but due to the limited nature of their authority, the thin material base of the mission, and the accommodations they had to make to the persistence of the temporal ordering of the Māori economy, CMS missionaries in Te Ika a Māui hardly fit Nanni's description of evangelicals at the edge of the empire as the "most zealous emissaries" of temporal reform.[152]

Indeed, missionaries were consistently anxious about the fragility of the mission and the slow impact of their work. Many of the missionaries were worried about the ability of Māori to fashion novel interpretations of their teachings, but they were also pleased that the gospel was gaining ground, a prospect that had seemed unlikely in the early 1820s. The early years of the mission were difficult and troubled. The settlement of mechanics and their families at Hohi, which Marsden imagined as an exemplary Christian community, was plagued by bitter conflicts over status, access to resources, and morality. More important, the mechanics remained economically dependent on Māori. Settled on a difficult strip of unproductive land under Rangihoua pā, they were unable to dictate the terms of trade or payment for work, were uncertain in their ability to procure labor, and accommodated themselves to the economic significance of slavery within the Māori world. For their part, the rangatira of Te Hikutu and the other northern alliance hapū placed little value on Christian thought, but they appreciated the mission station's position within a set of British networks that brought novel commodities, new tools, and prized weapons into the Bay of Islands. Just as the common folk who occasionally worked for the missionaries were able to control their labor inputs (and payment), these rangatira were certain of their ability to control their relationships with the British, a confidence most evident in Hongi Hika's 1820 visit to England to source weapons, iron ore, preachers, and settlers to enhance his wealth, military power, and mana.

Against this very particular set of relationships, Marsden's vision of the missionaries using the "Civilized Arts" to teach Māori the values of "industriousness" failed. Into the early 1820s, Marsden remained resolute in his belief in the efficacy of his "Civilization" strategy, but the mechanics were increasingly vehement in their rejection of this policy.[153] In 1821 Thomas Kendall told Marsden,

> I think you expect too much from measures of a temporal nature. You seem to give more encouragement to husbandry and agriculture and to be more zealous respecting them than you are about churches and schools. You have always attended chearfully to applications made to you for cattle &c even after some had been destroyed by the natives, but you have not always seen your way so clearly respecting churches & schools. . . . If I might be permitted to give my opinion, I should say, that so far as the ultimate object of the society is concerned, one pound laid out in the support of a school is of more advantage than two, or perhaps than five, laid out in Cattle, &c.[154]

Kendall's critique anticipated a seismic shift in the CMS policy toward New Zealand. In 1823 Henry Williams was appointed to lead the New Zealand mission, and he implemented a new set of priorities from his base at Paihia. Before Williams left Britain, the CMS stressed the primary importance of religious teaching over "civilization." In a language very different from Marsden's favored economistic idiom, the society told Williams that his mission in New Zealand had "no secular object in view, but

[was] desirous of bringing glory to God by advancing the kingdom of his Son."[155] Edward Garrard Marsh, of Hampstead Chapel and Oriel College, warned Henry Williams against the kind of secular entanglements that had been so central in Marsden's career in New South Wales and which had been so influential in dictating Marsden's vision of how the mission to Māori should proceed.

> The first thing that seems desirable [for the missionary], is to disencumber himself of every thing which could prove a temptation to him in the way of his duty: for, though earthly weapons cannot help you in this warfare, they may hinder you, like the armour of Saul, girt upon the limbs of David: and the Christian must put them off him, as David did; remembering the advice of St. Paul—No man that warreth entangleth himself with the affairs of this life, that he may please him who hath chosen him to be a soldier.[156]

Under Williams, new emphasis was placed on the translation of scripture, in the printing of educational and biblical texts, and in extending the mission to reach out to unevangelized communities. While he had been warned off "secular" entanglements, Williams was aware that economic independence was crucial if the missionaries were to have standing in Māori eyes. From 1826, the mission began to enjoy greater material security after the launching of the *Herald*, which tempered the mission's economic dependence on Māori. In effect, from the mid-1820s the missionaries began trying to reposition themselves as not being dictated to by local politics, a shift which began to have tangible consequences with the foundation of the Waimate station. As their evangelization began to gain significant purchase, the missionaries also became more confident in stressing the novelty of their message and emphasizing the authority of the Bible, the value of literacy, and the power of their "new" way of thought and action. These reorientations certainly raised the mana of the mission in Māori eyes, and missionaries, especially Henry Williams, begin to take on role of mediators in local conflicts. As Judith Binney has observed, "Maori attitudes altered towards the missionaries only when they ceased to be certain that they controlled Pakeha and their goods, and when their own confidence in their ability to choose and manipulate the elements of civilization introduced to them began to fail."[157] What is striking is that Māori were willing to accommodate Christianity into their understandings of time and cosmology, and these aspects of indigenous mentalities were reworked more readily than were economic ideas and practices. But there was no neat, coherent, and all-encompassing cultural shift. Change was uneven and unpredictable, and missionaries lived with considerable uncertainty. Marsden's vision of the "useful arts" and "civilization" quickly taking root in New Zealand was not actualized, and missionary attempts to regulate and remake Māori society remained often uncertain well into the 1830s.

The fundamental precariousness of the evangelical project in New Zealand was repeatedly exposed by members of the missionary communities whose actions undercut the cultural ideals and social boundaries that mission stations were supposed to embody. The possibility of missionary transgressions had shaped the mission from the outset. Samuel Marsden worked hard to ensure that the New Zealand mission would not replay the spectacular failure of the first Missionary Society mission in the Pacific, where social boundaries melted away and various missionaries were drawn into a range of inappropriate sexual relationships. But despite Marsden's stress on the primacy of the Christian conjugal family, sexual restraint, and social discipline, from the outset the CMS mission was plagued by recurrent conflict and sexual relationships that contravened the boundaries of marriage. Mission families and their associated workers struggled hard, but routinely failed, to achieve the goal of making the mission stations models of Christian happiness and order.

In fact, for many evangelicals, the actions of some within the community embodied the human corruption that was a key element of the Calvinist worldview.[1] Thomas Kendall was dismissed by the CMS in 1822, when it became clear that he had established a relationship with Tungaroa, a daughter of the Rangihoua tohunga Rākau and the sister of Ruatara's wife, Rahu. This was not the first controversy that had swirled around Kendall. He had returned to Britain on an unapproved voyage in 1820 and had alienated his fellow missionaries through his close connection with the powerful rangatira Hongi Hika, and his relationship with the CMS broke down over Kendall's commercial relationships with Māori and his unwavering defense of the musket trade. Kendall's career in New Zealand had been consistently turbulent. His running conflict with the convict blacksmith Walter Hall boiled over in mid-1816, with Hall shooting at Kendall. Kendall engaged in a fistfight with Richard Stockwell, another convict laborer attached to the mission, in June of that year. This physical confrontation was linked to another transgression that disturbed the mission. Stockwell had an affair with Kendall's wife, Jane, which culminated in the birth of a son Samuel, in that same month.[2] The close and intimate domestic spaces that were characteristic of the early mission, which saw Stockwell living with the Kendalls, perhaps promoted such liaisons. Less sensational and protracted controversies plagued the early history of missionary work in New Zealand. John Butler, the superintendent of the mission in New Zealand from 1819, was dismissed for drunkenness, and a host of accusations, including rape and an addiction to alcohol, swirled around the confrontational Wesleyan William White. Gossip, rumors, innuendo, allegations, and outraged reports of wrongdoing litter the mission archives.[3] And while many scandals focused on male missionaries who formed sexual relationships with Māori, it is clear that some missionary wives were drawn to the "tall and muscular forms" of Māori men even if the gendered and racialized codes of behavior that structured the mission precluded acting on such desire.[4]

The meaning and consequences of transgression can be discerned through a close reading of the most protracted scandal that rocked the mission: the dismissal of William Yate, in 1836, as a consequence of allegations that he established sexual relationships with a number of young Māori men and boys under his tutelage. Rather than following Judith Binney to interpret Yate's actions as the product the anxiety produced out of the conflict between his desire and his sense of own sinfulness, I locate Yate's transgressions in the overlapping webs of relationships that he fashioned.[5] Given Yate's movements between Britain, New South Wales, and New Zealand, I adopt a mobile analytical strategy, following Yate, the claims made against him, and his own persistent campaign to rehabilitate his name.

My approach also breaks with the existing work on Yate, which has been preoccupied with the question of Yate's sexual identity and has read the meaning of his transgression primarily through the question of homosexuality.[6] Rather than abstract sexuality from broader social relationships and treat it as a discrete and self-contained domain, I suggest that the scandal around Yate was profoundly shaped by the broader social dynamics and conflicts that he set in motion. Yate imagined himself as ensnared in a conspiracy and as a victim of injustice. Yet this public persona ultimately lacked credibility, not only because it set aside the rectitude and humility expected of a missionary, but also because Yate continued to maintain an intimate relationship with another man.

I also read the controversy around Yate within the context of the relationships he formed with Māori boys and young men against Yate's various interactions with Māori more generally and the ways in which he made sense of these social engagements. Yate valued his closeness with Māori as way of engaging with a people he understood as vital and expressive, even though he was also convinced of Māori fallenness. This proximity was central to Yate's authority, both as an author of a pioneering ethnographic treatment of Māori society and in his role as a missionary. As teacher, preacher, spiritual guide, and "father," Yate believed in his own ability to lead Māori out of heathenism, to transform their beliefs and practices. However, Yate exploited this position of authority to initiate a series of sexual connections that seem to have involved duplicity and coercion.

In highlighting questions of power, I offer a reading different from much of the writing on Yate, which has been primarily concerned with his sexual "identity" and that has seen him as challenging both the racial and sexual prejudices of his missionary peers. Thus, I do not attempt to frame Yate as a kind of cultural ancestor in the way in which some New Zealand writers have been drawn to Yate as a figure who chafed against sexual repression and racial boundaries.[7] Rather, I place him at the center of a series of overlapping debates about the ways in which missionaries should modulate intimacy, the consequences of certain types of sexual acts, and how such transgressions could be best managed. The scandals that surrounded Yate were seen to be a real and mortal danger to the evangelical project in New Zealand, and, as such, they occasioned feverish cultural and political work by missionaries on the ground, church authorities in Australia, and the Anglican hierarchy in Britain. As Peter Stallybrass and Allon White have argued, transgressive actors and practices are typically "despised and denied at the level of political organization and social being." But rather than being of marginal importance, transgressions function as "instrumentally constitutive of the shared imaginary repertoires of the dominant culture." Yate's case thus exemplifies Stallybrass and White's argument "that what is *socially* peripheral is so frequently *symbolically* central."[8]

Marsden and the Ideal Missionary

In fact, the very framing of the New Zealand mission was a reaction to the failure of the Missionary Society's initial Pacific mission, which was destabilized by moral lapses and sexual transgressions. In elaborating his scheme for New Zealand, Marsden was deeply concerned with the "character" of missionaries, explaining his vision of the ideal missionary in a letter he sent to the CMS in April 1808.

> A Missionary should also be naturally of an Industrious turn, a Man who could live in any Country by dint of his own labor, an Industrious Man has great Resources in times of difficulty and Danger in his own mind, great difficulties will easily be surmounted by an Industrious Man, while very small ones will overwhelm an Idle Man with Despair. It is worthy of Remark that in all my observations on Mankind I have rarely ever known an Industrious Man become an Idle one, or an Idle Man Industrious. A Missionary's Habits of Industry ought to be fully established or he will be found totally unfit for the arduous Work of the Mission in a country where nothing has been done before him. It will also require great Prudence and Circumspection in a Missionary to govern a Savage Mind, upon which his own very Existence will depend. His difficulties will many of them be new, and much greater, and more numerous than he can possibly imagine or foresee; on this account he will require great patience and perseverance to bear up under them.[9]

Marsden's stress on these moral qualities was undoubtedly inflected by the scandal-ridden failure of early missionary activity in Britain's Pacific empire. In November 1800 Marsden criticized the early missionaries who relocated to New Holland (Australia) after the failure of the Missionary Society's first foray into the Pacific. Marsden was convinced that these men were ill-suited to the moral responsibilities of evangelization: "Some of the missionaries which have come to this colony are the opposite characters they are profane in their lives and conduct, they are totally ignorant of mankind, they possess no education they are clowns in their manners." In the same letter Marsden offered some critical thoughts on the progress of the Missionary Society's mission to the Pacific and set out his vision of missionary work. Marsden noted that in initiating the mission to Tahiti the directors of the

Missionary Society were driven "by the purest and best of motives."[10] However, the dispositions of its initial party, Marsden suggested, were ill-suited to missionary work, and the unmarried mission workers were also vulnerable to sexual temptation. Many of the single missionaries sent to the Pacific by the Missionary Society on the *Duff* in 1796—including Francis Oakes, John Cock, Benjamin Broomhall, and Edward Main—established sexual relationships with Polynesian women. Reverend Thomas Lewis established a close relationship with a Tahitian woman and was ostracized from the mission.[11] Most notably, George Vason, the unmarried Nottinghamshire brickmaker stationed on Tongatapu, deserted the mission, adopted local dress, became tattooed, and took several wives as he adopted the social trappings of the Tongan elite.[12] Oakes and Cock, after abandoning the mission, slept with prostitutes in New South Wales, acts that underlined their turn away from the moral regulation that was central to missionary identity.[13]

As he took on an important role in the rebuilding of British missionary work in the Pacific mission in the wake of these scandals, Marsden placed heavy emphasis on the importance of marriage as the foundation for evangelization. In 1811 the directors of the Missionary Society sent a letter that stipulated that the Tahitian mission should be rebuilt and that "none but married Miss[s] should be sent from Port Jackson."[14] The family was to be the building block of missionary theory and practice. This was, at one level, an extension of evangelical social thought. For British evangelicals, the family was a devotional unit, knitted together by family prayers, discussion of biblical precepts, and the reading of scripture. Faith and practice reinforced and enhanced family ties. Of course, established economic organization and everyday social practice reinforced the centrality of the family for British evangelicals. As Catherine Hall notes, they came from a "society in which family enterprises were at the heart of economic, social and cultural life. They were used to a world that was physically organised around the family, to which men, women, and children each contributed in their particular ways."[15] Families also made manifest God's vision of the social order and offered a template for social relationships more broadly. The first issue of the Church Missionary Society's *Missionary Register* published in 1813 explained that "the husband and wife, the father and son, the master and servant, at once learn from it their respective duties. . . . Rulers become the fathers of their people, and subjects cheerfully yield obedience."[16]

Both hierarchy and mutuality ordered families. The uneven distribution of power within families defined social roles and underpinned the structural relationships between husbands and wives, parents and children, and siblings.

Evangelicals like Hannah More emphasized the divine basis of difference and the social importance of dependence. She argued that "the very frame and being of societies, whether great or small, public or private, is jointed and glued together by dependence. Those attachments which arise from, and are compacted by, a sense of mutual wants, mutual affection, and mutual obligation, are the cement which secures the union of the family as well as of the State."[17] Such ideals, which were routinely espoused by evangelicals during the early nineteenth century, were articulated in the face of real fluidity and instability. Industrialization, urbanization, and the extension of mobility produced a wide range of household configurations. The idealization of the family thus was in part an anxious assertion in the face of economic change and the successive debates over morality triggered by the sexual and political scandals that punctuated the Regency era and the early years of Victoria's reign.[18] These anxieties, as well as the longer history of missionary transgressions in the Pacific, are important contexts for understanding the scandalous case of William Yate.

Yate's Early Career

William Yate was born on 3 November 1802 and baptized in the parish of St. Mary Magdalene in Bridgnorth, Shropshire. After completing an apprenticeship as a grocer, he attended the CMS training school at Islington, where he became a deacon in December 1825, and was ordained as a priest by the CMS in May 1826. This was followed by one year as a curate at St. Swithin's Church in east London. When ordained, Yate had been granted a special dispensation to serve in the colonies, and he realized this calling when he sailed for service in New Zealand, reaching Paihia on 19 January 1828.

The missionary community in the Bay of Islands warmly welcomed Yate. He arrived against a backdrop of turbulence and uncertainty, as the powerful rangatira Hongi Hika was ill. Missionaries were fearful about the possibilities of war and for their own security, fears that reflected the lingering legacy of the sacking of the Methodist Wesleydale mission just over a year before. In this context, Yate seemed to bring new optimism and energy to the mission. Henry Williams's journal for Sunday, 20 January 1828, recorded that the newly arrived Yate addressed the congregation at Paihia "in a most pleasing manner."[19] His wife, Marianne Williams, saw Yate's presence as a "comfort" and greatly enjoyed the "most delightful exhortation" he delivered when he preached at Paihia in May 1828.[20] Henry Williams signaled the only note of disappointment relating to Yate on their first meeting, when he noted, "We were introduced to Mr. Yate but were sorry to learn that there was no Mrs. Yate."[21]

The leaders of the CMS envisaged William Yate as playing a central role in the continuing expansion of the mission. Within a fortnight of his arrival Henry Williams observed, "We feel our hands much strengthened already. It is very encouraging to see such men amongst us."[22] Marianne Williams quickly noted that Yate had particular facility for teaching Māori children. During the mission's general examination at Kerikeri in 1829, Yate not only administered the sacrament of Communion but also delivered a special speech to the assembled Māori children. Marianne Williams reported,

> Mr Yate addressed the children as Mr Yate only can, for he has quite a talent for talking to little children, explained what that wise man Solomon meant, when he said that children were like asses' colts, even the young donkeys at Kerikeri.
>
> He told them that their friends in England thought much about them and prayed for them, that they might have new hearts and become good and wise.... After all was over the boys literally had a scamper like so many wild colts up and down the front of Mr Yate's house until bed time.[23]

Yate's popularity among the mission community was well and truly secured on this occasion, when he supplied gowns, aprons, and bags for all the prize-winning female native pupils.[24]

Although he quickly proved himself to be an effective teacher, powerful preacher and engaging presence, his primary responsibility was the supervision of the translation of passages of scripture and prayer into te reo Māori and to oversee their production as printed texts. Yate labored intensively in his efforts to master te reo and in the preparation of draft translations for which he drew on the extensive expertise of some of his senior colleagues. In 1830 Yate crossed the Tasman Sea to Sydney to supervise the printing of a collection of teaching texts for the mission, which included the Ten Commandments, a variety of biblical selections, two catechisms in Māori, and nineteen hymns.[25] This volume provided the New Zealand mission with its first substantial Māori text. In that same year, Yate oversaw the production of the first work printed in New Zealand, a catechism *Ko Te Katekihama III*, but it was only when the trained printer William Colenso arrived, in 1834, that the Paihia printing establishment operated with any efficiency and reliability.[26]

By the time Colenso took up his position, Yate had become less popular with his colleagues. Yate could be charming, but he was also self-absorbed and stubborn. These characteristics violated the ideals of sacrifice and brotherliness that were integral to the work of the mission, as leaders such as Henry Williams attempted to replace the quarrelling and conflict of the mission's early years with stability and order. Yate's manner, which was confident, assertive, and at times playful, caused growing unease among the New Zealand missionaries. Yate's decision to sail back to England in June 1834 exacerbated these anxieties. Yate's journey was ostensibly undertaken to raise funds for the mission, but he had no official support for this initiative, and the New Zealand-based missionaries felt that Yate's actions were arrogant, prideful, and disrespected the importance of fraternity in Christ's work.[27]

Yate's *Account* and His Visit to Britain

En route to London, Yate drafted a firsthand description of New Zealand, entitled *An Account of New Zealand and of the Formation and Progress of the Church Missionary Society's Mission in the Northern Island*.[28] The Church Missionary Society in London eventually sanctioned a preface to *An Account of New Zealand*, which emphasized that the volume was "the result of personal observations by the Rev. W. Yate, during his residence of seven years" in New Zealand. His "systematic" account, the CMS contended, was "well calculated, both to convey much new information, and to fix in the mind of every Christian reader a deeper interest in the sacred cause of Missions."[29]

In the first half of his volume Yate adopted the pose of an authoritative observer, offering an extensive and detailed account of the North Island's geography, resources, and peoples. It was a lively contribution to the tradition of missionary ethnography that William Ellis had refined in his landmark *Polynesian Researches* (1829). As a narrator, Yate assumed a much more intrusive position in the second half of the volume, where he detailed the transformation of Māori as a result of missionary work. Here "I"—Yate as the narrator—was much more prominent in ordering the narrative, as was Waimate, the last mission station that Yate was posted to.[30] In *An Account of New Zealand* Yate placed himself at the forefront of the missionary drama, reframing the history of the New Zealand mission and positioning himself as a self-proclaimed missionary hero. This detailed and often sensational work proved popular with the English public, and it was quickly reprinted.

Riding the volume's success, Yate undertook a speaking tour of England, Scotland, and Wales, attracting large audiences as well as generous contributions to the CMS from many evangelical congregations. He cultivated connections with the Anglican elite, meeting the Bishop of London and the Archbishop of Canterbury. At one of Yate's meetings, held at Ramsgate in October 1835, the Duchess of Kent and her daughter, Princess Victoria, were in the audience.[31] The extent of Yate's quickly won fame was such that on several occasions King William IV expressed a wish to speak with him, finally granting him a private audience in January 1836 at the Brighton Pavilion. In an interview that lasted over an hour, which convinced Yate that the King had read his book with care, the King quizzed Yate on New Zealand, the mission, and Māori. The King was certainly interested in New Zealand's status: "He then enquired whether the natives would quietly submit to have their country colonized and assured me that it was only for information that he enquired and that as long as he had anything to do with it no more colonies should be added to the British Crown for he had now more than he knew what to do with, or than his shoulders would bear."[32]

Thanks to the success of Yate's book and his ability as a public speaker, he assumed for a moment the mantle of being the leading British expert on New Zealand and an authority on colonization more generally. Yate's public authority was further cemented during the following month, when he gave evidence on New Zealand, Australia, and the Pacific before the 1835–36 Select Committee on Aborigines, chaired by the leading humanitarian and abolitionist Thomas Fowell Buxton.[33]

News of Yate's publication and his metropolitan fame was met with a hostile response from the CMS missionaries in New Zealand, who resented Yate's hyperbolic descriptions of Māori and the inflated characterization of his own role in the mission's progress. Yate used his talks on the New Zealand mission to raise funds, but these contributions were specifically solicited for "Mr Yate's Church at the Waimate," a project that not only suggested that the Waimate mission was Yate's personal domain, but had little support from the New Zealand-based missionaries.[34] Several missionaries complained to the CMS that Yate's endeavors were self-seeking and were not supported by his brethren. William Wade told the CMS secretary Dandeson Coates that Yate "was indeed by all accounts the one of the last in the mission whom the Missionaries would have designated as their faithful representative, either by word or by mouth."[35] In a similar vein, Richard Davis also expressed his chagrin: "Had Mr Yate visited England by the sanction of your local Com[mitt]ee, your Missionaries would now have deeply felt their responsibility, but their opinion on that subject was neither asked officially nor privately. . . . Had the Missionaries in New Zealand wished to have sent home to the Parent Com[mitt]ee one of their body as their representative, Mr Yate would not have been chosen for that office."[36]

But Yate had produced a text that was crafted to meet the expectations of a British reading public that had an appetite for tales of savagery and the trials of missionaries. The tone of the book upset Yate's colleagues in New Zealand; in a district meeting held in August 1836 his peers recorded that they were "entirely ignorant" of Yate's plan to publish and that they felt that "many statements" in *An Account of New Zealand* were "incorrect, & by no means presenting a view of the State of the Mission, or of the character, manners, and customs of the New Zealanders." The committee resolved that a review of *An Account of New Zealand* should be produced for the CMS, and it was this resolution that presumably led to the drafting of William Wade's scathing assessment of Yate's work.[37] Wade attacked Yate's vanity and his tendency to emphasize the most sensational aspects of Māori culture. Concerned at the "injurious impressions" that Yate's book could create of both Māori and the mission, Wade wrote,

> That the book contains "much new information" we do not deny. Many things in it are altogether new and marvelous to those who have had more opportunity than the Author ever had of knowing the habits, character, &c. of the New Zealanders. We are prepared to shew that Mr Yate's statements are not the result of his personal observations—that he has displayed his own ignorance and want of information—that the work abounds in exaggerations and misrepresentations—and that Self stands prominently throughout the volume.[38]

Other missionaries echoed this line of argument. George Clarke wrote to the CMS complaining, "Mr Yate has, strictly speaking, little or no claim upon the Waimate settlement, he has culled the labours of his noiseless brethren the Catechists & with considerable clamour has invited the public to see what he has done."[39]

There is no doubt that Clarke and Wade would have also been alarmed by Yate's evidence before Buxton's Select Committee on Aborigines, which produced a dramatic picture of Māori society. The committee asked Yate, "What is the character of the New Zealand inhabitants, so far as you have come into contact with them?" His brief response condensed the most sensational tropes that had been routinely deployed by European travelers to characterize Māori society: "We found them decidedly a savage people, addicted to cannibalism, to murder, and to every thing which was evil."[40] While the evangelical missionaries in New Zealand were deeply committed to evaluating and transforming Māori society, by the mid-1830s they were routinely producing detailed and sophisticated assessments of the people they lived among. While Yate's "New Zealand experience" and his hyperbolic accounts of life on the frontier might have won him a fleeting moment of renown in the metropole, his trip home to Britain forever alienated him from the New Zealand mission.

Prince Regent and Sydney

Some of the negative responses to Yate's work were undoubtedly prompted by the increasing speculation on the nature of Yate's relationship with his Māori charges and the allegations concerning Yate's conduct when he returned from London. Veiled rumors hinting at Yate's improprieties dated back to 1832, but in June 1836 word of a scandal concerning Yate swept through Sydney after he disembarked from the *Prince Regent*, which had carried him from England with his sister Sarah.[41] On his arrival in New South Wales, Yate agreed to stand in place of the chaplain of St. James' Church, who had died suddenly, until a new appointment could be made. Yate was excited by this possibility. He swiftly produced a pamphlet that encouraged parishioners to support his confirmation in the role, and he boasted to the CMS about the popular demand for this text.[42]

But this prospect was quickly snatched away as W. G. Broughton, the new Bishop of Australia, informed Yate that rumors were circulating about his conduct aboard the *Prince Regent*, and that as a consequence Yate was suspended. Broughton explained to Yate that talk had spread through Sydney regarding the "marked intimacy" between Yate and the ship's third mate, Edward Henry Denison.[43] Yate had shared a cabin with Denison, and the two men were lodging together in Sydney. There were also suggestions that Yate had behaved inappropriately with another crew member.

Richard Taylor, a fellow CMS missionary who had sailed on the *Prince Regent* en route to New Zealand, was the primary force behind these allegations. Taylor repeated to Samuel Marsden, the patriarch of the CMS mission, the reports of several passengers who described the close physical relationship between Yate and Denison. Taylor told Marsden that Yate had stayed in Denison's apartment ashore and had shared Denison's bed inside his locked cabin during the voyage. Taylor informed the informal inquiry into Yate's conduct that the missionary and Denison routinely shared inappropriate displays of affection, enjoyed holding hands, and were prone to fits of giggling. He also recorded that they liked to share a hammock.[44]

Taylor's report was the culmination of the tense and difficult relationship that had developed out of the fledgling friendship that initially taken shape between the two missionaries on board the *Prince Regent*.[45] Yate was buoyed by the great success of his English tour, and as a result, he cast himself as the senior figure in the party of mission workers and their families sailing for New Zealand. Conversely, Taylor, who traveled with his wife, Caroline, and their four children, had a difficult voyage: Caroline struggled with the heat of the tropics; they were all seasick and hated the seaboard food; and the children were very "peevish and fretful." They were afflicted by bed bugs and ringworm, making the proximities of shipboard life difficult to bear.[46] Yate seemed to have little sympathy for the Taylor family and was self-absorbed. When the window of Yate's cabin was broken by the force of a swell, Yate remained ensconced in his hammock writing in his journal—scribbling "O the pleasures of the sea"—while Taylor and crewmen worked urgently to stem the leak and contain the water damage.[47] On another occasion Yate surprised Taylor, leaping onto him without warning despite the fact Taylor had already injured his back climbing the ships' rigging for exercise.[48] If the voyage was physically and emotionally difficult for Taylor, it was exciting and transformative for Yate. Not only was he basking in the glory of his audience with the king and the success of *An Account of New Zealand*, but the bonds he had forged with Denison also energized him. Robert Aldrich has suggested that shipboard license was an important context within which the connection between Denison and Yate formed.[49]

Once in Sydney, Taylor reported on what he saw as the shipboard improprieties of Yate and forwarded to the CMS information that he had received from another *Prince Regent* crewman, Dick Deck. This recounted an incident when Denison, Yate, and Deck shared a bed after landing in Sydney until "there had been so much tickling that [Deck] was obliged to get out of bed and sleep on a sofa in the next room in order to obtain any rest."[50] Broughton suggested to Yate that he should return immediately to England, but Yate decided to remain in Sydney to contest the accusations made against him.[51] In his journal during December 1836, Yate imagined that Taylor's charges were simultaneously the product of his desire for what Yate imagined as "his" post at St. James' Church and the result of the debased nature of morality in the New South Wales colony.

> I became the victim of the most unprincipled conspiracy. A diabolical conspiracy which had for its end not only my removal from this scene of my labours that a man who envied me may take possession of my place but my utter ruin. Had this envious person who was foremost in this infamous plot only told me that he wished to occupy my post

at St James', and could have shown me that he was capable of undertaking the whole of its duties I would have given it up. But Mr Taylor was imbued with the spirit of New South Wales even before he arrived there and he found so many kindred spirits in this apostate land that he was strengthened and encouraged to persevere in his unholy works his works of darkness.[52]

Yate also suggested that the colonial environment together with the effects of old age had convinced Samuel Marsden of his guilt.

I, however, thought that Mr Marsden acted from principle—and I attribute all his late proceedings to the extremely infirm state of his mind—to his utter want of recollection in every *recent* event—to the easy manner in which he is now worked upon—and to the natural suspicion of his mind being heightened by the situation which he has held, and the society in which he has been placed. As a magistrate which he was in this colony for many years he was accustomed to give credit to all the abominable tales which one Convict told of another. With him to be accused was always to be found guilty. He condemned every man against whom there was a shadow of a charge.[53]

While some of Yate's fellow passengers offered him support, he partly incriminated himself by providing copies of his private correspondence with Denison to establish the propriety of the relationship. That correspondence revealed an unusually close bond, with Denison's letters to Yate addressing him as "My dearest friend, my *Father*" and "Friend of my bosom."[54] Denison's letter also confirmed that they had shared a hammock aboard the *Prince Regent*. During the voyage, Yate himself had penned an unusual letter to the CMS which extolled Denison's virtues: "I very particularly wish to mention to you the name of our third mate Mr Edwin Henry Denison and to say that I never met a man more anxiously attentive to his duties than he has been." Yate suggested that Denison could be used by the society as a secure conduit for shipping packages or goods to the colonies in the future.[55] But if this letter stressed the value of Denison to the worldly work of the mission, Yate framed his relationship with the crewman in much loftier terms. As the *Prince Regent* approached Sydney, Yate penned a final "farewell address" to complete a sequence of love poems he had drafted en route to Australia. Yate imagined an undying love sanctified by Christ himself.

We live—for ever shall we live
Death died when Christ the Saviour rose

The grave has no more thorns to give
Tis now a bed for sweet repose.

A bed where you and I shall sleep
Locked in the arms of mutual love
Nor aught shall we in our slumbers break
Till waked by Thunders from above.

Then on the wings of love we'll fly
To heaven that pure that bless'd abode
Mount to the throne, the throne on high
And hear the welcomes of our God.

For ever then we'll join our songs
Loud shall our Hallelujahs ring
The Saviour's name dwell on our tongues
Christ only—always—Christ our King.[56]

This poem, which frames spirituality in an eroticized language of physicality, suggests that Yate saw his attachment Denison in the highest possible terms. And it perhaps helps explain Yate's anger, as what he experienced as the genuineness of "mutual love" was imputed with a base quality that was at odds with the theological and spiritual significance he saw in his relationship with Denison.[57]

Yate saw nothing of significance in the transgressions—symbolized by the locked door and shared hammock—of the carefully modulated forms of intimacy that were acceptable within the missionary circle. But Broughton suspended Yate from public ministry in mid-August 1836 on the grounds that Yate was "guilty of prevarication and falsehood" and initiated a fuller investigation of the charges relating to Yate's behavior on the *Prince Regent*.[58] After an inquiry in late September offered strong evidence about the affectionate relationship that had developed between Yate and Denison, Broughton extended Yate's suspension in early November 1836.[59]

The Four Depositions

Yate's protestations of innocence were further undercut when depositions from four young Māori men and boys who had been under Yate's pastoral care arrived in Sydney. These four accounts confirmed they had engaged in a range of sexual behaviors with the missionary, including mutual masturbation and oral sex, which Yate on occasion had rewarded with tobacco.[60]

These depositions were the product of an investigation conducted by the missionaries in New Zealand. But it seems very likely that at least some of Yate's colleagues had been aware of rumors and allegations regarding his sexual misconduct for several years previously. In 1832 Yate himself wrote to the CMS warning them that Captain William Brind, a whaler and master mariner who had settled in the Bay of Islands and who was closely connected to the rangatira Rewa, was intending to level charges against the missionary. Brind had been in a running conflict with the missionary establishment because of his sexual relationships with Māori women, his role in encouraging "prostitution" in the Bay of Islands, and his close connections to the disgraced Thomas Kendall.[61] Yate told the CMS,

> [Brind] says he will write to the Committee and charge me with crimes of a most gross and horrid nature, and he has actually given the natives presents to confirm what he writes. When I heard of his accusations, which are far too abominable even to be mentioned I referred the whole matter to my brethren at Waimate and Kerikeri. . . . They made every consistent enquiry and found that the whole arose from the evil distortions of Cap. B—.[62]

Once the news of Taylor's allegations about Yate's actions aboard the *Prince Regent* reached the missionaries in New Zealand, local Māori were quick to confirm the missionaries' worst fears. In fact, several Māori were insistent in claiming that they had previously informed missionaries about Yate's habits. In September 1836 William Wade explained to the CMS that

> The matter appears to have been universally known among the natives, and every one is astonished that it could have been kept so long from us, as natives commonly keep no secrets. But . . . the missionaries so decidedly refuse in general to lend any ear to the native reports, and what little had been said about Mr Y. was so sharply checked as being slanderous and false, that the natives would find little encouragement to make any further exposé, especially with the sense of shame which some of them possess.[63]

Two years later, Joel Samuel Polack, the leading trader in the Bay of Islands, also wrote that Yate's conduct "was *reported to the brethren* for several years by the natives," but that the missionaries had initially tried to suppress the whole issue: "The subject was *even forbidden to be mentioned*." [64] In September 1836 Clarke offered two explanations for these stories not resulting in action against Yate. First he explained to Marsden that "certain accusations had been made against him [Yate] by Mr White of the Wesleyan Mission" and noted that in light of these accusations the "Missionary Brethren" believed that Yate "had acted with a degree of indiscretion which had given occasion to the enemy to blaspheme."[65] Clarke also suggested that some Māori has been reluctant to make allegations against Yate because information was "concealed under the expectation of Mr Yates return[ing] with large rewards" for his intimates.[66] Conversely Richard Davis recorded in his journal that "things have been muttered for some time about, but I was in the hopes it was nothing of a criminal nature, as I had frequently observed a volatile playful spirit in Mr Yate."[67]

William Wade, Richard Davis, and George Clarke conducted an investigation and solicited information from Māori about Yate's behavior. Richard Davis's journal for October 1836 recorded the moment when Māori at Waimate confronted him over Yate.

> After service some of the natives drew round me for conversation & wished me to point out to them the hymns of which —— was the author, in order that they might erase them and O! how much I was made to feel by their observing that we should be very quick in pointing out to them the nature of sin as revealed in the Bible, in order that they might know what was sinful and what was not. One of them observed that they saw things which were wrong in us, as several efforts had been made by them from time to time to make known ——'s wickedness, but they were always told that they were people who seldom spoke the truth. I took the opportunity of asking them whether the crime alluded to was previously known among them. They acknowledged it was. I asked if they never observed what was said on the subject in Romans 1. They replied: "We have seen it, but as you never spoke to us on the subject, & knowing Y—— was continually practicing his wickedness, we thought some other crime must be alluded to."[68]

Deeply troubled by the affair, Davis sought out further information and recorded that he "examined, or rather conversed" with various Māori in the Bay of Islands and "found them all uniform in their accounts and statements."[69] His journal for late September and October 1836 recorded that numerous Māori in both the coastal and interior Bay of Islands testified about Yate's sexual activity.[70] Wade echoed these findings: "Native after native has been questioned, and not one jarring testimony has been found. It is of no use for Mr Y to say that native testimony is not to be depended on. Most of the young men who have been examined are trustworthy baptized natives who themselves were drawn in by the wretched man's persuasions and rewards, without being conscious of the detestable nature of the crime into which he was leading them." Moreover, Wade suggested that these practices were not some recent development: "It appears that not only on board the 'Prince Regent,' but on the 'Sovereign' on his first coming out, and at Tonga, whither he went in quest of Mr C. Davis, did he carry on his infamous practices."[71] George Clarke also explained to the CMS that he had learned that "the abominable practices of the individual in question began soon after he came to the land. That every station in which he resided has been polluted by them. That they were carried on at the native villages which he visited and even in the road to those villages and shocking to relate that he introduced to Christian Baptism the very natives; who both before and afterwards were the misguided partakers in his guilt."[72]

Although this missionary investigation was not entirely systematic, it did identify a large group of young men who claimed to have had sexual contact with Yate. Richard Davis was deeply distressed when he learned that several of the young men he had known from their childhood had been drawn into relationships with Yate, recording in his diary that he was suffering sleeplessness and a fever as he collected more evidence relating to Yate. On 12 October 1836, his journal entry concluded that accounts of Yate's "vile purposes . . . of a most awful nature" suggested that "these must be last days."[73] The British resident James Busby suggested that Yate had established connections with more than sixty Māori, while William Williams suggested that the number of men and boys involved was between fifty and a hundred.[74] As part of this investigation, the missionaries took depositions from at least four Māori, but it seems that more may have been collected as Marsden wrote to the CMS suggesting that the four he would forward "would be sufficient to prevent his return [as a missionary]."[75]

Contrary to Judith Binney's suggestion that these texts "did not contain substantial evidence" against Yate, the four depositions were stark and frank in recording various encounters between Yate and young men and boys connected to the mission.[76] Toataua's deposition noted that he "was a little boy" when he was first "taken by Mr. Yate into his house."[77] According to Toataua, Yate was insistent in initiating sexual contact during a trip to Hokianga en route to Port Jackson: "We arrived at the Puru, he urged me there but I was not willing. We arrived at the Tatainga and slept there. In the evening he urged me and said, Let us go among the fern. We went. He said to me, Pull off your trousers. He saw my penis and said it was no bigger than a rats tail, and we did titoitoi [mutual masturbation]. He gave me one pipe and one fig of tobacco."[78] Toataua also recorded that Yate's sexual advances were accompanied by threats of violence. He recalled that during a journey to the south, William Williams left the party and Yate and he arrived at Puriri, near the Waihou River.

> I slept in the tent of Mr Yate we slept together. He said to me, Cast off your garments. I went and slept under his clothes. He said to me, Take hold of my penis. He laid upon me and —— with his hand and with my hand. ——————. We slept till break of day. In the morning he began again that work. ——————. I said to him, I am going out. He said to me, I will flog you on the back. I was going outside. He laid hold of me and dragged me by my hand into the tent, and we titoitoi. That ended there. I went outside and he gave me one pound of tobacco as a payment.[79]

In a similar vein, the deposition of Philip Tohi, a redeemed slave who had earlier been a correspondent of Yate, recorded both Yate's insistence and his use of threatened violence.

> He ordered me and said, Go let us two go to my room upstairs. I stood at the door of his room. He said to me Come in, don't be ashamed. I was obstinate, because I was a stranger to his proceedings then. He said to me, Don't be obstinate, I'll break your head. He then came and took my hand and dragged me on to his bed. The buttons of my trowsers were undone and of his also. We lay together on the bed. We took hold of each others' penis ka titoitoi maua [he and I masturbated together]. . . . He gave me ten rings. I cannot count how many times I went to him.[80]

Samuel Kohi's deposition offers some insights into how Yate explained his desires to Māori. As Kohi recalled, at the Kerikeri mission station,

> [Yate] saw me and said to me, Come up (stairs) to my room to see the picture of my sister who shall be a wife for you. I went up and stood by the side of his bed. He said to me, you see my sister, she shall be a wife for you. He said to me, Pull off your clothes. I said to him, For what purpose? He said to me that we may copulate. I replied, I do not understand what you are going to do. He said to me, All Europeans act thus while they are single men. Then because they sleep with their wives this practice is left off. But as for me my wife is this, my a hand. I said to him, By whom were you taught this practice? He said to me, By my father was I taught this practice in my childhood. I said to him, that will do, I am not willing, I am going away. I am afraid lest Mr Davis should be angry with me for delaying to carry his

coat to Mr Hamlins house. He replied, Remain, kia titoitoi taua [we mas-
turbated together]. . . . I will give you six pipes. I was not willing because I
was ashamed. That was all[.] I came away. I ran off.[81]

Kohi's deposition detailed the range of strategies that Yate used to induce
this relationship. Not only did he lure Kohi to his room with a most unlikely suggestion (that Kohi might see the portrait of Yate's sister, who he
might marry in the future), but he also used a range of arguments and inducements to enable the creation of a sexual connection. It is difficult to
know how to read the suggestion that Yate's father "taught" him. One possibility is that Yate was offering an antecedent that would legitimate this
sexual contact. Yate himself conspicuously positioned himself as a "father"
to Māori, and his journals are studded with references to "his boys." While
other missionaries did occasionally talk about the "boys" and "girls" connected to the mission, none used these terms with the frequency or affection of Yate. Moreover, Māori associated with Yate also used the language of
kinship, often addressing him as "Father." Again, some Māori did address
other missionaries as "Father" and their wives as "Mother," but Māori letters
to missionaries used a wide range of salutations, whereas the letters to Yate
were consistently addressed to "Father, Mr. Yate," "Our father, Mr Yate," "My
Father," "Our Father," and "Father."[82] These letters laced together reflections
of Christian teaching (especially sin), the power of writing, and the affective
bonds that linked these Māori to the missionary, giving the corpus a unique
tone.[83] Above all, they are powerful testament to Yate's very real charisma
and his effectiveness in engaging Māori in conversation about Christianity.

Like Philip Tohi, Samuel Kohi did establish an ongoing sexual relationship with Yate. His deposition explained,

On another occasion, when prayers were over while we were at the
Kerikeri, he said to me, Let us go (you & I) to my store and there we will
"titoitoi." We went there. He said to me, Take hold of my penis, titoitoi
with your hand. He said to me, undo the buttons of your trousers. I undid
them, he took hold with his hand & I with my hand took hold of his penis,
and titoitoi. He gave me six pipes and six figs of tobacco on the Sabbath
day as payment. I went to him three times before my baptism, and since
my baptism I have been many times, more than I can count.[84]

Across these depositions, Yate's words and actions were far removed from
the idealized language that framed the texts around his relationship with
Denison. Yate was domineering, insistent, and violent; in these depositions,

the relationships between Yate and the young men were not couched in a language of love nor were they invested within any spiritual or theological meaning. This is particularly clear with regard to one incident recorded in Pehi's deposition.

> Once at Pateretere, when we went to bathe. He said to me, If a woman makes her appearance, be strong to drag her, be strong to drag her as a woman whom we may lie with. He then said to me, A woman will not appear quickly for you and me. Let us go and bathe. He pulled off his trousers He called to me, Come down into the water I'll break your head with my penis The deposition then goes on to state that he, Mr Yate had a venereal connexion with the deponent, peni in ore imposito, promising to give him a pound of tobacco.[85]

The abrupt shift in this section of Pehi's deposition from first to third person reminds us that it is impossible to gain unmediated access to a "Māori perspective" on Yate. The extant sources are shaped, transmitted, and, in this case, translated, by the missionaries who investigated Yate's actions. This is not to say that they have been subject to conscious distortion. The depositions were carefully individuated and crafted with care to capture the rhythms as well as the content of reported speech, and they were not shaped into the seamless, flowing narratives that evangelicals often valued. But not only have the depositions themselves been mediated, but these texts together with the other archival fragments that record Yate's work in New Zealand, suggest that he established a variable range of relationships with Māori. Yate played a variety of social roles within the communities he worked among, and it is almost certain that Māori in the Bay of Islands offered a range of readings of him. But there is little doubt that a number of these relationships transgressed the moral and spiritual codes that guided missionary work. The depositions clearly point toward Yate's insistence and coerciveness and his willingness to exploit the ways in which he had positioned himself as a "Father" and a "Friend."

Legal Matters

Back in Sydney these depositions, together with Yate's refusal to sever his connection with Denison, convinced the Anglican establishment of Yate's wrongdoing. However, on reviewing the evidence, Francis Fisher, the Crown Solicitor in Sydney, suggested that despite the "disgusting details" they recorded, "it seems more than probable that the crime of sodomy cannot be proved against him according to law" and decided that a legal prosecution for sodomy should not proceed.[86] The acts recorded—mutual masturbation and oral sex—did not technically constitute sodomy.[87] Although in some British contexts "sodomy" could refer to all sexual relations between males, in British civil law a legal definition of "sodomy" as anal intercourse had taken shape in Elizabethan times and had been repeatedly reasserted into the 1820s. In reality, most prosecutions focused on such acts between men, but from the eighteenth century a number of men were also tried for having sexual connections with women in this manner.[88] In fact, not long before the Yate scandal broke, important new legislation shifted British legal definitions. The 1828 Offences against the Person Act included a revision of the evidentiary standards relating to sodomy cases, removing the old requirement, which dated from Elizabethan times and revealed the strong Christian underpinnings of the law, that seminal emission was necessary for the crime of sodomy to be committed.

If that shift in definition expanded the definition of sodomy and made such charges easier to prove, Charles Upchurch has noted the 1827 Larceny (England) Act was an even more significant transformation of the legal regimes that defined illegal sexual behavior. This legislation included "sodomy" within a broad catalogue of "infamous crimes," but also criminalized a wide range of acts between men which could be understood as revealing an "Intent" to commit sodomy, defining "every Solicitation, Persuasion, Promise or Threat" used to enable sexual connections between men as a criminal act. This was a major reconceptualization that marked a clear rupture in statute law.[89] Upchurch has demonstrated that in the 1820s and 1830s the charge of "attempted sodomy" was much more common than a prosecution for sodomy itself. Such charges could be brought on relatively limited evidence and were frequently laid by men of "modest means" against men of standing.[90]

The Crown Solicitor could have proceeded with charges against Yate under the enhanced provisions of the 1827 Larceny Act, which automatically became part of colonial law in New South Wales, or could have followed British common law practice and pursued the charge of attempted sodomy, as there is no doubt that the depositions exceeded the prevailing British evidentiary standards identified by Upchurch.[91] Previous scholars have generally believed that Fisher's decision was indicative of the weakness of the case against Yate, an argument that is at odds with the content of the depositions and that ignores the context within which the decision was undertaken.[92] Fisher elected not to proceed against the backdrop of growing anxieties over the supposed prevalence of same-sex relationships in colonial New South

Wales. According to Ernest Slade, the superintendent of the Sydney convict barracks in the mid-1830s, sexual acts between men were more prevalent in Sydney than "in any part of the civilised world," and William Ullathorne, the influential Catholic priest based at Parramatta, told the Molesworth Select Committee on Transportation in 1838, "This Colony is worse than the ancient city of Sodom."[93] The idea that the convict system had spawned a monstrous sexual order was a key line of argument by the colonial reformers at the forefront of the antitransportation movement.[94] Perhaps these worries encouraged the Crown Solicitor to apply an unusually high evidentiary standard and thereby avoid a sensational case that would have suggested that such practices were not restricted to a criminal class, but had also flourished among the Anglican hierarchy.

The decision of the Crown Solicitor closed off the possibility of trying Yate for sodomy in New South Wales. But the CMS's Parent Committee found that by remaining in Sydney rather than following Broughton's recommendation to return to England to clear his name, Yate had "refused to have the very painful reports which were in circulation investigated."[95] On these grounds, it suspended Yate in November 1836. Only after his suspension did Yate return to England, on 17 December 1836. He sailed on the *Ulysses* with his sister, Sarah, as well as with Denison, the only three passengers to embark in Sydney.[96]

Yate's departure brought the Crown Solicitor's decision into public question. A long editorial in the *Sydney Gazette* published on the day of Yate's departure announced that Yate was leaving on the *Ulysses*. According to the *Gazette*,

[This news] has surprised us exceedingly, inasmuch as it comes within our knowledge, that only a few days ago, voluminous despatches have been received from the British Resident at New Zealand, containing some 50 or 60 affidavits of the most conclusive character, and accompanied by certificates from the body of Missionaries there, naming a great number of witnesses who are ready to come forward at once, to substantiate a whole host of charges of the most serious and awful nature. How the government, with the knowledge of these facts, can assist or connive at the escape of Mr. Yate after this we know not and yet we are informed such is the case, but confess we can scarcely credit it. But we *will* enquire; for acquainted as we are with all the circumstances, with the fact too, that the Governor, the Colonial Secretary, and Crown Solicitor have had a meeting on the subject, the public will not be satisfied, unless, without further delay Mr. Yate is immediately apprehended, and put upon his trial before a jury of his country[men].

The *Gazette* raised the question of status in determining the handling of Yate's case: "If the Government disregard them [the depositions] it will be at the total hazard of its reputation, for we see no reason why the laws should not be administered alike impartially to the rich and poor, to the high and the low. Let us hope that in this case, there will be no desire to deviate from straight forward a course."[97]

Missionary Interpretations

In the wake of their investigations, the missionaries in New Zealand did not share whatever doubts that the Crown Solicitor in Sydney may have harbored. As George Clarke explained to Samuel Marsden when he forwarded the four depositions, questioning Māori had "elicited facts which place it beyond the possibility of a doubt that Mr Yate was during his residence in this land habitually guilty to an awful extent of the crime alluded to [in] Rom[ans] I.27."[98] The information uncovered by the missionary investigation horrified Yate's fellow missionaries. "Never was there a more awful case than that of Yate," wrote William Wade in September 1836, "and never did the Church of Christ receive a deeper wound at the house of her friends. . . . What a scandal will it bring upon the Church of Christ! and how will the very name of poor New Zealand shrink in public estimation!"[99] In the following month, the long-serving CMS missionary Richard Davis lamented to his journal, "Alas! alas! what a monster of iniquity we have had amongst us!"[100] Davis was convinced that William Yate had indulged in "conduct . . . of the most revolting nature."[101] In November 1836 Davis wrote to the CMS recording the impact of the scandal: "All is awfully dark, deeply distressing & most mysterious. Alas! Alas! What is human nature not capable of! The chastening hand of the Lord is upon us. . . . My mind has been so overwhelmed that I have had no heart to attend to my common duties. The cause of Christ is awfully disgraced—the missionary character is disgraced—we are disgraced & the stigma will be brought upon our dear children when we are no more."[102]

The accusations about Yate's transgressions on the *Prince Regent* and his relationship with his Māori congregationalists were discussed and written about at great length by Yate's fellow CMS missionaries, their spouses, and European travelers. Essentially these contemporary responses to Yate were a discourse of containment, since these mainly evangelical writers strove to limit the disruptive effect of Yate's behavior on both Māori and European morality. In 1836 William Wade's review of Yate's *An Account of New Zealand* was composed to rebut the "injurious impressions" that Yate's work could create; otherwise, he wrote, "we would leave the book to that oblivion into which it must sink."[103] According to the most telling passage in the review, "The result of the investigation is now but too well known, and must forever stamp with infamy the writings of one, who under the garb of priesthood has been wallowing in *worse than beastly sins*."[104] Wade emphasized Yate's irresponsibility as a religious teacher, as his use of the phrase "under the garb," with its implications of duplicity and concealment, suggested that Yate exploited his position to gratify his own desires. More important, however, Wade considered Yate's actions to be essentially unnatural, because Yate's relationships with men stripped Yate of his humanity. Yate, and all men like him, were envisaged as being lower than animals, "worse than beastly." Yate, and those like him, were carnal, unrestrained, and immoral creatures who contravened God's vision, as they, in the words of the apostle Paul, left "the natural use of the woman . . . men with men working that which is unseemly."[105]

Polack reiterated similar themes in his depiction of Yate. Polack, like Marsden, was convinced of Yate's guilt as "a mass of information was furnished by the New Zealanders, of sufficient weight to crush a host."[106] In his *New Zealand: Being a Narrative of Travels and Adventures*, Polack interrupted his description of the mission's success to note the "case of a late missionary," relegating Yate to a nameless position, where his actions were more important than his name or identity.[107] Polack insisted that Yate's actions brought "disgrace" to "the cause to which he was attached, but [also to] humanity itself."[108] For many of Yate's contemporaries, including Polack, this transgression jeopardized his fundamental identity as human, as he slipped to the status of beasts and abominations.

While same-sex relationships imperiled the spiritual status of the participants, the missionaries also believed that they resulted in more readily visible and tangible dangers. William Wade hinted at this when he wrote, "We tremble for the consequences among the poor natives. . . . When this Achan is removed from the camp of our little Israel, we do yet hope that the mischief which has come upon us through him may be averted."[109] In a letter to Marsden, William Williams suggested that the sicknesses and diseases that periodically wracked Māori were divine retribution for Yate's action: "The wrath of God has been upon us. There has been much sickness among the natives for some years past and we wondered at the cause."[110] This letter caused Samuel Marsden a great deal of concern about the state of the New Zealand mission, prompting him to embark on a brief visit to New Zealand to monitor any ill effects Yate's actions might have had on the moral character of the Māori.[111]

Other missionaries attempted to use Yate's transgressions to reaffirm the moral authority of Christianity. In October 1836 Richard Davis used the story of Judas to remind Waimate Māori that weakness was to be found even among Christ's apostles. He also explained the parable of the tares, "and again alluded to ——'s case," suggesting that Yate was the tare among the good seed of the mission, a metaphor that identified the fallen missionary as a "son of the evil one."[112] Ironically, Yate himself had perhaps alluded to this parable in *An Account of New Zealand*, where he suggested that the "enemies of the mission" came from within, suggesting that as "the number of Labourers [in the mission] was increased; and some, influenced by the spirit of the wicked one, early crept in among the faithful few. So far, indeed, did some of them dishonour the self-denying doctrines of the Cross, which they had been sent here to teach, that no less painful a plan could be adopted, than an ignominious erasure of their names from the list of the Society's Labourers."[113] Men like Thomas Kendall and the Wesleyan William White were the tares among the good seed of the mission.

The Yate affair was particularly distressing for the recently arrived missionary Benjamin Yate Ashwell. Ashwell was distantly related to Yate, and he saw the scandal as besmirching the family name. Ashwell fell into a deep depression as the evidence stacked up against Yate and attributed his physical weakness to the stress that the Yate affair had caused him. In December 1836 Ashwell finally wrote to the CMS on this issue, expressing concern for Yate's sister and outlining his desire to forever sever connections with Yate himself.

You have doubtless heard of the painful circumstances the Mission has been placed in by the awful conduct of Mr. Yate. This is a blow which has for a season paralized my almost every energy and overwhelmed me with grief and sorrow not only as regards the cause of the Gospel which is the first consideration but also as respect His family to whom I am related. Miss Yate is indeed my much loved and valued friend. I do not know any one in whom I have seen more of the Spirit of Christ. She is also devotedly attached to her poor guilty brother whome she believes to be innocent, therefore much injured by the voice of slander. My heart bleeds for her, but this is a subject too painful to write upon. The chief object of this letter is to request that the name of Yate and even the letter Y may be omitted and erased in all letters and packages sent to me by the Society for it is a name justly abhorred in New Zealand.[114]

Ashwell signed this letter "B. Ashwell," rather than "B. Y. Ashwell" as he had previously. Ashwell's erasure of his middle name foreshadowed the large-scale collective effort of the missionaries to extirpate any trace of Yate from the mission.

The Vale of Achan

In August 1837, when Marsden was visiting New Zealand and the inquiry into Yate's conduct uncovered evidence suggesting that Yate had established sexual relationships with a large number of young Māori men, a group of CMS workers gathered at Waimate. They razed Yate's small cottage, destroyed his property, and even killed his horse, Selim. They gathered the books that belonged to Yate, which were held in the main Waimate mission house, and ripped out their nameplates, a purging that echoed the earlier request of Māori at Waimate that Richard Davis expunge the hymns translated by Yate.[115] These acts initiated a week of prayer and fasting, as the missionaries remained deeply anxious about the state of the mission as a result of Yate's actions.

By this time, the missionaries called Yate's dwelling and the surrounding land the "Vale of Achan," referring to the figure of Achan in the Book of Joshua, who was widely known as "Achan the troubler" in Yate's time.[116] According to the Book of Joshua, Achan had retained an ingot of gold and a garment from Jericho, when all of the plunder was to be dedicated to God.[117] The Israelites determined that Achan's selfishness had resulted in divine punishment for the whole community, as thirty-six Israelites died in their first failed attempt to conquer the city of Ai. As a result, Achan was punished by death. Achan's wrongs not only led to his own execution, but also resulted in the killing of his extended family and the destruction of their possessions, along with Achan's own goods and animals. The Israelites thus expunged all traces of the "troubler." The reenactment of these Old Testament punishments at Waimate stood as a powerful emblem of the missionaries' efforts to limit the disruptive effect of William Yate's transgressions. The missionaries' actions not only illustrated their continued commitment to God, but also underscored the particular anxiety that attached to sexual acts that transgressed the "natural order."[118]

While Ashwell wanted to excise the Yate name, and at the same time as the missionaries in New Zealand worked hard to contain what from their perspective were the destabilizing effects of Yate's transgression, Yate himself continued the battle to restore his name after he learned that in February 1837, when he was still en route to England, the CMS had officially dissolved its connection with him.[119] Yate fulminated against the Church Missionary Society, which he described as "a prejudiced, deceitful and ungrateful set of men and are not worthy of that trust which is at present reposed in them. But the day will come when a judgement will take place between us and then it will be seen who is right and who is wrong."[120] For its part, the CMS refused to give Yate the official enquiry he demanded. But the CMS also never made the reasons for Yate's dismissal public, nor did it want Yate to become the center of legal proceedings, even though some missionaries, especially William Williams, were convinced that Yate would have been found guilty of sodomy if his case had been tried and that Yate may well have been executed.[121]

Yate continued to maintain his innocence and nurtured a strong sense of injustice. He was upset that fellow missionaries, especially Taylor, were moving forces in the scandal. Yet Yate himself had played an important role in the controversy around the Wesleyan missionary William White. This earlier sequence of accusation and counter-accusation laced together charges that White was guilty of sexual impropriety and rape with an intense conflict between White and the additional British resident in Hokianga, Thomas McDonnell, over trade and authority in the region.[122] White arrived in Sydney in August 1836, after being found guilty of "loose and immoral conduct" by a jury of Europeans in Hokianga, and there he met Yate.[123] Yate had earlier made allegations about White's drunkenness, but after meeting the intimidating Wesleyan in person, Yate recanted those contentions.[124] Yate's vacillation may have contributed to White's ability to convince the Wesleyan authorities in New South Wales that he had been wrongly accused. Thus, White returned to New Zealand at the very point when the only Wesleyan who initially doubted the case against White, William Woon, finally admitted that the weight of evidence against White was damning.[125]

Yate's vacillation helped delay White's final dismissal from the Wesleyan mission until 1838, but he worked hard at winning support for his own cause, writing letters and printing pamphlets in 1838 and 1843. The pamphlet *Letter to the Committee of the Church Missionary Society* (1843) was an extended defense that rested on a critique of the CMS's handling of his case. It did not offer any explanation for the content of the depositions, reflecting Yate's confidence that the CMS would not want to reignite the scandal by making those texts public.[126] Ultimately, Yate's mission to clear his name was driven by the ways in which the scandal constrained his career. After his return to England, he was unable to find a secure post, largely because the Bishop of London repeatedly moved to block his appointment and did not want Yate to publically officiate again. It was only in 1840 that his career was partially rehabilitated, after he was willing to take up a post in the northwest of Ireland, in the parish of Donagh, County Donegal, where he served until the end of 1841.[127] At that point, it seemed that Yate would finally be able to return to a permanent appointment in England, as he was subsequently appointed as the chaplain for the Workhouse of St. James' Church in Westminster. But it became clear that the Bishop of London would have preferred Yate to remain in the wilds of Donegal, as he stripped Yate of the post in Westminster before he could take up the position.[128] It was not until 1846, when he took up a post in the abandoned St. John's Mariner Church in Dover, that he acquired a secure appointment, and he continued to minister at St. John's until his death in July 1877.[129]

Social Connections and Scandal

Yate's drive to clear his name was weakened by his ongoing relationship with Denison, which, of course, had precipitated the whole scandal. Allegations about Yate's relationships with Māori youths were made only after the scandal regarding the *Prince Regent* had taken hold and Bishop Broughton had extended Yate's suspension. Nevertheless, Yate remained committed to his friend while in Sydney, and he traveled back to Britain with both his sister and Denison. This decision eroded support for Yate in Anglican and missionary circles. Marsden noted, "Mr Yate has been condemned by his friends for taking his Associate with him to England."[130] During the passage to Britain, Yate affirmed his special bond with Denison: "Notwithstanding all I would not that what has taken place between us should not have taken place, even if it were possible to undo it. I have gained a friend though I may thereby have lost a name."[131] As Yate began to try to restore his reputation on his return to London, the three travelers initially stayed together in Stepney, and Yate and his sister subsequently lived in the house next to Denison's, when they moved on from their initial lodgings.[132] In July of that year, Yate holidayed with Denison's family in Cornwall, and in September 1837 the trio moved to a cottage in St. Arvans where they remained until September 1838.[133] During the remainder of 1838 and 1839, the party of three subsequently moved to Poole, Parkstone, and Farnham. The strength of Yate's connection to Denison appeared to continue casting a shadow over his social standing, as in Parkstone and Farnham the Bishop of Salisbury prevented Yate from officiating over divine service.[134] It is telling that when Yate finally received his appointment in Donegal, he traveled alone. Although he remained in contact with Denison, it seems that Yate may have finally realized that the openness and intensity of their friendship was incompatible with his position in the Church.[135]

Robert Aldrich has observed that there was "something of the 'coming-out story'" in the Yate case.[136] This formulation is a productive anachronism, as it draws attention to the ways in Yate's abiding connection to Denison not only underlined his own rejection of marriage, but rendered his same-sex attachment a matter of concern for church and public alike. The CMS probably did not pursue further investigations into the Yate case because they feared the effects of making his transgressions public, but Yate's continued bond with Denison certainly made it difficult to imagine him as a source of theological understanding, spiritual guidance, or moral example. Yate's long-standing refusal to give up this connection or at least mask its existence by keeping it private was a source of very real difficulty within a cultural landscape where the languages for speaking about same-sex relations were both heavily constrained and in flux, creating one of the key paradoxes of mid-nineteenth-century British culture.[137]

In the end, the significance of Yate and Denison reminds us that the Yate scandal did not hinge on technical legal questions about sodomy, but revolved around appropriate forms of homosocial connection in general. An extensive reading of the missionary records of the late 1820s and 1830s suggests that broader social connections and the processes of building and maintaining relationships were central in giving rise to this scandal. While Yate's gregariousness initially charmed key members of the missionary community in the late 1820s, his self-interest and his self-promotion—traits that were seen to contradict the fundamental values of evangelical missionary work—increasingly rendered him marginal.

The firm linkages between social relationships and Yate's compromised public standing are clear in a letter William Wade wrote to fellow missionary John Wilson in October 1836. Wade argued that Yate's assumption of the temporary position at St. James' Church encouraged him to "look down from his pinnacle of glory with a degree of contempt upon his brethren." But Yate's good fortune was not durable, as his pride and arrogance led him, Wade suggested, to "fall like Lucifer." Wade went onto suggest that Yate was not a unique case, telling Wilson, "You will be astonished to find one at the South also involved."[138] This "one" was Henry Miles Pilley, a carpenter and catechist who arrived in New Zealand in February 1834. Senior members of the CMS in

New Zealand were deeply concerned after hearing allegations that Pilley had engaged in "very indecent conduct with some of the European boys." It seems the allegations primarily focused on Pilley's voyage to New Zealand and drew from evidence from Philip Hansen King (the son of John King) and the Edmonds family.[139] On the basis of Henry Hodgkinson Bobart's and William Wade's investigation, a mission committee based in the Bay of Islands decided that Pilley was guilty and that he should be expelled from the mission. Wade noted, however, that communicating this decision and handling the fallout from the accusation fell to the leader of the mission, Henry Williams, and that these processes were difficult. He noted that the mission leaders had decided that "as little as possible should be said about the original charge" in order to minimize the anxieties within those mission families whose children were connected to Pilley. As a result, when Williams traveled to inform Pilley of the investigation, Pilley denied all wrongdoing and demanded an investigation, convincing some of the missionaries based in the south of his innocence, while others, such as Thomas Chapman, were convinced that he was "a most depraved young man."[140] But Pilley was swiftly dismissed from the mission, and his case generated a thin paper trail, limited contemporary comment, and no substantial scholarly investigation.[141]

The relative silence around Pilley and the lack of scandal around this case helps us make sense of the Yate case. One clear divergence was that Pilley was young, unordained, and a minor worker on the southern frontier of the mission. While a collection of Pilley's letters from the New Zealand mission field was published in Britain, that work had limited circulation, mainly among readers in the vicinity of his native Cheltenham, meaning that his work did not have the reach of Yate's *An Account of New Zealand*. Pilley was less central in the mission's function, and unlike Yate, he had no real public standing in New Zealand, in New South Wales, or in Britain itself. Moreover, Pilley's position meant that he was unable to build extensive or significant alliances to contest the allegations against him for any length of time, and he did not have access to the skills or connections that had helped enhance Yate's profile in 1835 and 1836.

Perhaps most important, Pilley's transgressions seemed to have been relatively contained. They were of a sexual nature, but he had a limited web of social connections within the mission. In Yate's case, conversely, his significant role within the mission on the ground and the extensive connections he fashioned in Britain meant both that the allegations were more contentious and that he was able to proclaim his innocence to a wide range of acquaintances, friends, and allies. Although scandals in the first half of the nineteenth century frequently turned on questions of sexual morality, they were almost never solely about sex, but rather raised fundamental questions about social organization, the distribution of power within a society, and the relationship between the supposedly private arrangements of intimate life and public roles and reputations.[142] So the divergent social position and connections of the subjects at the center of these controversies partly explains the different ways in which these issues entered, or did not enter, public life. It also seems that due to the desire to protect the reputation of those missionary families whose children were connected to Pilley, this investigation was kept within the hierarchy of the CMS establishment within New Zealand and essentially involved the relatively discreet investigations of Bobart and Wade. Where the missionaries were ultimately happy to mobilize Māori voices to incriminate Yate through the production and distribution of depositions, they had no desire to depose their own children in the same manner as the young Māori men who had had relationships with Yate. Pilley returned to New South Wales, where he was eventually married, in 1842—ironically, in St. James's Church in Sydney.

"Unnatural" Connections

Pilley's marriage brings us back to the question of conjugality. The primacy of Christian marriage in evangelical theology and missionary practice must be central to any explanation of why an insistence on the "unnatural" and anarchic character of same-sex relationships was at the heart of the missionary response to Yate. Evangelicals were familiar with a wide range of biblical texts, which constructed Christian marriage as the proper locus for the expression of sexual desire while condemning a wide range of other sexual behaviors as immoral and unnatural.[143] However, biblical injunction was not the only force that prompted missionaries to condemn same-sex relations as unnatural and corrupting. This moral discourse on sexuality should also be viewed against the religious and ideological frameworks that circumscribed and shaped its production.

Nineteenth-century Anglican evangelicalism subscribed to a moderate form of Calvinism and thus developed out of a tradition that did not oppose the expression of sexuality, as long as these desires found expression in the correct context.[144] Evangelicalism maintained the traditional Christian stress on the importance of marriage as the relational structure, which was expected to contain sexual activity. Procreation continued to be the primary, but not the only purpose for sexual relationships. Sex within marriage provided a means of spiritual elevation, intimate companionship and a means of experiencing sensual fulfillment.[145] The following extract—from a letter written by Charles Baker, a CMS missionary in New Zealand, to William Colenso, a CMS missionary whose adulterous relationship with his Māori servant Ripeka led to his dismissal from the CMS in 1852—clearly illustrates the privileging of sex within marriage: "On the birth of your second child you separated yourself from your wife's bed. Here, I conceive, commenced your ruin. . . . [I] urged the fulfilment of your matrimonial obligations—Your Brethren heard with grief of your sleeping in separate rooms & expressed doubts as to the results."[146]

While evangelicals like Baker valued sex within marriage, they were, however, fierce opponents of sexual activity outside marriage. They believed that love within the bonds of matrimony checked the dangers of unrestrained sexual desire, directing sex away from selfish lust toward mutual respect and spiritual communion. Christian marriage effectively tempered the sexual drive, limiting selfish sensuality, and made sex serve moral and spiritual ends.

Thus, when sex occurred outside the context of loving marriage and the marriage bed, evangelicals feared that "God's gift" would lose its innocence and become sinful.[147] Baker expressed this sentiment when he attacked William Colenso's adulterous relationship:

> I will name some of those circumstances that strike me as of a very aggravating character. Your neglecting your lawful wife: cohabiting with another woman under the same roof where your wife dwelt—with the wife of your old servant & it appears that this guilty practice has been of long continuance.
> What awful apostacy from God has your conduct discovered![148]

Baker condemned Colenso's affair with Ripeka as corrupt and sinful, because it dislocated sex from its proper locus in Christian marriage. The contrast with his earlier statement on "matrimonial duties" is indicative of evangelical attitudes toward sexuality both within and outside the confines of marriage.

Through the consistent use of the natural-unnatural hierarchical opposition, missionaries attempted to contain Yate's transgression and reinscribe the boundaries he had contravened. Thus, Yate's transgression was absorbed into a moral discourse that presented Christian monogamy as the sole permissible form of sexual expression. This myth—which created an eternal, universal, and "unalterable hierarchy of the world"—tried to contain the vast range of contradictory behaviors that the missionaries' contemporaries, including Yate, engaged in.[149] This need was most keenly felt at the margins of the empire, in places such as New Zealand, where the very existence of societies which organized desire and intimacy along different lines posed an implicit challenge to this conception of sexuality, which constantly represented itself as the normative and divinely ordained form of sexual organization.

Missionary teaching and translated portions of scripture that stressed the centrality of marriage and procreation were the key planks of this regulated order. Through his translation and printing work, Yate himself played a role in establishing linguistic and textual frameworks for recoding Māori understandings of sexual relationships. In 1833 Yate worked closely with Edward Parry Hongi in Sydney, preparing and printing scriptural translations. Hongi had a long connection with Yate and had named his daughter Sarah Yate Hongi after the missionary and his sister.[150] Philip Granger Parkinson has noted that here again Yate's legacy was ambiguous. Among the biblical texts they translated were Romans 1:27 and 1 Corinthians 6:9–10, passages which excluded from the kingdom of God those who sought sexual pleasure beyond marriage (including those who are "effeminate" and "abusers of themselves with mankind").[151] Parkinson notes that Yate and Hongi coined the term *wakawahine* (to make like a woman) in their translation of 1 Corinthians 6:9–10. This term not only suggested a certain gendered reading of same-sex intimacy, but was itself a lewd macaronic or bilingual pun. They combined the causative prefix *waka*—which is now typically rendered *whaka* (the initial "wh" is pronounced as a labiodental fricative "f")—with *wahine* (woman), such that for speakers of both te reo Māori and English, the new term suggested "fuck-a-woman."[152] Although William Williams revised the translations of the New Testament that he had undertaken with Yate to expunge his influence, this coinage has proven durable: it remains in use in 1 Corinthians 6:9 and is used today by some within the Māori LGBT community.[153]

The Persistence of Transgression

William Yate continues to occupy an important place in New Zealand's cultural landscape; his case has been an important site from which successive generations of artists, writers, and scholars have made arguments about the nature of colonialism, the relationships between race and sexual desire, and the place of sexuality in the making of New Zealand culture. In the 1830s, however, his transgressions once again underlined the centrality of marriage to the evangelical project and to the regulated order for which missionaries strove. Connections with young European males led to Pilley's downfall. He had been a staunch advocate of the importance of marriage and hoped that the CMS would help him find a suitable wife. In July 1835 he asked for assistance to return to Britain to find a spouse and complained about the dangers of being a single missionary: "I would with great humility say that it is the worst thing possible to send a single man to New Zealand: if he be not possessed of great grace [he] is very likely to fall into the traps which are continually put in his road by native females."[154] In the wake of the Yate and Pilley cases, the CMS Southern District Committee resolved "that from the late awful circumstances . . . it is deemed highly important that the single men of this mission be recommended to withdraw from the land as early as possible."[155]

But such issues would not disappear. In 1840, a Wesleyan mission in the south of the South Island was established by James Watkin, who carried with him the taint of the sexual relationship he had established with a "native" woman while stationed in Tonga, and his replacement, Charles Creed, had transgressed in a similar fashion.[156] Transgressions continued to plague the CMS: Seymour Mills Spencer was suspended from the CMS between 1844 and 1849 for allegedly establishing an improper relationship with a Māori woman at the Ruakareo mission station at Tarawera; the operation of a CMS school for half-caste children near Ōtawhao in the Waikato from 1847 was plagued by claims of sexual impropriety by Europeans working under the authority of missionaries; William Colenso was dismissed from the CMS in 1852, after it became known that he was the father of the baby boy born to his family's servant Ripeka Meretene; the sexual relationships that Ralph Barker established with Māori women while stationed at Waiapu, on the east coast of the North Island, led him to resign his position in haste in 1853.[157] And in 1852 St. John's College, which had been established by Bishop Selwyn, was closed after it was discovered that Seth Frank Ward, a recently ordained deacon, had broken his vows, pursuing "evil practices" that quickly became widespread "among the scholars."[158]

Thus, transgression was a persistent problem. The repeated uncovering of these infractions sapped the morale of the mission and undermined the ability of missionaries to claim moral authority for the regulated social and sexual order that they urged Māori to adopt. At one level, these heterodox relationships were enabled by the structure of missionary work. Mobility was a key aspect of evangelization, and missionaries traveled extensively, as they journeyed to sites of intertribal conflict, established new stations, distributed texts, completed regular circuits to preach and heal, and explored new districts. This to-ing and fro-ing meant that missionaries were constantly building new social connections as well as maintaining old links. And given the material and social contexts of both missionary and Māori culture, missionaries by necessity were forced into proximity and social intimacy with their native teachers, guides, and traveling companions. They routinely shared fuel, food and drink, clothes and sleeping quarters. This deep implication in the Māori world opened up possibilities for missionaries to form intimate connections with those to whom they ministered. Breaches of missionary monogamy were taken all the more seriously, as they were understood to contravene the bedrock of the mission's program: the missionary as exemplar and model Christian conjugal family.

Heterosexual sex outside marriage was seen as sinful, but it was often understood as "natural," echoing the lack of restraint that was seen to typify non-Christian and noncivilized communities. Those missionaries who strayed from their marriages in heterosexual relationships were often able to rebuild their careers. When missionaries were dismissed, it was often because their sexual indiscretions followed in the wake of broader social conflict, as in the case of Kendall, White, Colenso, and Yate.[159] Same-sex relationships presented a challenge of a different order to the missionary project. The "unnaturalness" of such connections was held to imperil both the missionary community and native congregants and converts. Same-sex desire was understood to be a contagion that could not only introduce corrupt practices to naïve native peoples, but had also literally disseminated illness, disease, and death. All traces of these vectors had to be purged from the community as the destruction of Yate's property, the killing of his horse, and Ashwell's excision of his middle name, "Yate," demonstrates.

In fact, all transgressions of the Christian conjugal ideal at the heart of evangelization called the mission into question. Conversion was not only about introducing God's word to Māori, but also about remaking Māori as people, transforming how they acted in the world and the ways in which they organized their lives. The missionary code of social regulation, which stressed marriage, literacy, work, sobriety, and turning away from war and slavery, was not just a matter of social convention, but also effectively enacted theological understandings and biblical precepts in the world. Given their commitment to the vernacularization of Christianity and the creation of a native church, missionaries understood that Māori converts would access God through their native tongue and the printed Māori Bible, and that their version of Christianity would be distinctive. Such translations were both necessary and cause for anxiety. But missionaries remained consistent in their emphasis on the centrality of Christian marriage and conjugal monogamy, which they saw as channeling desire to higher purposes. The primacy of marriage remained a key site for theological and social debate between missionaries and Māori well into the second half of the nineteenth century. Creating a regulated and ordered Christian community required constant restraint and consistent policing. Translating these goals into reality was an extremely difficult undertaking, as the transgressions of missionaries like Yate demonstrated all too clearly.

P rotestant missionaries working in northern New Zealand hoped
not only that their stations could serve as "enchanters' wands"
that would regulate and eventually transform Māori social practices,
but also that their work would remake Māori cosmologies. For missionaries, understanding Māori views of death was a crucial element in
their attempts to create a vernacularized Christianity in northern New
Zealand. They quickly realized that native conceptualizations of death
provided an important way of grasping Māori understandings of the
human condition and the relationship between the natural and supernatural worlds. These beliefs, of course, were the very things that the
missionaries hoped to reshape, reform, or supplant with a new cosmology built around the conflict between good and evil, God's love, and the
atoning power of Christ's sacrifice. However, Māori never passively accepted these new interpretations of the order of things. Although some
key elements of evangelical belief and practice rapidly gained ground in
the 1830s, the transformation of Māori deathways was only partial; it was
the negotiated outcome of both sustained cross-cultural conversations
about what it is to be human and fraught, occasionally violent, conflicts
over the ways in which death should be understood and managed.

Examining the place of death between cultures in northern New
Zealand between 1815 and 1840 is significant in terms of both the tem-

poral and spatial parameters of the existing historiography on death. This focus has a particular value given that this period falls between studies of "early modern death" and "Victorian death." The early nineteenth century occupied an awkward position in the groundbreaking study of death in the European tradition by Phillipe Ariès, who framed the period marking the shift in deathways from the early modern ("the death of the Self") to the modern ("the death of the Other"). Julie Rugg has also framed the period as a transitory age where modern deathways emerged, as death became more secularized, increasingly subject to state regulation, and reshaped by the new importance of the cemetery, the undertaker, and the feelings of the bereaved.[1] In spatial terms, the historiography of death has also largely been focused on shifts in European and American understandings of the meaning of death and funerary practices. There have been comparatively few studies of cross-cultural encounters in challenging established Western deathways or that have paid close attention to the ways in which empire building and evangelization invested death with new significance for colonized communities.[2]

The key studies of death in Anglophone colonial spaces have generally suggested that the transplantation of inherited traditions to the colonies were marked by little disruption or contestation. David Hackett Fischer's study of folkways in seventeenth- and eighteenth-century North America demonstrated that distinctive regional deathways were transmitted without substantial disruption from different parts of the United Kingdom and Ireland to the New World. *Albion's Seed* suggested that the deathways of Anglo-Celtic colonists in New England, the Chesapeake, Virginia, and the Appalachian backcountry were not called into question by contact with Native Americans or enslaved Africans, nor were they substantially transformed by the act of migration itself, or the cultural distance from the United Kingdom.[3] In a similar vein, Pat Jalland's landmark study of death in Australia suggested that there was little engagement between Aborigines and colonists over the meaning of death. As the transformation of Aboriginal death practices is largely beyond the purview of Jalland's study, the key argument in her work in terms of cross-cultural engagements around death is that European colonists exhibited little interest in Aboriginal deathways, "except when they were anxious to plunder Aboriginal burial places to collect skulls and skeletons."[4] Conversely, influential works on Māori deathways, from Elsdon Best's 1905 essay on Māori eschatology to R. S. Oppenheim's authoritative 1973 monograph, have attempted to reconstruct "traditional" beliefs and customs and pay limited attention to the historical development of cultural practice.[5]

In forwarding this volume's general concern with "bodies in question," I explore the significance of death in the engagement between evangelical missionaries and Māori, suggesting that death was a crucial window for both missionaries and Māori into each other's worlds. Erik Seeman's landmark study of death in the early modern Atlantic demonstrated the centrality of death in framing cross-cultural understandings and suggested that death was "one of the most important channels of communication between peoples of different cultures."[6] More broadly still, Vincent Brown's history of death in colonial Jamaica has suggested that "attitudes towards death often lie at the heart of social conflict," an observation that certainly also applies to the Bay of Islands between the 1810s and 1830s.[7] Out of the contests over death I explore, new visions of the order of things took shape, and the alteration of deathways was a particularly significant element in the reordering of Māori cultural practice in the Bay of Islands during the 1830s. I begin by examining the place of death in the Protestant missionaries' worldview and highlighting some significant ways in which burial practices on the mission stations diverged from practices in Britain. I suggest that these modifications were, at least in part, the product of the missionaries' awareness of the social importance of Māori deathways and more especially their apprehension of the cultural weight of tapu. I then reconstruct the development of missionary ethnographies of death, highlighting the elements of Māori deathways with which they were preoccupied, how ethnographic knowledge was ordered, and the ways in which that knowledge underwrote the growing ability of missionaries to challenge established Māori practices and was shaped by its insertion into metropolitan print culture.

Death in the Evangelical Imagination

Death stood near the heart of evangelical thought and practice. Christ's death on the Cross was fundamental to evangelical teaching. John Wesley had argued that this atoning death was central to understanding Christianity and was "the distinguishing point between Deism and Christianity."[8] Evangelicals emphasized the doctrinal centrality of the Crucifixion, arguing that Christ died as a substitute for sinful humanity. David Bebbington has shown that the idea of "substitutionary atonement" was a defining characteristic of early nineteenth-century evangelical thought. Christ's atoning sacrifice made salvation possible, and for many evangelicals, gratitude for Calvary was an important element of their love for Christ.[9] Thomas Haweis—the influential evangelical Rector of All Saints, Aldwincle, Northamptonshire, co-founder of the Missionary Society, and a regular correspondent with Samuel Marsden—expressed evangelical understandings of death clearly in his extensive writings.[10] Haweis told his evangelical audience that because of original sin, humans were "as weak to resist the efforts of disease and sickness, as the chaff to endure the furious blast of the whirlwind."[11] Those "ungodly" individuals who did not recognize their own sinfulness and refused to struggle against Satan's power were destined to be "pointed out as the object of scorn and abhorrence to saints and angels; and be doomed to live for ever as an outcast from God; with devils in hell."[12] But he also reminded them that the "comfort and relief of the sinner depends on the all-sufficiency of the Redeemer," and Christ's sacrifice, he argued, allowed believers to find "deliverance from [their] fears, peace from the accusations of conscience, comfort in death, and after death life everlasting."[13] For Haweis, the essence of evangelical belief was a commitment to the figure of the crucified savior. One of his hymns made the promise of the crucifixion especially clear.

From the cross uplifted high,
Where the Saviour deigns to die,
What melodious sounds I hear!
Bursting on my ravish'd ear!
Love's redeeming work is done,
Come and welcome, sinner come.[14]

The pivotal importance of the Cross—what Bebbington has identified as evangelicalism's distinctive "crucicentrism"—was clear in the influential handbook *The Christian Ministry* by the Anglican evangelical Charles Bridges, which suggested that "Christ Crucified" was "the soul of the Christian system."[15] For evangelicals, the crucifixion linked sinfulness and salvation in a powerful way. John King expressed this in his typically direct manner when he noted that he taught his Māori congregants "the Missery of Man by Sin, & the Happines to be Obtained by Jesus Christ."[16]

Thus, death was a central thread in evangelical thought as theologians explored key doctrines relating to sin, assurance, and atonement.[17] From 1760, Enlightenment critiques of Christianity and the growing authority of doctors began to erode the Church's control of popular understandings of death in Britain, but evangelicals continued to frame death within the cosmic struggle between God and Satan and the promise of Heaven and the fearful torments of Hell.[18] At the same time, it is clear that evangelicalism's emphasis on the need to account for one's time, its stress on an active engagement with the world, and its insistence on the importance of experience produced a new urgency around the individual's responsibility for their earthly actions.[19] This sense of accountability invested illness and death with particular significance, as the deathbed became the site of reckoning where faith and action would be subject to divine judgment.

In the middle of the nineteenth century, this evangelical concern with the experience and fate of the ailing individual was an important element in the reworking *ars moriendi*, the art of dying well.[20] The Protestant reformulation of this long-established tradition afforded less of a role to the clergy than did its Catholic antecedents as it produced a clear model of the "good death," in which pious individuals expressed fortitude and faith as they prepared to face death surrounded by their loved ones in a Christian home. According to this ideal, the good Christian would repent, bid farewell to their family members, and accept God's will as they looked forward to the promise of joining God and their family in Heaven. Suffering and death were to be understood as part of God's plan, and the firm believer would face these pains with penance and grace. Implicit within this model, however, was the possibility of a "bad death," one in which the unprepared or unrepentant individual did not account for their sinfulness and were unable to embrace God's love and the promise of the Cross. Where the faithful and penitent would join in union with God and their families in Heaven, these unfortunates would suffer God's judgment and be sent to Hell for all eternity.[21] More liberal English Protestants had begun to express their discomfort with the idea of eternal damnation by the 1840s, as they saw the "eternal fire" of Hell as being incompatible with the loving God of the New Testament, but for evangelicals from the 1810s through to the 1840s, the horrors of Hell remained a central tenet of their faith and a key element of their psyche.[22]

The letters and journals of Protestant missionary workers and their families in northern New Zealand suggest that these understandings of the meaning of death were transplanted from Britain with little disruption. These frameworks were particularly important, as death and disease were central to the experience of missionary families in the Bay of Islands, even if the environment posed few epidemiological challenges to Europeans in the way that West Africa, India, or parts of the Caribbean did.[23] Even if they did not face the threats of tropical diseases in the warm but temperate north of Te Ika a Māui, the missionaries still lived in a death-haunted world. Within the missionary community, infant mortality rates were high. Given the absence of experienced midwives, limited medical expertise, and the isolated nature of the stations, the delivery of newborns was difficult and dangerous.[24] Missionary wives lost many babies: the archives feature numerous references to miscarriages and stillbirths.[25] The mothers themselves also faced considerable danger: both Marianne Williams and Sarah Fairburn almost died from severe hemorrhaging after birth, and several missionary wives suffered from life-threatening puerperal fever in the wake of delivery.[26] These risks, together with the pressures resulting from having large families, meant that missionary wives tended to die at a younger age than their husbands. In southern parts of the North Island, the life expectancy of missionary wives was in the early forties, whereas their husbands tended to die in their early seventies. The extant biometric data for early missionaries working in the north of the North Island produces a more moderate divergence, where husbands outlived their wives by nine years on average.[27] Given that most missionary wives were significantly younger than their husbands, this inverted British norms of life expectancy, wherein, on average, women significantly outlived men.[28] Missionary children, for their part, were not only prone to the usual childhood illnesses, but also to injury and death from the relative freedoms that they enjoyed. The King family lost three children, George and Martha Clarke lost two, and the Ashwell, Turner, Shepherd, White, Puckey, Whiteley, Woon, and Hobbs families all suffered the loss of one child before or during 1838.[29] Death was even more common beyond the confines of the mission, where the missionaries routinely interacted with adventurers, traders, and seamen. Due to the perils of maritime life and the long-term consequences of the sex and alcohol available at Kororāreka and Ōtuihu, these Euroamerican men died regularly. Missionaries were frequently called to minister to men who were sick, injured, and expected to die, and in many instances both Wesleyans and Anglicans buried sailors, whalers, and other men drawn to the ports of northern New Zealand. These men were frequently buried alongside members of missionary families in the graveyards of the mission stations.

But most strikingly, in the 1810s, 1820, and early 1830s the missionaries operated within Māori communities where death seemed ubiquitous. Violence was meted out to slaves as an instrument of control and punishment, and slaves were also sacrificed when particularly high-ranking individuals died. Slavery escalated in the far north as a result of the raids of Ngāpuhi leaders to the south from 1818. Large numbers of captives were brought back to the north and missionaries observed the execution of prisoners, as well as observing the absorption of many into agricultural and domestic labor.[30] Most important, missionaries lived among Māori communities that were ravaged by illnesses and diseases. They witnessed the death of great rangatira, like their patrons and protectors Ruatara, and numerous slaves and commoners perished as Eurasian diseases—measles, influenza, whooping cough, and tuberculosis—exacted a devastating toll on Māori communities that had no immunological experience of these pathogens.[31] The missionaries were aware that large numbers of Māori died during the first two years after Marsden's first sermon on Christmas day 1814, and from the outset of the mission, they expressed an ongoing concern about the health of individual Māori and the overall health of the native population as a whole.[32]

Confronted with death on a regular basis, missionaries and their families continued to stress the centrality of Christ's sacrifice, the threat of Hell, and the promise of Heaven to make sense of human mortality. All missionary families dealt with grief, whether it was produced by the news of death within their families at home in Britain, deaths within the missionary family itself, or the deaths of Māori closely associated with the mission. Some historians have suggested that high mortality rates, especially the high rates of infant mortality, reduced the psychic toll of death and minimized grief. But work by Linda Pollock on parental affection and by Pat Jalland on infant death have undercut Lawrence Stone's assertions that the "omnipresence of death" in the premodern period limited the amount of "emotional capital" invested in children and that in turn children did not invest too deeply in any adult.[33] While some letters and journal entries greeted news of death with composure, others made painfully clear the grief that missionaries in New Zealand experienced when they lost family members, especially children.[34] A telling example of this suffering and the evangelical effort to embrace the spiritual meaning of death is Benjamin Yates Ashwell's letter to the cms in 1838, informing the society of the death of his daughter.

> Were it not for the consoling and heart cheering truth that "God is love" I should now be swallowed up by overmuch sorrow, for it has been my painful task to follow to the grave our beloved, our only child. Last week on June 13th she was taken ill about 4 o'clock in the morning, at 10 o'clock the same morning she was a corpse. Every means was used but in vain. Congestion of blood on the brain had during the night gradually taken place, a rupture of a vessel on the brain ensued. Convulsions and death were the consequences.
>
> My beloved wife was enabled to say during this trying season "Father, Thy will done" and we both found strength according to our day. Yet, Dear Sir, Poor Nature will cry out and we may weep for "Jesus wept." Our sweet placid happy child had entwined herself around our hearts, her little winning ways, and happy disposition, had made her a great blessing, and to be parted from her forever in this world is no small trial. Sure

I am that there is but one tie stronger or sweeter than that of a parent. We feel this stroke deeply, very deeply, but we do know that our Heavenly Father loved His children too well to leave them unchastised. He will not inflict one unnecessary pang. Oh that we may improve by this affliction and learn the meaning of it. Our hearts bleed, but faith believes and I trust we are *enabled* to say "Father glorify Thy Name."[35]

This letter reveals Ashwell's conviction that his child's death had meaning, but that comprehending the meaning of the death amid trauma and pain was extremely difficult, a struggle intensified by the affective bonds that connected him, his wife, and their "sweet placid happy child."

Jalland has argued that in the face of the powerful grief that wracked mourning families, British churches produced large bodies of consolation literature, which taught parents that while the death of a child was a painful way to learn submission to God's will, the child had left the wicked and sinful world for a "better place."[36] Most evangelicals found consolation in the prospect of reunion after death and God's judgment. In 1828 George Clarke received a letter from his father informing him that two of his brothers had died. He responded, "Soon, soon, my dear parents, we must follow, and oh! That it may be with hopes full of immortality, of uniting again as one family, to recount all the acts of mercy to us in this lower world, and to praise him who hath loved us and redeemed us and put us in possession of the Everlasting rest."[37] In the following year Clarke wrote to his father to tell him about the death of his own daughter, Martha Elizabeth: "It has pleased our heavenly Father to call away our infant daughter, about 3 months old, to join—I hope—my two brothers who are gone before. Thus, dear Father, we are constantly reminded that this is not our rest."[38] A decade later, Susan Maunsell wrote to her friend and correspondent Eliza Langham, explaining her view of death and the afterlife: "We are both I trust on our journey to a far distant country where sooner or later we shall both arrive, never again to regret the want of each other's society and though always possessing never satiated because this corrupt nature will be left behind, and we shall be clothed with purity and glory."[39] Boyd Hilton has suggested that during the middle of the nineteenth century, evangelicals increasingly imagined Heaven in domestic terms, as a "cosy fireside" where deceased members of the family were reunited in the glow of God's love.[40] Clarke's and Maunsell's visions of Heaven were not yet entirely domesticated; Heaven was certainly the site where families would be reunited, but it remained a space whose very existence remained a potent reminder of god's sovereignty.

The palpable sense of struggle in Ashwell's letter suggests that despite the consolations of God's love and the prospect of eternal life, death was traumatic for missionary families. At the end of his life, George Clarke Jr, the eldest son of George and Martha Clarke, reflected on the death of his little sister, Martha Elizabeth, whom his father had written about in 1828.

A sister was born into the family, who died in three months from whooping cough. An incident, associated with her death, made a lasting impression upon me. It always comes back to me with the sight and smell of cabbage roses, and is a sort of faint musk to my memory. My father had a short time before got a box of plants from Sydney, among them some precious cabbage roses, the first I suppose that were grown in New Zealand. . . . My father carefully planted and tended them until the buds began to form. I remember his taking me by the hand, nipping off a half open bud, and then our walking into the study and his putting the flower in the dead baby's hand. I can not be sure, but I should think that was the first of our sweet English roses that ever bloomed in New Zealand. Then, too, by way of improving the occasion, I had to learn a hymn beginning—
    "Tell me, Mamma, and must I die
    "One day, as little baby did?"
that, I don't think I have seen for over sixty years, but I have not quite forgotten it yet.[41]

This narrative underscored both the affective power of death and the significance of death as a didactic moment: Martha Elizabeth's dying could be an occasion on which George Jr would be educated about the significance of mortality. The hymn he learned, "About Dying," was written by the sisters Jane and Ann Taylor, popular nonconformist hymn writers. The mother's section of the hymn, which replies to the child's queries about death, explicated evangelical views of death very clearly.

'Tis true, my love, that you must die;
The God who made you, says you must;
And every one of us shall lie,
Like the dear baby, in the dust.

These hands, and feet, and busy head,
Shall waste and crumble quite away:
But though your body shall be dead,
There is a part which can't decay:

That which now thinks within your heart,
And made you ask if you must die,
That is your soul—the better part—
Which God has made to live on high.

Those who have lov'd him here below,
And pray'd to have their sins forgiv'n,
And done his holy will, shall go,
Like happy angels, up to heav'n:

So, while their bodies moulder here,
Their souls with God himself shall dwell:—
But always recollect, my dear,
That wicked people go to hell.[42]

With regard to bodily culture, it is important to note that "About Dying" stressed the corruptibility of the human body and the transience of material existence. The body was a vessel for the soul—"the better part"—which was durable, unlike the body that was destined to molder, crumble, and decay.

Evangelical Practices

The Taylors' hymn taught George Clarke Jr. that sin and death were intimately connected. But it also offered hope that his soul and that of his sister would live with God, the Heavenly Father, "like happy angels." In this regard "About Dying" echoed the theological arguments of evangelical thinkers like Haweis who suggested that for the saved, death facilitated a reunion with the divine.[43] For this reunion to occur, burial rites were important; as Haweis suggested, "The decent care of burial is profession of our hope of the resurrection of the body." At the same time, however, discharging the correct observances for burial was not an end in itself: "Whilst we are all so solicitous in general for a burying-place for our bodies in earth, let it quicken us to greater solicitude, to secure a resting place for our souls in heaven."[44]

How, then, did the missionaries in northern New Zealand bury their dead? While evangelical understandings of the meaning of death were smoothly transplanted to the mission stations, established burial practices could not simply be recreated. The interment and commemoration of the dead beyond the formal frontier of empire was restricted and confined. The Protestant missionaries working in New Zealand had left behind a Britain that celebrated its soldiers, sailors, statesmen, and great national figures through public spectacles, impressive statues, and splendidly solemn tombs. By 1800, this tradition has been re-created in some parts of the empire. In established imperial cities like Calcutta, monuments to dead Britons were a prominent feature of the colonial landscape; tombs, funeral statuary, and monuments were important assertions of social status and a means of celebrating individual sacrifices for the cause of civilization and empire.[45]

The harnessing of deathways to an imperial patriotism was simply not possible in northern New Zealand in the 1810s and 1820s. Of course, Protestant missionaries were frequently skeptical of the power of the state and were certainly not inclined toward the ostentatious displays of social status in life or death. But, most important, on the New Zealand frontier, missionaries, traders, and sailors were forced to adjust significant aspects of their deathways because they were inhabiting a landscape that was framed by the operation of tapu and that was already heavily encoded by Māori habitation and conflict. Angela Middleton has suggested that missionaries generally denied the power of tapu, and as a result they understood the local landscape as profane.[46] Yet the operation of the mission stations required significant accommodations to the power of tapu in the Māori world.

This was also the case with deathways. In 1817 Thomas Kendall made it very clear to Samuel Marsden that missionary relationships with Māori and the landscape were constrained by tapu, especially the forms of tapu produced by death and the practices associated with it.

> In selecting a portion of land for a settlement, it would be advisable to take care that it be as clear as possible of what the natives call the wahhe taboo [wāhi tapu]. Wherever a person has breathed his last, or his bones have been laid for a time, there is always a piece of timber set up, if there is no tree already growing, to perpetuate his memory. This wahhee taboo is not suffered to be molested, and is held sacred both by friends and strangers. Amongst the natives, the least disrespect paid to their sacred relics or religious ceremonies and customs is considered a sufficient ground for a war by enemies and for a public debate by friends.[47]

Patu Hohepa has observed that traditional practices had "spread layers of tapu for the dead" over the Bay of Islands. The landscape was punctuated by the tapu places where war canoes carrying fallen warriors landed, the tapu sites where bodies were prepared for display or burial, the tapu areas where exhumed bones were painted with ochre, and the highly tapu locations where bodies were buried and bones were finally interred.[48] Kendall's letter clearly conveys the ways in which the missionaries had apprehended this power and felt constrained by its presence within the landscape.

Kendall further explained that the missionaries had already inadvertently become embroiled in conflict over the violation of tapu. "My colleague, Mr. Hall, and Mrs. Hall, suffered at Whitangee on account of the disrespect which had been paid by Warrakkee's people to some sacred relic, and not on account of any ill-will which the assailants entertained towards them."[49] In January 1816, a taua muru (plunder party) had raided the Halls' new base at Waitangi, throwing William Hall to the ground, threatening him with taiaha (long wooden clubs) and mere (short flat clubs), and then striking Dinah Hall in the face when she came to her husband's assistance, temporarily blinding her. The party stripped the mission house of its bedding and took tools, cooking utensils, an axe, and two guns.[50] This act of plunder was targeted at the Halls because they were living on land that had belonged to the recently deceased rangatira Waraki. It seems that Waraki's death, together with the vulnerability of the Halls, provided an occasion for a rival group to exact utu for an earlier infraction of tapu by Waraki's people.

This attack on the Halls underlined both the cultural weight of tapu and the vulnerability of the mission. Even as they were critical of tapu, missionaries recognized its power and were generally scrupulous in their efforts to avoid any infractions of wāhi tapu. As Grant Phillipson has noted, negotiations for the CMS to purchase land from rangatira affirmed that missionaries were to respect wāhi tapu.[51] Against this backdrop, missionaries realized that burials could not be made in just any location, nor was it possible to establish a cemetery in a centralized location convenient to the various stations that developed in the 1810s and 1820s. Essentially, missionaries decided that the burials that they conducted had to occur within the confines of mission stations. In the CMS case, this practice began in July 1816. William Hall's diary records the sudden death of Sarah Shergold, the wife of one of the mission sawyers, on the evening of 24 July 1816.[52] Although Hall and the other missionaries had witnessed many Māori deaths, Shergold was the first European who had died since the foundation of the mission. Hall reflected, "It is to be feared we have thought ourselves too secure and not been thankfull enough for mercies." Hall spent the following day preparing the coffin and the grave, which was dug at an unspecified location within the station at Hohi (Ōihi).[53] Hall's brief note for July 26 provides no detail about the burial service, other than noting that all the members of the settlement attended the funeral.[54] During the following week, Hall "commenced making a palisading to put around the grave," but it seems that this burial site received no other markers.[55] This precedent was followed at other stations, where missionary burials occurred within the confines of the station. At Kerikeri, the first burial, in 1820, occurred near the back boundary of the garden attached to John Butler's house; later burials were located in the graveyard near the schoolhouse-chapel that was opened in 1824.[56] At Whangaroa, the Turners' eleven-month-old son was buried in the garden that the missionaries at Wesleydale station had established inside the station's inner fence.[57] At the Mangungu station, the Wesleyans set aside a flat area of land above the Hokianga River in May 1829, when they buried two sailors from the *Roslyn Castle*.[58]

Thus, from the outset, mission graveyards were close to the mission houses, an arrangement that echoed practices in some other colonial sites, such as Jamaica, where the small and scattered nature of the British population encouraged whites to bury deceased kin within the boundaries of the family's property.[59] This arrangement was quite different from the urban landscapes that missionaries knew at home. In Britain in the early nineteenth century new cemeteries were carefully laid out at the edge of urban areas to minimize the risk of disease, which was believed to result from the miasma produced by decaying bodies.[60] This effectively produced a new distance between the living and the dead; Joseph Roach has argued that the rise of newly ordered cemeteries was an important way of circumscribing the cultural space afforded to the dead.[61] As cemeteries became more ordered, park-like, and increasingly perceived as formal sites of commemoration, a new segregation emerged that the hardened boundaries between the worldly life and the afterlife. This shift, which played out in the decades up to the 1860s in North America, Britain, and much of Europe, was not initially replicated in New Zealand mission stations.[62] Although the precise location of Sarah Shergold's grave at Hohi is unclear, John and Hannah King chose to bury their sons, Thomas Holloway (in 1818) and Joseph (in 1823), in the grounds attached to their house. During the 1820s and 1830s, they were joined by a significant number of Europeans and Americans who were buried at Hohi, seemingly in ground adjacent to where Shergold may well have been interred.[63]

The boundaries that the missionaries worked hard to construct between themselves and men of the sea were relaxed at death: sailors, whalers, and adventures were admitted into mission graveyards without hesitation. In some cases missionaries invested considerable time and energy in these efforts. William Hall had entertained Captain West of the whaler the *Indian* in January 1822. The following month West was crushed in the mouth of a harpooned whale and died painfully. Hall buried West in his garden alongside Mr. Wilson, the chief mate of the *Indian*, who also died suddenly in the Bay of Islands. Hall noted that he worked hard as he "erected a permanent and substantial paling round both graves at the Society's expense, and painted it white."[64]

Of course, at one level, the divergence between improvised missionary customs and the new forms of practice that were calcifying in Britain reflected the small scale of mission settlements. Missionary practice had more in common with older, rural traditions that were based around the village church and its graveyard. At the same time, however, it is also clear that due to the spatial location of missionary work beyond the formal frontiers of empire, the proximity of hastily constructed graveyards to mission houses and churches had special value. This reconnection of the living and the dead allowed missionaries to maintain close ties with lost children and deceased spouses in a foreign land. This was made clear in the debate over the future of the Hohi mission station in the late 1820s. Henry Williams argued that the decline of the population in the northeast of the Bay of Islands meant that Hohi should be disestablished, a move that would save the CMS money and focus its resources on the more central mission stations. John King opposed this suggestion. He conceded that they should move, but only less than a mile away, to the flatter ground at Te Puna, which sat just to the west of the Rangihoua pā. King emphasized not only the importance of the relationships he had established with the Rangihoua people, but also the special connections he had to the region. As he reminded the CMS, "Our two little Boys are buried in our Garden [at Hohi] and would have to be removed by us, or the natives would disturb them there is no doubt as we have known one instance of the same, this is the principle thing [I] feel."[65] In suggesting that the graves of his sons might be "disturbed," King was referring to the recent disinterment of Ann and Nathaniel Turner's young son during the sacking of the Whangaroa station. The missionaries had been horrified to discover that the grave was broken open, with the baby's remains left exposed on the mission's grounds and, according to the Wesleyan James Stack, its body hacked to pieces. Both the Wesleyans and CMS missionaries attempted to keep the details of this incident from Ann Turner, and in the wake of this trauma, Nathaniel Turner hoped to sever his connection to New Zealand by joining the WMS mission in Tonga.[66] King's arguments about the importance of the burials at Hohi and Turner's reluctant return to the New Zealand field in 1836 suggest that graves quickly became important sites for mediating Europeans' relationships to the landscape.[67] But where the interment of iwi (bones) reinforced the primacy of whakapapa and tribal connections to specific takiwā (spaces, districts) for Māori, European burial sites were central in fashioning familial connections to particular settlements during the 1820s and 1830s. The durability of such connections is especially clear in the case of the King family. John King himself was buried at Hohi after his death, in 1854. He joined his wife, Hannah, who was interred in the burial ground in 1851, and in subsequent years their daughter-in-law Mary Eliza King and their sixth and seventh sons, Samuel Leigh and James, were also laid to rest at Hohi.[68]

One of the important constraints on missionary burial practices was the absence of consecrated ground. After his return to Sydney, in 1836, from a sojourn in England, the Archdeacon of New South Wales, W. G. Broughton, was appointed as Bishop of Australia. An important aspect of his new powers was to consecrate churches and burial grounds—acts that could only be carried out by a bishop—and during his visit to the CMS mission in New Zealand in 1838–39, he extended these functions to the Bay of Islands. In January 1839 Broughton consecrated two established burial grounds in New Zealand: at Paihia and Kororāreka. In the lead-up to the service at Paihia on 4 January 1839, missionary families from around the Bay of Islands and from the inland stations traveled to witness the proceedings. The service, which took place in a lath and plaster church built in 1826–27, was well attended, and Charles Baker reported that Māori were drawn to the occasion despite the widespread illnesses that were afflicting local Māori communities.[69]

Broughton's arrival, on 21 December 1838, surprised the mission's printer, William Colenso, but Colenso quickly composed a four-page rendering of Genesis 23—the death of Sarah—a text that had been translated quickly, probably by William Williams.[70] This text recorded the death of Abraham's wife and Abraham's efforts to bury her. When Sarah died, Abraham was living among the Hittites at Hebron, and a Hittite named Zephron offered Abraham the cave of Machpelah and its adjoining field as a burial ground. Haweis's commentary on the chapter, in his influential *The Evangelical Expositor*, noted that as a stranger, Abraham was required to request permission to bury his wife among the Hittites. His application resulted in Zephron's "most generous offer" of the burial ground as a gift. But Abraham insisted on paying for the land, and this agreement established reciprocal relationships: Haweis noted that Abraham and the Hittites became "true friends."[71] Broughton's selection of this text implicitly suggested that the Old Testament compact was playing out again, as the missionary presence among Māori was the result of mutual consent, and the lands they occupied were purchased from local rangatira.[72] The missionaries also would have understood Abraham's choice as affirming the commitment of the missionaries to

New Zealand; after all, Abraham himself was buried alongside Sarah, and over the following decades his son, daughter-in-law, grandson, and grandson's wife also would be interred there.[73] Producing a translated and printed Māori version of this text was certainly designed to stress the implications of both missionary land purchases and the role that burial sites played as signs of the CMS's long-term ambitions.

More generally, however, the missionaries hoped that graveyards and burials could having an exemplary function, demonstrating to Māori new ways of thinking about death and new ways of managing human remains.[74] John Butler made this very clear in 1820, when William Bean, a carpenter attached to the Kerikeri station, and his wife suffered the loss of their son. Butler decided to conduct the burial in his garden, and although the child was interred within the station, Butler hoped that local Māori would see this ceremony. His journal for 14 July 1820 reads,

> This afternoon, I buried Mr. Bean's child in my garden. All the Europeans attended, and walked in regular order, as this tender lamb was the first [illegible] that it hath pleased our Holy Father to take to Himself and shield in His bosom from our little flock at Kideekiddee. It was my particular request that everyone should attend, not out of any vain ostentation, but to show the natives the manner of a Christian burial. Part of this service was read in the house, and the remainder at the grave, and two appropriate hymns were sung on the occasion.[75]

Ethnography of Māori Death

John Butler's account of the burial of the Bean child indicates that the missionaries were aware of the innate performativity of ritual practice. The burial service not only allowed the young child to make the transition from worldly life to the hereafter, but served as an occasion on which the missionary community could display its beliefs and practices to Māori. Butler was well aware that the rituals would be a spectacle that would draw the attention of local Māori, an awareness that was particularly acute for all who lived in the Kerikeri basin. The basin's topography meant that it functioned as kind of natural amphitheater: the station was plainly visible from the landing points and headlands on both the north and south sides of the inlet, and a particularly commanding view of the station was offered from the elevated ground of Hongi's Kororipo pā. In turn, missionaries on the station grounds were able to see these various locations around the inlet and were accustomed to watching the movement of waka in the basin and activities at the pā from the mission.

While the particular landscape of Kerikeri facilitated these cross-cultural gazes, observation was fundamental to the project of evangelization more generally. Missionaries worked hard to build up their knowledge of the history, social structure, cultural practices, and cosmology of the people they lived among. This kind of knowledge was essential if they were to be effective translators of the gospel, powerful preachers able to engage Māori in public contestation over the authority of their old ways, and social reformers able to suppress the "vices" and "evils" that they saw as afflicting Māori society.

Given the importance of observation to missionary work, death took on a particular significance, as the missionaries understood it as a fundamental aspect of native culture and a key point of contention for their work in the transformation of Māori beliefs. In the 1810s and 1820s Protestant missionaries in New Zealand were frustrated by their inability to access Māori "religion." While they quickly formulated complex assessments of the characters of different rangatira, developed a basic understanding of the relationships between different kin groups, and assembled a picture of how local economies operated and rights were dispersed, they found it much harder to access Māori esoteric knowledge or develop insight into the operation of a host of ritual practices. Here again, missionary aspirations were checked by the operation of tapu. Within Māori society knowledge was not freely shared; the dynamics of knowledge transmission were carefully controlled and esoteric knowledge was shared only within the highly regulated regimen of the *whare wānanga* (school of learning). These established knowledge practices meant that few Māori in the far north were inclined to share their knowledge of the interaction between the natural and supernatural domains and how human action could shape the interaction between these permeable worlds. This led many missionaries to doubt that Māori actually possessed any systematic body of beliefs and practices that could be designated as a "religion"; rather, they believed Māori possessed an assemblage of superstitions and folk beliefs. The absence of religion—which the missionaries understood as an organized set of tenets, practices, and institutions—was seen to make Māori particularly susceptible to Satan, and missionaries routinely understood many Māori "vices" as manifestations of the power of the "Prince of Darkness."[76]

Although the transmission of key elements of traditional cosmological and genealogical knowledge occurred beyond the confines of the mission stations and many potent rituals were conducted in spaces closed to the missionaries, a host of practices relating to death did occur in plain sight. In part, this was a byproduct of the ways in which Māori dealt with the powerful tapu attached to death. Unlike the rituals associated with divination, war-making, or propitiating an angry atua—which were conducted in secluded locations, where the tohunga's incantations and rituals would not be disrupted and would remain secret—many of the practices relating to death occurred within open spaces where missionaries were able to observe proceedings.[77] Most important, missionaries were able to witness many of these practices because of the pivotal social role played by the *tangihanga*—burial and grieving practices—in affirming the connections that linked members of whānau, hapū, and iwi to each other.

Kendall and the Death of Ruatara

Soon after the establishment of the CMS mission at Hohi, in December 1814, the missionaries witnessed the decline and death of their patron and protector Ruatara. Ruatara's death provided the missionaries—especially Thomas Kendall, who exhibited a deep and sustained interest in Māori beliefs and practices—with significant insights into the ways in which illness and death were managed socially and offered fleeting glimpses of Māori cosmology as well. Judith Binney has noted that Kendall's early accounts of Māori beliefs were "almost always accounts of beliefs associated with death and burial."[78] There is no doubt that deathways offered missionaries some of their most significant insights into the Māori world.

Anne Salmond has suggested that local tohunga believed that Ruatara's illness reflected his confrontation with an "existential danger" (mate) that was physically manifest and that as a consequence, his hau (life force) was under threat. Conversely, the missionaries read his illness as a heavy cold that had led to inflammation and believed that he could be restored with food and drink. In Salmond's terms, this disjunction produced a "cosmological collision" over understandings of the body and the meaning of death.[79] Kendall produced a long narrative describing Ruatara's illness, its implications, and his eventual death. Kendall noted that the people of the Rangihoua pā believed that in his ill state their chief was highly tapu, as an "*Atua* had . . . entered into him." This meant that only tohunga could come into his presence; but Kendall was allowed to visit him as well, "after it had been settled upon that an European would not by his presence occasion the displeasure of the deity." Kendall visited Ruatara with a jug of rice water, believing that it might help restore him, and he engaged the rangatira on the meaning of death.

When I had given him a few spoonfuls and was desirous to empty the decanter in order that it might be replenished, his feelings were very much hurt. He said to me, "You are very unkind, Mr. Kendall. If the decanter is taken away, *atua* will kill me this very day." I told him the *atua* must be very cruel and reminded him of the God Whom we worshipped, Who was infinitely kind, and, as he had often heard, had given His own Son Who had suffered, bled, and died for the sin of man, in order than man might live and die happy. He made no reply to my observation.[80]

Ruatara's reluctance to engage with Kendall's argument can be read as a manifestation of his anxieties over his connection to the mission and the consequences of the foundation of the Hohi station. During the voyage of the *Active* from Port Jackson to the Bay of Islands in November 1814, the missionary party noted a marked shift in Ruatara's countenance: where he was once "lively and communicative," he suddenly became "quite dejected" and subject to a "morose melancholy." Eventually, Ruatara revealed that a colonist in Port Jackson had told him that the missionary settlement would ultimately destroy Māori, making a "once happy people . . . entirely extinct."[81] After receiving effusive reassurances from Marsden and the missionaries, Ruatara continued to act as the protector of the mission and remained interested in new agricultural practices, but he had little interest in missionary ideas and made the missionaries' dependence on him clear.[82] Ruatara's silence in the face of Kendall's explanation of the doctrine of the Cross was a telling portent of what the CMS missionaries would painfully learn over the next two decades: it was very difficult to encourage high-ranking chiefs like Ruatara to give up their old atua, the atua who were the very source of their power and status as rangatira.

Although Ruatara resisted Kendall's discourse on Christ, he was very important to the missionary's grasp of Māori views of illness and death. In the narrative of Ruatara's death he drafted in his journal, Kendall explained the supernatural elements that accounted for mortality: "In certain diseases upon the lungs, such as a violent cold which I believe was the case with Duaterra [Ruatara], The natives believe that *Atua* enters into the sick in the form of a Voracious reptile and though unseen preys upon the Vitals until the Breath is gone. As the Atua descends like a falling star so in time the Soul of the deceased ascends and becomes a Star in the firmament."[83] Here Kendall was beginning to develop some understanding of the interrelationships between atua and the humanity. Not only was Ruatara's death caused by atua, Kendall noted that as soon as he had died the people of Rangihoua referred to Ruatara himself as an atua. While it was not unknown for living rangatira to be understood as an atua, Kendall clearly believed after Ruatara's death his kin thought that he, too, was now a supernatural being, a being that was capable on intervening in the natural world.[84]

Kendall's narrative also detailed the response of Ruatara's kinsfolk to his death. He noted that Hongi was at the forefront of the ritual.[85] The rangatira

> held a blade of green Moca [muka: scrapped flax] which he had inten-
> tionally plucked up and waving the other he occasionally took hold of the
> hair of Duaterra as if eager to snatch him from the King of Terrors. Tears
> fell streaming down his cheeks as he began his lamentable theme. The Na-
> tives joined in crying but the grief of the relations was excessive. Dahoo
> [Rahu] (the head wife) was of all others the most unconsolable and her
> conduct has brought within my observation one instance more than the
> many I have before heard of, of the dreadful effects of Heathen supersti-
> tion, for on Saturday March 4th while the people were still mourning and
> cutting themselves according to their manner until their persons were
> besmeared with blood she sought and found an opportunity to put a pe-
> riod to her own existence by hanging herself at a short distance from the
> body of her departed husband. None of the natives nor even of her near
> relations appeared shocked or surprised at this incident. The mother it is
> true wept while she was composing the limbs of her daughter, for what
> mother would not weep, but she nevertheless applauded her resolution
> and the sacrifice she made for the man she so tenderly loved. Her father
> observed her corpse without any apparent concern; I could not discover
> a tear when it was brought before him. And her two brothers smiled on
> the occasion and said "it was a good thing at New Zealand. It is common
> for women to do this when their husbands die. They think they then go
> to them." It appeared strange to me that the family could suppress the
> feelings of human nature on such an awful occasion, as I had always hith-
> erto observed them very affectionate towards each other, and remarkable
> for their attention to the woman who was now no more.[86]

Here, Kendall stressed the inability of Māori to modulate their grief and what he saw as the excessive nature of their reaction to death. While evangelicalism prioritized feeling and experience over purely intellectual understandings of faith and the Bible, it suggested that emotions should be tempered and restrained. It might have been a feeling faith, but it was a rational one, too.[87] Most important, feelings should be harnessed to the seriousness of evangelicalism, its deep moral sensibility, its campaigns against vice and suffering, and its preoccupation with the doctrine of the

Cross.[88] For Kendall, the mourning that marked Ruatara's death evinced an extreme grief, a grief that was more ritualistic than substantive. *Haehae* (self-laceration), *tangi* (crying; lamentation), *pihe* (dirges), and *waiata tangi* (mourning songs) were all read as an intemperate and unrestrained emotionality that was made physically manifest. Here, Kendall's analysis bore the clear imprint of the increasing restraint that shaped the expression of grief within British culture. As life became more predictable and interpersonal violence declined in early modern Europe, greater stress was placed on civility, order, and self-composure. Comportment and self-regulation became key markers of both social standing and moral seriousness, as passions and appetites were increasingly reshaped into more orderly emotions.[89] For evangelicals, the suppression of violent or excessive emotions was a vital element of self-mastery, a control of both the body and feelings that was an important spiritual and social undertaking.[90] Conversely, for Māori, the very physicality of these expressions of grief were culturally meaningful. *Roimata* (tears) and *hupe* (mucus) were understood as salves for the pain of death.[91] Haehae, self-laceration which spilled highly tapu blood, was a powerful demonstration of love and esteem; these marks of grief, which were signs of affective connection with the deceased, could be made permanent when *ngārahu* (soot) was applied to the wounds, producing an inedible symbol of loss.[92]

Missionaries understood these practices as both uncivilized and in violation of Biblical injunction, but Kendall argued that Māori grief was insufficient as well as excessive.[93] He suggested that Ruatara's and Rahu's kin lacked the benevolent compassion to express sadness at the death of Rahu. He considered this a coldness that suppressed the "natural" feeling that should connect families, especially parents to their children. Both this absence and excess, Kendall contended, were clear signs of the power of "heathenish customs." These practices were not simply the product of Māori being in a state of nature, but rather reflected the power that Satan himself exercised over the unconverted: "Certainly the People here are held in a state of extreme bondage by the great Deceiver of mankind." [94] Because missionaries understood that death could be a portal to everlasting life with God and could potentially reunite pious families, they saw the visceral nature of Māori mourning practices as the direct consequence of the ascendancy of their old gods, who included Hine-nui-te-pō, the goddess of night, death and the underworld.[95]

Kendall's journal entry closed by detailing the interment of Ruatara and Rahu. He noted that they were placed upon a "stage" which was constructed where Ruatara had died and that Hongi and seven other chiefs enclosed the stage with rails and boards. These high-ranking men were subsequently in an extremely tapu state and thus were not able to handle food. Hongi maintained these restrictions for two days, while Te Papa, Ruatara's tohunga, remained in this state for two months. For those two months, Kendall reported, Ruatara's kin would continue to publically mourn his passing, and he noted their audible "cries" and the "roaring" of visiting Māori who saw the site of Ruatara's interment.[96] In fact, six weeks later, on 15 April 1815, Kendall recorded that Ruatara's and Rahu's remains were removed for their final burial on his lands at Moturaha.[97] Reflecting on Ruatara's illness, his death, and the suicide of Rahu, as well as on the rituals he had witnessed, Kendall suggested, "The veneration of the New Zealanders for the dead is extraordinary. A native who can speak English asserts, it is like our going to church. I cannot say positively the dead are worshipped, as I become acquainted with the language I shall better understand the real purport of the funeral ceremony."[98]

Elaborating the Ethnography of Death: Cosmology

Kendall was aware of the limits of his own knowledge and comprehension, but Ruatara's death allowed him to quickly assemble some detailed observations about deathways at Rangihoua. While Kendall's knowledge was never shaped into a coherent printed account, he shared his understandings with the other missionaries and established a basic framework for interpreting the place of death in the Māori world. Within Kendall's narrative we can identify three recurrent points of observation that gave this developing ethnographic archive shape: the cosmological significance of death; the relationship between status and death; and the management of death through mourning practices and interment customs.

Ruatara's death taught the CMS missionaries that Māori in the Bay of Islands believed that illness and death were a result of the action of atua in the world. These potent agents could act on their own or they could be brought into te ao mārama by human action. In the northeastern part of the Bay of Islands, in 1822, John King heard the story of a rangatira called Paka. Paka's death was attributed to malevolent witchcraft that directed the power of atua at Paka. After Paka's death, a tohunga performed a ritual that allowed him to identify the person responsible for this mākutu (witchcraft). Subsequently, the tohunga suggested that Paka's family should sacrifice two people to assuage Paka's angry spirit. A young man named Te Huringa, who King had taught to spin twine, was responsible for enacting one of these sacrifices, and now, several years later, he came to King because he was ill and was convinced that he would die. Te Huringa suggested that his illness was a result of having eaten off a mat that a girl he killed wore and that as a result of this infraction of tapu, an atua was angry with him.[99] In making sense of this complicated sequence of events, King made two important observations. First, he saw in the tohunga a reflection of the "*cunning-man* or *conjurer*," who he had heard about many times in his "own country." Second, he went beyond stressing this cultural equivalence to suggest that Te Huringa's story demonstrated that "the natives in general ascribe their illness & death" to magic and to the atua's intervention in worldly affairs.[100]

The story of Paka and Te Huringa also underscored a lesson that Kendall had drawn from Ruatara's death: that for some Māori at least, death marked a person's transition from being a human in te ao mārama to becoming an atua. But during the 1820s and 1830s, most Māori suggested to missionaries that after death their wairua (spirit) journeyed to the north to Te Reinga, the northern tip of Te Ika a Māui, from where it descended into the underworld and afterlife. Less than two weeks after Te Huringa told King his story, he died. At this time, local Māori informed King that "the spirit hovers about the body & place of the deceased untill the third day, when the priest prays and directs the spirit to the reinga a place at the north cape where the natives say the spirits go and descend, they suppose after death they are in a similar state as when in sleep & in dreems in this life, or, that they possess after death what they have dreemed of."[101] Later in the same month, King was told that entry into the underworld beyond Te Reinga was not guaranteed. King had been visiting a man named Maku, who was on the verge of death. A group of his friends gathered to mourn him, and one of them fired a gun three times at the moment it seemed that Maku was expiring. Within an hour, he had revived; King was told that he had recovered because "his spirit went to the Reinga, but his departed Friends would not let him enter."[102] This narrative suggested that for some Māori, other wairua could intercede before the deceased's wairua joined Hine-nui-te-pō. The following month, another local offered another reading of the afterlife: he told King that "a man dies his spirit goes to the *Reinga*, there grows up to maturety, plants sweet Potatoes, haves many children, fight & c—dies the second time & has no more life, returns not, nor revives no more—."[103] These accounts of the wairua's voyage to Te Reinga provided an important base for missionary critiques of Māori cosmology in the later 1820s and 1830s.

Ethnography of Death: Rank

Ruatara's death gave the CMS party a clear understanding of the strong ritual prohibitions and substantial mourning rituals that marked the death of a significant rangatira. Over the following years, however, they realized that there were significant divergences in Māori deathways according to social station. Very quickly they recognized that the death of taurekareka (slaves) were marked with no mourning and scant ritual injunctions. Most important, they learned that the killing of slaves had few social or spiritual consequences for the highborn. The fate of slaves rested entirely with their masters. Not only were taurekareka dislocated from their traditional land, the bones of their ancestors, and their own atua, but the kinfolk of enslaved individuals traditionally understood them as mate—socially and spiritually dead. Given the consequences of capture, there was little likelihood that utu would ever be sought for the mistreatment or killing of an enslaved individual.[104]

Missionary letters and journals record numerous acts of violence directed toward captives. For example, at Whangaroa, in 1823, John Hobbs was interrupted by the news that "that not far distant from our house the natives had killed a slave and were then roasting him." Leaving the station, Hobbs found a slave, whom he described as "a fellow mortal," roasting on two large logs. Hobbs was informed that the slave was old and that he had been killed by his master who found him "disagreeable," as the taurekareka "had become troublesome through old age and infirmity." The slave's master, in response to the slave's complaints, struck him with an axe before placing him on the fire.[105] Where the killing and eating of high-ranking individuals was rarely spontaneous or hasty, the marginal social status of slaves rendered them extremely vulnerable.[106] This was brought home to Hobbs the following year, when a rangatira from Whangaroa used a billhook, which Hobbs had earlier repaired, to kill a slave for taking kūmara.[107] This use of extreme violence to discipline or punish slaves was relatively common. In 1820 John Butler recorded the killing and eating of a slave at Kerikeri after he was accused of theft.[108] In 1822 John King noted that a high-ranking woman at Rangihoua pā had killed a slave for taking kūmara, and in 1824 he recorded two such deaths near Hohi in one week.[109] Missionaries also recognized that slaves could be killed during conflicts between high-ranking individuals: King observed that a female slave was killed near Hohi after her master's wife learned that her husband had left her to live with another of his spouses.[110] This vulnerability persisted after slaves entered into connection with missions; they remained subject to the threat of violence from their former owners and from high-ranking Māori in the locality.[111]

Moreover, King and other missionaries noted that when slaves were killed or died, the kinds of rituals that marked Ruatara's death were not observed: little care was taken with the disposal of slaves' remains.[112] This reflected the slaves' loss of mana and tapu. In comparative terms, their remains were not powerful or dangerous.[113] King believed that while high-ranking individuals would be buried temporarily, prior to the final interment of the bones, the remains of free people of low rank would simply be placed or buried in the ground. The bodies or remains of dead slaves might be not be formally disposed of at all.[114] Until the mid-1830s, these variations in deathways provided missionaries with some of the clearest evidence for the importance of social differentiation and the centrality of tapu in Māori society.

Missionaries saw these traditions as marking the inherent corruption of a society that had not yet heard the gospel; they were manifestations of the essential qualities of the Māori mind in its unreformed state. However, the violence directed toward slaves was almost certainly connected to the rapid expansion of slavery in the early nineteenth century. This transformation reflected two dimensions of cross-cultural contact. First, with the extension and intensification of warfare from the late 1810s through to the 1830s, large numbers of captives were taken by the powerful taua, armed with muskets, who pushed south from the Bay of Islands. Success in war and the accumulation of captives and slaves were crucial manifestations of a rangatira's mana.[115] Second, slavery grew in importance as rangatira retained larger numbers of war captives to labor in furnishing British, Australian, and American vessels with timber, processed flax, pork, and agricultural produce. Slaves provided the labor that drove forward the agricultural revolution initiated by Te Pahi and Ruatara and extended and intensified by Hongi Hika.[116] This amplified use of slave labor allowed the extension of kūmara plantations and the cultivation of introduced food plants, especially potatoes, on a massive scale. The resulting increase in the agricultural surplus enabled Hongi to trade potatoes for muskets and powder from European and American ships and to redirect labor resources toward frequent long-distance raids to the south.[117] The missionaries witnessed the return of taua with retinues of captives. While many of these prisoners were put to work in Hongi's cultivations, significant numbers were killed either as offerings to Tū-mata-uenga, atua of war, or as sacrifices for Ngāpuhi toa (warriors) lost in battle. Missionaries, especially at Kerikeri, were witnesses to these killings. The promontory on which Kororipo pā itself stood, which the missionaries referred to as "Shunghie's Dock," was the site where prisoners from the Ngāpuhi raid on Mokoia were executed. From the Kerikeri station, missionaries also witnessed the killing of war captives at a canoe landing on the northeast side of the Kerikeri basin.[118] These executions were not indiscriminate: captives were offered to specific atua, and those who carried out the killings were prepared for the task and subsequently ritually cleansed by tohunga.[119] The ritual killing of these captives in clear view of the Kerikeri station during the first half of the 1820s was an open repudiation of the claims of missionary teaching.

The missionaries also became aware that slaves were in particular danger when high-ranking individuals were ill or dying. In the 1820s, slaves would be sacrificed if a high-ranking individual was seriously ill or died. When a high-ranking man named Tuhi died in 1824, John King noted that one slave was sacrificed when he fell ill and that several more would be killed to mark his death.[120] In a similar vein, when news of the death of Hāre Hongi, Hongi Hika's son, reached Ngāpuhi in 1825, Hongi Hika's wife immediately killed her prized female slave. In some instances, it appears, slaves were killed at the completion of death rites to accompany high-ranking individuals on their voyage into the next world.[121] More generally, however, such killings had a ritual purpose. These practices reflected the highly tapu nature of rangatira, a desire to assert the mana of the deceased, the need to appease demanding atua, and the need to win the favor Tū-mata-uenga of in times of conflict.[122] The missionaries soon recognized that the deaths of high-ranking individuals were moments of great risk; not only could they potentially realign the balance of power between the different kin groups that the missionaries worked with, but the highly tapu nature of rangatira meant death also marked a reconfiguration of the relationship between atua and te ao mārama.[123] Rangatira themselves saw these sacrifices as important forms of spiritual protection and signs of their own status. For some high-ranking individuals, such as the rangatira and tohunga Tohi Tapu, the abandonment of human sacrifice was a very real transformation of their chiefly practice, a shift that was indicative of the ways in which engagement with missionaries resulted in significant cultural change even when it did not lead to actual conversion to Christianity.[124]

Ethnography of Death: Interment and Mourning

Ruatara's death and interment provided the missionaries with many insights into the ways in which northern Māori communities handled death. Over the subsequent decade, they extended this knowledge as they observed tangihanga from a distance and, on many instances, were invited to attend tangihanga by local rangatira. Four months after Ruatara's death, Thomas and Jane Kendall visited the tangihanga for a man named Te Waimuri. Thomas Kendall's journal entry suggests that he had quickly felt confident in his grasp of Māori deathways: "The corpse was placed in an upright posture as is usual. The face had been oiled in order to make the marks of the tattooing clear, the hair had been cut, and was neatly tied up and ornamented with feathers."[125] Missionary narratives such as this paid considerable attention to the physical preparation of the deceased and the material culture associated with death. John King noted in his journal in 1822 that when a high-ranking man died, the widow often lived in a "small house called the ware-taua" (whare tauā). While in this "house of mourning," the widow wove mats that would be used to wrap the bones of the deceased when they were exhumed in the future. These mats, King noted, were called "watu-tangi knitting-crying" (*whatu tangi*) or "kakahowroimate, mat of tears, or bed-wet-with tears-while-makeing a mat of sorrow" (*kaka roimata*).[126] King also noted that mats were used to wrap the deceased for their primary burial and that in the Bay of Islands waka (canoes) were frequently used to hold the remains of high-status individuals during primary burial.[127] Most detailed accounts of Māori deathways also discussed the exhumation of remains and secondary burial, which occurred from two months to many years after the initial interment.[128]

Missionary narratives followed Kendall's lead in paying considerable attention to the ways in which Bay of Islands Māori responded to death. At Te Waimuri's tangi, Kendall noted that as visitors approached the location where Te Waimuri was on display, "they kneeled down in a row in front of the dead body. They then commenced the usual battle cry, cutting their persons and speaking to the deceased."[129] John King was alarmed by the mourners' haehae on this occasion: "The people around him [Te Waimuri] was crying & cuting themselves in an horrid manner, there appeared to be half a pint of blood on the ground, which ran from their faces breasts & harms [arms]."[130] In October 1825 Nathaniel Turner and John Hobbs visited a tangi near Whangaroa. Hobbs again noted the practice of haehae and offered some explanation of its significance: "Many of the natives [were] crying around partially covered with blood, a strong demonstration of the love of his friends manifested by their cutting themselves with a flint, and at the same time a strange evidence of the pride and vanity of others who assisted in the formal ceremony."[131] Missionaries quickly attempted to suppress haehae, but had little success until the late 1830s in limiting the occurrence of this ritual.

The other element relating to mourning that the missionaries were particularly concerned with was *whakamomori* (suicide). It was not uncommon for individuals to kill themselves after losing a loved one. While this seems to have been more prevalent for women, there is evidence that some husbands took their lives after their wives died and that some men also attempted to kill themselves when their friends, brothers, and fellow warriors died.[132] In his journal in 1822 John King reflected that it was commonplace that "the wife hangeth herself at the death of her husband, so the husband hangeth himself at the death of his wife, but this occurs but very seldom, tho it is held as a very good thyesing thus to shew their love of the deceased, to a husband, to a father or mother, Brother, &c."[133] Three years later, he felt more able to offer insight into the logic of whakamomori.

> Nahui hearing that her husband is killed in battle, tied her child up in the hut, the slaves hearing the child groan rushed in & cut the child down & saved its life—she told Mrs K[in]g to day that she reasoned within herself thus, my husband is dead, I will hang myself but who will nurse & feed my child, so I intended to hang my child & then myself, in this manner they are driven to desperation and death—[134]

This was a deeply troubling practice. Evangelicals saw suicide as a manifestation of Satan's power in the world, as well as a crime against God that made manifest the most unimaginable excesses of pride and selfishness.[135]

For evangelical missionaries, the practice of whakamomori was the strongest proof of Kendall's argument that Māori were incapable of modulating their grief. In their eyes, this was simply part of the larger inability of Māori to master their emotions, a deficiency that stemmed from the continued hold of the "Prince of Darkness" over their minds and bodies. King complained that old and young alike "often hang themselves up, on very frivolous occasions" and that this extreme action was frequently a response to "vexation."[136] In a similar vein, William Puckey complained to the CMS in 1839, after a rash of four suicides near the Kaitaia station. He saw these acts as overwrought responses to small social infractions: in each case there was significant evidence that suggested that the individual concerned had committed theft. Puckey went beyond King, however, to note that these acts reflected the power of shame and embarrassment in Māori society: "Their shame was so great they could not bear the idea of being looked upon as thieves therefore they shot themselves."[137] Whakamomori might be a response to experiencing whakamā (shame, embarrassment), but as Maori Marsden has noted, it also could be the ultimate act of self-assertion in the face of injustice or social constraints.[138] More generally, however, missionaries saw these acts as reflecting the general lack of self-mastery among Māori. Hobbs summed up this view when he suggested that during tangi, he had witnessed "a great deal of inconsistency."[139] The teachings of the missionaries offered not only a new cosmology, but also a social order that would reshape both the physical and emotional culture of the *tangata whenua* ("people of the land," Māori).

Disputing Death: Te Reinga

Ethnographic knowledge was a central tool for missionaries who wished to contest and reform Māori deathways. An excellent example of the strong connections between ethnography and missionary critiques of Māori cosmologies and cultural practices is offered by missionary voyages to Te Reinga, the Leaping Off Place, at the far north of Te Ika a Māui. This site occupied a central position in the cosmology of Māori who believed that the wairua (spirits) of the deceased proceeded from this place to the underworld and then onto Hawaiki, the ancestral homeland. As in the case of John King's encounters with Te Huringa and Maku, missionaries frequently heard about Te Reinga when attending to the ill. The desire of missionaries to help the ill and to minister to the dying was at times contested by Māori. In such disputes, the power of Te Reinga could be mobilized against missionary teaching. In December 1832 Henry Williams visited the settlement of Ōtuihu, where he encountered an old woman hostile to missionary teaching who reminded Williams of the "witches of former days." Nevertheless Williams was pleased to have the encounter, as the woman had "a great deal of news to impart." The woman, who Williams believed functioned as a kind of local "oracle," ignored the missionary's teaching "and amused herself and others occasionally by a pukana, one of their hideous stares, accompanied with a Satanic grin and twirl of the tongue." As she rejected the authority of the missionaries' words, she invoked the "excellency of the Reinga as having conversed with many from thence."[140]

Such collisions between old gods and new, long-established ways of thinking and the new order that missionaries were trying to sponsor became more common in the 1830s as the CMS mission expanded, vernacular literacy spread, growing numbers of missionary texts circulated, and enthusiastic

Māori attached to the mission began to propound the gospel. One of the most dramatic of these confrontations occurred in December 1834, when the CMS catechist William Puckey led an expedition to Te Reinga. Puckey had come to the far north early in 1834 to establish the Kaitaia mission under the mantle of the most powerful Muriwhenua rangatira Panakareao, who belonged to Te Patu hapū of the Te Rarawa iwi. Panakareao had risen to preeminence in the far north in the middle of the 1820s, and he exercised considerable authority, with some members of the Te Aupōuri and Ngāti Kuri iwi recognizing his mana, as well as the Te Rarawa iwi with whom he primarily identified. He oversaw the preparation of the land for the Kaitaia mission station and organized its transfer to the missionaries. He had a strong interest in Christianity and, perhaps, an even stronger desire to build commercial and political connections with Europeans.[141]

Accompanied by six Māori men from the Kaitaia station and Matengā (Marsden) Paerata, a powerful Te Rarawa rangatira of the Te Patukoraha hapū, Puckey lead an expedition north in December 1834. The primary aim of the voyage was to visit the Te Aupōuri communities that were settled on the long thin strip of land running north from Rangaunu harbor to Te Reinga, but visiting Te Reinga itself was important secondary goal.[142] This desire quickly caused conflict. At Houhora, little more than a third of the way to Te Reinga, a local rangatira who had learned the party's intention confronted Paerata, telling him, "'I am come to send you and your white companion back again, for if you cut away the "aka" or roots of the Reinga, the whole Island will be destroyed; but your white friend will not.' He moreover said to Paerata, 'Do not suffer your friend to cut away the ladder by which the souls of our forefathers were conveyed to the other world.'"[143] Puckey, Paerata, and the rest of the party were not persuaded by this argument, nor did this exchange prevent a significant number of local people from attending the service that Puckey held that afternoon. In the wake of this encounter, Puckey reflected,

The whole body of New Zealanders, although composed of numerous tribes who for the greater part are living in malice, hateful and hating one another, yet all firmly believe in the Reinga (which is at the north cape) as the one only place for their departed spirits. It is their belief that as soon as the soul leaves the body, it makes its way with all speed to the Western coast: if it be the spirit of a person who resides in the interior, he takes with him a small bundle of branches of the palm tree, as a token of the place where he resided; if one who lived on the coast, he takes with him a kind of grass which grows by the sea side, which the spirit leaves at different resting places, on its road to the Reinga.[144]

The debate at Houhora anticipated the cosmological questions that would recur for the party of travellers. Even the most routine tasks of journey—gathering firewood and setting the nightly fire—could spark larger questions. When the party rested at Waimahuru, a small creek, the campfire burned out of control, destroying one of the party's packages of supplies. The fire had been set by two young men in the party who were closely connected to the Kaitaia mission, and they had used wood that they gathered from two whare near the campsite that were considered tapu. In the wake of the fire, a local guide who had joined the group read this as a sign of the anger of the atua and informed Puckey that he had not yet begun to believe in the Christian God.[145] In addressing Puckey, the guide perhaps misread the situation: it is possible that it was the young "mihinere" (missionary) Māori who were testing the authority of the old gods and ways, rather than Puckey himself.

As they proceeded north along Te Oneroa-a-Tōhē (Ninety Mile Beach), the party looked out for a green *wakaau* (token fashioned out of flax), which would be a sign that a spirit of a recently deceased individual had passed en route to the Reinga. Puckey himself looked for such signs, but found none, suggesting not only that he was keen to contest these ideas but that he also saw the existence of wakaau as at least a credible possibility.[146] The next day, as they approached Te Reinga, they ascended the hill known as Haumu, where they found many dried wakaau. Puckey's local guide suggested that spirits who rested on the hill before completing their voyage to Reinga had deposited them. Puckey challenged the local man, asking, "If it were not possible for strangers who passed this way, to do as my natives were then doing, which was every one twisting green branches, and depositing them there as a sign that they had stopped at that notable place. This is a general custom with the natives, whenever they pass any remarkable place."[147]

On 9 December, the party made its way to Te Reinga itself and looked at the aka, the roots the wairua clutch on their descent into the underworld. They then moved a hundred yards farther along the coast, to Motatau, where they observed a large clump of seaweed, which Puckey was informed was "the door which closed in the spirits in the Reinga." The guide explained that at this location all the fish were "quite red, from the Kokowai (or red ochre) which the natives bedaub their bodies and mats with."[148] Here, Puckey was unnerved, recognizing the legitimacy and potency of Māori beliefs about Te Reinga.

The scenery around the place I stood, was most uninviting, and not only so, but calculated to inspire the soul with horror. The place has a most barren appearance, while the numerous sea fowls screaming, and the sea roaring in the pride of its might, dashing against the dismal black rocks, would suggest to the reflecting mind, that it must have been the dreary aspect of the place, which led the New Zealanders to choose such a situation, as this for their hell.[149]

Puckey's party quietly and quickly returned to Kaitaia station by the same route. Puckey was surprised by the stormy welcome that awaited the travelers. After their departure, "rumours were spread among the tribe that I had gone to cut away the Aka of the Reinga." This issue aroused great debate within the community at Kaitaia: those keen to protect the old ways had threatened to "way lay" Puckey's party on the return. But Puckey also reported that some who had begun "to feel a little enlightenment" responded by asking, "And what of it, if the ladder is cut away: it is a thing of lies, and the spirits never went there?" In return, some older men, more attached to the old ways and less receptive to the novelty of missionary teaching, suggested that these forms of understanding could perhaps coexist: "'It is very well for you to go to the Rangi (or Heaven), but leave us our old road to Reinga, and let us have something to hold on by, as we descend, or we shall break our necks over the precipice.'"[150]

But a willingness to allow both forms of belief—in the authority of Te Reinga and the promise of Christian Heaven—was not widely felt. Almost a month later, conflict erupted again, as a group of forty men, from an unspecified location and kin-group, visited and challenged Paerata. A hui (ritualized meeting) took place, and some of the visitors suggested that Paerata's property should be plundered because he had threatened the power of Te Reinga and the old ways. Paerata, an effective orator, then rose and spoke for two hours, recounting the journey in great detail. He reassured the hui that the path to Te Reinga and Te Reinga itself had not been disturbed, meaning that the "the road still lay straight" for those who believed in the old ways. But Paerata himself now believed that Te Reinga was an "absurdity" and confessed, "'There is another Hell which I am afraid of, the one which burns with fire and brimstone.'"[151]

Later missionaries, including William Colenso, Joseph Matthews, and William Wade, travelled to Te Reinga from 1839 and were more confident than Puckey in dismissing its power. But the hui at Kaitaia and Paerata's speech remind us that it was often those Māori who embraced Christianity—not missionaries themselves—who were the most potent and potentially authoritative critics of established cultural codes and social norms. Māori converts and evangelists were often more assertive and zealous in their rejection of the traditional order. When Colenso visited Te Reinga in March 1839, one of the young Māori Christians who traveled with him was keen to cut off "a piece of this very sacred root [aka]" for the missionary; it was only the strong winds that prevented him from attempting to do so. Colenso himself inspected Te Reinga closely from several vantage points and read scripture aloud to declaim his faith, but he was also fully cognizant of the site's tapu status.[152] These incidents are potent reminders that although the presence of missionaries precipitated cultural change, Māori were primary agents in the actual spread of Christianity, and that the growing authority of the Bible was dependent on the willingness of converts to openly challenge tikanga (rules, protocols) and ritenga (custom).[153]

In light of this argument, it is not surprising that it was possible to discern the beginnings of a shift in Māori deathways around the Bay of Islands from the mid-1820s, as those Māori families with some connection to missions began to reassess their established practices in light of their new affiliations. Even before Puckey's journey, there were significant indications that some Māori were making adjustments to their beliefs and practices around death. By 1832, it was clear that Māori connected to the Paihia station were increasingly willing to follow Christian burial practices: in some cases they were buried in locations close to their normal residences, while in others they were interred within the mission station's cemetery.[154] Some Māori who maintained links to missionary families at Paihia but never formally converted nevertheless returned to the mission when they knew that death was imminent and signaled that they preferred the rites of the missionaries.[155] More generally, from late 1832, around Paihia we can see in the journal of Henry Williams an extended set of debates over deathways. Even those who were resistant to missionary teaching were now drawn into such discussions.[156] On several occasions, disputes broke out about whether missionaries should bury Māori Christians or whether their families should take their deceased whanaunga (relatives) and maintain older practices. By 1835, it seems, Henry Williams and other cms missionaries were routinely winning such arguments, and the whānau (families) of the deceased ultimately recognized that Christian burial reflected the importance their kinfolk's connection to the missionaries.[157]

A clear example of this dynamic comes from Te Puna mission station. In June 1833 Witirua, the daughter of the Rangihoua rangatira Wharepoaka, died at Rangihoua pā. When John and Hannah King visited Wharepoaka, he told them "'You have brought her up, she belongs to you, it is for you to say how she shall be buried.'" Witirua had lived with the Kings for over ten years and had developed strong links to the family. John King and his son built a coffin and buried Witirua at Rangihoua inside a paling enclosure. Wharepoaka gave the Kings the authority to make this decision even though some Rangihoua Māori wished for her death to be handled "according to the custom of N.Z." King explained that these dissenters looked "upon burying in the ground a Chief or his Children as very degrading," yet Wharepoaka set aside these arguments of his people and instead prioritized the connection that both Witirua and he had to the mission. Moreover, he cemented these bonds further by giving over another daughter to live with the King family.[158] These were significant shifts that marked the clear beginnings of the Christianization of Māori life, a process that was certainly uneven in time and space, but which was beginning to gain ground in the Bay of Islands in the mid-1830s.

Māori Death Composed

At the same time as they were beginning to gain increased influence over Māori beliefs and practices in the Bay of Islands, evangelicals began to organize the ethnographic knowledge they had pieced together into coherent accounts of Māori deathways. The landmark text here was William Yate's *An Account of New Zealand* (1835). While his fellow missionaries were critical of this volume's use to raise money for "Mr Yate's church at Waimate," it was certainly the most coherent and composed text produced by any individual connected to the New Zealand mission. Yate wove together his letters, journals, notes, and correspondence with Bay of Islands Māori into a lucid, if occasionally hyperbolic, narrative. His extensive treatment of death began with a more positive assessment of Māori deathways than had been offered by any missionary: "In no country can greater respect be shown for the dead than in New Zealand."[159] Yate then sketched the ways in which the remains of the deceased were prepared and displayed.

> When a chief dies, the event is immediately announced by a long-continued fire of musketry; and those friends who are not within hearing are sent for by special messengers, and are expected immediately to attend. The eyes of the corpse are closed by the father, mother, sister, brother, or nearest relative present; and the body is covered with the choicest garments which

any of them possess. After the first day, it is beaten by the brother with fresh flax, gathered for the purpose; and this is done with the intention of driving away any thing evil that may still be lingering about him: the spirit is then sung out of the body to the realms above; or, as they say, they know not whether it may not be to the regions below. The legs of the dead body are then tied up, in such a position as to cause the knees nearly to touch the chin. The hair is very neatly dressed, and decorated with feathers; and the body is then placed in a box lined with blankets, and painted outside with red ochre and whiting: it is exposed to the view of all who wish to see it, and the most bitter weeping and wailing is continued, night and day, till the sun has three times risen and set upon the earth.[160]

Where Kendall's long 1815 narrative of Ruatara was rich with specific detail, here Yate was synthesizing his own observations and established missionary understandings into a flowing, generalized account of Māori deathways, which attested to the maturation of missionary ethnography and which was certainly designed to cement Yate's own position as an authoritative interpreter of the Māori world for his British audience.[161]

Yate's explanation of Māori death customs followed Kendall's critique of the physicality of Māori mourning practices.

All the immediate relatives and friends of the deceased, with the slaves, or other servants or dependants, if he possessed any, cut themselves most grievously, and present a frightful picture to a European eye. A piece of flint (made sacred on account of the blood which it has shed, and the purpose for which it has been used) is held between the third finger and the thumb; the depth to which it is to enter the skin appearing beyond the nails. The operation commences in the middle of the forehead; and the cut extends, in a curve, all down the face, on either side: the legs, arms, and chest are then most miserably scratched; and the breasts of the women, who cut themselves more extensively and deeper than the men, are sometimes wofully gashed. The noise made during the time of this self-inflicted torment is truly affecting, and gives you an idea of boisterous sorrow nowhere else to be found. The cry is most hideous; and as one discordant note mingles with another, the mind naturally reverts to that place of outer darkness, where there is nothing but "weeping and wailing, and gnashing of teeth."[162]

This narrative combined finely grained ethnographic information—detailing how the flint was gripped by mourners, as well as the location, contours, and qualities of the incisions made on the body—with a rhetoric that emphasized the excess of these mourning rites. The diction of the passage is powerful: the sound of the tangi is "most hideous," and bodies are "wofully gashed" and wounded "most grievously." It is also full of vivid intensifiers: torsos were "most miserably" cut, and female breasts—potent signifiers of both maternity and female sexuality for British observers—were incised "more extensively and deeper" than male bodies.[163] Yate deployed these rhetorical strategies to produce powerful images in the imagination of his British readers, scenes that were designed to produce both horror and empathy. But these sentiments were not simply to be directed to the suffering bodies of the heathen; rather, Yate's use of biblical allusion reminded his readers that these practices were directly connected to the fate of individual souls. Yate suggested that the sights and sounds of the tangi had the power to move the Christian—they were "truly affecting"—but for the pious believer these rites *naturally* invoked the "weeping and wailing, and gnashing of teeth" of the "outer darkness" mentioned in chapters 8, 22, and 25 of the gospel of Matthew. The "outer darkness" was, of course, Hell, a place of complete separation from God, where Thomas Haweis suggested the damned suffered the "most poignant anguish" in that "place of torment."[164]

The careful construction and polished nature of Yate's reflections on Māori deathways were quite different from earlier missionary writings. The letters and journals of a missionary like John King, who had a limited education and was not a confident writer, offered condensed, fragmentary, and often elliptical insights into death in the Māori communities. King's writing in the 1810s and 1820s—with its characteristic incomplete sentences and reliance on simple conjunctions—was not highly ordered. Yate's *Account*, on the other hand, was the product of a very capable writer: Yate was widely read, an excellent preacher, and an enthusiastic poet. His *Account* moved deftly between genres, offering a sophisticated mix of ethnographic description, catalogues of flora and fauna, and an account of the progress of the mission. The complexity and ambition of the text is hardly surprising: it was probably at least partially modeled on William Ellis's landmark *Polynesian Researches* (1829) and was designed to complement John Hartley's *Researches in Greece and the Levant*, the second edition of which had been produced by Yate's publisher, Seeley and Burnside, in 1833. At the *Account*'s heart, as Lydia Wevers has noted, was "the gradual transformation of the savage and barbarous New Zealanders" as a result of the labor of CMS missionaries, especially Yate himself.[165]

Deathways were a key signifier of this transformation. Yate's *Account* offered a clear contrast between what he framed as the hellish sounds and scenes of the tangi, and the good Christian deaths of converted natives. In recounting these good deaths, Yate was moving from the conventional ethnographic description of traditional manners and customs to offer an assessment of the mission's progress, documenting the ways in which the gospel elevated Māori moral and spiritual sentiment. Here, Yate drew on the didactic death narratives that were the staple of British evangelical periodical literature.[166] These accounts offered models of good deaths and attested to the power of evangelicals to bring the "heathen" at home closer to God. These conventions were easily extended to recount the deaths of native converts and spiritual enquirers in the colonies. Yate's *Account* deployed the "good death" tradition to demonstrate the progress of the mission, but to ensure that the advances made by the mission were entirely clear to British readers, he first offered a model of a "bad death."

He also recounted the death of Paru, a Ngāi Tāwake rangatira. Yate told his readers that Paru was "a man of a bold and daring spirit; savage in his disposition; and reckless of the consequences of any of his actions, either to himself or others." He did not heed missionary teaching, and he was reluctant to receive their medicine when he became ill: "He placed his whole confidence for his recovery in the superstitious rites of the priests, whose tapues and other observances and requirements, in the end, greatly hastened his death. He had heard many times of the truths of our holy religion; and had been entreated again and again, while in comparative health, to lay hold of the hope of everlasting life set before him in the Gospel; but he rejected every overture of mercy."[167] Paru's narrative concluded with Yate asking him about the fate of his soul. "The answer which I received from Paru to this important question was rather a lengthy one: they were the last words he ever spoke— the last earthly sounds he ever uttered, except the long, deep, hollow grown of death.—'I shall go to hell,' said he, with terrible emphasis, 'I shall go to hell. Wiro [Whiro, a malevolent atua who reigned in the underworld with Hinenui-te-pō] is there, and I shall be his companion for ever.' . . . Paru, to the very last, turned his back upon the only way of salvation."[168]

Conversely Yate offered Coleman Davis Aoheke as "an instance of a very different kind . . . the scene of the dying Christian, whose redeemed and sanctified spirit was borne through the portals of death, 'on angels' wings, to heaven' and who rejoiced in the prospect of eternal glory, which was, in a manner, revealed to him, even before he had done for ever with time!" Yate explained that Aoheke had been captured in war, but that his master in the Bay of Islands allowed him to reside at the Paihia station after the CMS made a payment to "redeem" him.[169] Aoheke exhibited an interest in Christianity, and Yate prompted him toward Christ.

> "Is it true," he one day asked me, "is it indeed true, that Christ is willing to save sinners; and that He is desirous of saving sinners?" My answer was—"Yes; he is able and willing to save to the uttermost all that come unto God by him." "Ah, ah!" said he, "it is good, it is good;—then I shall be saved! Jesus will not send my soul to hell. Ah, ah! my heart is light now: it was dark before, but now it is light: fear made my heart dark; and sin made me afraid—afraid of God; afraid of you; afraid of death; afraid of judgment. Oh, Mr. Yate! since I have thought at all, I have always been afraid."

After Aoheke became ill, he was worried about the spiritual state of his wife and children and requested that Yate baptize them. Aoheke was too weak to witness the service, but was relieved to hear of the baptism as he approached death.

> He died in a full persuasion that his sins were washed away in the blood of Jesus. No cloud seemed to overshadow his path to glory; and no thoughts of this world seemed to banish, for a moment, the thoughts which possessed his mind, of the world which is to come. Thus died Coleman Aoheke, redeemed by the servants of God from the slavery of an earthly master; and redeemed by God himself from the still more dreadful slavery of sin, the world and the devil.[170]

Yate offered Aoheke's death to British readers as clear evidence of the new light that the gospel was bringing to New Zealand. Working closely within received representations of Christian death in British print culture, Yate suggested that, ultimately, evangelical notions of the "good death" transcended place and culture. The assertiveness of Yate's *Account* was a long way from the fragmentary observations, fleeting analysis and spatial embeddedness that was the stock-in-trade of CMS letters and journals. Its confidence was also at odds with the limits and anxieties of those mundane daily forms of writing in which missionaries attempted to record Māori deathways, texts which revealed the difficulties of comprehending a radically different worldview and that recorded the weight of a native tradition that prevented the easy replication of British practices on the ground in northern New Zealand, far beyond the formal frontier of British sovereignty.

Conclusion

In this chapter I have made three key points. First, I have highlighted the divergences between Māori and missionary understandings of death. For the Anglican and Wesleyan families settled on mission stations, death was a painful reality of life, but they also understood it as a moment where the good Christian was united with God and reconnected with deceased family members. The pathway to Heaven was opened up, of course, because of Christ's own death: evangelicals understood his crucifixion as a sacrifice that atoned for humanity's sinfulness. Second, I have suggested that while missionaries were able to transplant their cosmological understanding of death to northern New Zealand with no significance alterations, their burial practices were significantly modified. Partly as a result of the small scale of mission settlements and their scattered distribution in the far north, missionaries initially conducted burials in their gardens and then, from the mid-1820s, in graveyards adjacent to mission chapels. In effect, this meant that children, European workers, and native Christians were buried in close proximity to missionary homes, a practice that reversed British trends, where there was a growing separation between the worlds of the living and the dead. Most important, I have demonstrated that this distinctive pattern reflected the missionaries' awareness of the importance of tapu and the strength of Māori deathways, as well as a real apprehension regarding the security of their burial sites.

My third argument was that for missionaries, deathways functioned as a vitally important window into Māori cosmology, ritual practice, and social order. From the outset of the mission, missionaries recorded their observations about local understandings of death, their burial traditions and mourning customs. Although Thomas Kendall had assembled some understanding of Māori deathways during the mission's first year, taken as a whole this body of ethnographic knowledge grew slowly and haphazardly until the mid-1830s. By that time, however, the missionaries were more confident in challenging Māori beliefs, including Te Reinga's special place in Māori cosmology. This confidence was fortified by the growing willingness of those Māori who were connected to the mission in various ways—as patrons, "native teachers," converts, or frequent visitors—to challenge established beliefs and the power of the old atua. I concluded by assessing the ways in which William Yate ordered and reshaped this knowledge as he compiled *An Account of New Zealand* for a British audience, producing a work that stressed the centrality of death in Māori worldviews and using the conventions of the "good death" to underscore the progress made by the mission in the1830s. Such ethnographic texts would come to have real political power in the imperial metropole in the 1830s, as a series of arguments over the vitality of Māori and their capacity to withstand "contact" with Europeans came to stand at the center of fierce debates over the desirability of formally colonizing New Zealand.

Six

THE POLITICS OF THE "ENFEEBLED" BODY

Even though it formally remained beyond the territorial reach of British authority, New Zealand was firmly entangled in the world of the empire by 1830. Explorers, naturalists, sealers, whalers, traders, and missionaries had all been active along the costs of Te Ika a Māui and Te Wai Pounamu. Their activities, their published narratives, handwritten reports, journals, letters, maps, and sketches had laced Māori and New Zealand into the empire. Māori themselves were also active participants within the empire. Many sought out the new foods, tools, and weapons that Europeans possessed; rangatira regularly visited Poihākena (Port Jackson, Sydney); some cultivated relationships with the governors of New South Wales, influential churchmen like Marsden, and even the king of England; and still others traveled widely, visiting the islands of the Pacific, India and Britain itself. But these various forms of mobility and the connections they engendered did not create a flat, fully integrated, and seamless imperial domain. While Māori still typically exercised control over such encounters on the ground in Te Ika a Māui, their ability to ultimately direct the long-term consequences of these relationships was heavily constrained by British commercial power and military capacity and the sheer scale of British society (when measured against te ao Māori).

By the 1830s, some Britons were increasingly concerned about the consequences of these engagements for Māori, against the backdrop of growing metropolitan interest in New Zealand's colonial potential. But the question of New Zealand was just one significant imperial issue, as intense debates over the objects of empire-building and a sequence of crises in colonial authority brought the empire into question. In December 1831 slaves went on strike and then rebelled in Jamaica. This uprising was brutally repressed, and widespread reprisals were targeted at both slaves and the Baptist missionaries, who were seen as destabilizing the plantation system. Three years later, the Sixth Frontier War broke out in the Cape Colony, intensifying settler antipathy to the Xhosa and providing an opportunity for the extension of the colony's frontier to "open up" more land for sheep farming.[1] In 1837 rebellion erupted in Lower and Upper Canada, as both French and British colonists unsuccessfully fought against the elite interests that dominated colonial government. As the decade closed, the East India Company went to war with the Qing empire, after Lin Zexu, the new imperial commissioner at Canton, had attempted to close down the company's lucrative but illegal trade in opium. At the same time, in an effort to secure the northwestern frontier of its Indian empire, the East India Company launched its disastrous war against the Afghans. These insurrections and wars were widely debated, as accounts produced by both colonial opinion makers and non-Western critics of British expansion circulated back to the center of the imperial system, and a staggering range of metropolitan editorial comments, newspaper reports, commercial magazines, missionary periodicals, and pamphlets dissected the state of the empire.

Within this domestic political landscape saturated by signs of empire, New Zealand emerged as an important site of concern and contestation in the 1830s. In the years following the foundation of the CMS, the society's agents produced a variegated archive that described Māori social organization. Elements of this archive began to appear in metropolitan print culture from 1815, when missionary presses began to compose and circulate carefully crafted accounts of missionary endeavors in New Zealand. The steady trickle of news and information from New Zealand back to the United Kingdom became a regular flow in the mid-1820s, as the establishment of Wesleyan mission in 1823, the expansion of CMS activity beyond the Bay of Islands to Muriwhenua, Thames-Hauraki, the Bay of Plenty, and East Cape, and the intensification of the connections between New South Wales and New Zealand created new sources of knowledge, thickening the imperial knowledge store about New Zealand's geography, its resources, Māori leaders, and their "tribes." By the mid-1830s, both New Zealand and Māori were increasingly "known" in the metropole. Maps inscribed the outlines of New Zealand into the archives of imperial geography with increasing detail and confidence.[2] Engravings in travel narratives and popular evangelical magazines introduced British readers to distant places like Whangaroa, Kerikeri, and Waimate.[3] And leaders like Waikato, Tītore, Tuai, and Hongi Hika were key figures in the detailed evangelical publications that narrated the dramatic developments on distant mission stations.[4] At the same time, a new body of colonial promotional literature, which laced together heavily edited reportage from the New Zealand frontier with schemes for colonization, suggested that New Zealand was an ideal, perhaps even the very best, field for large-scale settlement by Britons and the investment of British capital.[5]

James Belich has emphasized the political significance of the narratives circulating in Britain, arguing that the metropolitan government was "increasingly inundated by reports" about New Zealand from 1830, reaching "a crescendo in 1837–8." These reports, he argues, framed contact in New Zealand as a "fatal impact," with Māori society on the brink of collapse because of disease, alcohol, intertribal conflict, and the malignant cultural influence of escaped convicts, whalers, and traders. This image of an indigenous society in a state of crisis induced through contact with Europeans was pivotal in prompting British intervention in 1840. Belich suggested that although the Colonial Office was by its very nature a skeptical and cautious institution, it was in effect a "blind giant," reliant on information produced on the frontier to guide its policy-making decisions.[6] In Belich's view, the sheer volume of these accounts of frontier lawlessness convinced the British government that it was, in the words of the British prime minister Lord Melbourne, a "fatal necessity" to formally colonize New Zealand.[7]

While Belich has not developed this argument at length, he was undoubtedly correct in emphasizing the power that the sheer volume of reports, pamphlets, and narratives from the southern Pacific exercised in Britain and in highlighting the importance of their framing of cross-cultural contact as a "fatal impact." Here I build on Belich's suggestive insights by explicating the nature of these proliferating accounts of cross-cultural contact, these thickening ribbons of text that linked the islands and people of New Zealand to Britain.[8] I reconstruct the knowledge-production networks that produced and disseminated these narratives, by mapping the key points of conflict and analytical registers that shaped debates over New Zealand's place within the empire. I offer a reading of representations of the physical and moral consequences that Māori experienced because of their encounters with Europeans, embedding my assessment of these representations in political debates and processes that encompassed the New Zealand frontier, the colonial administration in New South Wales, and key institutions (the Colonial Office, the House of Commons, and House of Lords) and organizations (the New Zealand Company and the Church Missionary Society) within Britain itself.

This close attention to both the imperial structures and metropolitan cultural currents that framed competing understandings of Māori culture and New Zealand's place within the empire sets the analysis that follows apart from recent New Zealand historiography. By recovering the ways in which the Māori body threaded through the larger debates over empire, trade, and cultural difference within the empire in the 1830s, this chapter firmly reconnects New Zealand's history with both the broader development of the empire and British politics of bodily reform. What follows then is offered as a counterpoint to both narratives that define the 1830s as a prelude to the main action of a national story and to analyses that reduce New Zealand's place within the empire during the 1830s to readings of the debates that swirled around Colonial Office records.[9] In fashioning the arguments that are developed below, I have drawn significant inspiration from recent work by feminist scholars who have opened up new perspectives in diplomatic history, such as Kristin Hoganson and Emily S. Rosenberg, by emphasizing the importance of culture in shaping policy-making, foregrounding the role of cross-cultural representation, the power of rhetoric and metaphor, and gender not just as "contexts" but as drivers of international conflict and imperial interventions.[10] Following the lead of this work, this chapter examines the anxieties over empire-building that fed the intense exchanges over New Zealand in the 1830s, mapping the recurrent concerns as well as lines of conflict within the debates about the desirability of colonizing New Zealand between competing interest groups in Britain, New South Wales, and on the frontier itself.

Central to my analysis are the types of texts that Thomas Laqueur identified as "humanitarian narratives," narratives that focused on the suffering of another's body in order to engender compassion and to urge ameliorative action. These narratives documented suffering in close detail to draw a direct causal link between an evil, the victim, and a benefactor. This form of narration, Laqueur argued, was central in enabling the various humanitarian groups that espoused social reform from the end of the eighteenth century, as well as playing an important role in reshaping understandings of both the human condition and the nature of politics in the wake of the Enlightenment.

I trace the cultural and political significance of these accounts of pain by embedding them within the culture of sensibility and the new power attached to "sympathy," an emotion that Stuart Tave identified as "an essential force" in shaping cultural production and political life in the late eighteenth and early nineteenth centuries.[11] As I argue, this mode of narrating pain, illness and death was increasingly deployed as a way of representing Māori during the 1820s and 1830s, and the circulation of images of the physical suffering inflicted by Europeans upon Māori produced a broad consensus among British observers that Māori communities were enfeebled and powerless. I also examine the development of the competing discourses of "protection" that drew on both humanitarian narratives and debates over depopulation as their evidentiary basis. In examining the elaboration of a sequence of plans for the extension of British sovereignty and colonial governance over New Zealand from 1837, I end by highlighting the role of the discourse on "protection" in convincing the Colonial Office of the need for intervention and ultimately in providing the legitimating basis of colonization.

Humanitarian Narratives

In an influential 1989 essay, Thomas Laqueur sketched the lineaments of a distinctive new form of narration that he identified as a product of the Enlightenment. From the confluence of the empirical revolution of the seventeenth century, the rise of scientific medicine during the eighteenth century, and the emergence of humanitarianism, a new way of understanding pain and suffering emerged. Whereas pain had previously been seen as an essential element of the human condition, from the middle of the eighteenth century humanitarians worked to alleviate pain and suffering where possible—especially when that bodily experience was produced or inflicted by various "social evils" (ranging from alcohol to the excesses of the industrial system) or unjust laws. To document the causes, nature, and effects of these "social evils," advocates of reform recorded physical distress with a newfound specificity, providing extensive and vivid detail to enable their readers to visualize the plight of the narrative's subject.[12] Whether they took the form of published social enquiries, medical records, obituaries, or even novels, humanitarian narratives were explicitly political texts. Their finely grained accounts of the reality of pain and misery were central in critiquing moral laxity, directing social reform, and establishing the need for state intervention.[13]

Laqueur's essay had a firm metropolitan focus, framing these narratives as an important force in the reshaping of the culture of moral feeling within the United Kingdom itself. He does note the role of these narratives in directing reform efforts toward marginalized groups within Britain (such as paupers, young children, and miners), as well as suggesting that this form of narration was closely related to abolitionism. There is no doubt, however, that this form of narration was a powerful tool within the broader context of the empire as well, where economic systems and political structures operated within even more complex cultural landscapes marked by multiple forms of cultural difference. Humanitarian narratives became increasingly important during the 1820s and 1830s, as evangelicals and humanitarians were critical of what they saw as the excesses of settler colonialism and used these textual conventions to record indigenous suffering and to argue for the remaking of the empire into a progressive moral and spiritual enterprise. Within this context, the wounds inflicted on individual "natives"—whether the Xhosa notable Hintsa, who was killed by British soldiers while in custody in 1835, or on the Ngāi Tahu chief Te Maiharanui, who was kidnapped and murdered in New Zealand, or Ngāti Ruanui's Oaoiti, who was tortured— were upheld as potent emblems of the evil that flourished where the empire lacked a sound moral and spiritual basis.

Any sustained reading of missionary texts from New Zealand reveals a range of texts that fit into this form of narration highlighted by Laqueur. One of the most striking examples comes from the journal of the Wesleyan missionary John Hobbs, who was stationed at Whangaroa in the mid-1820s. In his diary entry for 19 January 1824, he noted,

> This evening called to witness an instance of barbarity and cruelty such as I never before beheld. In the evening we went over to the village to see a Cook Ke [kuki: slave] whom we had been informed was nearly murdered by her cruel and unfeeling master. On our arrival made inquiry and were surprised to see a little girl sitting wrapped in her garment apparently unconcerned and comfortable, whom they informed us was the person hurt. On approaching nearer were struck with horror to behold a dreadful wound upon the right hand which had caused the forefinger to drop down in the palm of the hand and the end of the knuckle bone was entirely bare, the thumb also nearly cut off. We had no sooner perceived this than we discovered another large wound stretching from the side of the face behind the ear about three inches long, and being cut in an oblique manner the underside dropped out downwards, forming a cut about two inches wide and 7/8 of an inch deep leaving the jawbone in sight which stopped the hatchett with which the wounds were inflicted.

They told us there was another in the back, but this was not more than two inches long, half an inch wide and not very deep. In this mangled condition this monster of iniquity left her to suffer the pains which are consequent upon so desperate an outrage, I suppose not caring whether she would live or die. Thus does a New Zealander tyrannise over the children of those whom they wantonly murder and eat. This child was brought from the East Cape as a slave taken in war. The cause of this conduct was that she saw him (committing adultery) and spoke of it, which made him feel thus vile and mad.[14]

Hobbs's diary entry clearly fits within of Laqueur's typology of humanitarian narratives. First, these texts were characterized by their very careful rendering of physical suffering, where the extent and severity of wounds, the physical effects of fevers and diseases, and the physical sensation of pain are recounted through rich detail, often with a very strong evocation of the sensory experience of those of who witnessed the suffering: the sounds, smells, and, most of all, the sights that communicated pain. Here, the wounds inflicted on the kuki are recounted with considerable specificity: the peculiar angle of the forefinger, the exposed bone, the severed thumb, the large wound from behind the ear running parallel to the jawbone, as well as an unseen wound on her back. The extent of these wounds are itemized carefully: their width, depth, and length are all described with precision, allowing both the author and any reader of this account to conjure up a detailed image of the extent and gravity of these injuries. This concern with the precise and accurate rendering of the trauma—what Laqueur terms the "reality effect"—reflected evangelicalism's profoundly empirical orientation.[15] David Bebbington has noted that the British evangelical tradition was heavily influenced by the Scottish "common sense" philosophy of Thomas Reid and Dugald Stewart and, as such, placed great emphasis on observation, experience and empiricism.[16]

This empiricism was, in turn, closely related to the second feature of post-Enlightenment culture that shaped humanitarian narratives and their reception: the culture of sensibility. Made manifest in literature, in new social sites (like the coffeehouse), and in the political domain, the culture of sensibility was defined by the new stress it placed on feeling, openness, and the importance of refined manners, a set of values that which reshaped British understandings of masculinity in particular.[17] Although this reordering of emotional codes and social norms was contested by some who feared that emotional expressiveness was effeminizing, the growing concern with the evils of social distress and pain enabled critiques of forms of abuse and cruelty that had previously been tolerated and generated new concern for suffering marginal social groups.[18]

Central to a culture of sensibility was "sympathy," the ability to identify with fellow humans, which Edmund Burke described as "a sort of substitution, by which we are put into the place of another man."[19] We can see this in Hobbs's diary, where his detailed itemization of the bodily suffering of the kuki not only reflected the Enlightenment tendency to use visualization as a way of conceiving another's pain, but was also shaped to solicit sympathy from the reader. [20] Hobbs's moral indictment of the evils of slavery—which emphasized the vulnerability of the kuki because of her age and gender, as well as the deep immorality of her violent and adulterous master—had power because its detailed reportage of the kuki's wounds reinforced his status as an eyewitness and the resulting veracity of the image that his text could fashion in the reader's mind. Adam Smith in his *The Theory of Moral Sentiments* (1759), explained the importance of witnessing bodily suffering, whether through reading a narrative or being an eyewitness: "By the imagination we place ourselves in his situation, we conceive ourselves enduring all the same torments, we enter as it were into his body, and become in some measure the same person with him."[21] For Smith, as James Chandler has observed, "the fundamental virtue to be refined or 'polished' in commercial society . . . is a capacity for putting ourselves in the place or 'case' of another"—a virtue that was quickly called upon when that "other" was suffering.[22]

Hobbs was, of course, the product of an evangelical tradition that had been very receptive to the culture of sensibility. The grand dame of British evangelicalism, Hannah More, celebrated "Sweet Sensibility" in a 1782 poem, stressing the value of true feeling when it was given shape and direction by religious commitment.[23] While the culture of sensibility in some contexts produced an introspective "collective cathartic weeping," "sympathy" also directed emotions and actions outward from the self, toward what Hannah More termed "principle" or "the virtue of *action*."[24] Thus, humanitarian narratives such as Hobbs's spoke to an evangelical audience already receptive to evocations of suffering and appeals to their finely tuned sense of sympathy. Missionaries and their supporters were accustomed to a specifically evangelical version of the heroic "man of feeling" identified by Karen Halttunen. Halttunen argues that this ideal type was defined by his "tender-hearted susceptibility to the torments of others" and demonstrated his virtue through his efforts to ameliorate the suffering of others.[25] By the time Hobbs was writing, evangelical missionaries' understanding of their role as reformers was defined by an interweaving of empiricism and emotion, reason and sentiment. This very particular cultural sensibility, in turn, powerfully shaped the ways in which they understood and represented the communities they evangelized.[26]

While it is possible to identify a range of missionary texts that fit key elements of this form of narration, I would not suggest that humanitarian narratives dominated the archives produced by Protestant missionaries in New Zealand.[27] My reading of missionary manuscripts suggests that it is in fact far from the case. Short notes about the weather and the daily routines of preaching, farm work, and correspondence, terse comments about food stocks, complaints about the absence or poor quality of paper, fabrics, or building materials, elliptical comments about happenings at the nearby pā, or days of silence were the stock-in-trade of missionary archives. Nor was the humanitarian narrative's careful mix of empiricism and emotion the dominant register of missionary writing; frustration, fear, anxiety, and boredom were actually more common. But on occasions when missionaries were moved by witnessing a local practice they found particularly offensive or had identified as a real obstacle to Christianization, or when they were operating within a context of social conflict—whether warfare between or violence within kin-groups—they did compose narratives that accord with the features identified by Laqueur.

Therefore, while curt journal entries focused on the rhythms of mission life may be more representative of the overall tenor of missionary sources, "humanitarian narratives" deserve particular attention because these discursive forms exercised considerable cultural and, within a political context charged by "reform" and abolition, political power. We can usefully think of missionary letters, journals, and reports as "mobile inscriptions" that were designed to be carried by ship from the Bay of Islands to Samuel Marsden in New South Wales or to the Church Missionary Society in London in order to account for evangelization and its progress. But as Samuel Marsden and the CMS itself received these texts, they were aware that vivid accounts of Māori suffering or, conversely, missionary successes could be powerful agents for religious and political mobilization within Britain itself, encouraging both financial support for the mission and calls to curb the excesses of imperial power.[28]

Humanitarian Narratives in the Metropole

It was because of their ability to move people that humanitarian narratives were significantly overrepresented in the accounts of Māori society circulating within Britain.[29] Narratives of this type were widely disseminated in

Britain by various evangelical and missionary periodicals, particularly the multidenominational *Missionary Register* in the case of the CMS and *Missionary Notices* in the case of the WMS. These substantial monthly periodicals were read by those who subscribed to missionary societies, as well as by a moderate-sized readership of evangelicals and middle-class readers interested in the empire. But evangelical organizations were also committed to disseminating accounts of the heathen to the broadest possible audience, including the urban, working-class members of their congregations. To reach these audiences, they produced small, accessible pamphlets that were either inexpensive or free.

From 1816, for example, the Church Missionary Society published its cheap *Missionary Papers* four times a year; these four-page publications, designed as tools for teaching, cost one shilling per one hundred copies or just a single penny for an individual text.

New Zealand featured prominently in this series, with accounts of the rangatira Hongi and Tuai, Māori material culture, and the Kerikeri mission station being published between 1816 and 1830.[30] Another account relating to New Zealand, a biography of "Mowhee" or Māui, was published in midsummer 1818. As a young boy, Māui was fascinated by the stories of Tuki Tahua and Ngāhuruhuru's travels to Norfolk Island. In 1806, at the age of nine or ten, Māui left his kinfolk in the southern Bay of Islands, traveling to Norfolk Island on a whaler.[31] While on Norfolk Island, he was cared for by the local harbormaster, John Drummond, who enrolled Māui in a day school, where he learned English, reading, writing, and arithmetic.[32] The Drummonds shifted to Liverpool, near Port Jackson, and after working for a short time as a shepherd, Māui settled with Samuel Marsden at nearby Parramatta. In Parramatta, he lived alongside other high-ranking Māori from Te Tai Tokerau (the far north of Te Ika a Māui), and he continued his studies under the supervision of Thomas Kendall, leading up to his baptism, in 1813: this made Māui the first Māori Christian convert, some twelve years before the first conversion in New Zealand with the baptism of Christian Rangi in September 1825.[33] In late 1814 he sailed back to the Bay of Islands with Marsden on the voyage that established the first CMS mission at Rangihoua. After functioning as Marsden's key translator, he stayed in the Bay of Islands for a brief time only, leaving around July 1815 to sail to London.[34]

The *Missionary Paper*'s narrative recounted these details of Māui's early life in some detail, before presenting an account of his time in London and his painful death in December 1816. Basil Woodd, the renowned evangelical preacher and a leading supporter of the CMS from his pastorate in Marylebone, was both the "superintendent" of Māui while he lived in London and the author of the *Missionary Paper*'s biography of the Māori traveler. Woodd's narrative stressed the depth of Māui's continued engagement with British education and evangelical Christianity in London, recording his studies in the day school run by "Mr. Hazard" and his commitment to Christianity. Woodd suggested that the combination of Māui's schooling in useful knowledge, his devotion to scripture, and his desire to immerse himself in evangelical institutions had great effect. He "discovered great tenderness and humility, an ardent thirst for all useful knowledge, a perfect compliance with the advice of his instructors, and a devout ambition to qualify himself to be useful in his own country."[35] In short, Woodd suggested that Māui was remade as civilized, educated, and disciplined. Woodd underscored both Māui's intellectual ability, highlighting Māui's developing abilities as a draughtsman, his study of Euclidean geometry, and his moral seriousness, which was evident in the contrast between his enthusiasm for Sunday school and his lack of interest in public spectacles, like the Lord Mayor of London's procession. Woodd recounted Māui's desire to help the effort of Christianizing Māori and emphasized his thorough rejection of heathenism. When Māui encountered a "collection of Indian Idols," Wood recalled, he declared, "'Oh! What a blessing it is to be delivered from these vanities, to serve the living and true God!'"[36]

This conversion narrative heightened the impact of the final page and a half of the narrative, which related Māui's death in detail. His physical decline started with the onset of winter, and as the "damp and foggy weather of November greatly tried his constitution," he was suddenly afflicted with consumption. After a brief recovery, he again struggled with severe illness, an abrupt downturn in his health that Woodd dramatically linked to "mysterious Providence": *Dust thou art, and unto dust shalt thou return!*" Terrible pains in his head and back afflicted Māui; then his face became swollen, and he suffered from the ill effects of dysentery. Woodd fashioned a vivid account of the approach of death. He recorded that visiting Māui was difficult as his room was, "from his disorder, offensive in the extreme." Māui succumbed, finally, to a "malignant putrid fever: his blood oozing from every pore, and his countenance covered with purple spots." Woodd reassured his readers that Māui met his death as a good Christian, recognizing his status as a sinner and trusting in the grace of God. Woodd hoped that Māui's life and death might be a meaningful moment in the development of the mission: "Mowhee is dead: but his work is not yet done. Let his Grave address his Countrymen. Who can tell, but they may yet hear and believe!"[37] Māui's grave addressed at least one Englishman; in October 1818, the blacksmith James Kemp, writing from Wymondham in Norfolk, offered his services to the CMS, emphasizing that his desire to serve in New Zealand was strong "since I read the account of the Death of Mowhee, a native of New Zealand."[38]

This account of Māui's death not only drew at least one new missionary to the field, but it also marks an important rupture in the ways in which Europeans represented Māori. In the wake of Cook, British texts had primarily defined Māori by their masculinity—in fact, a "hard" hypermasculinity defined by martiality and the resolute nobility of Māori chiefs, a nobility forged in the cut and thrust of warfare and oratory.[39] More sensationally, in the British imagination, Māori masculinity had been defined by tā moko (tattooing), the taking of heads as trophies, and cannibalism: all of these practices exhibited a kind of emotional and physical excess that echoed Thomas Kendall's discussions of Māori mourning practices. Now, in the mid-1810s, British evangelical publications offered a new model of Māori masculinity: the educated, civilized Māui who embodied the seriousness of a remade man. The engraved portrait that accompanied Woodd's narrative emphasized Māui's status as transformed man. Produced by the drawing master and master engraver William Austin (1721–1820), Māui's portrait represented him as well-groomed, serious, and clothed in respectable dress: his hair is neatly cut, and he wears a good quality double-breasted coat and a neat shirt and tie, fastened close at his throat. The refined Māui stood in direct contrast to earlier visual representations of Māori culture, which focused on moko, weapons, haka, and the semi-naked warrior, as well as the sensational images of heathen gods and barbaric rites that frequently graced the cover of *Missionary Papers*.

But in the figure of Māui a double shift occurred. Not only did the narration of Māui's conversion serve as a counterpoint to the warrior-chief model, but the account of his death suggested that Māori were fragile, vulnerable to illness, and frail. Over the coming two decades, accounts of dying Māori became increasingly common in metropolitan publications and shaped Euroamerican understandings of Māori in general.[40] Many narratives documented the impact of epidemic diseases in New Zealand, highlighting the effects of consumption on Māori and emphasizing the vulnerability of those Māori who traveled beyond New Zealand's shores. While such accounts of dying "natives" reflected one of the very real consequences of cross-cultural engagement for Māori, they also reflected the particular power of narratives of suffering that culminated in death.[41] Accounts of death had particular power, as Laqueur notes: "The corpse, more so even than the vivified flesh, enabled the imagination to penetrate the life of the other."[42] Moreover, not only did death grip the reader's imagination, but the dead subject in many ways was easier to fashion into a narrative; not only was there no possibility for the dead to contest the accuracy of the account, but also it is much easier to shape a life story that had a definitive ending that could be invested with real social meaning.

A striking counterpoint to the exemplary moral seriousness of Māui was the Ngāre Raumati rangatira Tuai, whose life and death was recounted in the midsummer 1826 issue of *Missionary Papers*. Tuai had lived with Marsden in Parramatta in 1813 and later, in 1817, traveled to England with Titere.[43] Both young travellers became ill, and the CMS relocated them to Shropshire for the benefit of their health. Their rural retreat did not last long, however, because in the wake of Māui's death, the CMS was convinced that that wellbeing of the rangatira was "much endangered by the climate of this country," a danger which offset the chief's deep interest in observing all aspects of British culture.[44] The rest of the narrative focused on Tuai's turn away from the deep interest in education and Christianity he had exhibited in England and his prominence in the wars of the 1820s.[45] While the account quoted George Clarke's observation that "Tooi's eyes sparkled at the sound of the names of Mortimer, Pratt, and Bickersteth," it ended by stressing his apostasy. His tribe was in tatters as a result of war and was powerless as its leader lay ill. His tribesmates tried to avert his death by sacrificing a slave, then killed four more after his death. The engraving of Tuai in the *Missionary Papers* stressed his retreat from Christianity and his return to "country ways." In marked contrast to the image of the remade Māui, Tuai's hair was long and dressed with feathers, he wore a korowai (cloak), and he appears as a quintessential warrior, with a mere tucked into his belt and a taiaha (staff-like weapon) grasped firmly in his right hand.

Māui and Tuai were joined by many other ill and dead Māori in the archive of British print culture in the 1820s and early 1830s. Representations of Māori in metropolitan periodicals placed heavy emphasis on bodily suffering and death, particularly when it arose from the complex cluster of interhapū conflicts and long-distance taua (war expeditions) that were reshaping New Zealand's political demography. The complexities of these campaigns, displacements, and migrations were far from clear for many missionaries in Te Ika a Māui itself, and the specificities of these dynamics were of limited interest to those based in Britain, who instead read these conflicts as markers of the innate "character" of Māori. In such narratives, cannibalism was the most potent signifier of native savagery. This reading was at odds with that developed by Samuel Marsden, who had clearly grasped by 1819 that the practice of eating defeated enemies was a way of achieving utu (revenge, balance) as well as a mechanism for absorbing their mana.[46] More broadly, some missionaries, especially Octavius Hadfield, understood such conflicts as being governed by "established rules" and saw in them the operation of indigenous understandings of justice and political organization, but metropolitan evangelical journals conveyed missionary reportage which offered an image of political instability and cultural excess, replete with vivid images of body-covered battlefields, masses of enslaved prisoners, baskets of human flesh, and cannibal feasts.[47] Here, the physical suffering of the heathen was seen as the product of evils embedded within Māori society; social practices such as slavery, whakamomori (suicide), the execution of slaves, the taking of heads as trophies, warmaking, and cannibalism were read as emblematic of the moral corruption of "natural man" and evidence of Satan's hold on Māori.[48] These narratives were a rallying cry for missionary work. In producing a Hobbesian view of "native" life as brutal and short, periodicals like the *Missionary Register*, *Missionary Papers*, and *Church Missionary Record* stressed the great distance between these unconverted communities and the social norms and moral codes cherished by their evangelical and "civilized" readers.

Even though these texts were produced by evangelical organizations that argued that Māori were God's children and, as such, were capable of being saved in the same manner as Britons, metropolitan missionary publications tended to produce the cultural differences that were seen to separate the evangelized from the evangelizers. As Karen Halttunen suggests, "Although spectatorial sympathy claimed to demolish social distance, it actually rested on social distance," a distance produced both by accessing the suffering through the intermediary of a written text and by the social distance of the imagined middle-class reader.[49] The cultural gaps produced by these narratives were not only central in consolidating the "rule of difference" within the empire, but also carried a very specific theological weight. Within a specifically evangelical context, the emphasis on difference was important in that it affirmed the doctrine of means. As it was most fully articulated by William Carey, the doctrine of means stressed the need for Christians to exercise their agency to bring non-Europeans the gospel and to bring them to Christ.[50] This doctrine was simultaneously an affirmation of a universalist vision—where salvation was open to all humanity—and a framework for understanding evangelization that emphasized the role of missionary while downplaying the agency of the heathen. This theological vision not only energized the desire of British evangelicals to extend their mission to people like Māori, but also encouraged them to believe that they had a responsibility both to reform non-Christian societies and, when those societies were threatened by outside forces, to protect them.

The Problem of the Frontier

During the 1830s, another notable shift occurred in British representations of Māori. Whereas the "humanitarian narratives" that circulated within the empire in the 1810s and 1820s focused on the suffering produced by "social evils" within Māori society itself, a new emphasis was placed on the physical suffering and moral ill-effects that came from *outside* Māori society, from contact with Europeans. The supposed immorality of Europeans in the Pacific had, of course, been a long-articulated concern of Samuel Marsden, but in the 1830s humanitarian narratives became more widely used by evangelicals and humanitarians in their critiques of the immorality of the British imperial system. Within a metropolitan context charged by the politics of "Reform" and a cultural climate reshaped by the power of abolition, narratives documenting indigenous suffering carried new political weight.

Samuel Marsden's detailed, if rather scrambled account of the *Elizabeth* affair was an important impetus to the appointment of Busby as the British resident in the Bay of Islands in 1832, even though the events he narrated took place in Te Wai Pounamu and the south of Te Ika a Māui. Captain John Stewart of the brig *Elizabeth* entered into an arrangement with the Ngāti Toa rangatira Te Rauparaha and Te Hiko, which would allow Ngāti Toa to avenge the killing of Te Hiko's father, Te Peehi Kupe, at Kaiapoi during Ngāti Toa's raid into the *rohe* (domain) of Ngāi Tahu in early 1830. In return for a cargo of muka (prepared flax), Stewart agreed to convey a large taua of Ngāti Toa warriors to Horomaka (Banks Peninsula). With the Ngāti Toa warriors hidden below decks, Te Maiharanui was lured aboard to discuss trading flax for a consignment of muskets and gunpowder. After he went below decks, Te Maiharanui was captured and constrained, allowing Te Rauparaha to taunt him. The Ngāi Tahu rangatira's daughter, Ngā Roimata, and wife, Te Whē, were also lured aboard and caught. Then, at night, Stewart and an armed crew from the *Elizabeth* conveyed the Ngāti Toa taua ashore, and Te Rauparaha's men raided and burned the Ngāi Tahu settlement of Takapuneke before launching subsequent raids on other settlements on Banks Peninsula. Many Ngāi Tahu were captured and enslaved, while many more were killed (perhaps up to three hundred). As the *Elizabeth* sailed back to Kapiti to collect Stewart's payment,

Te Maiharanui and Te Whē killed Ngā Roimata to prevent her being used as a hostage by Ngāti Toa. Once the *Elizabeth* arrived in Kapiti, Te Maiharanui and Te Whē were taken ashore to witness Ngāti Toa consume the "baskets of flesh" gathered at Takapuneke. After Te Rauparaha finally delivered the promised muka, Stewart turned over Te Whē and Te Maiharanui to Ngāti Toa, and they were conveyed to Waitohu, where they were tortured and killed, allowing the widows of Te Peehi and other high-ranking Ngāti Toa warriors to drink their blood, marking the extraction of utu (balance, revenge) for Te Peehi Kupe's death at Kaiapoi.[51]

Stewart's entanglement in conflicts between Māori caused widespread concern, for both Europeans and Māori. Although Bay of Islands Māori had few connections to the complex rivalries and indemnities that interlaced the history of Ngāti Toa and Ngāi Tahu in this period, they expressed a deep concern over the impact that the *Elizabeth* affair might have on cross-cultural trade and worried that Stewart's direct involvement in resolving *take* (the causes of war) set a dangerous precedent. As a result, Wharepoaka of Rangihoua traveled to Sydney to convey the concerns of the northern chiefs directly to Governor Darling.[52] But the protestations of Wharepoaka and the testimony of two of Te Maiharanui's kin, Pere and Ahu, had less impact than the power of the written word within an imperial system that valorized the archive and which was finely attuned to narratives that recounted human suffering. From Parramatta, Marsden drafted a letter to Governor Darling expressing the anxieties of the northern chiefs and underscored both his own concerns and the destabilizing effect of European shipping on Māori society. Marsden's letter to Darling, a letter which significantly shaped British understandings of New Zealand through the 1830s, was prefaced by an insistence that the *Elizabeth* affair had created a "great anxiety in the minds of the natives in general, and they look for redress and protection to the British Government."

At the heart of Marsden's letter, however, was the cruelty inflicted on Ngāi Tahu and the physical suffering of Te Maiharanui. Marsden recorded that once Te Maiharanui had gone below decks of the *Elizabeth*, he "was laid hold on, and his hands were tied fast; at the same time, a hook with a cord to it was struck through the skin of his throat under the side of his jaw, and the line fastened to some part of the cabin; in this state of torture he was kept for some days until the vessel arrived at Kappetee."[53] What is striking about Marsden's account when it is read the against the depositions collected in Sydney— which were gathered from Pere as well as from William Brown (crewman on the *Elizabeth*), John Swan (the *Elizabeth*'s carpenter), and Joseph Barrow

Montefiore (the influential Sydney merchant)—is the very specificity of its account of physical suffering and the powerful image of the Ngāi Tahu chief in irons and restrained by a cord threaded through his throat.[54]

The failure of the government of New South Wales to effect a prosecution of Captain John Stewart or the *Elizabeth*'s mate, Clementson, elicited considerable discussion and anxiety in Britain. Viscount Goderich, secretary of state for war and the colonies, wrote to Darling in January 1831, clearly setting out the moral implications of the *Elizabeth* affair. Goderich articulated a pessimistic vision for the future of Māori in light of his reading of the character of the convicts of the Australian colonies and of British sailors.

> It is impossible to read, without shame and indignation, the details which these documents disclose. The unfortunate natives of New Zealand, unless some decisive measure of prevention be adopted, will, I fear, be shortly added to the number of those barbarous tribes, who, in different parts of the Globe, have fallen a sacrifice to their intercourse with civilised men, who bear and disgrace the name of Christians. When for mercenary purposes, the native of Europe, minister to the passions by which the savages are inflamed against each other, and introduce them to the knowledge of depraved acts and licentious gratifications of the most debased inhabitants of our great cities, the inevitable consequence is, a rapid decline of population preceded by every variety of suffering. Considering what is the character of a large part of the population of New South Wales and Van Diemens Land; what opportunities of settling themselves in New Zealand are afforded them by the extensive intercourse which has recently been established, adverting also to the conduct which has been pursued in these Islands by the Masters and crews of British vessels . . . I cannot contemplate the too probable results without the deepest anxiety. There can be no more sacred duty than that of using every possible method to rescue the natives of the extensive islands from the further evils which impend over them, and to deliver our own country from the disgrace and crime of having either occasioned or tolerated such enormities.[55]

These anxieties, brought to a head by the *Elizabeth*, convinced Goderich that Māori were in need of "protection" and that some form of British intervention was necessary to protect Māori interests.

The nature of that intervention, however, was constrained by international law and a succession of rulings that clearly defined New Zealand's status in the eyes of the British Crown. British claims to sovereignty over

New Zealand had been consistently repudiated for six decades after Cook claimed for Britain the North Island in November 1769 and the South Island in January 1770. Most notably, in 1817 New Zealand, along with Tahiti and Honduras, was formally recognized by Parliament as being "not within His Majesty's Dominions."[56] This position was reaffirmed in Commissioner Bigge's report of 1823, which recognized the existence of indigenous hereditary rulers who exercised authority "to which known limits are assigned" and affirmed that under British law, "New Zealand was a place not within the dominions of His Majesty."[57] Shortly before the *Elizabeth* sailed from England, this understanding was underscored in a minute, drafted by James Stephen of the Colonial Office, that clearly identified Māori as the "owners & sovereigns of the soil."[58]

James Busby, Independence, and "Protection"

The Colonial Office decided that the best solution would be the appointment of a British Resident in the Bay of Islands. James Busby, a viticulturist and a minor state functionary in New South Wales who made his reputation through his informative reports to the Colonial Office on colonial affairs, was appointed to promote commerce and oversee the activities of British subjects in New Zealand. Busby's appointment was primarily the product of the Colonial Office's concerns for both Māori welfare and British commerce in the wake of the *Elizabeth* affair, but it was also partially a response to the "King's Letter." In October 1831 British missionaries, traders, and many leading Bay of Islands rangatira were concerned by rumors circulating in Sydney that suggested that France intended to annex New Zealand, fears that seemed to materialize when the French naval vessel *La Favorite* arrived in the Bay of Islands. Thirteen northern chiefs drafted a letter to King William IV, emphasizing the close contacts that had developed between Māori and Britain and requesting the King to become "a friend and guardian of these islands."[59]

On his arrival in New Zealand, in May 1833, Busby carried a reply drafted by Goderich on behalf of William IV, which informed the chiefs that Busby's purpose was to "afford his protection to the inhabitants of New Zealand, against any acts of outrage which may be attempted against them by British subjects, it is confidently expected by HIS MAJESTY, that on your parts you will render to THE RESIDENT that assistance and support, which is calculated to promote the object of his appointment, and to extend to your country all the benefits which it is capable of receiving from its friendship and alliance with Great Britain."[60]

Busby's appointment marks a crucial turning point. The British government now had an official on the spot, and in Busby they had a functionary who was an enthusiastic informant for the government of New South Wales and the Colonial Office. The Colonial Office's bureaucracy depended on regular reportage from the empire's frontiers, knowledge which they used as the basis for the letters they drafted, speeches they wrote, and decisions they made. In the early nineteenth century, this stream of information became a flood. In 1824, for example, the Colonial Office received 964 letters from New South Wales and Van Diemen's Land, and dispatched 1,104 in return (up from 83 received and 15 dispatched in 1806).[61] Knowledge was the backbone of imperial governance, and the Colonial Office was a central knowledge-producing node within the imperial system. Busby's regular correspondence meant that the Colonial Office was provided with a regular and detailed flow of information from the most distant frontier of British influence.

Busby's letters and reports spliced together empirical detail—recording the provenance, crew size, and tonnage of shipping in the Bay of Islands—and emotive generalizations. While Busby occasionally produced accounts of individual Māori suffering that fit Laqueur's model of humanitarian narratives, his dispatches were more typically framed within a discourse on depopulation. In an 1837 letter to the secretary of state, Busby painted an alarming picture of social crisis and population decline, produced by the combination of alcohol, tobacco, venereal disease, prostitution, and infanticide. Despite his protestation that it was not simply "intercours with Europeans" that was responsible for depopulation, his detailed discussion of mortality underlined cross-cultural contact as the primary cause of decline. Even infanticide, he argued, was largely a response to pregnancies arising from the sex trade stimulated by growing numbers of Europeans visiting New Zealand's shores. In short, Busby argued that "district after district has become void of its inhabitants" and urged Britain to extend its "efficient protection" over Māori to prevent "permanent anarchy."[62]

Busby had initiated one important innovation that he hoped would provide some security for Māori. Fearful of the intentions of Baron Charles de Thierry, who planned to establish an independent colony based on his landholdings in the Hokianga and who styled himself as New Zealand's "Lord and Governor," Busby arranged for an assembly of thirty-four chiefs to gather in late October 1835. With the aid of several missionaries, Busby explained the threat posed by de Thierry and French influence, and encouraged the chiefs to sign a Declaration of Independence (He Wakaputanga o te Rangtiratanga o Nu Tirene). In the declaration, the chiefs were styled the "United

Tribes of New Zealand," and they asked for William IV to be the "parent of their infant State" and to function as its "Protector from all attempts on its independence." It is important to underscore that while this declaration was recognized by the Colonial Office, from the outset Busby envisioned the declaration as marking a crucial step toward formalizing Britain's responsibility for New Zealand, rather than marking the establishment of a fully independent Māori nation that would stand outside the empire. In his letter forwarding the declaration to the Colonial Office, Busby made it clear that he saw the declaration as an instrument by which Britain could assume imperial trusteeship for Māori and thus place New Zealand firmly within the orbit of British imperial influence. Busby suggested that if Britain confirmed the property rights of Māori, then "the Chiefs might be led to enact, and to aid by their influence and power, the enforcement of whatever Laws the British Government might determine, to be most advantageous to the Country." Busby thus saw the possibility that Britain could establish "a System of Government supported by Military Force . . . based upon the principle of protecting a Nation in its minority, and preserving it from those evils to which the intercourse of a Civilised people, would, under the Circumstances expose its simple Inhabitants."[63]

In short, Busby argued, "the establishment of the Independence of the Country under the protection of the British Government would be the most effectual mode of making the Country a dependency of the British Empire in everything but name."[64] Less than three months after the signing of the declaration, in January 1836, Busby wrote again to the secretary of state for the colonies, reaffirming the necessity for the British government to extend its "protection" over Māori.

> They are perfectly convinced of their incapacity to govern themselves, or to cope unaided with the novel circumstances to which they are constantly exposed by the encroachments of their civilised visitors.—They have as yet confidence in the British Government, and if protected in the enjoyment of their Landed property, and their personal rights: they would I am sure gladly become the subjects of the King of England; and yield up the Government of their Country to those who are more fitted to conduct it; and not only feel, but acknowledge the blessings which they would derive from equal Government and impartial laws.[65]

While Busby had been instrumental in ensuring that Māori sovereignty was confirmed, he clearly imagined a future in which the substance of that authority would be alienated and New Zealand incorporated into the empire so that Māori might enjoy the beneficent protection of the rule of law, British justice, and the might of Britain's military.[66]

The Humanitarian Moment: The Buxton Committee

Busby's reports coincided with the appointment of parliamentary select committees in Britain to inquire into the effects of colonization on indigenous peoples. The famous 1835–37 Select Committee on Aborigines, chaired by the leading evangelical abolitionist Thomas Fowell Buxton, compiled a massive body of evidence relating to British colonies of settlement, and the committee's report offered a powerful critique of colonial governance and settler morality. Elizabeth Elbourne has suggested that the establishment of the committee and its final report need to be read as "contingent interventions," produced out of the intersection of a series of ongoing transnational discourses about the morality of British empire building, the power of an extensive set of evangelical and missionary networks, and a moment in British politics shaped by the 1832 Reform Act and the 1833 abolition of slavery.[67] This contingency is very clear in the make-up of the committee. Its chairman, Thomas Fowell Buxton, was an Anglican evangelical with close connections to influential Quaker networks through his marriage to Hannah Gurney who had emerged by the mid-1830s as the leading British champion of "humanitarian" reform. Buxton had publicly opposed the death penalty, supported the protection of animals, advocated the reform of criminal law and the prison system, was a founder of the Society for the Mitigation and Gradual Abolition of Slavery (1823), and, most famously, led the fight against slavery in Parliament in the wake of Wilberforce's retirement in 1825, a fight that culminated in the Slavery Emancipation Act in 1833.[68]

During the 1820s and early 1830s, Buxton developed a strong interest in the plight of "Aborigines" within the British empire.[69] This was stimulated by John Philip, the director of the London Missionary Society, who drew Buxton's attention to the marginal position of Khoisan laborers in the Cape Colony, and Buxton quickly used his influence to pressure the colonial secretary Sir George Murray to "emancipate" the Khoisan and to grant them equal legal status with whites.[70] Encouraged by Philip and a fellow member of the Anti-Slavery Society, Thomas Pringle, Buxton devoted considerable effort to exploring the position of colonized groups within the empire, reading Colonial Office records with skepticism and, with the help of his daughter, building up and maintaining an extensive network of colonial informants.[71] Armed with up-to-date information, Buxton became a powerful advocate for the "protection" of African communities against the depredations of South African settlers and argued more broadly that white settlement should be restricted throughout the empire and that "reparations" should be paid to indigenous communities through the provision of programs that would promote civilization and Christianity.[72] Buxton's advocacy initially focused on the Colonial Office, but in 1834 he brought the condition of "Aborigines" to Parliament's attention, and in July 1835 he successfully argued the case in Parliament for establishing a select committee to enquire into the issue.[73]

The committee included Buxton's son-in-law Andrew Johnston; Joseph Pease, a Quaker who was married into the family of Anna Gurney (Buxton's cousin and the intimate of his sister Sarah Maria); Buxton's old abolitionist ally Charles Lushington; and George Grey, who Buxton knew from his dealings with the Colonial Office. Zoe Laidlaw has shown how the committee was shaped by Buxton's extensive network of connections, stressing the pivotal role played by the Buxton women in gathering and shaping information in the lead-up to the hearings.[74] Despite this careful management, a significant rift shaped the committee's proceedings, as a group who advocated for the interests of white colonists, including the distinguished military man Sir Rufane Shaw Donkin and a young William Ewart Gladstone, countered those sympathetic to Buxton's agenda.[75] Although Donkin and Gladstone ensured that that pro-colonist evidence was heard, Buxton and his network effectively used the committee as an occasion to "incite discourse," to produce new knowledge and publicize established critiques of settler morality within a forum that by its very definition carried significant political weight.[76] With this aim in mind, Buxton was identifying potential witnesses and working out specific questions and what additional sources to procure six months before the committee met.[77] This faith in the power of information to persuade and to guide imperial governance was in keeping with Buxton's moderate and constitutionalist vision of reform, an approach that depended on his close knowledge of the political process and his extensive political networks, which linked him both to powerful Westminster power-brokers and to leading Quaker, evangelical, and humanitarian interest groups.

Although New Zealand was outside the formal remit of the committee, it did feature prominently in the committee's hearings.[78] William Yate gave extensive testimony, highlighting Busby's lack of power and the immorality of the non-mission-based Europeans in New Zealand. Yate suggested that contact with Europeans was "highly demoralizing," as the presence of a large number of ships resulted in the "interference with the daughters and wives of the natives," stimulated Māori interest in alcohol, and fed the trade in muskets and gunpowder.[79] In response to his portrait of an indigenous community wracked by moral decline and social crisis, Yate was asked, "Did you ever know a case in which, when the facts were really sifted, the fault did not originate with the Europeans?" Yate's answer was intended as a powerful exoneration of Māori: "Not one case has ever come under my own observations, never under any circumstances, but what the Europeans have been the aggressors, or have committed some breach in a known New Zealand law." In assigning the "original fault" to Europeans in all cases of cross-cultural conflict, Yate in effect denied the ability of Māori to be active social agents, presenting an image of a passive people markedly at odds with missionary journals, including Yate's own, that dwelt at length on the difficulties of "managing" Māori on mission stations, the willingness of many Māori to engage with and contest missionary teaching, and, most important, their ability to dictate the terms of the commercial, sexual, and social relationships they fashioned with European sojourners in the far north of the North Island.[80]

Yate also provided sensational evidence that seemingly confirmed the Colonial Office's fears about Europeans interfering in conflicts between indigenous groups. In addition to providing a version of the *Elizabeth* affair that had been recounted to him "by hundreds of the natives," Yate recalled an incident where Rewa, the Ngāi Tāwake rangatira, showed him a parcel of "corrosive sublimate" that had been given to him by the captain of a "New South Wales trading vessel." According to Rewa, the captain suggested that the powder could be added to food that he might provide to his enemies from Tauranga in a hākari, enabling him to kill 300 or 400 at one time and allowing Rewa's people to be "able to get possession of their lands."[81] Yate also provided evidence relating to the role of Europeans in encouraging the trade in preserved heads and the desire of the master of the HMS *Buffalo* to be provided with Congreve rockets to use against Māori if the *Buffalo* was posted to New Zealand again.[82]

Yate's evidence of European violence and the inability of Māori to protect their interests was affirmed by other witnesses called by the committee. In response to Buxton's invitation to recount "any acts of cruelty and oppression, committed by Europeans on the natives," the secretary of the CMS, Dandeson Coates, read Marsden's letter to Darling into the committee's record of evidence.[83] This detailed account of Te Maiharanui's suffering echoed the evidence presented by William Barrett Marshall, assistant naval surgeon on the HMS *Alligator*. Under the command of Captain George Lambert, the *Alligator* had been dispatched to the Taranaki coast, by order of the Executive Council of New South Wales, to rescue the surviving members of the barque *Harriet*, which ran aground near Rahotu in April 1834. In addition to over sixty armed men, the *Alligator* carried the whaler John Guard, who had escaped from Ngāti Ruanui warriors following the wreck of the *Harriet* and was anxious to recover his wife, Elizabeth, and his two children. Before the committee, Marshall read from his published account of the voyage, recording the shooting and torture of the Ngāti Ruanui chief Oaoiti by John Guard and British sailors following the recapture of Elizabeth Guard and her baby.

> He [Oaoiti] was instantly seized upon as a prisoner of war himself, dragged into the whale-boat and despatched on board the Alligator, in custody of John Guard and his sailors. On his brief passage to the boat, insult followed insult; one fellow twisting his ear by means of a small swivel which hung from it, and another pulling his long hair with spiteful violence; a third pricking him with the point of a bayonet. Thrown to the bottom of the boat, she was shoved off before he recovered himself, which he had no sooner succeeded in doing than he jumped overboard and attempted to swim on shore, to prevent which he was repeatedly fired upon from the boat; but not until he had been shot in the calf of the leg was he again made a prisoner of. Having been a second time secured, he was lashed to a thwart and stabbed and struck so repeatedly that, on reaching the Alligator, he was only able to gain the deck by a strong effort, and there, after staggering a few paces aft, fainted and fell down at the foot of the capstan in a gore of blood. When I dressed his wounds, on a subsequent occasion, I found ten inflicted by the point and edge of the bayonet over his head and face, one in his left breast, which it was at first feared would prove what it was evidently intended to have proved, a mortal thrust, and another in the leg.[84]

Marshall's account clearly fits within the humanitarian narrative form, in that its dramatic reportage was balanced by careful empiricism, as he itemized the instruments used to inflict wounds on Oaoiti's body and the exact number and extent of those injuries. More specifically, Marshall's evidence fits neatly within the strong humanitarian tradition that had developed within sectors of the British navy, which Jane Samson has identified as being as crucial in shaping British understandings of the Pacific and the policing of imperial frontiers in the region.[85]

Buxton's select committee effectively operated as an extended attempt to build an authoritative archive that documented, to borrow Elizabeth Elbourne's phrase, the "sins of the settler."[86] These narratives of Māori suffering were very prominent in the committee's final report. Marsden's 1831 letter to Darling concerning the role of Captain Stewart in the Ngāti Toa raid on Horomaka was quoted at length in the final report, as was Goderich's letter to Darling, which lamented the ineffectual attempt to bring prosecutions in the wake of the *Elizabeth* affair and affirmed the need to "protect" Māori.[87] The committee's final report suggested that such evils inflicted on "Aborigines" by British citizens were comparable to those of slavery and that the immorality of settlers destroyed "Aboriginal" societies as well as being inimical to the construction of civilized colonies, the growth of commerce, and the cultivation of Christianity. In addition to castigating colonial governments over their lack of concern for their non-European charges, the report set out a series of principles that were designed to "govern our intercourse with those vast multitudes of uncivilized men, who may suffer in the greatest degree, or in the greatest degree be benefited, by that intercourse."[88] These measures—which included the restrictions on alcohol, tighter control of land sales, greater emphasis on education and religious instruction, and the administration of "native affairs" by central authorities—were designed to regulate the actions of British subjects, to ensure the "protection" of remaining indigenous polities, and, most fundamentally, to transform the empire into a moral and spiritual enterprise.[89] The report suggested that Britain had been "signally blessed by Providence" and that the empire was therefore underpinned by a deeper moral responsibility. God himself would judge how this responsibility had been discharged.

> He who has made Great Britain what she is, will inquire at our hands how we have employed the influence He has lent to us in our dealings with the untutored and defenceless savage; whether it has been emerged in seizing their lands, warring upon their people, and transplanting unknown disease, and deeper degradation, through the remote regions of the earth; or whether we have, as far as we have been able, informed their ignorance, and invited and afforded them the opportunity of becoming partakers of that civilization, that innocent commerce, that knowledge and that faith with which it has pleased a gracious Providence to bless our own country.[90]

In its discussion of the "South Sea Islands," the report firmly stated the committee's opposition to plans for the colonization of New Zealand.[91] Buxton was convinced that the committee's final report would prevent the extension of British imperial activity in the Pacific for the foreseeable future. In a letter to his brother-in-law, Joseph John Gurney, drafted on 25 June 1837, the day before the House of Commons ordered the committee's report to be printed, Buxton was confident that the committee had undercut the plans of the recently formed New Zealand Association, which promoted the settlement of New Zealand by British colonists, and that he had forestalled the possibility of New Zealand's colonization by Britain.[92]

Contesting Colonization: The House of Lords Select Committee

Buxton's optimism soon proved to be misplaced. The New Zealand Association proceeded with publicizing its plans for establishing settlements in New Zealand based on Edward Gibbon Wakefield's vision of "systematic colonization" and placed considerable pressure on the prime minister Lord Melbourne to smooth the way for its scheme. Although the association was offered a Crown charter for its activities in December 1837, it actively resisted the need to operate as a joint-stock company and in rejecting this clause of the charter pushed instead for the passing of an Act of Parliament to enable its colonization of New Zealand.[93] Against this backdrop, a House of Lords select committee was convened to "inquire into the present state of the islands of New Zealand, and the expediency of regulating the settlement of British subjects therein." This twenty-one-member committee comprised a much wider spectrum of interests and opinions than had Buxton's committee, and its hearings provided a crucial arena in which the impact of cross-cultural impact on Māori and New Zealand's future place within the empire were contested.

The Māori body—both in its "natural" capacity and in its transformation by cross-cultural contact—became a key site for debates that played out before the committee. Given the broader composition of this House of Lords committee and the lack of a Buxton-style conductor orchestrating the witnesses and choreographing the questions, the 1838 hearings roamed over a wider terrain than the 1835–37 committee. However, the humanitarian narratives collected by the Buxton committee resurfaced in 1838, particularly with the evidence of the Sydney-based merchant Joseph Barrow Montefiore. Montefiore was a passenger on the *Elizabeth* in 1831, and during his testimony, the committee twice questioned him over the torture and killing of Te Maiharanui. Montefiore was asked whether Te Maiharanui had been held "with a Hook put through the fleshy Part of his Chin." He answered, "It is impossible for me to say more than the Captain himself related to me; I was on board the Ship subsequently; the Story is bad enough without Aggravation. I saw the Chief; he was as fine a Man as ever I saw in my Life; had there been any Appearance of the Hook alluded to it could not have escaped my Notice."[94] Montefiore admitted that severe wounds had been inflicted on Te Maiharanui's legs and that he had objected to the placing of the Ngāi Tahu chief in irons. But Montefiore took the opportunity to challenge the sympathy that Marsden's letter and Coates's evidence before the Buxton committee had solicited for the suffering Ngāi Tahu rangatira. Montefiore recast Te Maiharanui as an unrestrained savage, a cannibal, and an enemy of Europeans. He told the committee that Te Maiharanui had not only killed leading members of Ngāti Toa, but had also "killed several White Men . . . and Four Years ago cut off, and ate, with his Comrades, the Boat's Crew of His Majesty's Ship Warspite."[95]

More generally, however, Montefiore stressed Māori physical prowess and their capacity as agriculturalists, seamen, and traders. The overwhelming thrust of his evidence was the ability of Māori to be absorbed in an imperial market economy, and he underlined both New Zealand's commercial significance for New South Wales and its suitability for colonization.[96] Similar points were made repeatedly by witnesses who had established trading interests in New Zealand or who were involved with the New Zealand Association. Joel Polack, the prominent trader based at Kororāreka, suggested that colonization should proceed, in part because Māori were perfectly suited to provide the labor for a fledgling colony: "No People will become better Farm Servants than the New Zealanders."[97] Polack contended that colonization would stabilize Māori society and advance the civilizing process: "A Colonization would employ their Minds as well as their Bodies."[98] It was not missionary education nor the Māori Bible that would uplift the indigenes, but rather absorption into a British-dominated colony, where Māori would seamlessly be incorporated as the working class: "They must have Europeans, and they must be employed by Europeans; they must have civilized Persons to employ them."[99]

Polack also suggested that colonial rule was needed to impose order on the lawless Europeans, to give shape to a proper "society," and, most fundamentally, to "protect" Māori. He argued that in fact colonization was already under way, with the missionaries acquiring large tracts of land and a growing population of former convicts, sailors, and adventurers settling in the Bay of Islands. This group was, Polack suggested, enacting "Colonization of the worst Kind." Without the formal extension of British sovereignty over New Zealand, the future for Māori was bleak, as the "present European Population now residing in New Zealand will destroy, will extirpate and annihilate, the People; it cannot be otherwise."[100] Francis Baring, a member of the New

Zealand Association whose family had substantial commercial interests in the "East," also argued that "the Necessity of colonizing arises completely out of the Nature of the Population which is now there, and which makes Colonization indispensable."[101] The Reverend Samuel Hinds, a high church Anglican who was unsympathetic to missionary opposition to "systematic colonization," also eloquently forwarded the New Zealand Association's case that formal colonization would "regularize" contact with Māori. Hinds suggested that Britain was "imperatively called upon to establish a Colony, or rather to establish organized Society in New Zealand, because at this Moment an irregular Process of Colonization [is] going on there."[102]

Polack, Baring, and Hinds did not believe that the acknowledged sovereignty of Māori rangatira should be an obstacle to this scheme. Other advocates for the New Zealand Association suggested Māori would actively welcome colonization. Charles Enderby, a member of the association and owner of a leading Pacific whaling firm, argued that Māori would be willing to yield "all sovereign Authority," as "they would wish to have some Laws laid down by which they might be themselves protected; they would not be disposed to interfere with it [colonization]."[103] The New Zealand Association was pleased with the evidence provided by "Nayti," Te Whaiti of Ngāti Toa, who had traveled to Europe on a French whaler, then settled in Chelsea, where Wakefield encouraged him to learn English, preparing him for his later role as a key translator for the New Zealand Company.[104] When asked by the committee about how Māori would view colonization, Te Whaiti initially stated that he did not "know what [his] Countrymen would like." But he then also suggested, "I think they would like it [colonization] too, because they like even the bad People now. I think they would like Gentlemen."[105] Wakefield must also have been delighted when the former CMS catechist John Flatt contravened his former society's official opposition to the New Zealand Company's plans by suggesting that if colonization was "accompanied by some System and Regulation of Law," Māori would then "receive them [settlers] with open Arms."[106]

But this view was not uncontested in these hearings. The first witness, John Liddiard Nicholas, who had accompanied Marsden on his 1814 voyage to the Bay of Islands to establish the mission at Hohi, told the committee that "the Chiefs are exceedingly jealous of their Independence." Nicholas argued that while a rangatira might appreciate the "Protection of the Colonists against other Tribes," if colonization did occur, no rangatira would "be interfered with in the Management of his own People."[107] John Watkins, a surgeon who visited the Bay of Islands and Hokianga in 1833–34, confirmed that Māori were "very much alarmed at the Idea of their Country being taken away from them, and their being reduced to Slavery; but they were very anxious to have something done to increase their knowledge, and to allow their Independence at the same Time to remain."[108] Not surprisingly, the staunchest critique of the association's plan and the strongest defense of the sovereignty of rangatira came from Dandeson Coates, the secretary of the Church Missionary Society. In his extensive evidence, Coates questioned the intention of extending British sovereignty. He stated bluntly that "to acquire Sovereignty in that Country would be a Violation of the Fundamental Principles of international Law, New Zealand being, to all Intents and Purposes, an independent State."[109] Coates's critical reading of empire and the clear distinctions he tried to draw between missionary work and imperialism was a clear move away from Marsden's tendency to conflate mission and empire in the 1810s: Coates certainly did not want missionaries to be tarnished by the "sins of the settler."[110]

During the hearings of the House of Lords Select Committee, Coates returned to the strategy he used before Buxton's committee, mixing passionate commentary with the recitation of long extracts from various sources produced on the New Zealand frontier that he wished to be entered into the committee's minutes. This evidence was used to highlight the growth of missionary schools and the extension of the mission to new regions beyond the Bay of Islands, to record the role of missionaries as peacemakers, and to stress the progress of the mission, progress that Coates believed would be lost if colonization proceeded.[111] Coates's emphasis on the "civilizing" effects of the mission created a strong tension in his evidence. Despite his insistence on Māori capacity for civilization and their embrace of Christianity, Coates questioned Māori ability to enter into the kinds of legal arrangements that colonization would necessitate. His position contrasted markedly to missionaries on the ground, who generally stressed the clarity of Māori understandings of both property and sovereignty. Coates suggested that any agreement that required the "Cession of the Sovereignty of the Tribes . . . would be a Violation of moral Obligation." In short, Coates believed it "to be utterly impossible that a Set of Barbarians, like the Natives of New Zealand, can by any Explanation, however honestly given, be made to comprehend the ultimate Consequences of the Transaction [the cession of sovereignty], and that therefore such an Arrangement is essentially inequitable, and such as the British Government could not with Propriety make themselves Parties to."[112]

Coates continued to ground his opposition to any scheme for the colonization of New Zealand in his skeptical reading of the long history of empire building. He bluntly told the committee, "European Colonization, in every Instance, as far as my Acquaintance with the History of Colonization goes, has resulted in the most disastrous Consequences to the Aborigines of those Countries which they have so colonized."[113] Coates believed that incidents like the *Elizabeth* affair and the impact of Europeans on Māori health and mortality confirmed that this pattern was already playing out in New Zealand. Māori required protection from Europeans, protection best provided by the continuation of the Protestant missions, the restriction of further settlement, and the strengthening Busby's of position as resident.

The starkly divergent views of New Zealand's place within the empire proffered before the House of Lords select committee meant that the committee's report could not clearly endorse either the New Zealand Association's or the missionary societies' opposition to systematic colonization. But in delivering a short report—essentially one paragraph—that simply suggested that Britain's connection with New Zealand was "a question of public policy which belongs to Her Majesty's Government," the House of Lords committee effectively opened the door for colonization. This was very important given that the report was published shortly after the New Zealand Association's aspirations were dealt a severe blow. The bill that would have enabled their colonization of New Zealand was roundly defeated in the House of Commons because it offered little formal protection for Māori interests and did not provide sufficient definition of the Association's liability for the proposed colony.[114] Thus, where Buxton's committee offered a stinging critique of colonial governance and the lack of virtue displayed by British settlers, the House of Lords committee did not enunciate any principled critique of colonization, but neither did they suggest that the extension of Britain's imperial reach was in violation of the high moral code invested in Britain by Providence. In effect, the House of Lords committee's noncommittal report shifted the ground away from a lingering attention to indigenous suffering and in the process provided the New Zealand Association a reprieve, a second chance that it used to radically reinvent itself as the joint-stock New Zealand Company.[115]

In the wake of this report and the defeat of the New Zealand Association's bill, the responsibility for deciding New Zealand's fate fell to the Colonial Office. As the 1830s drew to a close, the Colonial Office set Britain's policy within a metropolitan context where reformist and humanitarian interests were starting to lose ground. Buxton—the leading humanitarian in the House of Commons—lost his seat in the 1837 election, Melbourne's Whig government was hamstrung after the failure of its Jamaica Bill in May 1839, and attitudes toward humanitarianism and the culture of sensibility were hardening. The very term *humanitarianism* began to be used as a pejorative, as sensitivity to the suffering of others was cast as effeminate and ineffectual.[116] This shifting cultural ground was shaped by the rise of new forms of racism; understandings of the non-British objects of humanitarian sympathy were viewed with skepticism, as both the Anglo-Saxon revival and polygenist anthropology began to gain ground. At the same time, a new expansive energy drove British imperial ambition, feeding conflicts throughout the empire. Not only was the East India Company fighting wars in Afghanistan and locked into conflict with the Qing empire, but settlers in South Africa were demanding the annexation of Natal, and there was widespread fear that Mehmet Ali might be able to create a French-sponsored empire spanning much of north Africa and the Middle East. Within this context, James Stephen described working in the Colonial Office as "living . . . in a tornado."[117]

"Protection" and Colonization

Within this turbulent context, the Colonial Office responded to the flow of information from the New Zealand Company (which emerged out of the earlier New Zealand Association), which recorded the growth of the white population, increasing land sales, and the "demoralization" of Māori, by appointing a consul. While the New Zealand Company began working on a revised scheme for colonization and purchased the *Tory*, Captain William Hobson accepted the position of consul to New Zealand in February 1839. By August, when it seemed that the New Zealand Company was contemplating colonization and the establishment of a settler state with no official sanction, the Colonial Office upgraded Hobson's appointment to Lieutenant Governor. Hobson, an Anglo-Irish naval officer who had served in both the West and East Indies and who had spent much of 1837 in New Zealand commanding the frigate HMS *Rattlesnake*, would play a pivotal role in Britain's formal intervention in New Zealand. Not only did Hobson oversee the negotiations surrounding the Treaty of Waitangi in 1840, but he was a key figure elaborating the discourse of "protection" that was central in shaping that document. Hobson's appointment was largely the product of his New Zealand experience and the influential report he had sent to the Colonial Office late in 1837. Hobson's report adopted models from British India as a template for controlling British activity in New Zealand and for the "protection" of Māori interests. He suggested that two or three delimited areas of land could be purchased and through a treaty be placed under British jurisdiction. The factories would be overseen by an appointed head, who would also serve as a consul to the local rangatira. Through the factories, Hobson argued, Britain would simultaneously sow the seeds of civil government and impose firm boundaries on British activity in New Zealand, in addition to providing a "safe retreat" from inter-iwi conflict.[118]

This 1837 plan was an important contribution to the discourse of protection. The need for Britain to "protect" was clearly articulated by Marsden in 1831 and affirmed by Goderich in 1832. Throughout the mid-1830s, Busby asked for more power in order to be able to "efficiently" protect Māori. And Thomas Fowell Buxton was convinced that his report had "protected" Māori from the fate of colonization. Hobson's appointment was a key material outcome of this discourse: Māori were now to enjoy greater security as the ineffective Busby was to be replaced and Britain's diplomatic presence in New Zealand was to be strengthened. Immediately on his appointment, Hobson repudiated his factory plan as a model for achieving protection and the imposition of control on British subjects settled on the New Zealand frontier. In a letter to the Colonial Office he reflected, "From the first moment of my acquiring any knowledge of the actual condition of New Zealand it was clear and evident to my mind, that the tide of Emigration which had already begun to flow towards the Country, would eventually oblige Her Majesty's Ministers to extend to it, in some shape or other, the protection of British laws." But he felt now that the India-derived model of "factories" was "insufficient for the full accomplishment of the object," as it would leave other parts of the islands open to encroachments by "other Nations," and British subjects outside the likely boundaries of any factories that could be created had already purchased "vast tracts" of land. In light of these reasons, Hobson now advocated a much more aggressive and extensive form of "protection": "I can suggest no remedy, unless Her Majesty's Government at once resolve to extend to that highly gifted land the blessings of civilisation and liberty, and the protection of English law, by assuming Sovereignty of the whole country, and by transplanting on its Shores, the Nucleus of a Moral and Industrious population."[119]

Although there was some prevarication within the Colonial Office, in early 1839, over the exact measures to be implemented with regard to New Zealand, this vision of colonization as a form of "protection" was increasingly consolidated. In March 1839, James Stephen wrote to the new parliamentary undersecretary, Henry Labouchere, setting out basic understandings regarding New Zealand, now that colonization was understood as being "at least an inevitable measure." Stephen suggested that intervention was necessary because New

Zealand was "in fact, colonised by British subjects of the worst possible character, who are doing the greatest possible amount of evil with the least possible amount of good, and who are living under no restraint of Law of Government." Stephen explained that "two cardinal points" must govern the establishment of a "regular colony in New Zealand." Colonization should be aimed at the "protection of the Aborigines" and sow the seeds of self-government among colonists.[120]

A letter from the secretary of state, the Marquess of Normanby, to Hobson in August 1839 reaffirmed this position. Normanby emphasized that Britain recognized that New Zealand "as a sovereign and independent state" and that it was not the queen's intention to "seize on the islands of New Zealand, or to govern them as a part of the dominions of Great Britain, unless the free and intelligent consent of the natives expressed according to their usages, shall be obtained." Normanby continued, explaining the need for intervention: "Believing, however, that their own welfare would, under the circumstances I have mentioned [growing migration and frontier lawlessness], be best promoted by the surrender to her Majesty of a right now so precarious and little more than nominal and persuaded that the benefits of British protection, and of laws administered by British judges, would far more than compensate for the sacrifice of a national independence which they are no longer able to maintain."[121] This was a crucial argument. Here, Normanby was drawing on the image of the suffering Māori and its constant reiteration in various published humanitarian narratives and the official archives collated by select committees and the Colonial Office itself. Māori were no longer able to protect themselves, they could not exercise their "national independence," and colonization was in their best interest. In her telling reading of this letter, Claudia Orange suggests that "had the Maori people been presented as more capable . . . British intervention could have been scarcely justified."[122]

The idea of "protection" was prominent in the treaty concluded at Waitangi in February 1840 and eventually signed by over five hundred rangatira from the majority of iwi throughout New Zealand. The preamble to the English version of the treaty stated that Queen Victoria was "anxious to protect their just Rights and Property and to secure to them the enjoyment of Peace and Good Order," while the Māori version suggested that the treaty reflected the queen's desire to "preserve to them their chieftainship and their land" and ensure that "peace may always be kept with them and quietness." The first article saw the chiefs cede "absolutely and without reservation all the rights and powers of Sovereignty" ("give up entirely to the

Queen of England for ever all the government of their lands" in the Māori version). The second article guaranteed to rangatira the "full chieftainship of their lands, their settlements, and all their property," while stipulating that the Crown had the right of preemption on all future land purchases. The third and final article returned to the theme of protection. The English text stated that the Queen "extends to the Natives of New Zealand Her royal protection" in addition to the rights of British subjects, while the Māori version guaranteed that the "Queen of England will protect all the Maoris of New Zealand."[123] Protection had become the legitimating device for empire and was to be a central and contentious concern for Governors who oversaw New Zealand's development as a British colony over subsequent decades.[124]

Conclusion

The Treaty of Waitangi has been heralded as both the "most striking example" of Victorian imperial humanitarianism and "the founding document of New Zealand as a bi-cultural society."[125] But when viewed within the context of the debates over New Zealand in the 1830s, rather than seen within an optimistic reading of empire or a national history cast in a bicultural mold, the treaty must be viewed very differently. In terms of Victorian humanitarianism, the signing of the treaty and the colonization of New Zealand marked a substantial retreat from the Buxton report. In articulating a skeptical reading of the morality of settler colonialism, Buxton's report argued against the territorial extension of the empire and questioned the very ethical basis of the creation of settler colonies. Most important, the eighth principle of the report was entitled "Treaties with Natives Inexpedient." It read,

> As a general rule, however, it is inexpedient that treaties should be frequently entered into between the local Governments and the tribes in their vicinity. Compacts between parties negotiating on terms of such entire disparity are rather the preparatives and the apology for disputes than securities for peace: as often as the resentment or the cupidity of the more powerful body may be excited, a ready pretext for complaint will be found in the ambiguity of the language in which their agreements must be drawn up, and in the superior sagacity which the European will exercise in framing, in interpreting, and in evading them. The safety and welfare of an uncivilized race require that their relations with their more cultivated neighbours should be diminished rather than multiplied.[126]

On the basis of its reading of the history of treaty-making within European empires, Buxton's committee saw treaties as tools that enabled expansion rather than preventing it and, in effect, argued that "protection" should ideally take the form of the restriction of contact.[127] The drafting of the Treaty of Waitangi offered a very different vision of protection. While article 2 of the treaty recognized "rangatiratanga" and allowed traditional leaders to continue to exercise some authority, the "national sovereignty" of Māori, which had been recognized since the 1810s and which had forestalled any formal intervention in New Zealand on an extensive scale, was extinguished. This alternative reading of "protection" ultimately transcended the recognition of Māori sovereignty and functioned as an instrument that finally consolidated British imperial authority in the region.[128]

So Britain's colonization of New Zealand was recoded as form of humanitarian intervention. Māori—supposedly fragile, weak, and diminishing by the day—were to be protected from the ravages of uncontrolled contact with Europeans through British law, their new rights as British subjects, and a system of regularized land sales that would actually greatly expand the scope and consequences of cross-cultural engagement. I have attempted to explore some of the cultural forces and political debates that shaped this vision of Māori as enfeebled and in need of protection. The new cultural weight attached to sympathy and the evangelical harnessing of the culture of sensibility to their reformist project underpinned the new forms of sympathetic identification that were so prominent in British antislavery agitation, campaigns for prison and factory reform, and in the far-reaching critiques of colonization articulated by Thomas Fowell Buxton and Dandeson Coates. At the core of this political tradition was a deep concern with bodily suffering and the need to alleviate physical pain through the cultivation of pure morality, true Christianity, and the enacting of "good" laws to restrict the debilitating consequences of "social evils," whether these occurred in Britain itself, within the empire, or, as in New Zealand's case, beyond the imperial frontier. The political importance attached to "sympathy" and the deepseated concern with the physical suffering of Māori suffused the passionate critiques of the New Zealand Association and of the immorality of British settler colonies, reaching their peak in 1837–38.

Ultimately, however, I have suggested that this moral and political sensibility was actually pivotal in enabling the formal colonization of New Zealand. By 1840, it seemed self-evident that Māori needed protection. I have shown that this "need" and the ultimate decision to formally colonize New Zealand were the products of extended public debate and a long and convoluted political process. At the heart of these exchanges over New Zealand's place within the empire was the figure of the suffering native, whose enfeebled body became the grounds for debate about the consequences of British enterprise in New Zealand and how the consequences of cross-cultural contact should be managed.[129] While Māori were able to contest missionary teachings about death, they were less able to shape their representation in metropolitan print culture or control the long exchanges between the Colonial Office and various interest groups that led finally to the decision to sign the Treaty of Waitangi. Although Māori did occasionally participate directly in these processes—as seen in Pere's and Ahu's depositions in Sydney after the *Elizabeth* affair, the "King's Letter," and Te Whaiti's evidence before the House of Lords select committee—these debates were primarily waged between a range of British groups and were largely shaped by the idioms and concerns of metropolitan politics.

Within a context charged by concern with physical suffering and the need for social reform, narratives that recounted Māori pain convinced many British observers that the Māori were unable to govern themselves and to control the consequences of their engagement with Europeans. By the late 1830s, debates over New Zealand were battles over what form protection should take. The radical position of the House of Commons "Report on Aborigines," which documented Māori physical suffering in considerable detail and opposed the colonization of New Zealand, was dismissed. Where that committee's report identified treaties as coercive tools that favored the interests of Britain and its colonists, the formal colonization of New Zealand was ultimately sanctioned by a treaty that framed the alienation of sovereignty as an act of protection, designed to defend the interests of an enfeebled people. As British settlement proceeded in the 1840s, however, colonists soon realized that Māori were not as enfeebled as they had been led to believe and were entirely capable of contesting the shape of the developing colonial society.

Conclusion BODIES AND THE ENTANGLEMENTS
OF EMPIRE

C ross-cultural exchanges, debates, and conflicts have been at the
heart of this book. Rather than framing the relationships that
developed between missionaries in the north of Te Ika a Māui as simply "encounters" or "meetings," I have read these relationships as entanglements produced by the incorporation of Te Ika a Māui into the
commercial, religious, and political networks of the British empire
in the wake of Cook's first Pacific voyage. Even though New Zealand
was not formally colonized until 1840, Cook and his crew quickly
recognized New Zealand's utility for empire. Their writings, maps,
sketches, engravings, and reports emphasized the commercial acuity
of Māori, as well as the potential of the islands of New Zealand for
imperial activity and future colonization. Of course, these inscriptive
artifacts—which circulated widely across Europe over the subsequent
decades—were themselves born out of the engagements between Britons and tāngata māori, but once they circulated within Europe, they
functioned as powerful mobilizations that helped convince British
moneymen, imperial agents, and missionaries of the opportunities
that the southern Pacific offered. Textual production and circulation
helped lay the foundations for the making of empire itself.

But it was the kidnapping of Tuki and Huru in 1792 that initiated
sustained contact and durable relationships between Bay of Islands

Māori and British imperial authorities, primarily those based in New South Wales. The CMS mission to New Zealand emerged from these engagements, which underpinned an important traffic in knowledge, skills, technologies, plants, and people between the Bay of Islands and New South Wales. The immediate context for the genesis of the mission were the connections that developed between Samuel Marsden and northern rangatira as a consequence of the manākitanga that Marsden offered the men on their visits to Poihākena (Port Jackson) and the promise that missionaries would introduce Māori to new ideas and things. From the beginnings of the mission on the ground in the Bay of Islands in December 1814, missionaries and Māori were linked by complex, shifting, and often unpredictable forms of connection: they were woven together by work and trade, prayer and worship, travel and commensality, conversation and argument, and mutual concern in times of illness and death. These threads of association often had lasting and unforeseen consequences. Once people and places were entangled, or perhaps ensnared, in the webs of empire, it was difficult to control cross-cultural connections, and it was impossible to unpick history: linkages might atrophy or be severed, but it was not possible to erase their consequences and ramifications.

I have suggested that one of the fundamental consequences of these new cultural entanglements was that they called the body into question. Those Māori drawn into the ambit of the mission encountered a group of Europeans who espoused a bodily regime fundamentally different from the practices embedded in te ao Māori. They wanted hair to be cut short, suggested that the use of shark oil and ochre to dress the body was unhygienic, encouraged Māori to wear shirts and jackets, and believed that ideally a single family should inhabit a house and that it was best for husbands and wives to sleep in a private section of the dwelling, separate from their children. For their part, missionaries not only found that it was hard to get Māori to follow these new models, but that it was difficult for their own families to maintain many of the practices that they understood as routine parts of "civilized" life. This was especially the case in the early years of the mission, when large missionary families dwelt in small whare, which made it difficult to uphold ideas about privacy and regimes of domestic order and cleanliness.

Throughout this book, I have suggested that proximity was central to mission work. Sharing water, food, and meals; coordinating the physical labor of dressing timber and building houses; sheltering and sleeping alongside Māori within whare; learning te reo; and teaching the "useful arts," domestic skills, and literacy all brought missionaries into close contact with Māori. *Entanglements of Empire* has affirmed Margaret Jolly's insistence that the "brush of bodies" was central in shaping patterns of cross-cultural engagement within the Pacific.[1] But, again, these moments of contact should not be understood as fleeting, as merely of transitory significance: even brief encounters could have lasting consequences, material or metaphysical. In the Bay of Islands missionaries worked hard to shape the meaning and outcomes of these relationships, especially given their growing concerns about the bodily and moral effects of Māori encounters—often of the most intimate kind—with the Euro-American whalers, sailors, and traders who visited the Bay of Islands. Indeed, missionaries in the Bay of Islands were vocal critics of the demoralizing impact of contact with these other outsiders and vehemently opposed plans to colonize New Zealand. They hoped to restrict contact between Māori and Europeans in order to maximize their control of the direction of social change within Māori communities.

But, of course, the presence of missionaries themselves was culturally disruptive and precipitated change. Just as evangelicals at home worked hard to remake British society, the intention of British Protestant missionaries was to reform and transform cultures they evangelized on the frontiers of the empire. Missionaries functioned as a kind of cultural irritant.[2] They attempted to engage indigenous and colonized populations in conversation, incited them to explain and justify their beliefs and practices, insistently asked questions about established ways of doing things, and encouraged new ways of talking and thinking about both the supernatural and human worlds. These forms of talk could be powerful; after all, talk is central to defining, maintaining, and remaking social relationships.[3] Māori undoubtedly reworked the Bible in new and creative ways from the 1830s, but although redeemed slaves, "native teachers," and enthusiastic converts were vital in the spread of Christian texts and thought, the missionaries were key facilitators of these changes. But even as their project sponsored critical reflection on established beliefs and the social order, missionaries were not able to entirely control the ways in which Māori readers interpreted scripture or to dictate the social vision of either Māori converts to Christianity or the followers of the succession of Māori prophets who emerged in the wake of Papahurihia.[4]

Historians of early New Zealand have often produced blunt readings of these dynamics, framing evangelization as a primarily a project of cultural destruction or, in recent decades, as a form of "cultural imperialism." Keith Sinclair, who was instrumental in establishing New Zealand as a research area from the 1950s to the 1980s, argued that missionary work resulted in "immediate temporal harm" for Māori, suggested that missionary ideas were "more destructive than bullets," and believed that evangelization had irrevocably demoralized and destabilized te ao Māori by 1840.[5] In her important studies of the transgressive missionaries Thomas Kendall and William Yate, Judith Binney consistently emphasized the fundamental incompatibility between evangelicalism and Māori culture, and highlighted the missionary desire to "destroy" the cultural underpinnings of Māori life.[6] In his landmark Māori history of New Zealand, Ranginui Walker also argued that missionaries were the "advanced party of cultural invasion" and were committed to undermining Māori communities and their cultural traditions.[7] Such readings recognize that missionaries were committed to a project of cultural change, but the evidence presented in *Entanglements of Empire* suggests that such arguments too neatly conflate missionary work with the project of empire-building and also offer misleading assessments of the sources, directions, and consequences of cultural change.

At its heart, evangelization was a project of cultural reform grounded in the vernacularization of Christianity. In other words, the ultimate object of the missionary was not "Anglicization," but rather the translation of the Bible into te reo Māori and the creation of strong communities of Māori Christians. Such translations were designed to precipitate cultural change within Māori society. But the articulation of this aspiration does not mean that missionaries were in a position of cultural dominance. *Entanglements of Empire* has demonstrated the extent to which missionaries were required to work with Māori, to immerse themselves in the logics of Māori language and culture, and to make substantial accommodations to Māori practices and beliefs. For example, in the 1810s and 1820s CMS missionaries were unable to undermine the importance of slavery and had to work under the protection and in close concert with rangatira who had large and growing numbers of war captives. But missionaries were also alive to the possibilities of turning Māori concepts to their own advantage, as when missionaries like Henry Williams turned tapu into an instrument that could be used to establish the sanctity of the Sabbath, which was translated as "rā tapu."

If assessments of missionary work that simply frame it as a form of cultural imperialism fail to reckon with the centrality of translation to this project, they also produce unduly neat and simple maps of cultural change that imagine power and influence being wielded by missionaries on Māori. Readings that emphasize the ability of missionaries to create European spaces, to remake Māori bodily cultures, to eradicate cannibalism or tattooing, to fundamentally recast indigenous social relations, and to dictate the means and ends of cultural change too readily accept, or at least echo, the most confident assertions of missionary literature, which was typically published in Britain and for a largely British audience.[8] A central concern of mine has been to explore the consequences of the missionaries' deep implication within Māori communities and the ways in which the development of the mission was shaped by Māori kin-group connections and rivalries. In *Entanglements of Empire* I have suggested that this immersion in the Māori world was both fundamental to the operation of the mission and an obstacle to the growth of the mission in the 1810s and 1820s. I have shown that this challenge emerged out of the personal connections between Marsden and the Bay of Islands rangatira who underwrote the foundation of the mission and who imposed significant constraints on the mission's development from the establishment of the community at Hohi (Ōihi). Similarly, I have suggested that the limited material base of the mission and the inability of the missionaries to dictate the terms of labor and trade until after 1826 meant that Māori demonstrated only limited interest in Christianity, valuing instead the missionaries as commercial brokers who operated from a position of weakness. This situation began to change after the mission established a sounder economic base in the second half of the 1820s and because of the growing ability of missionaries to operate with greater freedom from the patronage and control of rangatira, especially Hongi Hika. Nevertheless, it was Māori attached to missions—as workers, converts, or even chiefly patrons—who were the most potent critics of the old gods and old ways of doing things, a dynamic entirely glossed over by arguments that attribute cultural change to the "cultural imperialism" of missionary work.

Thus, social change within Māori communities around the Bay of Islands was not the simple consequence of a missionary "crusade to destroy" Māori belief systems, but rather was the outcome of translation, conversation, and debate.[9] Those exchanges have been central in *Entanglements of Empire*, wherein I have been committed to offering a close reading of the archives of evangelization. I have historicized the development of missionary writing and ethnographic knowledge, paying close attention to both the mentalities and social relationships that framed missionary texts.

The quotidian forms of missionary writing—letters, journals, reports, and minutes—that form the archival spine of *Entanglements of Empire* were rarely seamless, confident, and tightly constructed works. Rather, such texts—unlike the more composed and highly crafted missionary publications printed in Britain—were frequently broken up by some pressing task, interrupted by the interjections and demands of "the natives," and punctuated by accounts of tense exchanges over everyday matters and weighty cosmological questions.[10] And the common image of missionaries as confident reformers and potent cultural imperialists does not capture the emotional warp and weft of missionary texts, wherein uncertainty, anxiety, and even fear coexist with confident assertions and forceful criticisms of "heathen practices." These worries reflected both missionary doubts about the efficacy of their work—concerns that were only rarely printed in popular missionary texts and fundraising propaganda—and their deep awareness that they could never fully control the outcomes of their efforts.[11] Missionaries recognized the power that rangatira wielded, reflected on their dependence on native patronage, and were concerned about the ways in which native teachers and printed texts—two of the key instruments for disseminating Christian teaching—wrenched the interpretation of the gospel out of missionary control, generating a range of new readings of the Bible that were frequently difficult to counter.

Therefore, at the heart of this book, has been a story about the exchange of words between missionaries and Māori. Words and ideas moved between individuals and through communities as a result of biblical readings, sermons, and the circulation of printed portions of scripture. Such occasions often initiated dialogue, and missionaries found themselves answering the insistent questions that were posed in return by Māori engaged with Christian ideas. New ideas were also spread through quiet conversations about life and its meanings, which sprang up between missionaries and Māori as they worked, traveled, and rested, as well as through the stern injunctions of missionary teachers and wives who sought to discipline their Māori charges. In return, some Māori gave texts back to missionaries. These were letters that sought clarification of missionary teachings; requested explanation of Scripture; asked for Bibles, books, paper, slates, pen, and pencils; entreated missionaries to visit, to establish schools, and to support the construction of chapels; and inquired after the missionary and their families. And some Māori wrote to discuss their spiritual struggles or to announce their own transformation and their embrace of the gospel.[12]

But words could travel vast distances beyond Te Ika a Māui, especially if they were written on paper and carried by ship. A key point I have made in *Entanglements of Empire* is that Māori typically had much less control over how Europeans represented them in written texts than they had over Europeans in face-to-face encounters on the ground in Te Ika a Māui itself. It is certainly true that the power and aspirations of Māori imprinted many missionary diary entries and letters quickly penned in the Bay of Islands, but Māori could not control the more composed and polished forms of missionary writing, especially those texts printed and circulated in Britain, far removed from the struggles of the Bay of Islands. Some Māori themselves became skilled writers in this period, but they produced small numbers of texts that circulated beyond the shores of Te Ika a Māui. Not only were Māori overshadowed as producers of written knowledge about their own lands and peoples, but their texts had to be translated into English and to be championed by missionaries, humanitarians, or influential political figures to invest them with any authority within a British political landscape increasingly saturated by print.

This disjuncture between the ability of Māori to influence the pattern of cross-cultural contact in the Bay of Islands and their relative powerlessness to control how they were represented within metropolitan print culture stand as crucially important reminders of the unevenness of the cultural terrain of the empire. The rapid reversals of opinion in the metropole about the prospects of colonization between 1838 and 1840 also make clear the very real stakes attached to imperial entanglements and the power of writing. I have suggested, however, that the entanglements of empire were important drivers of change within Māori communities around the Bay of Islands from at least the late 1790s, if not from the first encounters with the *Endeavour* in 1769. This position is at odds with James Belich's argument that empire effectively remained a "myth" in New Zealand until the conclusion of the wars of the 1860s, which finally firmly established British sovereignty. The entanglements of empire reconstructed here have clearly demonstrated that Māori life and future opportunities were being shaped by forces well beyond New Zealand's shores prior to formal annexation and the beginnings of systematic colonization.[13] Legislation that defined New Zealand's legal position and delineated the authority of colonial authorities in New South Wales over the southern Pacific, policies that governed imperial trade and the operations of British shipping, and the oscillations of markets in Britain and its empire all came to provide deep structures that shaped the opportunities and choices that Māori leaders had. Some important work on cross-cultural engagements in the north has suggested that there were few limits to Māori "agency" and that Māori could embrace new plants, commodities, tools, and ideas with no significant changes to the "Māori order."[14] The evidence I have presented in *Entanglements of Empire* challenges such an image of unbroken cultural continuity and unconstrained action. More broadly still, it is crucial to recognize that the reality of imperial connections meant that Māori agency did operate within a broader set of communication, transportation, commercial, and political networks that Māori could not control, even if they could exploit the opportunities presented by the operation of such structures.

Thus the entanglements of empire before 1840 neither destroyed Māori culture nor left it untouched. Literacy, the Bible, and Christian teachings were important new cultural introductions that Māori evaluated, debated, and deployed, at the same time as they were incorporating pigs, potatoes, iron, and muskets into te ao Māori. None of these things could be used and deployed without cultural consequences: older ways of thinking, acting, and organizing life had to be modified or abandoned as these novelties were naturalized as part of the material, social, and intellectual repertoire. The extant archival evidence suggests that processes of accommodation and adaptation were rarely seamless and smooth, and that such changes almost always had some unexpected impacts.[15] At the same time, missionary life in northern New Zealand was underwritten by negotiation and cultural accommodations. British ways of speaking, acting, and organizing life could not simply be replicated and reproduced, because of the tyranny of distance, the economic insecurity of the mission, and the reality that missionaries were living among and working with Māori.

From 1840, these relationships would shift again. Although some connections between missionaries and Māori were durable—such as the connections created by the marriage of missionary descendants into Māori families from the middle of the nineteenth century, especially around Kaitaia—the onset of formal colonization, the significant erosion of rangatiratanga (chiefly power) by the colonial state, and the demands of colonists for land and the full assertion of British sovereignty undercut the authority of missionaries and tended to push Māori to the margins of the developing colonial society.[16] The entanglements of empire had been transformed into the struggles and calcifying inequalities of a colonial order, which would quickly lead to open warfare in the Bay of Islands and to deep lines of fracture within both Māori and colonial communities. But as the colonial order took shape, the Bible and missionary Christianity were naturalized as Māori and were important seed-beds of Māori social action and political thought.

One of the dialogues provided in the 1820 *Grammar* compiled by Kendall with Hongi Hika and Waikato explored the question of whether European missionaries could become part of Māori communities. In the exchange, the teacher posed the question "Ka máodi tía te pákehá?" ("Are the Europeans naturalized?") This could be translated as "Are the Europeans or missionaries 'made normal'?"—that is, were they integrated into the community? The pupil's answer in the dialog reflected the uncertainty around the nature and future of the mission in 1820: "K'wai óki 'au ka kite?: How can I tell you?" After 1840, there was no need to ask whether newly arrived colonists wanted to become part of te ao Māori: their aspirations were clearly divergent from the more ambiguous aspirations of the missionaries. Generally, colonists did not seek to be immersed in Māori life: they only occasionally wanted to learn te reo Māori; few worked at a daily level in close proximity with Māori; and they were not interested in building sustained relationships with them. It is one of the tragic ironies of New Zealand's colonial past that missionaries—who for so long were implacable opponents of colonization—were in fact pivotal in entangling Māori in the webs of empire in the first place. In 1820 missionaries were ambivalent figures positioned between cultures, translating between worlds. But while their legacies—substantial and important as they are—have become clearer with time, the figure of the missionary remains ambiguous two hundred years after that first sermon at Rangihoua.

NOTES

Abbreviations

AJHR   Appendices to the Journals of the House of Representatives

ATL   Alexander Turnbull Library, Wellington

AWM   Auckland War Museum and Library

CMS   Church Missionary Society

CN/L   Series of mission books containing correspondence from the CMS

CN/M   Series of mission books containing correspondence to the CMS

CN/O   Series of original papers and correspondence relating to the CMS mission
          RHC Hocken Library and Collections, Dunedin, New Zealand

HRNZ   Robert McNab, ed., Historical Records of New Zealand

HWJ   Henry Williams, The Early Journals of Henry Williams

JBL   John Butler, Earliest New Zealand: Journals and Correspondence of John
          Butler

JKLJ   Letters and Journals of John King, PC-0152, HC

JHD   "Diary of John Hobbs," MS 144, AWM

KempLJ   Letters and Journals of James Kemp, MS-0070, HC

ML   J. R. Elder, ed., Marsden's Lieutenants

RCO   Records of the Colonial Office, National Archives, Kew, London

RDLJ   Richard Davis, Letters and Journals, MS-0066, PC-0066–0068, HC

SMCP   Samuel Marsden Collected Papers, HC

SMLJ   Samuel Marsden, Letters and Journals of Samuel Marsden

TKL   Thomas Kendall, Letters etc. 1816–1827, PC-0151, HC

WHD   William Hall, Private Diary, 1816–1838, Micro-MS-0853, ATL

WHLJ   Letters and Journals of William Hall, 1819–1832, MS-0067, HC

WFC   Williams Family Collections, qMS-2225, ATL

WMS   Wesleyan Missionary Society

WWP   William White Papers, MS 329, AWM

WPP   William Puckey Papers, MS 250, volume 1, AWM

WYC   William Yate Correspondence, Microfilm: 10096:1, HC

WYJ   William Yate Journal, Microfilm: 10096:2, HC

Introduction. Bodies in Contact, Bodies in Question

1. Initial reactions to the arrival of Europeans in the far north are recorded in "Nga Uri a Tapua me Kapene Kuki," in John White, "The Ancient History of the Maori, His Mythology and Traditions. Nga-Puhi. Volume 10 (Maori), From MS Papers 75, B 19 and B 24," printed as *The Ancient History of the Maori: Volume 9*, sections 71–72. This Māori text is reproduced with a modern parallel translation as "The First Pakehas to Visit the Bay of Islands," *Te Ao Hou* 51 (1965): 14–18. The authorship of this narrative is discussed in the letter from Ormond Wilson, *Te Ao Hou* 52 (1965): 2. See also Horeta Te Taniwha's account of the *Endeavour's* arrival at Whitianga, which is available in parallel English and Māori texts in *Te Ao Hou* 52 (1965): 43–49.

2. On "tangata maori," see Kendall, *A Korao no New Zealand*, 22–23. For evidence of the adoption of "Maori" in the place of "New Zealander" or "native," see Henry Williams, Journal 14 October 1833, HWJ, 332–33; Markham, *New Zealand or Recollections of It*, 117; log entry for 20 April 1836, in Anson, *The Piraki Log (e Pirangi ahau koe)*, 33. It seems that this shift toward using "Maori" in the place of other terms began in letters and journals produced on the New Zealand frontier, rather than in published texts produced for British audiences. This is a different analytical strategy than that recently adopted by Damon Salesa who prefers to use "Tāngata Whenua" to "Māori" for this period (*Racial Crossings*, 23–24). The use of macrons to distinguish long and short vowels, which are central in defining meaning in te reo Māori, has only been common in the last two decades. When quoting material I follow the original usage.

3. Marianne Williams, Journal 15 July 1824, WFC, ATL.

4. See, for example, John King to CMS, 4 November 1819, JKLJ, HC; Richard Taylor, Diary 7 February 1830, MS-Papers-0254–12, ATL. Also see Thorne, *Congregational Missions and the Making of an Imperial Culture in Nineteenth-Century England*, 29.

5. Nicholas, *Narrative of a Voyage*, 1:79, 97, 122, 129, 294; Hohepa, "My Musket, My Missionary, and My Mana," 196–98.

6. Cited in Lineham, "This Is My Weapon," 178.

7. See, for example, John Hobbs, Diary 27 November 1823, JHD, AWM; Jane Williams, Journal 3 February 1840, in Porter, *The Turanga Journals*, 90; John Butler, Journal 22–24 December 1819, Church Missionary Society, Archives Relating to the Australian and New Zealand Missions, 1808–1884, mission books containing correspondence to the CMS, Hocken Microfilm, CN/MI, HC.

8. For examples of the creolization of missionary English, see Henry Williams, Journal 7 September 1832 and 11 December 1832, HWJ, 258, 267. Henry Williams called his brother William "Parata," a Māori transliteration of "brother." On linguistic and racial connections, see Ballantyne, *Orientalism and Race*, 62–65.

9. Anon., "New Zealand: The Aborigines and Their Language," *Fisher's Colonial Magazine and Colonial Maritime Journal* 2 (January–April 1843): 455–57; E. Wakefield, "The New Zealand Language," *Fisher's Colonial Magazine and Colonial Maritime Journal* 2 new series (1845): 281.

10. See, for example, Luke 8:15, Romans 2:15, and Matthew 5:8, 12:34, and 15:18.

11. Wariki to George Clarke and William Yate, in Yate, *An Account of New Zealand*, 268–69.

12. These arguments were grounded in biblical injunctions, most explicitly in Leviticus 19:28.

13. *The Missionary Register* (June 1822), 252.

14. Nicholas, *Narrative of a Voyage to New Zealand*, 1:9–10.

15. Nicholas, *Narrative of a Voyage to New Zealand*, 1:10.

16. *Missionary Papers*, 1816, Michaelmas (III), unpaginated.

17. This claim about the mission's suppression of the practice was made by Yate, *An Account of New Zealand*, 150. It is more likely that the practice declined, albeit unevenly in time and space, from the 1840s, due to a complex conjuncture of forces, including the growth of colonial settlement and the pressures of colonial capitalism, the calcification of Māori congregational identities, and the development of indigenous modernities that selectively reworked aspects of "tradition."

18. The difficulties that missionaries pose for self-consciously modern and liberal New Zealanders is neatly sketched by Belich, *Making Peoples*, 135.

19. Foucault, *The History of Sexuality*, 17.

20. Foucault, *The History of Sexuality*, 18.

21. For a critical reading of this conflation, see Canning, "The Body as Method?"

22. This formulation reworks Tony Ballantyne and Antoinette Burton's "Introduction: Bodies, Empires, and World Histories," in Ballantyne and Burton, *Bodies in Contact*, 7. Also see Gallagher, *The Body Economic*; Poovey, *Making a Social Body*.

23. Canning, "The Body as Method?," 500.

24. Stoler, *Race and the Education of Desire*, esp. 7–8.

25. See Ballantyne and Burton, *Bodies in Contact*.

26. Dieffenbach, *Travels in New Zealand*, 2:118.

27. Maori Marsden notes that this status is "reinforced by endowment with mana." He thus sees mana as following tapu and as being produced when "the spirit

of gods fell upon the person and filled or possessed him." For Marsden, mana is best understood as "spiritual authority." Maori Marsden, "God, Man and Universe: A Māori View," in *The Woven Universe*, 5–7.

28. See, for example, Yate, *An Account of New Zealand*, 137; Polack, *Manners and Customs of the New Zealanders*, 2:108–9. For a useful discussion on the "contagious" nature of tapu, see Best, *Maori Religion and Mythology*, 16, 19.

29. See the *pēpeha* (traditional saying) that recalls the Waikato tohunga Kiki: "Ngā uri a Kiki whakamaroke rākau" [The descendants of Kiki who withered trees]. Or the pēpeha relating to the tapu shadow of the chief Hae: "Whati ngā ope a Mōkau." Pēpeha 2085 and 2664, in Mead and Grove, *Ngā Pēpeha a ngā Tīpuna*, 335, 425.

30. Biggs, *Maori Marriage*, 15.

31. Te Awekotuku, *Mana Wahine Maori*, 45.

32. Brubaker, *The Limits of Rationality*, 23–24; Gardella, *Innocent Ecstasy*, 9; Bebbington, *Evangelicalism in Modern Britain*, 63–65.

33. See, for example, Chapman, "Fiction and the Social Pattern," 36; Colgan and McGregor, *Sexual Secrets*, 5; Binney, *The Legacy of Guilt*; Sargeson, "An Imaginary Conversation."

34. The inhabitants of Waokena were responding to the rather literal translation of this text offered by missionaries, which emphasized the actual physical punishment of the body, rather than the spiritual control or mental repression of bodily desire. Richard Taylor, Journal 18 December 1845, qMS-1987, ATL.

35. Guha, *Elementary Aspects of Peasant Insurgency in Colonial India*.

36. Jones and Jenkins, *He Kōrero*, 119.

37. Dening, "The Comaroffs Out of Africa," 476.

38. Anne Salmond, *Two Worlds*; Anne Salmond, *Between Worlds*.

39. O'Malley, *The Meeting Place*. Examples of the work on gender include Rountree, "Re-making the Maori Female Body"; Middleton, "Silent Voices, Hidden Lives"; Tanya Fitzgerald, "Fences, Boundaries and Imagined Communities"; and Tanya Fitzgerald, "Creating a Disciplined Society." The key starting points for the older debate over conversion are Owens, "Christianity and the Maoris to 1840"; Binney, "Christianity and the Maoris to 1840: A Comment."

40. Ballantyne, *Orientalism and Race*; Ballantyne, *Between Colonialism and Diaspora*; and Ballantyne, *Webs of Empire*.

41. The text that typically accompanies this image says that the "design by Cliff Whiting invokes the signing of the Treaty of Waitangi and the consequent interwoven development of Maori and Pakeha history in New Zealand as it continuously unfolds in a pattern not yet completely known."

42. I should also note Nicholas Thomas's important *Entangled Objects*, which made an important contribution to the study of exchange relationships and material culture in the Pacific.

43. Hamilton, *Terrific Majesty*, 3–4.

44. Nuttall, *Entanglement*, 1.

45. Nuttall, *Entanglement*, 1, 3.

46. Lynn M. Thomas, *Politics of the Womb*, 19.

47. I have elaborated that argument with regard to place in a pair of essays: "Thinking Local" and "On Place, Space and Mobility in Nineteenth-Century New Zealand."

48. Note that Angela Middleton's recent vision of the "entwined" histories of Kororipo pā and the Kerikeri mission is very local in scale and does not conceive of these entanglements as being firmly connected to broader imperial networks. Middleton, *Kerikeri Mission and Kororipo Pā*.

49. On events and the "speeding up" of time, see Sewell, *Logics of History*.

50. For two historiographical statements, see Ballantyne, "Religion, Difference, and the Limits of British Imperial History," especially 449–51; and Ballantyne, "The Changing Shape of the Modern British Empire and Its Historiography," especially 451–52.

51. Stocking, *Victorian Anthropology*, xii–xiv.

52. The notion of the "global overlay" is drawn from Adshead, *Central Asia in World History*, 4. On empires as producing "entangled pasts," see Ballantyne, *Between Colonialism and Diaspora*.

53. Tsing, *Friction*.

1. Exploration, Empire, and Evangelization

1. Glen, "Those Odious Evangelicals"; Andrew Porter, *Religion Versus Empire?*; Stanley, *The Bible and the Flag*; compare to Sinha, *Colonial Masculinity*.

2. Most notably in the work of Anne Salmond: *Two Worlds* and *Between Worlds*.

3. Stoler and Cooper, "Between Metropole and Colony"; Cox, *Imperial Fault Lines*.

4. Massey, *For Space*.

5. Sissons, Wi Hongi, and Hohepa, *The Pūriri Trees Are Laughing*.

6. See Williams and Frost, "*Terra Australis*," 1–3.

7. Williams and Frost, "*Terra Australis*," 9–11.

8. See, for example, the discussion of John Dee, in E. G. R. Taylor, *Tudor Geography*, 279–80.

9. Schilder, *Australia Unveiled*.

10. "Instructions for the Skipper Commander Abel Jansen Tasman," 13 August 1642, in Sharp, *The Voyages of Abel Janszoon Tasman*, 30.

11. "Instructions for the Skipper Commander Abel Jansen Tasman," 13 August 1642, in Sharp, *The Voyages of Abel Janszoon Tasman*, 33.

12. "Tasman's Journal of the Voyage of 1642–1643," 13 December 1642, in Sharp, *The Voyages of Abel Janszoon Tasman*, 116.

13. See Anne Salmond, *Two Worlds*, 74–84; Mackay, *A Compendium of Official Documents*, 1:39–45.

14. Anne Salmond, *Two Worlds*, 78–83.

15. "The Haalbos-Montanus Account of the Voyage of 1642–1643," in Sharp, *The Voyages of Abel Janszoon Tasman*, 42–43; "Tasman's Journal of the Voyage of

1642–1643," 5 and 6 January 1643, in Sharp, *The Voyages of Abel Janszoon Tasman*, 144–45; "The Sailor's Journal of the Voyage of 1642–1643," 5 December 1642, in Sharp, *The Voyages of Abel Janszoon Tasman*, 278–79. This final source, produced by an anonymous and unidentified sailor on the *Heemskerck*, survives only as a copied manuscript and the copyist confused the dates of the voyage. He believed that the refit in Mauritius lasted for just a day, rather than a month and a day; thus the chronology of this text is one month behind the other records of the journey.

16. "Tasman's Journal of the Voyage of 1642–1643," 19 December 1642, in Sharp, *The Voyages of Abel Janszoon Tasman*, 124.

17. "Tasman's Journal of the Voyage of 1642–1643," 19 December 1642, in Sharp, *The Voyages of Abel Janszoon Tasman*, 122–23.

18. This was aimed at calculating the distance of the sun from the Earth, which would allow the distances between all the planets to be calculated.

19. Cook, *The Voyage of the Endeavour*, cclxxxii.

20. Cook, *The Voyage of the Endeavour*, cclxxxiii.

21. David, *The Charts and Coastal Views of Captain Cook's Voyages*; Joppien and Smith, *The Art of Captain Cook's Voyages*.

22. For a useful recent treatment of Tupaia, see Vanessa Smith, "Joseph Banks's Intermediaries."

23. Banks, *The Endeavour Journal of Joseph Banks*, 2:3. In a similar vein, Cook stressed the potential value of "immense woods on the verge of the Thames River." Cook, *The Voyage of the Endeavour*, 207.

24. Banks, *The Endeavour Journal of Joseph Banks*, 2:9–10.

25. Cook, *The Voyage of the Endeavour*, 276.

26. Cook, *The Voyage of the Endeavour*, 278.

27. Cook, *The Voyage of the Endeavour*, 204.

28. Cook, *The Voyage of the Endeavour*, 243.

29. Hawkesworth, *An Account of the Voyages Undertaken by the Order of His Present Majesty*, 3:437–40. Following both Banks and Cook, he noted, however, that Te Ika a Māui appeared more fertile and suited to settlement than Te Wai Pounamu.

30. Hawkesworth, *An Account of the Voyages Undertaken by the Order of His Present Majesty*, 3:438.

31. See, for example, *Annual Register* (1774): 27–42; *London Magazine* 43 (1773): 319–20.

32. Salesa, "Afterword."

33. Joppien and Smith remind us that even Hodges' dramatic and romantic landscapes were seen as having potential value in exploiting New Zealand's natural resources, including mineral deposits (*The Art of Captain Cook's Voyages*, 2:23).

34. Journal 26 November 1773, in Forster, *The Resolution Journal of Johann Reinhold Forster*, 3:429.

35. Charles Clerke, "RESOLUTION: Log kept by Lieutenant Charles Clerke, towards the South Pole. Discovery and surveying, Pacific, Australia, west coast of North America," Adm 55/103, f. 71, National Archives, Kew, London.

36. George Vancouver, Journal 20 November 1791, in Lamb, *A Voyage of Discovery to the North Pacific Ocean and Round the World*, 364.

37. George Vancouver, Journal 20 November 1791, in Lamb, *A Voyage of Discovery to the North Pacific Ocean and Round the World*, 365.

38. McCalman, *A Natural, Commercial and Medicinal Treatise on Tea*, 24. Also see his discussion of Cook drinking "tea" (101).

39. *Parliamentary History*, vol. 24, 1783–85, columns, 755–57.

40. J. Thomson to H. Dundas, 22 November 1792, RCO 201/7, 360–64, National Archives, Kew, London.

41. "Plan by Messeurs Franklin and Dalrymple for Benefiting Distant Unprovided Countries," in Franklin, *Political, Miscellaneous, and Philosophical Pieces*, 37–38.

42. "Plan by Messeurs Franklin and Dalrymple for Benefiting Distant Unprovided Countries," in Franklin, *Political, Miscellaneous, and Philosophical Pieces*, 38.

43. Anne Salmond, *Between Worlds*, 36.

44. Anne Salmond, *Between Worlds*, 40.

45. On the broad imperial impact of the information collected by Cook, see Ballantyne, "Empire, Knowledge, Culture."

46. Matra to North, 23 August 1783, RCO 201/1, ff. 57–61, National Archives, Kew, London.

47. Quoted in Frost, *The Global Reach of Empire*, 155.

48. Frost, *The Global Reach of Empire*, 183–84; and Frost, *Botany Bay Mirages*.

49. These maritime networks are discussed in Blainey, *The Tyranny of Distance*; and Bach, *The Maritime History of Australia*, 45–69. On the importance of Bengal to the colony, see Broadbent, Rickard, and Steven, *India, China, Australia*. On New South Wales's Pacific connections, especially to Tahiti, see Maude, *Of Islands and Men*, 185–94; and Newell, *Trading Nature*, 178–90. Newell uses the term "ocean-minded" (180).

50. Gammage, "Early Boundaries of New South Wales"; Ryan, "Was New Zealand Part of New South Wales, 1788–1817?"

51. Morton, *The Whale's Wake*, 108. Cook's voyages were instrumental in initiating sealing in New Zealand. Soon after the *Resolution* arrived in Dusky Sound in 1773, Captain Cook had a seal killed: its flesh was used as food for the crew, while its oil was used for lighting and its hide in rigging.

52. See McNab, *Murihiku and the Southern Islands*, 38–48.

53. The best reconstruction of sealing in New Zealand is Ian Smith, *The New Zealand Sealing Industry*.

54. Bladen, *King and Bligh*, 88.

55. McNab, *Murihiku and the Southern Islands*, 48; Bladen, *Hunter and King*, 630.

56. Edgar Thomas Dell, 1795, RCO 201/18, 7–19, National Archives, Kew, London; Anne Salmond, *Between Worlds*, 234–51.

57. Anne Salmond, *Between Worlds*, 252–81.

58. Frost, *Botany Bay Mirages*, 55.

59. Philip Gidley King, Letterbook, c187, 59, Mitchell Library, State Library of New South Wales, Australia.

60. King recorded that he felt for his captives as "a Father & a Husband," because of the "daily lamentations of Two sensible men, who were continually reminding me of my Promise [to return them home] & repeating their anxious fears, respecting the safety of their familys" (Philip Gidley King, Letterbook, c187, 225, Mitchell Library, State Library of New South Wales, Australia). On Tuki's map, see Anne Salmond, *Between Worlds*, 222–26; Binney, "Tuki's Universe."

61. On language, see King in HRNZ, 2:543–44. Tuki also told King that Cook's map of New Zealand omitted the Hokianga River, which, he informed King, was home to "Pine trees of an immense size."

62. This point on the importance of the manākitanga of King and his mana in Māori eyes is well made by Anne Salmond, *Between Worlds*, 226.

63. Eustace Carey, *Memoir of William Carey D.D.*, 18.

64. Whitcombe, *A Sermon Preached in the Parish-Church of Walesby*, 12.

65. Whitcombe, *A Sermon Preached in the Parish-Church of Walesby*, 12–13.

66. Haweis, "The Very Probable Success of a Proper Mission to the South Sea Islands."

67. Yarwood, *Samuel Marsden*, 1–21, 283–85; Purnell, *Magdalene College*, 171–80.

68. Marsden to Reverend Josiah Pratt, 24 March 1808, Records Relating to the New Zealand Mission. General inwards letters, March 1808–November 1812, MS-0498/001/001, HC.

69. Samuel Marsden to Reverend Josiah Pratt, 7 April 1808, Records Relating to the New Zealand Mission. General inwards letters, March 1808–November 1812, MS-0498/001/003, HC.

70. Samuel Marsden to Reverend Josiah Pratt, 18 June 1808, Records Relating to the New Zealand Mission. General inwards letters, March 1808–November 1812, MS-0498/001/007, HC; Samuel Marsden to Reverend Josiah Pratt, 28 June 1808, Records Relating to the New Zealand Mission. General inwards letters, March 1808–November 1812, MS-0498/001/008, HC.

71. Jones and Jenkins, *He Kōrero*, 33.

72. King to CMS, 25 April 1810, Church Missionary Society, Archives Relating to the Australian and New Zealand Missions, 1808–1884, original papers and correspondence relating to the CMS, Hocken Microfilm, CN/O 61/28, HC.

73. Anne Salmond, *Between Worlds*, 386, 414; *Sydney Gazette*, 10 March and 21 April 1810; Ballara, "Te Pahi ?–1810," www.teara.govt.nz/en/biographies/1t53/te-pahi. In October 1810, Marsden was informed by a young Māori sailor that the real cause of the attack on the *Boyd* was the desire of Te Puhi to extract revenge on the ship and its crew for the mistreatment of Te Āra and his three companions, who had served aboard the ship. See Marsden to Pratt, 25 October 1810, in Harvard-Williams, *Marsden and the New Zealand Mission*, 31–35. Also see

Marsden's report on Te Āra's own testimony (Marsden to CMS, 15 March 1814, SMCP, "Correspondence, 1813–1814," PC-0118, HC).

74. Despite his relatively young age—he was about twenty-five years old in 1812—Ruatara assumed the mantle of leadership at Rangihoua. The heir of Te Pahi, "Ogateeree" (Hokatiri?), had disappeared, perhaps dying during the raid on Te Pahi's island in 1810. Ruatara seemingly inherited the mana of Te Pahi over the more senior Te Uri o Kanae, who was a less capable leader. See Angela Ballara, "Ruatara ?–1815," www.teara.govt.nz/en/biographies/1r19/ruatara.

75. Following Ian Smith and Angela Middleton's research, I will here prefer "Hohi," although I have, like most other historians, previously used "Oihi," following the lead of the influential editor J. R. Elder. See Smith and Middleton et al., *Archaeology of the Hohi Mission Station*.

76. Quoted in Bollen, "English Missionary Societies," 284.

77. M. H. Ellis, *Lachlan Macquarie*, 373.

78. Marsden to Scott, 2 December 1826, quoted in Gunson, *Australian Reminiscences and Papers of L. E. Threlkeld*, 2:347. Also see Gascoigne, *The Enlightenment and the Origins of European Australia*, 157.

79. On both the difficulties of improvement and significant innovations in north Yorkshire, see Overton, *Agricultural Revolution in England*, 114; Caunce, "Agriculture in North-Eastern England."

80. Marsden to Scott, 2 December 1826, quoted in Gunson, *Australian Reminiscences and Papers of L. E. Threlkeld*, 2:347.

81. Bollen, "English Missionary Societies and the Australian Aborigine," 271–72.

82. Bollen, "English Missionary Societies and the Australian Aborigine," 285.

83. Johnston, *The Paper War*.

84. Yarwood, *Samuel Marsden*, 112–13; Stapleton, *Elizabeth Marsden*, 14–16; Elizabeth Marsden to Mrs. Stokes, 1 May 1796, in Mackaness, *Some Private Correspondence of the Rev. Samuel Marsden and Family*, 15.

85. *Sydney Gazette*, 2 December 1804.

86. Reynolds, *With the White People*, 185.

87. J. B. Marsden, *Memoirs of the Life and Labours of the Rev. Samuel Marsden of Parramatta*, 84.

88. Marsden to Coates, 23 February 1836, SMCP, "Correspondence July 1835–February 1838," PC-0139, HC.

89. Marsden to CMS, 24 February 1819, SMCP, "Correspondence March 1818–May 1819," PC-0132, HC.

90. These issues are explored in an important discussion in Standfield, *Race and Identity in the Tasman World*, chaps. 5 and 6.

91. Marsden to Commissioner Bigge, 28 December 1819, in HRNZ, 1:449–50.

92. Samuel Marsden, "Observations on the introduction of the Gospels into the South Sea Islands: Being my first visit to New Zealand in Dec 1814," SMCP, MS-0176/001, PC-0030, HC. Governor King noted that Te Pahi's "every action and observation shows an uncommon attention to the rules of decency and

propriety in his every action, and has much of the airs and manners of a man conversant with the world he lives in." King's "Notes, 1806," in HRNZ, 1:264.

93. Samuel Marsden to Reverend Josiah Pratt, 7 April 1808, Records Relating to the New Zealand Mission. General inwards letters, March 1808–November 1812, MS-0498/001/003, HC.

94. Samuel Marsden, SMCP, "Observations on the introduction of the Gospels into the South Sea Islands," PC-0030, HC.

95. Samuel Marsden to Reverend Josiah Pratt, 7 April 1808, Records Relating to the New Zealand Mission. General inwards letters, March 1808–November 1812, MS-0498/001/003, HC.

96. Marsden to John Stokes, 26 November 1811, in Mackaness, *Some Private Correspondence of the Rev. Samuel Marsden and Family*, 44–45.

97. Gunson, *Messengers of Grace*, 270.

98. Davies to Missionary Society, 8 September 1813, London Missionary Society, "South Seas Letters 1812–1818: Minutes and Selected Records Relating to Australia and the South Pacific," Micro-MS-Coll-02-019, ATL.

99. Yarwood, *Samuel Marsden*, 111.

100. Hainsworth, *The Sydney Traders*, 158–60; Newell, *Trading Nature*, 178–90.

101. Steven, *Merchant Campbell*, 273, 279.

102. Marsden to Reverend Josiah Pratt, 7 February 1820, SMCP, "Correspondence July 1819–August 1821," PC-0134, HC. On Campbell's New Zealand connections, see Steven, *Merchant Campbell*, 31, 112–17, 145–46, 213–14, 231, 254, 283.

103. Yarwood, *Samuel Marsden*, 133; Newell, *Trading Nature*, 128, 188.

104. Marsden to Pratt, 22 September 1814, printed in *A Sermon Preached at the Parish Church of St. Andrew by the Wardrobe and St. Anne Blackfriars on Tuesday, 2 May 1815*, 625.

105. Quoted in Yarwood, *Samuel Marsden*, 158.

106. Marsden to Reverend Josiah Pratt, 24 March 1808, Records Relating to the New Zealand Mission. General inwards letters, March 1808–November 1812, MS-0498/001/001, HC. MS-0498/001/001, HC.

107. Marsden to Reverend Josiah Pratt, 7 February 1820, SMCP, "Correspondence July 1819–August 1821," PC-0134, HC.

108. Marsden to Reverend Josiah Pratt, 22 September 1820, SMCP, "Correspondence July 1819–August 1821," PC-0134, HC.

109. Marsden to Reverend Josiah Pratt, 24 March 1808, Records Relating to the New Zealand Mission. General inwards letters, March 1808–November 1812, MS-0498/001/001, HC. MS-0498/001/001, HC.

110. Marsden to Reverend Josiah Pratt, 9 May 1809, Records Relating to the New Zealand Mission. General inwards letters, March 1808–November 1812, MS-0498/001/020, HC.

111. Marsden to Macquarie, 1 November 1813, quoted in the *Missionary Register*, November 1814, 465–66.

112. Governor Macquarie, "Government Order," 1 December 1813, HRNZ, 1:316–18.

113. Governor Macquarie, "Government and General Order, 9th November 1814," HRNZ, 1:316–18, 328–29.

114. Marsden to CMS, 3 May 1810, in Harvard-Williams, *Marsden and the New Zealand Mission*, 28–29; Marsden to Pratt, in 18 November 1814, HRNZ, 1:330–31; Marsden to Miss Mary Stokes, 15 June 1815, in Mackaness, *Some Private Correspondence of the Rev. Samuel Marsden and Family*, 54–55; *A Sermon Preached at the Parish Church of St. Andrew by the Wardrobe and St. Anne Blackfriars on Tuesday, 3 May 1814*, 302–3; *Missionary Papers*, no. 3 (Michaelmas 1816), unpaginated; Kendall to Joshua Mann, 14 July 1817, and Kendall to Marsden, 1 August 1822, TKL, HC.

115. Marsden, Cartwright, and Youl to Pratt, 27 March 1817, SMCP, "Correspondence March 1817–August 1818," PC-0131, HC.

116. Marsden to Pratt, 20 November 1811, in Harvard-Williams, *Marsden and the New Zealand Mission*, 40–41.

117. Marsden to Ruatara, 9 March 1814, SMCP, "Correspondence 1814–1815," PC-0119, HC.

118. Jones and Jenkins, *He Kōrero*, 79. John Liddiard Nicholas suggested that the dress was a gift from Marsden himself. Nicholas, *Narrative of a Voyage to New Zealand*, 2:199.

119. See Marsden's use of the phrase "my friend" in correspondence about one of these rangatira: Marsden to John Stokes, 26 November 1811, in Mackaness, *Some Private Correspondence of the Rev. Samuel Marsden and Family*, 44–45.

120. Jones and Jenkins, *He Kōrero*, 126.

121. Jones and Jenkins, *He Kōrero*, 172.

122. Belich, *Making Peoples*, 140–55.

123. Samuel Marsden to Reverend Josiah Pratt, 24 March 1808, "Records Relating to the New Zealand Mission," MS-0498/001/001, HC.

124. Samuel Marsden, SMCP, "Observations on the introduction of the Gospels into the South Sea Islands," MS-0176/001, PC-0030, HC.

125. Nicholas, *Narrative of a Voyage to New Zealand*, 1:13–14.

126. Nicholas, *Narrative of a Voyage to New Zealand*, 1:24–25.

127. See Leach, "Four Centuries of Community Interaction and Trade in Cook Strait, New Zealand"; and Leach, "Prehistoric Communities in Palliser Bay, New Zealand."

128. Binney, "Tuki's Universe."

129. King's "Notes, 1806," in HRNZ, 1:263–4.

130. *Sydney Gazette*, 15 June 1806 and 12 April 1807.

131. Samuel Marsden, SMCP, "Observations on the introduction of the Gospels into the South Sea Islands," MS-0176/001, PC-0030, HC.

132. Kendall to Marsden, 25 July 1817, SMCP, "Correspondence March 1817–August 1818," PC-0131, HC.

133. On their interest in Christianity, especially the Sabbath, see Samuel Marsden, SMCP, "Observations on the introduction of the Gospels into the South Sea

Islands," MS-0176/001, PC-0030; Marsden to CMS, 19 Nov 1811, "Records Relating to the New Zealand Mission," MS-0498/008/240, HC.

134. Grove, "Te Whatanui"; Winiata, "Leadership in Pre-European Maori Society."

135. Anne Salmond, *Between Worlds*, 422.

136. Ballara, *Taua*, 397–98. Compare Ballara's cautious reading of the role of potatoes in providing the material base for the extension of Māori warfare—she suggests that they may have only become very significant in the 1830s—with Belich's more assertive reading in *Making Peoples*, 159.

137. Sissons, Wi Hongi, and Hohepa, *The Pūriri Trees Are Laughing*, 31–39.

138. See Ballara, *Taua*, 205.

139. See John Savage's comments about Te Pahi's use of potatoes (*Some Account of New Zealand*, 54–57).

140. Thomas Kendall, Journal 16 June 1814, "Thomas Kendall Journal 9 Mar 1814–13 Feb 1815," MS-Papers-0921, ATL.

141. Samuel Marsden, 19 October 1819, SMCP, "Rev. S. Marsden's journal of proceedings at New Zealand from July 29 to Oct 19, 1819," MS-0177/002, PC-0140, HC.

142. See Sissons, Wi Hongi, and Hohepa, *The Pūriri Trees Are Laughing*, 45; Ballara, *Taua*, 193.

2. *Making Place, Reordering Space*

1. Charles Darwin, Journal 23 December 1835, in Darwin, *Charles Darwin's Diary*, 368. After the completion of his visit to New Zealand, Darwin understood more clearly the importance of fern to Māori, and this was communicated in his *Journal of Researches into the Natural History and Geology of the Countries Visited by the H.M.S. Beagle*, 423, where he emphasized the dietary and nutritional importance of *aruhe* (fern root). On fern, see Best, *Forest Lore of the Maori*, 72–86.

2. Charles Darwin, Journal 23 December 1835, in Darwin, *Charles Darwin's Diary*, 367–69.

3. Charles Darwin, Journal 23 December 1835, in Darwin, *Charles Darwin's Diary*, 368–69.

4. Charles Darwin, Journal 23–24 December 1835, in Darwin, *Charles Darwin's Diary*, 370–71.

5. The capital, labor, and cultural reflection that was invested in the production of colonial respectability is at the heart of Robert Ross, *Status and Respectability in the Cape Colony*.

6. Graham, "'The Enchanter's Wand,'" 133.

7. Charles Darwin, Journal 23 December 1835, in Darwin, *Charles Darwin's Diary*, 370.

8. Charles Darwin, Journal 26 December 1835, in Darwin, *Charles Darwin's Diary*, 373–74.

9. Jacobsin-Widding, "Subjective Body, Objective Space."

10. Tsing, *Friction*.

11. This policy reflected a long tradition of Catholic missiology and was affirmed in the strong divide that Bishop Pompallier drew between "le bien naturel" (natural welfare) and "le bien spirituel" (spiritual welfare). Pompallier also insisted that missionaries did not work "au nom de quelque prince de la terre" (in the name of any earthly prince). See Pompallier, "Instructions pour travaux de la mission," 29 January 1841, POM 14-3, Auckland Catholic Diocesan Archives. Also see Thomson, "Some Reasons for the Failure of the Roman Catholic Mission to the Māoris," 169–70.

12. Tanya Fitzgerald, "Jumping the Fences"; Cathy Ross, *Women with a Mission*; Goldsbury, "Behind the Picket Fence"; Sinclair, *A History of New Zealand* (1969), 42.

13. Compare this reading with Tanya Fitzgerald's treatment of mission stations, which silences the powerful influence of Māori, especially influential chiefs like Ruatara and Hongi Hika, on the selection of sites, as she suggests that the positioning of stations simply reflected the missionaries' own priorities. Tanya Fitzgerald, "Fences, Boundaries, and Imagined Communities," 15.

14. McNab, *From Tasman to Marsden*, 105.

15. Savage, *Some Account of New Zealand*, 9, 54–56.

16. On the kidnapping of Atahoe and George Bruce, who functioned as Te Pahi's key intermediary, see Anne Salmond, *Between Worlds*, 349–67.

17. "Tippahee a chief of New Zealand," Sv/Mao/Port/14, Mitchell Library, State Library of New South Wales, Australia.

18. Ballara, "Te Pahi ?–1810."

19. Samuel Marsden, 19 October 1819, SMCP, "Rev. S. Marsden's journal of the proceedings at New Zealand from July 29 to Oct 19, 1819," PC-0140, HC; Samuel Marsden, n.d., SMCP, "Observations on the introduction of the Gospels into the South Sea Islands: Being my First Visit to New Zealand in Dec 1814," MS-0176/001, PC-0030, HC.

20. Jones and Jenkins, *He Kōrero*, 58, 61–62, 86.

21. Ballara, "Te Pahi ?–1810," www.teara.govt.nz/en/biographies/1t53/te-pahi; Marsden to CMS, 15 March 1814, in HRNZ, 1:320.

22. Angela Ballara notes that Marsden believed that Ruatara's father was Kaparu, Te Pahi's younger brother, while his mother was Hongi Hika's sister. But she suggests that in reality, Ruatara's father was "Te Aweawe of Ngati Rahiri and Ngati Tautahi sections of Nga Puhi, and his mother Tauramoko, of Ngati Rahiri and Ngati Hineira" ("Te Pahi ?–1810," www.teara.govt.nz/en/biographies/1t53/te-pahi). Also see Sissons, Wi Hongi, and Hohepa, *The Pūriri Trees Are Laughing*, 13.

23. Samuel Marsden, 19 October 1819, SMCP, "Rev. S. Marsden's journal of proceedings at New Zealand from July 29 to Oct 19, 1819," MS-0177/002, PC-0140, HC.

24. Nicholas, *Narrative of a Voyage to New Zealand*, 2:194–95.

25. Kendall to Secretary, 6 November 1816, SMCP, "Correspondence March 1816–February 1817," PC-0130, HC.

26. King to Secretary, 6 July 1815, SMCP, "Correspondence June 1815–October 1815," PC-0128, HC; William Hall, Journal 25 January 1816, WHD, ATL.

27. Marsden to Shunghee [Hongi Hika], 11 November 1823, SMLJ, 336.

28. Sissons, "Hongi Hika," 47.

29. Judith Binney, "Introduction," in Binney, Te Kerikeri, 10–12.

30. John King Diary (sent to Rev. Josiah Pratt), 16 August 1815, SMCP, "Correspondence October 1815–March 1816," PC-0129, HC.

31. Samuel Marsden, 17 August 1819, SMCP, "Rev. S. Marsden's journal of proceedings at New Zealand from July 29 to Oct 19, 1819," MS-0177/002, PC-0140, HC.

32. Samuel Marsden, 18 August 1819, SMCP, "Rev. S. Marsden's journal of proceedings at New Zealand from July 29 to Oct 19, 1819," MS-0177/002, PC-0140, HC. On Korokoro's kin and political affiliations, see Sissons, Wi Hongi, and Hohepa, The Pūriri Trees Are Laughing, 23, 42–48.

33. Samuel Marsden, 2 May 1820, SMCP, "Rev. Sam. Marsden's Journal from Feb 13 to Nov 25 1820," MS-0177/002, HC; Easdale, Missionary and Maori, 31; Sissons, Wi Hongi, and Hohepa, The Pūriri Trees Are Laughing, 39.

34. Samuel Marsden, 14 September and 24 September 1819, SMCP, "Rev. S. Marsden's journal of proceedings at New Zealand from July 29 to Oct 19, 1819," MS-0177/001, PC-0140, HC.

35. "Grant of land at Keddee Keddee by Shunghee Heeka to the Church Missionary Society, 4 November 1819," MS-0070/A, HC.

36. Sissons, "Hongi Hika," 48.

37. Archaeological evidence suggests that the material base of the mission communities at Hohi and Te Puna was relatively constrained. Smith and Middleton et al., Archaeology of the Hohi Mission Station; Middleton, Te Puna.

38. Kendall to Secretary, 6 November 1816, SMCP, "Correspondence March 1816–February 1817," PC-0130, HC.

39. Middleton, Te Puna, 69.

40. Turton, Maori Deeds of Old Private Land Purchases in New Zealand, 65–66.

41. Middleton, Te Puna, 70–71.

42. Henry Williams, Journal Thursday 11 January 1827, HWJ, 37.

43. For a clear early articulation of this argument, see George Clarke to the Secretary, 29 March, 1828, collected papers of and relating to George Clarke senior and family, "George Clarke [senior]. Letter and Journals. 1822–1849. Vol 1. Documents 1–57," PC-0054, HC.

44. Samuel Marsden, 7 August 1823, SMCP, "Rev. S. Marsden's journal from July 2 to Nov 1, 1823," MS-0177/003, HC; Sissons, Wi Hongi, and Hohepa, The Pūriri Trees Are Laughing, 39–42, 149.

45. HWJ, 31n.1. On this institution, which contained a "seminary for New Zealanders," see Jones and Jenkins, He Kōrero, chap. 12.

46. Samuel Marsden, 13 September 1819, SMCP, "Rev. S. Marsden's journal of proceedings at New Zealand from July 29 to Oct 19, 1819," MS-0177/002, PC-0140, HC.

47. Henry Williams, 24 October 1823, WFC, ATL.

48. Henry Williams, 13 November 1823, WFC, ATL. On Paihia's soil, see Thomas Chapman to CMS, 8 Sept 1831, Thomas Chapman Letters, Journals, Reports, 1830–1860, Church Missionary Society, Archives Relating to the Australian and New Zealand Missions, 1808–1884, original papers and correspondence relating to the CMS, Hocken Microfilm, CN/O 30, HC.

49. This vessel was wrecked in 1828, but was replaced by the *Karere* and, from 1835, the schooner *Columbine*. Frederic Wanklyn Williams, *Through Ninety Years, 1826–1916*, 9; Middleton, *Te Puna*, 225; Binney, "Christianity and the Maoris to 1840," 147.

50. Griffiths, "Boundaries of the Sacred," 39–40.

51. Henry Williams, Journal 6 January 1825, in Caroline Fitzgerald, *Te Wiremu/ Henry Williams*, 52; Coleman, *A Memoir of the Rev. Richard Davis*, 62–63.

52. Henry Williams, Journal 6 January 1825, in Caroline Fitzgerald, *Te Wiremu/ Henry Williams*, 52–53.

53. Nicholas, *Narrative of a Voyage to New Zealand*, 1:333.

54. Marsden to Hongi, 11 November 1823, SMLJ, 336; Parsonson, "The Expansion of a Competitive Society," 51.

55. Marsden to Hongi, 26 July 1824, SMLJ, 337.

56. Hargreaves, "Waimate-Pioneer New Zealand Farm," 38–45.

57. See the deed of "Kerekere Block 1, Mangonui District," in Turton, *Maori Deeds of Old Private Land Purchases in New Zealand*, 3.

58. Price, *Making Empire*, 16, 32n1.

59. Samuel Marsden, 26 December 1814 and 6 January 1815, SMCP, "Observations on the Introduction of the Gospels into the South Sea Islands," MS-0176/001, PC-0030, HC.

60. Marianne Williams, 6 October 1823, WFC, ATL.

61. *Church Missionary Record* (1832), 62; Markham, *New Zealand or Recollections of It*, 68.

62. King to Reverend Daniel Wilson, 15 February 1815, SMCP, "Correspondence, 1814–1815," PC-0119, HC.

63. Easdale, *Missionary and Maori*, 28, 32, 36.

64. Alexander McCrae, Journal 5 March 1820, in McCrae, *Journal Kept in New Zealand in 1820*, 19.

65. William Hall to CMS, 28 December 1820, ML, 243.

66. Middleton, *Te Puna*, 59–61.

67. Dandeson Coates evidence, 8 June 1836, *Report from the Select Committee on Aborigines* (1836), 522.

68. Thomas Kendall, 16–17, 21 October and 25 November 1822, Collected Papers, "Diary of Thomas Surfleet Kendall," MS-0071/072, HC.

69. Jeremy Salmond, "The Mission House, Kerikeri," 93–98.

70. See Robert Ross's discussion of how the use of halls and corridors to produce privacy by British colonists at the Cape diverged from Dutch models. Robert Ross, *Status and Respectability in the Cape Colony*, 81.

71. Standish, *The Waimate Mission Station*, 15–18.

72. Prickett, "An Archaeologist's Guide to the Maori Dwelling"; Makereti, *The Old-Time Maori*, 282–314.

73. Hanson and Hanson, *Counterpoint in Maori Culture*, 94–95; Prickett, "An Archaeologist's Guide," 120, 132.

74. Hanson and Hanson, *Counterpoint in Maori Culture*, 50, 94; Manihera, Pewhairangi, and Rangihau, "Foreword," 9.

75. Firth, *Primitive Economics of the New Zealand Maori*, 111.

76. King to Secretary, 6 July 1815, SMCP, "Correspondence June 1815–October 1815," PC-0128, HC; John King Diary (sent to Rev. Josiah Pratt), July 1815 (date illegible), SMCP, "Correspondence October 1815—March 1816," PC-0129, HC. The Kings also were primarily responsible for raising two of Wharepoaka's daughters.

77. John Butler, Journal 9 February 1920, JBL, 68.

78. Hanson and Hanson, *Counterpoint in Maori Culture*, 50, 79; Firth, *Primitive Economics of the New Zealand Maori*, 253–58; John King, Journal 1 December 1824, JKLJ, HC.

79. John Hobbs, Diary 24 October 1825, JHD, AWM.

80. Binney, *The Legacy of Guilt*, 57; Valerie Carson, "Submitting to Great Inconveniences," 62.

81. Kendall to CMS, 19 October 1815, Church Missionary Society, Records Relating to the New Zealand Mission, "General inwards letters, February 1813–December 1817," MS-0498/002, HC; Kendall to Joshua Mann, 14 July 1817, TKL, HC.

82. Kendall to Woodd, 16 October 1816, SMCP, "Correspondence March 1816–February 1817," PC-0130, HC.

83. Valerie Carson, "Submitting to Great Inconveniences," 62–64.

84. Marianne Williams, 22 September 1828, WFC, ATL.

85. Marianne Williams, 25 May 1830, WFC, ATL.

86. Marianne Williams, 25 May 1830, WFC, ATL.

87. Marianne Williams, 28 March 1828, WFC, ATL.

88. Henry Williams, Journal 8 November 1832, HWJ, 263.

89. Nicholas, *Narrative of a Voyage to New Zealand*, 1:87 and 2:41, 43–44, 10; Wade, *A Journey in the Northern Island of New Zealand*, 96 n.

90. Yate, *An Account of New Zealand*, 87; also see Hanson and Hanson, *Counterpoint in Maori Culture*, 50.

91. Henry Williams, Journal 11 February 1828, HWJ, 102; Tanya Fitzgerald, "Fences, Boundaries and Imagined Communities," 19.

92. John Butler, Journal 22–24 December 1819 and 3–4 January 1820, JBL, 63.

93. Nicholas, *Narrative of a Voyage to New Zealand*, 2:127

94. John Butler, Journal 26 May 1821, JBL; Marianne Williams, 11 January 1824, WFC, ATL.

95. Middleton, *Te Puna*, 176.

96. John King Diary (sent to Rev. Josiah Pratt), 31 August–1 September 1815, SMCP, "Correspondence October 1815–March 1816," PC-0129, HC.

97. King to Secretary, January 25 1816, SMCP, "Correspondence October 1815–March 1816," PC-0129, HC.

98. Easdale, *Missionary and Maori*, 41.

99. See Marianne Williams's comments on half of the community at Kawakawa being "decently dressed in English clothing" for divine service on 8 May 1836, in *Letters from the Bay of Islands*, 232–33. Also see Busby, *A Brief Memoir Relative to the Islands of New Zealand*, 61.

100. Easdale, *Missionary and Maori*, 45.

101. *Missionary Register* (1826), 616.

102. Eliza White to her parents, September 1833, cited in Middleton, "Silent Voices, Hidden Lives," 13.

103. Maunsell to Eliza Langham, 16 June 1838, Susan Maunsell, Letters, MS 93/111, AWM.

104. Jones and Jenkins, *He Kōrero*.

105. Easdale, *Missionary and Maori*, 32, 40.

106. Tanya Fitzgerald, "Fences, Boundaries, and Imagined Communities," 16–17.

107. For a sophisticated archaeological reading of such boundaries see Leach, "Horticulture in Prehistoric New Zealand."

108. Kendall to the Secretary, 14 December 1818, SMCP, "Correspondence March 1818–May 1819," PC-0132, HC; Kendall to Marsden, 27 September 1821, TKL, HC; Middleton, *Te Puna*, 144–45.

109. Kendall, *A Grammar and Vocabulary of the Language of New Zealand*, 68.

110. John King, Journal 10–11 February 1823, JKLJ, HC.

111. John King, Journal 17 December 1823, JKLJ, HC.

112. Hall to CMS, 3 Feb 1825, WHLJ, HC.

113. Middleton, *Te Puna*, 168.

114. John Butler, Journal 22–24 Dec 1819, Church Missionary Society, Archives Relating to the Australian and New Zealand Missions, 1808–1884, mission books containing correspondence to the CMS, Hocken Microfilm, CN/M1, HC.

115. King to Secretary, 6 July 1815, SMCP, "Correspondence June 1815–October 1815," PC-0128; William Hall, Journal 25 January 1816, WHD, ATL.

116. Easdale, *Missionary and Maori*, 32, 40.

117. Tanya Fitzgerald, "Fences, Boundaries, and Imagined Communities," 14–25.

118. William Hall, Journal 19 March 1816, WHD, ATL.

119. William Hall, Journal 23 and 25 March 1816, WHD, ATL.

120. Easdale, *Missionary and Maori*, 28–29, 31.

121. Hargraves, "Waimate Mission Farm," 5.

122. Middleton, *Te Puna*, 200–201.

123. Middleton, *Te Puna*, 145.

124. Jones and Jenkins, *He Kōrero*, 121, 162. Jones and Jenkins note that the *Grammar* was also underpinned by Tuai's earlier work with Kendall.

125. Jones and Jenkins, *He Kōrero*, 165–66; Hanson and Hanson, *Counterpoint in Māori Culture*, 123.

126. Kendall, *A Grammar and Vocabulary of the Language of New Zealand*, 69, 96–97.

127. Yate, *An Account of New Zealand*, 191; James Hamlin, Journal 12–18 May and 24 November 1830, "Collected papers of and relating to Reverend James Hamlin," PC-0040, HC.

128. Middleton, *Te Puna*, vi.

129. Massey, *For Space*, 63.

130. Compare with Tanya Fitzgerald's claim that there "was no possibility that either missionary or Nga Puhi could straddle both worlds, and the erection of fences presented a formal indication of the differences between these two worlds" ("Fences, Boundaries, and Imagined Communities," 16).

3. Economics, Labor, and Time

1. Porter, "'Commerce and Christianity'"; Stanley, "Nineteenth-Century Liberation Theology"; and Stanley, "'Commerce and Christianity.'"

2. Comaroff, "Missionaries and Mechanical Clocks," 3, 9. The argument about the indissoluble links between empire, evangelicalism, and capitalism is expanded in Comaroff and Comaroff, *Of Revelation and Revolution*. Jean Comaroff's work on independent African churches, *Body of Power, Spirit of Resistance*, also equates Christianity and capitalism, arguing that African resistance to Christian teaching was, in effect, resistance to capitalism.

3. Ballara, *Proud to Be White?*, 8–13; Robert Chapman, "Fiction and the Social Pattern," 36; Colgan and McGregor, *Sexual Secrets*, 5. More significantly, Judith Binney claimed that the aim of CMS missionaries was to "eradicate, by their actions and their words, the existing structure of Maori society." But the rich evidence that she presents in her study of cross-cultural contact in the 1810s and 1820s reveals the inability of the missionaries to actualize such a vision and, in fact, suggests that such a vision was not consistently held by the evangelists. Binney, *The Legacy of Guilt*, 2d edn., especially 32–33.

4. Elbourne, *Blood Ground*; and Elbourne, "Word Made Flesh."

5. Atkins, "'Kaffir Time'"; and Cooper, "Work, Class and Empire." My reading of these struggles over time at the edge of the empire diverges from Giordano Nanni's stress on the efficacy of the British colonization of time in Australia and South Africa. Nanni's work clearly establishes the centrality of time as a flashpoint in struggles over the shape of colonial cultures, but pays little attention to the texture of British temporal practices, and his vision of the authority of missionary and colonial temporal models is underwritten by a tendency to conflate evidence from disparate locations and points in time. Nanni, *The Colonisation of Time*.

6. Samuel Marsden, 9 January 1815, SMCP, "Observations on the introduction of the Gospels into the South-Sea Islands. Being my first visit to New Zealand in Dec 1814," MS-0176/001, PC-0030, HC.

7. Samuel Marsden, 10 January 1815, SMCP, "Observations on the introduction of the Gospels into the South-Sea Islands. Being my first visit to New Zealand in Dec 1814," MS-0176/001, PC-0030, HC.

8. Hunter to Grenville, 17 July 1790, Australia Parliament Library Committee, *Historical Records of Australia: Series 1*, 1:195.

9. Marsden to Stokes, 4 May 1810, in Mackaness, *Some Private Correspondence of the Rev. Samuel Marsden and Family*, 41–42.

10. Yarwood, *Samuel Marsden*, 79–80, 82–83, 98–99, 230–31.

11. Yarwood, *Samuel Marsden*, 219, 230.

12. Samuel Marsden, Journal 9 January 1815, SMCP, "Observations on the introduction of the Gospels into the South Sea Islands," MS-0176/001, PC-0030, HC.

13. De Vries, "The Industrial Revolution and the Industrious Revolution"; and De Vries, "Between Purchasing Power and the World of Goods." A skeptical response to this thesis is offered in Clark and Van Der Werf, "Work in Progress?"

14. Voth, "Time Use in Eighteenth-Century London"; and Voth, "Time and Work in Eighteenth-Century London."

15. Hudson, "From Manor to Mill." These values were also broadly shared by the earliest "mechanic" missionaries to New Zealand, who were born in the 1770s and 1780s.

16. Samuel Marsden, concluding observations, SMCP, "Observations on the introduction of the Gospels into the South Sea Islands," MS-0176/001, PC-0030, HC.

17. Brubaker, *The Limits of Rationality*, 23–24; B. S. Turner, *For Weber*, 315. Weber identified four forms of ascetic Protestantism: Calvinism, Pietism, Methodism, and the Baptist sects. Weber, *The Protestant Ethic and the Spirit of Capitalism*, 95.

18. Outler, "The Use of Money: An Introductory Comment," 263–65.

19. Wesley, "The Use of Money," in Wesley, *The Works of John Wesley*, 2:268, 273, 277.

20. Wesley, "The Use of Money," in Wesley, *The Works of John Wesley: Volume 2*, 273.

21. Wesley, "The Use of Money," in Wesley, *The Works of John Wesley: Volume 2*, 277.

22. Wesley, "The Danger of Riches," in Wesley, *The Works of John Wesley: Volume 4*.

23. Thompson, *The Making of the English Working Class*, 358. Also see A. D. Gilbert, *Religion and Society*, 85–86.

24. The Marsdens named their male children Samuel, Charles, and John. Yarwood also notes that the literacy of both Marsden's parents within a largely illiterate community also suggests that they were Methodists. Yarwood, *Samuel Marsden*, 5–7. Wesley preached against predestination arguing that it was a blasphemous reading of God's teachings, an argument that marked him off from both Anglican evangelicals and the Calvinist tradition of Wesleyan thought associated with George Whitefield.

25. Bradshaw and Ozment, "Work as Mission: Introduction," 4.

26. Bebbington, *Evangelicalism in Modern Britain*, 11; Outler, "The Use of Money," 263–64.

27. Macquarie, *A Letter to the Right Honourable Sidmouth*, 18.

28. 17 June 1791, *The Diary, or, Woodfall's Register*.

29. Bewick, *A Memoir of Thomas Bewick*, 82.

30. Compare this assessment with Patricia Bawden's resolutely optimistic reading of the early history of the mission, in "The Mechanic Missionaries."

31. Quoted in Stock, *The History of the Church Missionary Society*, 1:206–7.

32. Nicholas, *Narrative of a Voyage to New Zealand*, 1:365–66.

33. King to Daniel Wilson, 11 July 1815, SMCP, "Correspondence June 1815–October 1815," PC-0128, HC.

34. Nicholas records the genesis of these fears—"that the Missionaries then going, would shortly introduce a much greater number; and thus, in some time, become so powerful, as to possess themselves of the whole island, and either destroy the natives, or reduce them to slavery"—as the product of the "diabolical reasoning" of an anonymous opponent of the evangelical cause that Ruatara had met in New South Wales. Nicholas, *Narrative of a Voyage to New Zealand*, 1:40–43. King suggested that ultimately Ruatara's interests were primarily material: "Sowing Wheat, planting corn, makeing Farms was his favourite employ and the topic of his conversation, he wanted his people to be like White people to have Bread Tea Suger Clothing & etc." King to Daniel Wilson, 4 July 1815, SMCP, "Correspondence June 1815–October 1815," PC-0128, HC.

35. King to Daniel Wilson, 4 July 1815, SMCP, "Correspondence June 1815–October 1815," PC-0128, HC.

36. Kendall to Pratt, 6 November 1816, SMCP, "Correspondence March 1816–February 1817," PC-0130, HC; Nicholas, *Narrative of a Voyage to New Zealand*, 1:237.

37. Kendall to Marsden, 6 July 1815, SMCP, "Correspondence June 1815–October 1815," PC-0128, HC; Hall to Pratt, 21 and 26 January 1816, and Kendall to Pratt, 22 January 1816, SMCP, "Correspondence October 1815–March 1816," PC-0129, HC.

38. See Middleton, "Silent Voices, Hidden Lives," 26; Kath Hansen, *In the Wake of the Active*, 11–28.

39. Middleton, "The Archaeology of the Te Puna Mission Station," 151–52.

40. Kendall to Pratt, 20 and 23 January 1816, SMCP, "Correspondence October 1815–March 1816," PC-0129, HC. Marsden was quite clear that Kendall did not have any authority over the other two "mechanics" and insisted that they were "all equal in authority." Marsden to Pratt, 15 June 1815, SMCP, "Correspondence June 1815–October 1815," PC-0128, HC.

41. This is the original spelling. King to Pratt, 25 January 1816, SMCP, "Correspondence October 1815–March 1816," PC-0129, HC.

42. Willliam Hall to CMS, 22nd August 1816, SMCP, "Correspondence October 1815–March 1816," PC-0129, HC.

43. Kendall to Pratt, 22 January 1816, SMCP, "Correspondence October 1815–March 1816," PC-0129, HC.

44. King to Pratt, 25 January 1816, SMCP, "Correspondence October 1815–March 1816," PC-0129, HC.

45. King to Pratt, 25 January 1816, SMCP, "Correspondence October 1815–March 1816," PC-0129, HC.

46. William Hall, Private Journal 30 December 1816, WHD, ATL. On Elizabeth Kendall's infidelity, see Hall's report to Pratt, 6 April 1822, WHLJ, HC. Also see Binney, *The Legacy of Guilt*, 2d edn., 18.

47. William Hall, Private Journal 3 June 1816, WHD, ATL. It is interesting to note that this fight occurred just two days before Elizabeth Kendall gave birth to Samuel.

48. In 1822 William Hall summarized this event: "Mr. Kendall went to the smith shop and demanded admittance of a door that had been previously barred to keep out the natives, there being another entrance open at the same time at the other side of the house. Hall, hearing Mr. Kendall so violent, ran into his own house and brought out two loaded horse pistols and said he would shoot him if he forced the door open. Notwithstanding this Mr. Kendall put his hands under the bottom of the door and threw it off its hinges. The door fell in and I expected every moment to seen Mr. Kendall shot. However Hall did not fire, but Mr. Kendall jumped in with a sharp chisel in his hand and pushed Mr. Hall backwards into a tub that stood behind him and endeavoured to push the chisel into his belly. Hall's wife being present with a young child in her arms in betwixt them, and struck up Mr. Kendall's arms, and the chisel went into Hall's breast and again into his face and again into his head. Hall at the same time fired the pistol loaded with two balls. It set Mr. Kendall's raincoat on fire and grazed Mr. Hall's wife's arm a little above the elbow and they separated, and Hall was taken into his house and was confined six weeks in his room before he was able to do any work." William Hall, WHLJ. In this letter, Hall incorrectly dated this altercation as taking place in 1815.

49. William Hall, Private Journal 18–19 March 1816, WHD, ATL.

50. Binney, *The Legacy of Guilt*, 2d edn., 52.

51. Kendall to Marsden, 6 July 1815, SMCP, "Correspondence June 1815–October 1815," PC-0128, HC.

52. William Hall, Private Journal, 6 June 1816, WHD, ATL.

53. Binney, *The Legacy of Guilt*, 2d edn., 54.

54. Binney, *The Legacy of Guilt*, 2d edn., 51.

55. Also see the later comments on the use of tools as weapons by William White to WMS, 30 June 1824, quoted in Ballara, *Taua*, 398.

56. Nicholas was well aware of this after his visit in 1814–15. In his published account he noted, "Iron and fire-arms are by them held in greater estimation than gold and silver by us, and the most avaricious miser in Europe cannot grasp with such eagerness at a guinea or a dollar, as the New Zealander does at an axe or a musket." Nicholas, *Narrative of a Voyage to New Zealand*, 1:164–65.

57. John Butler, Journal 10–12, 14–16 February 1820, "Collected papers of and relating to Reverend John Gare Butler," PC-0053, HC; Baron de Thierry, "Historical Narrative of an Attempt to Form a Settlement in New Zealand," Grey Collection, MS 55, APL, 166, Auckland Public Library. On Kendall and Hongi's voyage to London and Port Jackson, see Binney, *The Legacy of Guilt*, 2d edn., 68–79; Cloher, *Hongi Hika*, 119–48.

58. See, for example, Marsden's comments on the value of small items such as "a needle or a nail." Marsden to Mrs. Stokes, 16 December 1817, in Mackaness, *Some Private Correspondence of the Rev. Samuel Marsden*, 68.

59. "Objects of Shunghee and Whykato in Visiting England," 14 August 1820, Church Missionary Society, Archives Relating to the Australian and New Zealand Missions, 1808–1884, mission books containing correspondence to the CMS, Hocken Microfilm, CN/M1, HC, 205–6.

60. Cloher, *Hongi Hika*, 140–41; Binney, *The Legacy of Guilt*, 2d edn., 73–74.

61. Binney, *The Legacy of Guilt*, 2d edn., 68. These other gifts included the engraved guns gifted to them by Charles de Thierry at Cambridge. Baron de Thierry, "Historical narrative of an attempt to form a settlement in New Zealand," Grey Collection, MS 55, APL, 166, Auckland Public Library.

62. Contrast this position of confidence, which lasted through to at least 1826–27, with Tanya Fitzgerald's suggestion that the missionaries established "hegemonic relationships" with Māori in the mid-1820s. Tanya Fitzgerald, "Fences, Boundaries and Imagined Communities," 16.

63. The establishment of the mission at Kerikeri is narrated in detail in Samuel Marsden, SMCP, "Rev. S. Marsden's journal of proceedings at New Zealand from July 29 to Oct 19, 1819," MS-0177/002 PC-0140, HC.

64. Francis Hall to Marsden, 20 October 1821, "Missionary Letters etc., F Hall 1821, H. Williams 1864," MS-0053, PC-0306/001-006, HC. Hongi may in fact have been suggesting that the missionaries were *kuki* (slaves or mere cooks).

65. Kendall to Marsden, 27 September 1821, TKL, HC. This argument was made within the context of debates over Kendall's role in the musket trade.

66. The allotment and organization of labor were prominent in the new instructions issued to the missionaries in 1819. See Marsden to Bigge, 28 December 1819, HRNZ, 1:453–58.

67. William Hall, Journal 20 April 1816, WHD, ATL.

68. See the toki, now in possession of the Bedggood family, photographed on p. 30 of Middleton, *Kerikeri Mission and Kororipo Pā*.

69. Middleton, *Kerikeri Mission and Kororipo Pā*, 30.

70. John Butler, Journal 19th February 1820, JBL, 72–73. Butler's official record of trade reminds us, however, that metal tools, especially axes and hoes, remained a central medium of payment. See Butler to Marsden, 18 September, 1823, JBL, 295.

71. Hall to CMS, 20 Dec 1820, WHLJ, HC.

72. Francis Hall to Marsden, 20 October 1821, "Missionary Letters etc., F Hall 1821, H. Williams 1864," MS-0053, PC-0306/001-006, HC.

73. See, for example, Makereti, *The Old-Time Maori*, 90. Makereti suggested that in "many cases slaves were men of high standing and exceedingly good looking. They were treated well by the chief and his people, and indeed, often married into the tribe." Here Makereti was really countering a common early British argument that slaves within Māori society constituted a separate caste or even race, marked by their physical and cultural inferiority.

74. Ballara, *Taua*, 28.
75. Hanson and Hanson, *Counterpoint in Maori Culture*, 179.
76. Hanson and Hanson, *Counterpoint in Maori Culture*, 182; Edward Markham, "Transcript of New Zealand or recollections of it by Edward Markham," MS-0085, HC, 81; Sinclair, *Laplace in New Zealand*, 84; John King, Journal 2 August 1822, JKLJ, HC.
77. Makereti, *The Old-Time Maori*, 82; Biggs, *Maori Marriage*, 57.
78. Hanson and Hanson, *Counterpoint in Maori Culture*, 178–79, 182–83; Parsonson, "The Expansion of a Competitive Society," 55.
79. There seems to have been no formal injunction against criticizing slavery issued to missionaries in New Zealand by the Church Missionary Society to parallel the restrictions put in place by missionary societies in the Caribbean.
80. Samuel Marsden, Journal 11 October 1823, SMCP, "Observations on My Fourth Visit to New Zealand," PC-0034, HC.
81. See, for example, John Butler, "Journey from Whangaroa by Whaleboat Oct.–Nov. 1820," MS-0557, HC.
82. John King, Journal May 25 1819, JKLJ, HC.
83. Yate, *An Account of New Zealand*, 289–90.
84. Henry Williams, Journal 28 and 29 December 1831, HWJ, 209–10; Nathaniel Turner's Journal, 20 November 1826, *Missionary Notices* 5 (1826–28), 292.
85. Marianne Williams, 10 August 1823 and 17 March 1824, in Marianne Williams, *Letters from the Bay of Islands*, 59, 82–83; Nathaniel Turner's Journal, 22–23 October 1826, *Missionary Notices* 5 (1826–28), 290.
86. John Hobbs, Diary 3 February 1824, JHD, AWM; Kemp to CMS, 19 January 1822, KEMPLJ, HC.
87. Ballara, *Taua*, 397.
88. King's Journal (sent to Rev. Josiah Pratt), 24th July 1815, SMCP, "Correspondence October 1815–March 1816," PC-0129, HC.
89. Hall to CMS, 22nd August 1816, SMCP, "Correspondence March 1816–February 1817," PC-0130, HC.
90. Hall to CMS, 22nd August 1816, SMCP, "Correspondence March 1816–February 1817," PC-0130, HC.
91. Richard Davis, Journal 17 December 1834, 25 September, 23 October, 2 November, and 11 December 1835, RDLJ, MS-0066, PC-066-0068, HC.
92. Evidence given by Dandeson Coates, 14 May 1838, in British Parliament, *Report from the Select Committee of the House of Lords*, 249, 254.
93. Coates, *The Principles, Objects and Plans of the New Zealand Association Examined*, 23–24.
94. This is important as debates over Māori capacity for labor have played a pivotal role in defining cultural difference in New Zealand. See the discussion in Ballantyne, "Writing Out Asia."
95. Firth, *Primitive Economics of the New Zealand Maori*, 180–83.
96. Makereti, *The Old-Time Maori*, 183.

97. Best, *Forest Lore of the Maori*, 48.

98. Mead and Grove, *Ngā Pēpeha a ngā Tīpuna*, nos. 38, 193, 416, 2606.

99. Grey, *Proverbial and Popular Sayings*, 17; H. W. Williams, *He Whakatauki, He Titotito, He Pepeha*, 47; Mead and Grove, *Ngā Pēpeha a ngā Tīpuna*, no. 880, 145 and no. 1290, 211.

100. Parata, *The Maori of New Zealand*, 16–19.

101. Thompson, "Time, Work-Discipline, and Industrial Capitalism."

102. Engels, *The Condition of the Working Class in England*, 202. On time and the working day, see Marx, *Capital*, book 1, part 3, chap. 10, 340–416.

103. Thompson, "Time, Work-Discipline, and Industrial Capitalism," 90.

104. Roediger and Foner have pointed out the need to modify his model for the "Atlantic's other shore." Roediger and Foner, *Our Own Time*, 1–5.

105. Hall to CMS, 22nd August 1816, SMCP, "Correspondence March 1816–February 1817," PC-0130, HC; King's Journal (sent to Rev. Josiah Pratt), 24th July 1815, SMCP, "Correspondence October 1815–March 1816," PC-0129, HC.

106. Firth, *Primitive Economics of the New Zealand Maori*, 64–66.

107. Firth, *Primitive Economics of the New Zealand Maori*, 57–63. Firth notes that for some Māori there were only ten named months in the traditional calendar, with this period of relative inactivity at the end of autumn resulting in "the absence of specific names for these last two months of the year" (62–63). Also see William Yate's perceptive comments in *An Account of New Zealand* (105–7), and his claim before the Select Committee on Aborigines that Māori were "decidedly industrious for savages" Yate's evidence, 12th February 1836, in British Parliament, *Report from the Select Committee on Aborigines (British Settlements)*, 538 (1836), 188.

108. Firth, *Primitive Economics of the New Zealand Maori*, 55. On the limited and declining significance of seasonality in late eighteenth-century Britain, see Voth, *Time and Work in England*, 93–99.

109. This continued into the mid-1830s when Christianity had begun to make inroads in many communities. See William White's letter of 5 February 1835 in *Missionary Notices* 8 (1835–38), 217.

110. Butler, Journal 27 October 1819, JBL, 45.

111. On affordability and quality of watches, see Adam Smith, *The Wealth of Nations*, 351; Macey, *Clocks and the Cosmos*, 34–36; Church, "Nineteenth-Century Clock Technology in Britain, the United States, and Switzerland," 618–19.

112. Henry Williams, Journal 5 August 1827, HWJ, 64.

113. McLean, "The Kerikeri Stone Store," 104.

114. John Hobbs, Diary, vol. 2, 37, WHD, ATL.

115. Bernard John Foster, "John Hobbs," in McClintock, *An Encyclopaedia of New Zealand*, 2:88–89.

116. Nanni, *The Colonisation of Time*, 16.

117. Puckey to CMS, 24 January 1834, WPP, AWM.

118. See, for example, Henry Williams, Journal 5 August 1827, HWJ, 64; Maunsell to Eliza Langham, 16 June 1838, Susan Maunsell, Letters, MS 93/111, AWM; Yate, *An Account of New Zealand*, 198.

119. Elbourne, *Blood Ground*, 141.

120. Wilberforce, *A Practical View of Christianity*, 103–7. Also see Roberts, "Making Victorian Morals?"

121. Hall, *White, Male and Middle Class*, 84.

122. *Proceedings of the Church Missionary Society*, 1810–12, app. 2, 102.

123. Stock, *The History of the Church Missionary Society*, 1:206.

124. Kendall to Pratt, 6 September 1814, SMCP, "Correspondence 1814—1815," PC-0119, HC.

125. Kendall, *A Grammar and Vocabulary of the Language of New Zealand*, 115.

126. John King, Journal 8 September 1822, JKLJ, HC.

127. John King, Journal 22 September 1822, JKLJ, HC.

128. John King, Journal 13 October 1822, JKLJ, HC.

129. John King, Journal 26 and 27 October 1822, JKLJ, HC.

130. John King, Journal 25 December 1823, JKLJ, HC.

131. John King, Journal 12 October 1823, JKLJ, HC.

132. *Missionary Notices* 4 (1823–25), 65.

133. Marianne Williams, Journal 1 April 1824, WFC, ATL.

134. Henry Williams to CMS, 10 November 1823, Church Missionary Society, Archives Relating to the Australian and New Zealand Missions, 1808–1884, mission books containing correspondence to the CMS, Hocken Microfilm, CN/M2, HC.

135. William White to his brother, 21 September 1824, WWP, 6–7, AWM.

136. *Missionary Notices* 4 (1823–25), 486.

137. Marsden to CMS, 19 November 1811, Samuel Marsden, Church Missionary Society: Records relating to the New Zealand mission, Reverend Samuel Marsden, Ivy Lane, to Reverend Josiah Pratt, Secretary," MS-0498/008/240, HC.

138. William White to his brother, 21 September 1824, WWP, 6–7, AWM.

139. William White to his brother, 21 September 1824, WWP, 52, AWM.

140. It seems that Hongi may have encouraged the attack on Whangaroa because he believed it would allow him to control that harbor's anchorages, allowing him to provide European ships with timber and opening up access to new supplies of muskets. But it was not simply Hongi's people who plundered the mission: several missionary sources confirmed that members of Ngāti Uru, including "boys" closely linked to the mission, were involved. For some contemporary accounts, see John Hobbs, Diary 10 and 13 January 1827, WHD, ATL; George Clarke, Journal, 24 January and 6 August 1827, Collected papers of and relating to George Clarke senior and family, "George Clarke [senior]. Letter and Journals. 1822–1849. Vol 1. Items 91–99," PC-0056, HC; Nathaniel Turner, Journal 9–10 January 1827, in *Missionary Notices* 5 (1826–28), 305–10.

141. See my discussion of Te Koki in chap. 2 of this volume.

142. Henry Williams, Journal 15 January 1827, HWJ, 39.
143. See William Williams, Journal 10 April 1827, Archives Relating to the Australian and New Zealand Missions, 1808–1884, mission books containing correspondence to the CMS, Hocken Microfilm, CN/O 96, HC; Henry Williams, Journal Monday 14 and 18 May, 20 June 1827, HWJ, 55, 56, 58.
144. Ballara, *Taua*, 199.
145. Ballara, *Taua*, 196.
146. Pickmere, *The Story of Paihia*, 10.
147. See, for example, Kendall, *A Grammar and Vocabulary of the Language of New Zealand*, 115, 119, 201.
148. James Stack, Journal 16 October 1825, MS-Papers-3306, ATL.
149. Henry Williams, Journal Sunday 31 August 1834, HWJ, 220–22.
150. Binney, "Papahurihia"; and Binney, *The Legacy of Guilt*, 2d edn., 230 n.114.
151. Nanni, *The Colonisation of Time*. In his "General Editor's Introduction" to Nanni's volume, MacKenzie notes that colonized groups were able to contest evangelization, but nevertheless suggests asserts that missionaries were the "shock troops" of empire and that they were pivotal in the "socialization processes of empire," a reading that too neatly equates the evangelical and imperial projects. John M. MacKenzie, "General Editor's Preface," in Nanni, *The Colonisation of Time*, xii.
152. Nanni, *The Colonisation of Time*, 16.
153. Tom Griffiths sketched these tensions in an underappreciated essay, "Boundaries of the Sacred," esp. 38–39.
154. Kendall to Marsden, 27 September 1821, TKL, HC.
155. Church Missionary Society, *Instructions of the Committee of the Church Missionary Society*, 11–12.
156. Church Missionary Society, *Instructions of the Committee of the Church Missionary Society*, 15–16.
157. Binney, *Legacy of Guilt*, 2d edn., 89.

4. Containing Transgression

1. See Richard Davis to CMS, 3 November 1836, Church Missionary Society, Archives Relating to the Australian and New Zealand Missions, 1808–1884, mission books containing correspondence to the CMS, Hocken Microfilm, CN/M9, HC.
2. Binney, *The Legacy of Guilt*, 2d edn., 66.
3. Wanhalla, "The 'Bickerings' of the 'Mangungu Brethren.'"
4. Most notably, see Marianne Williams's observation in the wake of settling Paihia: "I was too much fatigued to begin packing, and relinquishing an attempt to write, was glad of rest. The tall and muscular forms of the Newzealanders, flittered before my mind's eye, whenever I endeavoured to sleep." Marianne Williams, *Letters from the Bay of Islands*, 56, 7 August 1823. But also note Susan Maunsell's mixed reaction to the "familiarity" of a Māori man during a waka

voyage on her arrival. Maunsell to Eliza Langham, 3 December 1835, Susan Maunsell, Letters, MS 93/111, AWM.

5. Binney, "Whatever Happened to Poor Mr Yate?"

6. Wallace, *Sexual Encounters*; Aldrich, *Colonialism and Homosexuality*.

7. In addition to Binney's essay, see Sargeson, "An Imaginary Conversation."

8. Stallybrass and White, *The Politics and Poetics of Transgression*, 5–6.

9. Samuel Marsden to CMS, 7 April 1808, in Harvard-Williams, *Marsden and the New Zealand Mission*, 15–16.

10. Samuel Marsden, Letter to Captain Wilson, November 1800, G7753, National Library of Australia. In 1818 the Missionary Society was renamed the London Missionary Society.

11. Gunson, *Messengers of Grace*, 152–54.

12. Vason later "reconverted" and repented for his "lapse." He returned to Britain and served as the governor of the Nottingham gaol. Vason, *An Authentic Narrative of Four Years' Residence at Tongataboo*; James Orange, *Life of the Late George Vason*.

13. Gunson, *Messengers of Grace*, 153

14. Quoted in Davies, *The History of the Tahitian Mission*, 129.

15. Catherine Hall, *Civilising Subjects*, 93–94.

16. *Missionary Register*, January 1813, 1–2.

17. More, *Strictures on the Modern System of Female Education*, 186–87.

18. Anna Clark, *Scandal*; Kane, *Victorian Families*; Chase and Levenson, *The Spectacle of Intimacy*.

19. Henry Williams, Journal 20 January 1828, HWJ, 98.

20. Marianne Williams, 11 May 1828, in Marianne Williams, *Letters from the Bay of Islands*, 151.

21. Henry Williams, Journal 19 January 1828, HWJ, 98.

22. Henry Williams, Journal 10 February 1828, HWJ, 101.

23. Marianne Williams, 24 December 1829, WFC, ATL.

24. Jane Williams, 24 December 1829, WFC, ATL.

25. Parkinson and Griffith, *Books in Māori*, 35–36, work 11.

26. Parkinson and Griffith, *Books in Māori*, 36–38, work 12.

27. R. Davis to CMS, 10 June 1836, Church Missionary Society, Archives Relating to the Australian and New Zealand Missions, 1808–1884, mission books containing correspondence to the CMS, Hocken Microfilm, CN/M9, 496, HC.

28. Yate, *An Account of New Zealand*.

29. "Preface," in Yate, *An Account of New Zealand*, n.p.

30. Wevers, *Country of Writing*, 102–3.

31. Philip Granger Parkinson, "Our Infant State," 294.

32. William Yate, Journal 29 January 1836, WYJ, HC.

33. Evidence of William Yate, 12–13 February 1836, in British Parliament, *Report from the Select Committee on Aborigines (British Settlements)*, 538 (1836), 188–96.

34. Reverend F. Close to Yate, 15 December 1835, WYC, HC; Binney, "Whatever Happened to Poor Mr. Yate," 120.

35. William Wade to Dandeson Coates, 27 August 1836, "Missionary Letters etc., F Hall 1821, H. Williams 1864," MS-0053, PC-0306, HC.

36. Richard Davis to the Lay Secretary, June 10 1836, 496, Church Missionary Society, Archives Relating to the Australian and New Zealand Missions, 1808–1884, mission books containing correspondence to the CMS, Hocken Microfilm, CN/M9, 121/32, HC.

37. Meeting of Northern District, 30 August 1836, Church Missionary Society, Archives Relating to the Australian and New Zealand Missions, 1808–1884, mission books containing correspondence to the CMS, Hocken Microfilm, CN/M9, 121/32, 475, HC.

38. W[illiam] W[ade], "Review of 'An Account of New Zealand etc.' by the Rev. William Yate, Missionary of the Church Mission Society," 10 October 1836, WYC, HC.

39. George Clarke to CMS, 10 September 1836, Church Missionary Society, Archives Relating to the Australian and New Zealand Missions, 1808–1884, mission books containing correspondence to the CMS, Hocken Microfilm, CN/M9, HC.

40. Evidence of William Yate, 12 February 1836, *Report from the Select Committee on Aborigines (British Settlements)*, 538 (1836), 188.

41. On these earlier rumors, see Yate to CMS, 1 June 1832, WYC, HC.

42. See Yate, *To the Parishioners of St James' Church*; and Yate to Dandeson Coates, 19 July 1836, "Missionary Letters etc., F Hall 1821, H. Williams 1864," MS-0053, PC-0306, HC.

43. William Yate, Journal 22 June–15 August 1836, WYJ, HC.

44. Evidence of informal enquiry, now held among the Colenso Papers, qMS-0495–0503, cited in Binney, "Whatever Happened to Poor Mr. Yate," 118.

45. Richard Taylor, Journal 1 April 1836, vol. 1, Richard Taylor, Journals, 1833–1873, MS 302, AWM.

46. Owens, *The Mediator*, 18–19.

47. William Yate, Journal, 17 May 1836, WYJ, HC; Owens, *The Mediator*, 18.

48. Owens, *The Mediator*, 18.

49. Aldrich, *Colonialism and Homosexuality*, 228; Owens, *The Mediator*, 18.

50. Yarwood, *Samuel Marsden*, 272.

51. William Yate, Journal 16–31 August 1836, WYJ, HC.

52. William Yate, Journal December 1836, WYJ, HC. On 19 July 1836 Yate had written to Coates that Taylor was "a weak man, both in body and mind." Yate to Dandeson Coates, July 19 1836, "Missionary Letters etc., F Hall 1821, H. Williams 1864," MS-0053, PC-0306, HC. Marsden responded to Yate's allegations by advising the CMS secretary of "the very exemplary conduct of Mr Taylor as a Christian minister since his arrival in this Colony," and by expressing his hope that "the Society will not entertain any unfriendly feeling towards the Revd Richard Taylor from any malicious charges Mr Yate may have professed against the above gentleman." Letter from Marsden to William Jowett, 6 October 1837, WYC, HC.

53. William Yate, Journal December 1836, WYJ, HC.

54. Denison to Yate, 6 and 8 August 1836, cited in Binney, "Whatever Happened to Poor Mr. Yate," 116.

55. William Yate to CMS Secretaries, 4 June 1836, WYC, HC.

56. William Yate, Journal 1 May and June 5 1836, WYJ, HC.

57. Ryan Brown-Haysom has suggested that Yate might well have seen his relationship with Denison within the mold of the relationship between Jonathan and David and notes that there were several other close male relationships in the Bible that might have been understood by Yate as a kind of model for his bond to Denison. Ryan Brown-Haysom, "The Awful Fall of Mr Yate," unpublished essay in author's possession, 32. On David and Jonathan, see II Samuel 1:26.

58. Quoted in Philip Granger Parkinson, "Our Infant State," 301–2.

59. Binney, "Whatever Happened to Poor Mr. Yate," 188.

60. Depositions of Pehi, Tohi, Toataua, and Kohi, Colonial Secretary, Letters Received, 1837, 36/10481 in 4/2357.1, State Records of New South Wales. I am grateful to Ryan Brown-Haysom for initially providing me with copies of these depositions.

61. See, for example, Henry Williams, Journal 24 September 1827 and 24 October 1828, HWJ, 75, 147. On Brind, see Chisholm, "Brind, William Darby."

62. Yate to CMS, 1 June 1832, WYC, HC. Damon Salesa has noted that marriage was integral to the missionary project. Missionaries did not oppose interracial liaisons, but were fierce critics of what they called "concubinage," the unmarried cohabitation of Māori women with European men. Salesa, *Racial Crossings*, 79. For another reading, see Wanhalla, *Matters of the Heart*, 23–45.

63. Wade to Coates, September 28 1836, "Missionary Letters etc., F Hall 1821, H. Williams 1864," MS-0053, PC-0306, HC.

64. Polack, *New Zealand*, I, 147–48.

65. George Clarke to Samuel Marsden, 28 September 1836 enclosure in Crown Solicitor to Colonial Secretary, 14 December 1836, Colonial Secretary, Letters Received, 1837, 36/10481in 4/2357.1, State Records of New South Wales.

66. George Clarke to Samuel Marsden, 28 September 1836 enclosure in Crown Solicitor to Colonial Secretary, 14 December 1836, Colonial Secretary, Letters Received, 1837, 36/10481in 4/2357.1, State Records of New South Wales.

67. Richard Davis, Journal 26 September 1836, 558, Church Missionary Society, Archives Relating to the Australian and New Zealand Missions, 1808–1884, mission books containing correspondence to the CMS, Hocken Microfilm, CN/M9, HC.

68. Richard Davis, Journal 4 October 1836, 558, Church Missionary Society, Archives Relating to the Australian and New Zealand Missions, 1808–1884, mission books containing correspondence to the CMS, Hocken Microfilm, CN/M9, HC.

69. Richard Davis, Journal 26 September 1836, 558, Church Missionary Society, Archives Relating to the Australian and New Zealand Missions, 1808–1884, mission books containing correspondence to the CMS, Hocken Microfilm, CN/M9, HC.

70. Richard Davis, Journal 26 and 28 September 1836, and 6, 7, 9, 12, and 18 October, Church Missionary Society, Archives Relating to the Australian and New Zealand Missions, 1808–1884, mission books containing correspondence to the CMS, Hocken Microfilm, CN/M9, HC.

71. Wade to Coates, September 28 1836, "Missionary Letters etc., F Hall 1821, H. Williams 1864," MS-0053, PC-0306, HC. On 8 January 1831 Yate sailed on the *Active* for Tonga in search of Charles Davis. He returned to Paihia on 2 March.

72. George Clarke to Samuel Marsden, 28 September 1836 enclosure in Crown Solicitor to Colonial Secretary, 14 December 1836, Colonial Secretary, Letters Received, 1837, 36/10481in 4/2357.1, State Records of New South Wales.

73. Richard Davis, Journal 3, 6, 9, 11, and 12 October 1836, Church Missionary Society, Archives Relating to the Australian and New Zealand Missions, 1808–1884, mission books containing correspondence to the CMS, Hocken Microfilm, CN/M9, HC.

74. Williams to Marsden, 16 November 1836, cited in Binney, "Whatever Happened to Poor Mr. Yate," 114–15. Lee Wallace underplays the significance of this evidence from Māori, suggesting that "it seems the easiest thing in the world for these men of God to imagine Yate had shared sexual intimacies with each and every mission boy." Wallace, *Sexual Encounters*, 99.

75. Marsden to Coates, October 2 1837, SMCP, "Correspondence July 1835–February 1838," PC-0139, HC.

76. Binney, "Introduction," in Yate, *An Account of New Zealand*, xviii.

77. Despite the wording of this deposition, age was not a primary concern in the responses of the missionary community, the colonial authorities of New South Wales, or its Anglican establishment.

78. Deposition of Toataua, enclosure to George Clarke to Samuel Marsden 28 September 1836, enclosed in Crown Solicitor to Colonial Secretary, 14 December 1836, Colonial Secretary, Letters Received, 1837, 36/10481in 4/2357.1, State Records of New South Wales.

79. Deposition of Toataua, enclosure to George Clarke to Samuel Marsden 28 September 1836, enclosed in Crown Solicitor to Colonial Secretary, 14 December 1836, Colonial Secretary, Letters Received, 1837, 36/10481in 4/2357.1, State Records of New South Wales.

80. Deposition of Philip Tohi, enclosure to George Clarke to Samuel Marsden 28 September 1836, enclosed in Crown Solicitor to Colonial Secretary, 14 December 1836, Colonial Secretary, Letters Received, 1837, 36/10481in 4/2357.1, State Records of New South Wales.

81. Deposition of Samuel Kohi, enclosure to George Clarke to Samuel Marsden 28 September 1836, enclosed in Crown Solicitor to Colonial Secretary, 14 December 1836, Colonial Secretary, Letters Received, 1837, 36/10481 in 4/2357.1, State Records of New South Wales.

82. See letters 6, 11, 15, 19, in Yate, *An Account of New Zealand*, 254, 259, 262–63, 267; and letters 6, 11, 15, 19, in B[ennet], *Letters to the Rev. William Yate*, 15–16, 29–30,

39–41, 55. Parkinson notes that the original versions of these letters in te reo no longer exist.

83. Philip Granger Parkinson, "Our Infant State," 317; Binney, "Whatever Happened to Poor Mr. Yate," 113.

84. Deposition of Samuel Kohi, enclosure to Clarke to Marsden 28 September 1836, enclosed in Crown Solicitor to Colonial Secretary, 14 December 1836, Colonial Secretary, Letters Received, 1837, 36/10481in 4/2357.1, State Records of New South Wales.

85. Deposition of Pehi, enclosure to Clarke to Marsden 28 September 1836, enclosed in Crown Solicitor to Colonial Secretary, 14 December 1836, Colonial Secretary, Letters Received, 1837, 36/10481in 4/2357.1, State Records of New South Wales.

86. Crown Solicitor to Colonial Secretary, 14 December 1836, enclosure to Clarke to Marsden 28 September 1836, enclosed in Crown Solicitor to Colonial Secretary, 14 December 1836, Colonial Secretary, Letters Received, 1837, 36/10481in 4/2357.1, State Records of New South Wales.

87. The British Resident James Busby made a similar observation that Yate's case "was not rising to the full extent of the Crime which human laws have made penal, or which called down in times of old the divine wrath—It is this—that it did not take place *per anum* but it would appear merely by the instrumentality of the thighs." Busby to N.S.W. Colonial Secretary, 15 November 1836, 36/9924, quoted in Binney, "Whatever Happened to Poor Mr. Yate," 115.

88. Arthur N. Gilbert, "Conceptions of Sodomy and Homosexuality," 62–63.

89. Upchurch, *Before Wilde*, 91–93. Compare this with Parkinson's blunter claim that "oral intercourse" was not a criminal act. Philip Granger Parkinson, "Our Infant State," 302.

90. Upchurch, *Before Wilde*, 94.

91. Upchurch, *Before Wilde*, 94. On the applicability of the 1827 statute, see Gregory Woods's discussion of New South Wales's "automatic" adoption of English laws in effect before 25 July 1828. Gregory D. Woods, *A History of Criminal Law in New South Wales*, 121.

92. Binney, "Introduction," in Yate, *An Account of New Zealand*, xviii; Binney, "Whatever Happened to Poor Mr. Yate," 118–19.

93. McKenzie, *Scandal in the Colonies*, 149; British Parliament, *Report from the Select Committee on Transportation*.

94. Reid, *Gender, Crime and Empire*, 211; Gilchrist, "The 'Crime' of Precocious Sexuality."

95. Letter from Dandeson Coates to Major General Gordon, April 6 1837, Church Missionary Society, Home Letters Out, 5 July 1833 to 14 February 1838, CH/L2, Hocken Microfilm, 121/66, HC. The Home letter books of this period show that the Parent Committee was beset with correspondence demanding an enquiry into the circumstances of Yate's case.

96. *Colonist*, 22 December 1836, 7.

97. *Sydney Gazette and New South Wales Advertiser*, 17 December 1836, 2.

98. George Clarke to Samuel Marsden, 28 September 1836 enclosure in Crown Solicitor to Colonial Secretary, 14 December 1836, Colonial Secretary, Letters Received, 1837, 36/10481 in 4/2357.1, State Records of New South Wales.

99. W. R. Wade to Dandeson Coates, September 28 1836, "Missionary Letters etc., F Hall 1821, H. Williams 1864," MS-0053, PC-0306, HC.

100. Richard Davis, Journal 4 October 1836, 559, Church Missionary Society, Archives Relating to the Australian and New Zealand Missions, 1808–1884, mission books containing correspondence to the CMS, Hocken Microfilm, CN/M9, HC.

101. Richard Davis, Journal 26 September 1836, 558, Church Missionary Society, Archives Relating to the Australian and New Zealand Missions, 1808–1884, mission books containing correspondence to the CMS, Hocken Microfilm, CN/M9, HC.

102. Richard Davis to CMS, 3 November 1836, Church Missionary Society, Archives Relating to the Australian and New Zealand Missions, 1808–1884, mission books containing correspondence to the CMS, Hocken Microfilm, CN/M9, HC.

103. W[illiam] W[ade], "Review of "An Account of New Zealand etc." by the Rev. William Yate, Missionary of the Church Mission Society," 10 October 1836, WYC, HC.

104. W[illiam] W[ade], "Review of "An Account of New Zealand etc." by the Rev. William Yate, Missionary of the Church Mission Society," 10 October 1836, WYC, HC, emphasis added. For a dismissal of Yate's "hypocritical sanctity," see Richard Davis to CMS, 3 November 1836, Church Missionary Society, Archives Relating to the Australian and New Zealand Missions, 1808–1884, mission books containing correspondence to the CMS, Hocken Microfilm, CN/M9, HC.

105. Romans 1:27.

106. Polack, *New Zealand*, 2:148.

107. Polack, *New Zealand*, 2:147.

108. Polack, *New Zealand*, 2:147.

109. Wade to Coates, 28 September 1836, "Missionary Letters etc., F Hall 1821, H. Williams 1864," MS-0053, PC-0306, HC.

110. W. Williams to Marsden, 16 November 1836, cited in Yarwood, *Samuel Marsden*, 274.

111. Yarwood, *Samuel Marsden*, 274–75.

112. Richard Davis, Journal 2 October 1836 and 4 October 1836, 558, Church Missionary Society, Archives Relating to the Australian and New Zealand Missions, 1808–1884, mission books containing correspondence to the CMS, Hocken Microfilm, CN/M9, HC. The parable of the tares comes from Matthew 13:24–30 and 36–43. The text explains that during the final judgment, the angels will separate the "sons of the evil one," the tares, from the "sons of the Kingdom," the wheat. Davis also records that the first chapter of Paul's epistle to the Romans was also read to the Māori, presumably with a focus on its injunctions against "unnatural lusts."

113. Yate, *An Account of New Zealand*, 168.

114. Ashwell to CMS, 27 December 1836, Benjamin Yate Ashwell, Letters and Journals, MS-0860/001, HC.

115. Richard Davis, Journal 4 October 1836, 558, Church Missionary Society, Archives Relating to the Australian and New Zealand Missions, 1808–1884, mission books containing correspondence to the CMS, Hocken Microfilm, CN/M9, HC.

116. Richard Taylor, Journal 13 December 1836, vol. 1, Richard Taylor, Journals, 1833–1873, MS 302, AWM. On Achan, see Jonathon Edwards, *Practical Sermons, Never before Published*, 129; and see entries on Achan and Achor in Macbean, *A Dictionary of the Bible*.

117. Jacob 6:19, 6:24, and 7:11.

118. There are parallels between my reading and that of Lee Wallace. But Wallace shows relatively limited interest in the precise dynamics of relations within the mission and anachronistically frames missionary concerns with community boundaries as a concern with the foundation of a national community, suggesting that the missionaries imagined themselves as "proto-New Zealanders." Wallace, *Sexual Encounters*, 104.

119. A copy of this resolution, dated 24 February 1837, is included in WYC, HC.

120. William Yate, Journal 26 to 28 February 1838, WYJ, HC.

121. Williams to Marsden, 16 November 1836, cited in Yarwood, *Samuel Marsden*, 274.

122. Two recent treatments of this contest are Wanhalla, "The 'Bickerings' of the 'Mangungu Brethren,'" and Philip Granger Parkinson, "Our Infant State," chap. 13.

123. Nathaniel Turner, Letterbook 1836–1849, 17–19, 29–30, qMS-2065, ATL.

124. Philip Granger Parkinson, "Our Infant State," 283.

125. On Woon's initial sense of the case, see Woon to the Wesleyan Committee, 8 December 1835, letter 54, in Bruce Edwards, *A Bibliography of Material Relating to the Reverend William Woon*, Philip Granger Parkinson Papers, 2003–105–089, ATL. On his later belief that "he [White] is guilty," see Woon to Wesleyan Committee 14 November 1836, Letter 70, in Bruce Edwards, *A Bibliography of Material Relating to the Reverend William Woon*, Philip Granger Parkinson Papers, 2003–105–089, ATL.

126. Yate, *A Letter to the Committee of the Church Missionary Society*.

127. William Yate, Journal 2 June 1840–December 1841, WYJ, HC.

128. Yate, *A Letter to the Committee of the Church Missionary Society*, 37–49.

129. Binney, "Introduction," in Yate, *An Account of New Zealand*, xx.

130. Marsden to Coates, 31 July 1837, "Correspondence July 1835–February 1838," SMCP, PC-139, HC.

131. William Yate, Journal 16 to 31 August 1836, WYJ, HC.

132. William Yate, Journal 15 to 20 May 1837, WYJ, HC.

133. William Yate, Journal 29 June to 29 July 1837, 1 September to 6 November 1837, WYJ, HC.

134. William Yate, Journal 1 April to 31 December 31 1839, WYJ, HC.

135. In 1843 Denison, who had by that time settled in Yate's hometown of Brignorth, visited his old friend in London. William Yate, Journal April 23 1843, WYJ, HC.

136. Aldrich, *Colonialism and Homosexuality*, 228.

137. Cocks, *Nameless Offences*, 1–5.

138. Wade to John Wilson, 27 October 1836, "John Alexander Wilson—Letters from William Richard Wade," Wilson Family: Papers, MS-Papers-5512–14, ATL.

139. Wade to T. E. Northover, 21 July 1837, William R. Wade, Outwards Letters, Misc-MS-0323, HC. For an allusion to King, see Pilley, *The New Zealand Missionary*, 18.

140. Wade to T. E. Northover, 21 July 1837, William R. Wade, Outwards Letters, Misc-MS-0323, HC; Chapman to CMS, 8 August 1838, Church Missionary Society, "Mission Books—Letters Received CN/M11, CN/M12," Micro-MS-Coll-04-33, ATL.

141. Philip Parkinson has offered the fullest treatment of this case in "'A Most Depraved Young Man,'" where he suggests that the lack of a paper trail, including the large gaps in Pilley's papers, "may indicate deliberate suppression" (21).

142. This echoes, and reworks, Clark, *Scandal*, 1–3.

143. See for example Genesis 1:22, Leviticus 18:22, I Corinthians 6:9, I Timothy 1:10.

144. Bebbington, *Evangelicalism in Modern Britain*, 63–65.

145. Seidman, *Romantic Longings*, 58; Gardella, *Innocent Ecstasy*, 80–81.

146. Charles Baker, letter to Colenso, 25 November 1851, in Mary Baker, *Never the Faint Hearted*, 130.

147. Gardella, *Innocent Ecstasy*, 4–5, 7, 153.

148. Charles Baker, letter to Kendall, 25 November 1851, Mary Baker, *Never the Faint Hearted*, 130.

149. Barthes, *Mythologies*, 154.

150. Register of Baptisms, 27 December 1834, "Bay of Islands Missions/Waimate—Register: marriages (1823–1835), baptisms (1815–1835), burials (1821–1835)," R21906666, National Archives, Wellington.

151. Philip Granger Parkinson, "Our Infant State," 309–10. Romans 1:27: "And likewise also the men, leaving the natural use of the woman, burned in their lust one toward another; men with men working that which is unseemly, and receiving in themselves that recompence of their error which was meet." 1 Corinthians 6:9–10: "Know ye not that the unrighteous shall not inherit the kingdom of God? Be not deceived: neither fornicators, nor idolaters, nor adulterers, nor effeminate, nor abusers of themselves with mankind, Nor thieves, nor covetous, nor drunkards, nor revilers, nor extortioners, shall inherit the kingdom of God."

152. Philip Granger Parkinson, "Our Infant State," 310–11.

153. Philip Granger Parkinson, "Our Infant State," 310, 310 n.48.

154. Pilley to CMS, July 1835, cited in Philip Parkinson, "'A Most Depraved Young Man,'" 22 n.2.

155. Church Missionary Society, General Committee minutes, CN/M9, 533, Micro-MS-Coll-04-08, ATL.

156. Wanhalla, "The 'Natives Uncivilize Me,'" 29.

157. Binney, *Blain Biographical Directory of Anglican Clergy in the South Pacific*. On Ōtawhao, see Wanhalla, "The 'Natives Uncivilize Me,'" 1–2.

158. Philip Parkinson, "'A Most Depraved Young Man,'" 19.

159. Kendall's engagement in the musket trade and the ongoing conflicts he had with other missionaries were important factors that led Marsden to finally move against him. The Wesleyan William White was also engaged in unauthorized trade, waged a divisive running war with McDonnell, and was a persistently difficult colleague. Colenso had difficult relationships with his fellow missionaries, with the Anglican establishment from the 1840s, and with colonists who saw him as an obstacle to acquiring land from Māori.

5. Cultures of Death

1. Ariès, *The Hour of Our Death*; Rugg, "From Reason to Regulation."
2. One key exception is Seeman, *Death in the New World*.
3. Fischer, *Albion's Seed*, 111–16, 326–31, 517–22, 697–702, 813.
4. Jalland, *Australian Ways of Death*, 10.
5. Best, "Maori Eschatology"; Oppenheim, *Maori Death Customs*. Anne Salmond's essay on Ruatara is a notable exception to this. It foregrounds the place of death in the contact zone, but in many ways its primary interest is in anthropologizing rather than historicizing death. Anne Salmond, "Maori and Modernity."
6. Seeman, *Death in the New World*, 291.
7. Brown, *The Reaper's Garden*, 5.
8. Burtner and Chiles, *A Compendium of Wesley's Theology*, 79.
9. Bebbington, *Evangelicalism in Modern Britain*, 15–16; also see Ditchfield, *The Evangelical Revival*, 27. Bebbington notes that this position was increasingly rejected by liberal evangelicals from the 1870s, who argued that Jesus died as a representative of, rather than as a substitute for, humanity.
10. Welch, "Haweis, Thomas (1734?–1820)."
11. Haweis, *The Evangelical Expositor*, 1:14.
12. Haweis, *The Evangelical Expositor*, 1:13, 16.
13. Haweis, *Evangelical Principles and Practice*, 157–58.
14. Haweis, *Carmina Christo*, 175.
15. Bridges, *The Christian Ministry*, 223.
16. John King, Journal 26 March 1823, JKLJ, HC.
17. Jalland, *Death in the Victorian Family*, 21.
18. Rugg, "Reason to Regulation," 215. On the durability of evangelical views of deaths see Jalland, *Death in the Victorian Family*, 18–19; *Australian Ways of Death*, 51.
19. Rugg, "From Reason to Regulation," 215; Bebbington, *Evangelicalism in Modern Britain*, 10–12, 63–65. This moderate Calvinism preached salvation by faith alone and asserted that humans were responsible agents rather than simply objects of divine will.
20. Jalland, *Death in the Victorian Family*, 19.
21. Jalland, "Victorian Death and Its Decline," 230–36; Jalland, *Death in the Victorian Family*, 19–22.
22. Wheeler, *Heaven, Hell, and the Victorians*, 189–96.

23. See, for example, Brown, *The Reaper's Garden*.

24. Goldsbury, "Behind the Picket Fence," 60–61. Goldsbury notes that the Wesleyan Missionary Society records suggested that Catherine Leigh was to undertake a midwifery course, but it is unclear if she completed that training.

25. See, for example, Marianne Williams, 26 December 1829 and 25 April 1830 (on Sarah Fairburn), and 7 September 1830 (on Charlotte Brown), WFC, ATL. Also see Owens, *Prophets in the Wilderness*, 78.

26. Jane Williams, 24 April 1829 (on Marianne Williams), and Marianne Williams, 26 December 1829 (on Sarah Fairburn), WFC, ATL.

27. Porter, "All that the Heart Does Bear," 147. The figures for the far north are based on the biographical data provided for missionaries and their families in Peter Lineham's biographical appendix to *Mission and Moko*. Because we do not have reliable birth dates for many missionary wives, I have focused instead on calculating the average number of years between their arrival and death. This measure means that I have not examined data relating to single men and men who married after they arrived in New Zealand. In light of these exclusions, we have a sample of sixteen married couples arriving between 1814 and 1840: the male partner on average died 48.13 years after arrival, the female 39.62.

28. Heath, *Aging by the Book*, 9; Robert Woods, *The Demography of Victorian England and Wales*.

29. "Appendix 4: Recorded Deaths of Infants Born 1815 and 1837," in Goldsbury, "Behind the Picket Fence," 211.

30. Binney, "Introduction," in Binney, *Te Kerikeri*, 10, 14–15; Kemp to CMS, 19 January 1822, KempLJ, HC.

31. Salmond, "Maori and Modernity."

32. See, for example, "Mr Marsden's Queries to the Settlers at the Bay of Islands," 5 November 1819, HRNZ, 1:440.

33. Stone, *The Family, Sex and Marriage in England*, 651–52; Stone, *The Past and the Present*, 219; Pollock, *Forgotten Children*; Jalland, *Death in the Victorian Family*, chap. 6.

34. See, for example, Henry Williams fleeting note on receiving news of his mother's death. Henry Williams, Journal 19 June 1832, HWJ, 247.

35. Ashwell to CMS, 21 June 1838, Benjamin Yate Ashwell, "Letters and Journals of Benjamin Yates Ashwell," MS-0860/001, HC.

36. Jalland, "Victorian Death and Its Decline," 237–38.

37. George Clarke to W. Clarke Snr, 31 March 1828, George Clarke, Outward Correspondence, George Clarke Papers, MS-0250-5, ATL.

38. George Clarke to W. Clarke Snr, 4 February 1829, George Clarke, Outward Correspondence, George Clarke Papers, MS-0250-5, ATL.

39. Maunsell to Eliza Langham, 16 June 1838, from Manukau, Susan Maunsell, Letters, MS 93/111, AWM.

40. Hilton, *The Age of Atonement*, 336.
41. Clarke [Jr], *Notes on Early Life in New Zealand*, 14–15. Cabbage roses (*Rosa centifolia*) are also known as Provence roses. The importance of roses in the mission's cultural history is hinted at by Ruth Ross, "Old Roses for Waimate," www.rosarosam.com/articles/waimate/roses_for_waimate.htm.
42. Taylor and Taylor, *Hymns for Infant Minds*, 33. This volume went through forty editions by 1851. Also see Bowerbank, "Taylor, Jane (1783–1824)."
43. Haweis, *The Evangelical Expositor*, 1:40.
44. Haweis, *The Evangelical Expositor*, 1:41.
45. Travers, "Death and the Nabob."
46. Middleton, *Te Puna*, 48–50. Middleton does recognize, however, that the missionaries were forced to make accommodations to tapu in the early years of the mission.
47. Kendall to Marsden, 25 July 1817, SMCP, "Correspondence March 1817–August 1818," PC-0131, HC.
48. Hohepa, "Kerikeri, Tapu, Wāhi Tapu," 90.
49. Kendall to Marsden, 25 July 1817, SMCP, "Correspondence March 1817–August 1818," PC-0131, HC.
50. Hall to Marsden, 26 January 1816, SMCP, "Correspondence October 1815–March 1816," PC-0129, HC. On taua muru, see Ballara, *Taua*, esp. 103–11.
51. Phillipson, "Religion and Land," 64.
52. William Hall, Diary 25 July 1816, WHD, ATL. This, in fact, may have been Sarah McKenzie, who traveled to New Zealand on the *Active* in 1815. John Shergold was a passenger on that voyage as well. There is no evidence to suggest that either traveled with a partner, and I have been unable to locate any other reference to Sarah Shergold in material relating to the early Bay of Islands. See ML, 90, 95n12.
53. William Hall, Diary 25 July 1816, WHD, ATL. For a discussion of two burial grounds identified during archaeological work and recorded in a 1926 survey plan, see Smith and Middleton et al., *Archaeology of the Hohi Mission Station*, 85–86.
54. William Hall, Diary 26 July 1816, WHD, ATL.
55. William Hall, Diary 1 August 1816, WHD, ATL.
56. Easdale, *Missionary and Maori*, 119–20.
57. Owens, *Prophets in the Wilderness*, 83.
58. Williment, *John Hobbs, 1800–1883*, 90, 121.
59. Brown, *Reaper's Garden*, 89.
60. Tarlow, *The Archaeology of Improvement in Britain*, 113–14. For similar changes in the United States, see Yalom, *The American Resting Place*, 42–43.
61. Roach, *Cities of the Dead*, 49–51.
62. Etlin, *The Architecture of Death*, 163–90.
63. Smith and Middleton et al., *Archaeology of the Hohi Mission Station*, 85–86.
64. William Hall, Diary 13 February 1822, WHD, ATL.

65. King to CMS, 22 June 1829, Archives Relating to the Australian and New Zealand Missions, 1808–1884, original papers and correspondence relating to the CMS, Hocken Microfilm, CN/O 54, HC.

66. Turner, *The Pioneer Missionary*, 76–77, 160; Owens, *Prophets in the Wilderness*, 114.

67. For a similar point, see Peel, "Death and Community in a Colonial Settlement," 139.

68. Smith and Middleton et al., *Archaeology of the Hohi Mission Station*, 85.

69. Baker, Journal 1, 3, 4 January 1839, Charles Baker, Journal 1827–39, MS-0517/A, HC; Pickmere, *The Story of Paihia*, 49.

70. Colenso to CMS, 6 February 1839, William Colenso, Letters 1834–1853, PC-0059, HC; Church Missionary Society, *Order of Consecration of a Burial-Ground* (this is item 58 in Parkinson and Griffith, *Books in Māori*, 58). On Williams as the translator of this chapter, see Philip Granger Parkinson, "Our Infant State," 477.

71. Haweis, *The Evangelical Expositor*, 41.

72. See Deeds 71, 75–77, 81, in Turton, *Maori Deeds of Old Private Land Purchases in New Zealand*, 61–63; "Grant of land at Keddee Keddee by Shunghee Heeka to the Church Missionary Society, 4 November 1819," MS-0070/A, HC.

73. Genesis 47:30 and 50:13–14.

74. For a similar argument, see Deed, "Unearthly Landscapes," 51. For a specific discussion of this in the Wesleyan case, see Owens, *Prophets in the Wilderness*, 83.

75. Butler, 14 July 1820, JBL, 82.

76. Ballantyne, *Orientalism and Race*, 90–93. On Satan see, for example, see Davis to CMS, 29 April 1829, RDLJ, MS-0066, PC-066-0068, HC.

77. Best, *The Maori As He Was*, 76–77.

78. Binney, *The Legacy of Guilt*, 2d edn., 81.

79. Anne Salmond, "Maori and Modernity," 40.

80. Thomas Kendall, Journal 11 March 1815, SMCP, "Correspondence October 1815–March 1816," PC-0129, HC.

81. Nicholas, *Narrative of a Voyage to New Zealand*, 1:39, 41.

82. King to Daniel Wilson, 11 July 1815, SMCP, "Correspondence June 1815–October 1815," PC-0128, HC; also see Thomas Kendall, Journal 11 March 1815, SMCP, "Correspondence October 1815–March 1816," PC-0129, HC.

83. Thomas Kendall, Journal 11 March 1815, SMCP, "Correspondence October 1815–March 1816," PC-0129, HC.

84. Kendall observed that he was warned to stay away from wāhi tapu because "Atua" were buried there. Thomas Kendall, Journal 11 March 1815, SMCP, "Correspondence October 1815–March 1816," PC-0129, HC.

85. Kendall believed that Ruatara was Hongi's nephew. Samuel Marsden understood that Ruatara's father was Kaparu, the younger brother of the chief Te Pahi, while his mother was the sister of Hongi Hika. But it seems more likely that his father was Te Aweawe of Ngāti Rahiri and Ngāti Tautahi sections of Ngā Puhi, and that Tauramoko, of Ngāti Rahiri and Ngāti Hineira, was his mother. Ballara, "Ruatara ?—1815."

86. Thomas Kendall, Journal 11 March 1815, SMCP, "Correspondence October 1815–March 1816," PC-0129, HC.

87. Hilton, *The Age of Atonement*, 19–21; Bebbington, *Evangelicalism in Modern Britain*, 52.

88. Hylson-Smith, *Evangelicals in the Church of England*, 103.

89. Elias, *The Civilizing Process*, 129, 180; Dixon, *From Passions to Emotions*.

90. *Evangelical Magazine and Gospel Advocate* 8 (1837), 172; Wood, *Evangelical Balance Sheet*, 106; Blake, *Evangelicals in the Royal Navy*, 43–44.

91. The famous whakatauki states, "Ko roimata, ko hupe, anake ngā kai utu i ngā patu a aituā" [By tears and mucus only are the blows of death avenged]. Also see Hiroa, *The Coming of the Maori*, 417–18; and Best, "Maori Eschatology," 168.

92. Te Awekotuku, *Mau Moko*, 80–81.

93. Leviticus 19:28: "Ye shall not make any cuttings in your flesh for the dead, nor print any marks upon you."

94. Thomas Kendall, Journal 11 March 1815, SMCP, "Correspondence October 1815–March 1816," PC-0129, HC.

95. See, for example, William White to his brother, 21 September 1824, WWP, AWM; Henry Williams, Journal 28 March 1828, HWJ, 118; John Hobbs, Diary 8 October 1828, JHD, vol. 3, 287–88.

96. Thomas Kendall, Journal 11 March 1815, "Correspondence October 1815–March 1816," SMCP, PC-0129, HC.

97. Thomas Kendall, Journal 15 April 1815, SMCP, "Correspondence October 1815–March 1816," PC-0129, HC.

98. Thomas Kendall, Journal 11 March 1815, SMCP, "Correspondence October 1815–March 1816," PC-0129, HC.

99. Te Huringa clearly believed that the mat retained the tapu blood spilled during the killing. Te Rangi Hiroa offers interesting insights into the power of mats to retain tapu, in *The Coming of the Maori*, 416.

100. John King, Journal 23 July 1822, JKLJ, HC. This was hardly surprising, of course, given that humanity's mortality was the ultimate consequence of Māui's failure to defeat death. Māui attempted to reenter the womb of Hine-nui-te-pō to claim immortality for humans, but she was awoken by the laughter of the *pīwakawaka* (fantail) and crushed Māui. After the death of Māui, all humans were destined to die.

101. John King, Journal 2 August 1822, JKLJ, HC.

102. John King, Journal 28 August 1822, JKLJ, HC. For a similar exchange around the sick woman Tu, see John King, Journal 26 October 1824, JKLJ, HC.

103. John King, Journal 21 September 1822, JKLJ, HC.

104. Hanson and Hanson offer an even more negative assessment, in *Counterpoint in Maori Culture*, 181–85. Elsdon Best offered a more positive assessment of the right of slaves, while still recognizing the contingency of their fate, in *The Maori As He Was*, 89. Also see Mead, *Tikanga Maori*, 185.

105. John Hobbs, Diary 27 November 1823, JHD, volume 1, 8–10, AWM.

106. See Tuai's explanation to Dumont D'Uville on the absence of injunctions on killing slaves, in d'Urville, "Voyage de M. Duperry," 38. Also see Edward Markham, "Transcript of New Zealand or Recollections of It," MS-0085, 81–82, HC; Ballara, *Taua*, 177–78.

107. John Hobbs, Diary 3 February 1824, JHD, vol. 1, 30–31, AWM.

108. John Butler, Journal 26th August, 1820, JBL, 84.

109. John King, Journal 29 May 1822 and 21 June 1824, JKLJ, HC. Also see his entries for 9 December 1822.

110. John King, Journal 10 September 1824, JKLJ, HC.

111. Turner, Journal 21 Nov 1826, *Missionary Notices* 5 (1826–28), 292–3; Marianne Williams, Journal 11 February 1824 and 5 October 1824, in Marianne Williams, *Letters from the Bay of Islands*, 81, 93.

112. John King, Journal 30 July 1822, JKLJ, HC.

113. On this broad point see Hanson and Hanson, *Counterpoint in Maori Culture*, 183–84; and, more specifically, Best, "Maori Eschatology," 188.

114. John King, Journal 2 August 1822 and 30 July 1822, JKLJ, HC.

115. Petrie, *Chiefs of Industry*, 18, 67.

116. See John Savage's comments, in Savage, *Some Account of New Zealand*, 55–57, 96.

117. Belich, *Making Peoples*, 159. By 1814, Hongi had established large plantations of potatoes as well as kūmara, cabbages, turnips, pumpkins, and corn at Waimate. Nicholas, *Narrative of a Voyage to New Zealand*, 1:341. Also see Middleton, "Potatoes and Muskets."

118. Binney, "Introduction," in Binney, *Te Kerikeri*, 15.

119. John King, Journal 23 July 1822, JKLJ, HC; Ballara, *Taua*, 77–78.

120. John King, Journal 18 October 1824, JKLJ, HC. Note that this was not Tuai (or "Tooi"), who had visited England in 1818–19 with Tītere.

121. Sinclair, *Laplace in New Zealand*, 82–83; Hiroa, *The Coming of the Maori*, 429; Cloher, *Hongi Hika*, 230.

122. Ballara, *Taua*, 77; Hiroa, *The Coming of the Maori*, 485; Best, "Maori Eschatology," 158.

123. See Henry Williams, Journal 19 January 1827, 13 February 1827, 25 December 1827, 10 March 1828, HWJ, 40, 42, 93, 109–10. Also see Cloher, *Hongi Hika*, 224–25.

124. Henry Williams, Journal 24 June 1827, HWJ, 58. The trader Joel Polack suggested in the late 1830s that rangatira had turned away from the sacrifice of slaves as their labor was valued and the decline in war-making had reduced the supply of captives. Polack, *New Zealand*.

125. Thomas Kendall, Journal 23 July 1815, SMCP, "Correspondence October 1815–March 1816," PC-0129, HC.

126. John King, Journal 15 August 1822, JKLJ, HC.

127. John King, Journal 2 August 1822, JKLJ, HC.

128. See, for example, Samuel Leigh, Journal 1 May 1823, *Missionary Notices* 4 (1823–25), 203; John King, Journal 15 August 1822 and 16 June 1834, JKLJ, HC; John Hobbs, Diary 22 December 1823 (but describing 21 December), JHD, AWM.

129. Thomas Kendall, Journal 23 July 1815, SMCP, "Correspondence October 1815–March 1816," PC-0129, HC.
130. King, Journal 23 July 1815, JKLJ, HC.
131. John Hobbs, Diary 16 October 1825, JHD, AWM.
132. See, for example, Kendall's observations on Kaingaroa. Thomas Kendall, Journal 11 July 1815, SMCP, "Correspondence October 1815–March 1816," PC-0129, HC. Also see Cloher, *Hongi Hika*, 93.
133. John King, Journal 15 August 1822, JKLJ, HC.
134. John King, Journal 2 June 1825, JKLJ, HC.
135. Dowbiggin, *A Concise History of Euthanasia*, 35–36; Jalland, *Death in the Victorian Family*, 69–70.
136. John King, Journal 15 August 1822, JKLJ, HC.
137. Puckey to CMS, 21 September 1839, WPP, I, 55–56, AWM.
138. Mead, *Tikanga Maori*, 341; Hanson and Hanson, *Counterpoint in Maori Culture*, 142–45.
139. John Hobbs, Diary 16 October 1825, JHD, AWM.
140. Henry Williams, Journal 23 December 1832, HWJ, 269.
141. Ballara, "Pana-kareao, Nopera ?—1856."
142. William Puckey, "A Journal of an Expedition to Explore the Reinga or the Place of the Departed Spirits of the New Zealanders," WPP, I, 15, AWM.
143. William Puckey, 6 December 1834, "A Journal of an Expedition to Explore the Reinga or the Place of the Departed Spirits of the New Zealanders," WPP, I, 16–17, AWM.
144. William Puckey, 6 December 1834, "A Journal of an Expedition to Explore the Reinga or the Place of the Departed Spirits of the New Zealanders," WPP, I, 16–17, AWM.
145. William Puckey, 7 December 1834, "A Journal of an Expedition to Explore the Reinga or the Place of the Departed Spirits of the New Zealanders," WPP, I, 17–18, AWM.
146. William Puckey, 8 December 1834, "A Journal of an Expedition to Explore the Reinga or the Place of the Departed Spirits of the New Zealanders," WPP, I, 18, AWM.
147. William Puckey, 9 December 1834, "A Journal of an Expedition to Explore the Reinga or the Place of the Departed Spirits of the New Zealanders," WPP, I, 18–19, AWM.
148. William Puckey, 9 December 1834, "A Journal of an Expedition to Explore the Reinga or the Place of the Departed Spirits of the New Zealanders," WPP, I, 19, AWM.
149. William Puckey, 9 December 1834, "A Journal of an Expedition to Explore the Reinga or the Place of the Departed Spirits of the New Zealanders," WPP, I, 19, AWM.
150. William Puckey, 9 December 1834, "A Journal of an Expedition to Explore the Reinga or the Place of the Departed Spirits of the New Zealanders," WPP, I, 20, AWM.
151. William Puckey, 9 December 1834, "A Journal of an Expedition to Explore the Reinga or the Place of the Departed Spirits of the New Zealanders," WPP, I, 21–22, AWM.

152. William Colenso, Journal 31 March 1839, MS-0582, ATL. Colenso was especially aware of having accidentally infringed on tapu the previous night when staying at a small pā near a stream named Te Werahi. Colenso had drawn from a small pool of fresh water, violating the tapu of a "mirror pool" restricted for the use of the local rangatira. A hui was held about suitable punishments for Colenso, but he made a persuasive case about his own ignorance.

153. This is in keeping with recent research on the spread of Christianity in colonial Africa. See Brock, "New Christians as Evangelists."

154. Henry Williams, Journal 8 October 1832, 8 February 1834, 13 May 1834, 7 August 1834, HWJ, 260, 360, 373, 383.

155. Henry Williams, Journal 9 August 1833, HWJ, 326.

156. See, for example, Henry Williams, Journal 8 October 1832, 9 August 1833, and 29 September 1834, HWJ, 260, 326, 394.

157. Henry Williams, Journal 29 September and 1 October 1834, HWJ, 394. Also see A. N. Brown, Journal 28 November–6 December 1835, *Missionary Register* (July 1838), 341–42.

158. John King, Journal 5 June 1834, JKLJ, HC.

159. Yate, *An Account of New Zealand*, 135.

160. Yate, *An Account of New Zealand*, 135–36.

161. For a similar argument, see Wevers, *Country of Writing*, 102.

162. Yate, *An Account of New Zealand*, 136–37

163. Wilson, *The Island Race*, 178–85.

164. Haweis, *The Evangelical Expositor*, 2:389.

165. Wevers, *Country of Writing*, 103–4; Hartley, *Researches in Greece and the Levant*.

166. Jalland, *Death in the Victorian Family*, 21; Tolley, *Domestic Biography*, 85.

167. Yate, *An Account of New Zealand*, 282–83.

168. Yate, *An Account of New Zealand*, 284–85.

169. Yate, *An Account of New Zealand*, 286–87

170. Yate, *An Account of New Zealand*, 287–89.

6. *The Politics of the "Enfeebled" Body*

1. Lester, *Imperial Networks*, 62–65.

2. See, for example, "The Islands of New Zealand," engraved by J. and C. Walker; "New Zealand," drawn and engraved by W. and A. K. Johnston; "New Zealand (Cook's Strait) Current Basin," engraved by J. and C. Walker; "Bay of Islands"; "Wangeroa"; "New Zealand," engraved by James Wyld.

3. See, for example, "Wesley Dale, New Zealand," in Tyerman and Bennet, *Journal of Voyages and Travels*, 2:138; "Church-Missionary settlement at Kiddeekiddee, New Zealand," *Church Missionary Quarterly Papers* no. 59 (Michaelmas 1830); "Church Mission Station at the Waimate," *Church Missionary Quarterly Papers* no. 81 (Lady Day 1836).

4. "Tooi, a late chief of New Zealand," *Church Missionary Quarterly Papers* no. 42 (1826).

5. On the superiority of New Zealand, see Matthew, *Emigration Fields*. The sequence of plans for colonisation include De Thierry, *To the People of England*; *The British Colonization of New Zealand*; Peter Dillon, *Extract of a Letter from Chevalier Dillon to an Influential Character Here*; William White, *Important Information Relative to New Zealand*; and *Prospectus of the Scots New Zealand Land Company*.

6. Belich, *Making Peoples*, 185–87. On the cautious nature of the Colonial Office, see McLachlan, "Bathurst at the Colonial Office."

7. Belich, *Making Peoples*, 187.

8. "Ribbons of text" is drawn from Salesa, "Afterword."

9. The most important and sophisticated example of this kind of work is Hickford, *Lords of the Land*.

10. Rosenberg, "Revisiting Dollar Diplomacy"; Kristin L. Hoganson, *Fighting for American Manhood*.

11. Tave, *The Amiable Humorist*, 202–3.

12. Laqueur, "Bodies, Details, and the Humanitarian Narrative."

13. Laqueur notes, however, that these narratives did not necessarily result in action, as there was a marked tendency for the release of emotions elicited by the narratives to serve as an end in itself. He noted a tradition of criticism encompassing Dickens, Lukács, and Brecht that has suggested that these narratives actually fed sentimentality, rather than clearly directed moral action or, in the case of Brecht, revolutionary change. Laqueur, "Bodies, Details, and the Humanitarian Narrative," 202–3.

14. John Hobbs, Diary 19 January 1824, JHD, AWM.

15. Laqueur, "Bodies, Details, and the Humanitarian Narrative," 177.

16. Bebbington, *Evangelicalism in Modern Britain*, 59–60. It is worth noting, for example, that Henry Venn (1725-97)—founder of the Clapham Sect and father of John Venn, a founder of the CMS—argued that an individual should make sense of the world by drawing on their experience and *then* on scripture. Venn, *The Complete Duty of Man*, 33.

17. Here I am drawing on Barker-Benfield, *The Culture of Sensibility*; Pinch, *Strange Fits of Passion*; Markman Ellis, *The Politics of Sensibility*.

18. Halttunen, "Humanitarianism and the Pornography of Pain in Anglo-America Culture," 303. Also see Markman Ellis's treatment of slavery in the novels of sensibility, in *The Politics of Sensibility*.

19. Burke, *A Philosophical Enquiry into the Origins of Our Ideas of the Sublime and Beautiful*, 44.

20. On visualization, see Stafford, *Body Criticism*, 2, 21–22, 186–94. Also see Stafford, "Voyeur or Observer?"

21. Smith, *The Theory of Moral Sentiments*, 9.

22. Chandler, "Moving Accidents," 138.

23. "But if RELIGIONS's bias rule the soul, / Then SENSIBILITY exalts the whole." Hannah More, "Sensibility: An Epistle to the Honourable Mrs. Boscawen."

In a 1778 essay, More had attacked what she saw as the excesses of the culture of sensibility, warning against its particular dangers for young women and its potential to promote vice rather than virtue. But in this essay she celebrates "true genuine sentiment," arguing that it invested principle (what she saw as central to reforming action) with its "brightest lustre." More, "On the Danger of Sentimental or Romantic Connexions," in More, *The Works of Hannah More*, VI,6:295–307.

24. More, "On the Danger of Sentimental or Romantic Connexions." The phrase "collective cathartic weeping" is from Wahrman's discussion of early nineteenth-century reflections on the culture of sensibility in the late eighteenth century. Wahrman, *The Making of the Modern Self*, 39.

25. Halttunen, "Humanitarianism and the Pornography of Pain in Anglo-American Culture," 303.

26. John Wesley himself explained in 1768, "It is a fundamental principle with us that to renounce reason is to renounce religion, that religion and reason go hand in hand." John Wesley to Dr. Thomas Rutherford, 28 March 1768, in Wesley, *The Letters of John Wesley*, 5:364.

27. Among other examples of this genre are John King, Journal 4 June 1819, 29 May 1822, and 13 December 1823, JKLJ, HC; John Butler, Journal 14 November 1819, JBL, 49–50. Rod Edmond has drawn attention to the divergence between polished published texts by missionaries and the broader range of everyday missionary writing. Edmond, *Representing the South Pacific*, 17–18. A key exploration of missionary writing is Johnston, *Missionary Writing and Empire, 1800–1860*.

28. This draws from Latour, "Visualisation and Cognition."

29. It is important here to distinguish between the deep-seated fears and doubts that were generally kept out of metropolitan texts and the "troubles" and "tests" that were considered integral to the missionary's life. The Wesleyan *Missionary Notices* for November 1825, for example, prefaced its extract from New Zealand with an editorial comment saying that the letters from William White and Nathaniel Turner would "show the exercises, dangers, and capricious changes to which the messengers of peace are exposed among those warlike, ferocious, and untamed savages." *Missionary Notices*, November 1825, 545.

30. Account of Hongi, *Missionary Papers* (Michaelmas 1816); account of Māori material culture, *Missionary Papers* (Christmas 1816); "Memoir of Mowhee," *Missionary Papers* 10 (midsummer 1818); account of Tooi, *Missionary Papers* (midsummer 1826); account of "Kiddekiddee," *Missionary Papers* (Michaelmas 1830).

31. Māui was related to Tara, the principal chief of the southern alliance that dominated the region bounded by Kawakawa, Kororāreka, and Waikare.

32. While he was on Norfolk Island Māui took the name "Tommy Drummond."

33. Christian Rangi is typically identified as the first CMS convert, while the first Māori to convert to the teachings of WMS, Hika, was not baptized until January 1831. See J. M. R. Owens, "Christianity and the Maoris to 1840," 18.

34. Samuel Marsden, SMCP, "Observations on the introduction of the Gospels into the South Sea Islands: Being my first visit to New Zealand in Dec 1814," MS-0176/001, 33–34, HC; Samuel Marsden, Correspondence, 22 March 1813–13 June 1815, MS-0054, HC.

35. "Memoir of Mowhee," *Missionary Papers* 10 (midsummer 1818).

36. "Memoir of Mowhee," *Missionary Papers* 10 (midsummer 1818).

37. "Memoir of Mowhee," *Missionary Papers* 10 (midsummer 1818).

38. James Kemp to CMS Secy, 14 October 1818, Church Missionary Society, Archives Relating to the Australian and New Zealand Missions, 1808–1884, Home Letters to CMS Secretaries, Hocken Microfilm, CH/O 19, HC. Note that Kemp signed his letter "James Kempe."

39. This way of framing leading rangatira pervades Nicholas, *Narrative of a Voyage to New Zealand*.

40. This narrative, for example, reached an international audience, with an American edition being published in 1820 by the leading Connecticut-based children's author and publisher Samuel Griswold Goodrich. See the advertisement in the *Connecticut Mirror*, 8 May 1820, 3. This edition sold for 4 cents each, 42 cents per dozen, and $2.50 per hundred. Goodrich (1793–1860) was a bookseller and renowned author for children, publishing under the name "Peter Parley." He was based in Hartford, Connecticut, until he relocated to Boston in the mid-1820s.

41. The diversification and intensification of cross-cultural contact from the mid-1810s probably reduced the fertility of Māori women through the introduction of venereal diseases, as well as leading to a sequence of devastating epidemics, which resulted in significant population decline in some regions through the late 1830s.

42. Laqueur, "Bodies, Details, and the Humanitarian Narrative," 177.

43. Tuai later suggested that he had "enjoyed the favours" of one of Marsden's daughters while living in Parramatta. See Ollivier, *Extracts from New Zealand journals Written on Ships under the Command of d'Entrecasteaux and Duperry*, 139.

44. "Tooi, a Late Chief of New Zealand," *Missionary Papers* (midsummer 1826). On their visit to Britain, see Tuai and Titere, Letters, MS-Papers-0288, ATL.

45. These conflicts were primarily between Ngāre Raumati, the hapū of Korokoro and Tuai in the eastern region of the Bay of Islands known as of Te Rāwhiti-Pāroa, and Ngāi Tawake of Waimate. See Ballara, *Taua*, 180–81, 196–97. In 1820 Richard Cruise observed that Tuai offered a "continual boast of the atrocities he had committed," including cannibalism. Cruise, *Journal of a Ten Months' Residence in New Zealand*, 41.

46. Barber, "Archaeology, Ethnography and the Record of Maori Cannibalism," 263–64.

47. Octavius Hadfield, "System of Government among the New Zealand tribes," GNZ MS17, 112–14, APL.

48. Representative examples include *Missionary Register*, October 1822, 433–44 (on cannibalism and war); January 1823, 68 (on suicide, killing of slaves, and

cannibalism); November 1823, 504–6 (on the use of heads as trophies, slavery, war-making, the execution of slaves, and cannibalism).

49. Halttunen, "Humanitarianism and the Pornography of Pain in Anglo-American Culture," 309.

50. Carey, *An Enquiry into the Obligations of Christians to Use Means for the Conversion of the Heathens.*

51. This narrative is based on Edward Shortland, "Narrative of the origin and progress of the wars of Ngatitoa," in "Notes on Maori language, customs and traditional history," MS-0096, HC. Also see Te Kahu, "The Wars of Kai-Tahu with Kati-Toa."

52. Marsden to Darling, 18 April 1831, quoted by Dandeson Coates, in *Report from the Select Committee on Aborigines (British Settlements)*, 538 (1836), 482–83.

53. Marsden to Darling, 18 April 1831, quoted by Dandeson Coates, in *Report from the Select Committee on Aborigines (British Settlements)*, 538 (1836), 482–83.

54. Joseph Barrow Montefiore, Sydney merchant, deposition 5 February 1831; deposition of William Brown, crewman on Elizabeth; deposition of John Swan, ship's carpenter, sworn 7 January, HRNZ, 2:580–81, 584–85, 586–87.

55. Goderich to Darling, 31 Jan 1832, HRNZ, 2:598.

56. *Murders Abroad Act* (1817), 57 Geo III, c. 53, 27 June 1817, *Journal of the House of Commons*, 26–27 June, 1817, 418–19.

57. Bigge to Earl Bathurst, 27 February 1823, HRNZ, 1:589, 593.

58. James Stephen Minute, 25 May 1830, Records of the Colonial Office, New South Wales Original Correspondence, Correspondence, Original – Secretary of State, Individuals, etc., 1 January 1830 to 31 December 1830, RCO 201/215, folios 696–97, National Archives, Kew, London.

59. See encl. in Yate to Colonial Secretary, N.S.W., 16 November 1831, *British Parliamentary Papers*, (238) 1840, 7.

60. *Letter of the Right Honorable Lord Viscount Goderich.* See original 14 June 1832, Records of the Colonial Office, New Zealand Original Correspondence, Correspondence, Original – Secretary of State, Despatches and Individuals, 1 January 1830 to 31 December 1835, RCO 209/1, 104, National Archives, Kew, London.

61. See Young, *The Colonial Office in the Early Nineteenth Century*, 282–84.

62. Busby to Secretary of State, 16 June 1837, James Busby, "Official Letters to Various People, 1833–1870," qMS-0352, ATL.

63. Busby to Colonial Secretary, 31 October 1835, James Busby, "Despatches and Letters of James Busby 1833–1839," qMS-0345, ATL.

64. Busby to Colonial Secretary, 31 October 1835, James Busby, "Despatches and Letters of James Busby 1833–1839," qMS-0345, ATL.

65. Busby to Colonial Secretary, 26 January 1836, James Busby, "Despatches and Letters of James Busby 1833–1839," qMS-0345, ATL.

66. Contrast this reading to Paul Moon's assertion that the declaration "meant that New Zealand was constituted as a single sovereign state, under complete Maori rule, and separate from the British Empire." Moon here entirely disregards

Busby's broader vision of the meaning of the Declaration. Moon, *Te Ara Kī Te Tiriti*, 65.

67. Elbourne, "The Sin of the Settler." This view is in marked contrast to the readings of other historians—most notably Henry Reynolds—who see the committee as being representative of "metropolitan" views of indigenous rights. See Reynolds, *Frontier*; and Reynolds, *The Law of the Land*.

68. The range of Thomas Buxton's interest can be seen in a brief survey of his key works which include *The Distresses of the People*; *An Inquiry, Whether Crime and Misery Are Produced or Prevented by Our Present System of Prison Discipline*; *Severity of Punishment*; and *The African Slave Trade*.

69. See Buxton's own list of his areas of concern: Thomas Fowell Buxton, Papers, volume 16, 91e, GB 162 Bodleian Library of Commonwealth and African Studies at Rhodes House MSS. Brit. Emp. s. 444, Rhodes House Library, Oxford.

70. Elbourne, *Blood Ground*, 243–46.

71. Laidlaw, "'Aunt Anna's Report,'" 9–12.

72. Laidlaw, "'Aunt Anna's Report,'" 3–4. See, in particular, Thomas Fowell Buxton to Thomas Pringle, 14 January 1834, Thomas Fowell Buxton, Papers, vol. 12, 154, GB 162 Bodleian Library of Commonwealth and African Studies at Rhodes House MSS. Brit. Emp. s. 444, Rhodes House Library, Oxford.

73. *British Parliamentary Debates*, 3d series, xxix (14 July 1835), 549–53.

74. Laidlaw, "'Aunt Anna's Report,'" 1–29.

75. Donkin had served with distinction in the West Indies and against the Marathas in India before taking over the administration of the Cape Colony in 1820–21.

76. On "incitement to discourse," see Foucault, *The History of Sexuality*.

77. Charles Buxton, *Memoirs of Sir Thomas Fowell Buxton*, 186.

78. "YOUR Committee have proceeded to take Evidence, and their Inquiries have extended to Southern Africa, the Canadas, Newfoundland, New South Wales and Van Diemen's Land. They have also received some Information relative to New Zealand and the South Sea Islands, which countries, though not British Possessions, are continually visited by Subjects of Great Britain, and on which many of them reside." British Parliament, *Report from the Select Committee on Aborigines (British Settlements)*, 538 (1836), iii.

79. British Parliament, *Report from the Select Committee on Aborigines (British Settlements)*, 538 (1836), 197–98.

80. Yate's evidence, 12 February 1836, in British Parliament, *Report from the Select Committee on Aborigines (British Settlements)*, 538 (1836), 189–206.

81. Yate was pressed on the identity of the captain. He recalled that his name was Stewart, but confirmed that he was not the same "Captain Stewart" of the *Elizabeth* affair. Yate suggested that this event occurred around 1833. British Parliament, *Report from the Select Committee on Aborigines (British Settlements)*, 538 (1836), 193–96.

82. British Parliament, *Report from the Select Committee on Aborigines (British Settlements)*, 538 (1836), 195–96.

83. Coates giving evidence, 6 June 1836, quoting letter from Marsden to Darling, 18 April 1831. British Parliament, *Report from the Select Committee on Aborigines (British Settlements)*, 538 (1836), 481–84.

84. British Parliament, *Report from the Select Committee on Aborigines (British Settlements)*, 538 (1836), 439. Compare with Marshall, *A Personal Narrative of Two Visits to New Zealand*.

85. Samson, "The 1834 Cruise of HMS Alligator"; and Samson, *Imperial Benevolence*.

86. Elbourne, "The Sin of the Settler."

87. British Parliament, *Report from the Select Committee on Aborigines (British Settlements)*, 425 (1837), 17.

88. British Parliament, *Report from the Select Committee on Aborigines (British Settlements)*, 425 (1837), 75–77.

89. British Parliament, *Report from the Select Committee on Aborigines (British Settlements)*, 425 (1837), 77–81.

90. British Parliament, *Report from the Select Committee on Aborigines (British Settlements)*, 425 (1837), 75–76.

91. British Parliament, *Report from the Select Committee on Aborigines (British Settlements)*, 425 (1837), 86.

92. Buxton to Joseph John Gurney, 25 June 1837, Thomas Fowell Buxton, Papers, Volume 2, 131–38, GB 162 Bodleian Library of Commonwealth and African Studies at Rhodes House MSS. Brit. Emp. s. 444, Rhodes House Library, Oxford.

93. The best account of these complex negotiations remains Adams, *Fatal Necessity*, 91–120.

94. British Parliament, *Report from the Select Committee of the House of Lords, Appointed to Inquire into the Present State of the Islands of New Zealand*, 69.

95. British Parliament, *Report from the Select Committee of the House of Lords, Appointed to Inquire into the Present State of the Islands of New Zealand*, 55–56.

96. British Parliament, *Report from the Select Committee of the House of Lords, Appointed to Inquire into the Present State of the Islands of New Zealand*, 59, 60.

97. British Parliament, *Report from the Select Committee of the House of Lords, Appointed to Inquire into the Present State of the Islands of New Zealand*, 79–80.

98. British Parliament, *Report from the Select Committee of the House of Lords, Appointed to Inquire into the Present State of the Islands of New Zealand*, 87.

99. British Parliament, *Report from the Select Committee of the House of Lords, Appointed to Inquire into the Present State of the Islands of New Zealand*, 92–93.

100. British Parliament, *Report from the Select Committee of the House of Lords, Appointed to Inquire into the Present State of the Islands of New Zealand*, 87.

101. British Parliament, *Report from the Select Committee of the House of Lords, Appointed to Inquire into the Present State of the Islands of New Zealand*, 146.

102. British Parliament, *Report from the Select Committee of the House of Lords, Appointed to Inquire into the Present State of the Islands of New Zealand*, 125.

103. British Parliament, *Report from the Select Committee of the House of Lords, Appointed to Inquire into the Present State of the Islands of New Zealand*, 76–77.

104. Meredith, "Who Was Nayti?," 2.

105. British Parliament, *Report from the Select Committee of the House of Lords, Appointed to Inquire into the Present State of the Islands of New Zealand*, 115.

106. British Parliament, *Report from the Select Committee of the House of Lords, Appointed to Inquire into the Present State of the Islands of New Zealand*, 47.

107. British Parliament, *Report from the Select Committee of the House of Lords, Appointed to Inquire into the Present State of the Islands of New Zealand*, 10–11.

108. British Parliament, *Report from the Select Committee of the House of Lords, Appointed to Inquire into the Present State of the Islands of New Zealand*, 17.

109. British Parliament, *Report from the Select Committee of the House of Lords, Appointed to Inquire into the Present State of the Islands of New Zealand*, 243–44.

110. Elbourne, "The Sin of the Settler."

111. See, for example, the tables provided in British Parliament, *Report from the Select Committee of the House of Lords, Appointed to Inquire into the Present State of the Islands of New Zealand*, 185–86. Coates argued "that it is not the Want of a Colony that hinders the Progress of the Mission, but that Presence of the Colony will in all Probability present a Counteraction." British Parliament, *Report from the Select Committee of the House of Lords, Appointed to Inquire into the Present State of the Islands of New Zealand*, 255.

112. British Parliament, *Report from the Select Committee of the House of Lords, Appointed to Inquire into the Present State of the Islands of New Zealand*, 246.

113. British Parliament, *Report from the Select Committee of the House of Lords, Appointed to Inquire into the Present State of the Islands of New Zealand*, 246–47.

114. *British Parliamentary Debates*, 3d series XLIII (1838), 871–82.

115. Compare with Adams's reading which suggests that the House of Lords Committee "supported" the Buxton report. Adams, *Fatal Necessity*, 130.

116. This reached its apogee in the 1840s and 1850s. *Tait's Magazine* for 1850, for example, denounced "the puerile whimperings of an effeminate humanitarianism" (*Tait's Magazine* 17 [1850], 84). Most famously, however, Charles Dickens increasingly cast the term as a pejorative; his novel *Bleak House*, published in 1852–53, lampooned humanitarian concerns for non-Europeans through the figure of Mrs. Jellyby, whose attachment to Africans eclipsed her affective concern for her own family.

117. Stephen to Napier, 19 September 1839, Macvey Napier Papers, ADD, MS 34620, 382, British Library.

118. Hobson to Bourke, 8 August 1837, Records of the Colonial Office, New Zealand Original Correspondence, Correspondence, Original – Secretary of State, Despatches, Offices and Individuals, 1 January 1836 to 31 December 1837, RCO 209/2, 30–37.

119. Hobson to Glenelg, 21 January 1839, Records of the Colonial Office, New Zealand Original Correspondence, Correspondence, Original – Secretary of State,

Despatches, and Miscelleneous, 1 January 1839 to 31 December 1839, RCO 209/4, 87–88.

120. James Stephen to Henry Labouchere, 15 March 1839, Records of the Colonial Office, New Zealand Original Correspondence, Correspondence, Original – Secretary of State, Despatches, and Miscelleneous, 1 January 1839 to 31 December 1839, RCO 209/4, 326–28. For a new reading of the importance of humanitarianism in the shaping of colonial governance see Lester and Dussart, *Colonization and the Origins of Humanitarian Governance*.

121. Marquess of Normanby to Captain William Hobson, 14 August 1839, in Williams, *A Letter to the Right Hon. W. E. Gladstone Being an Appeal on Behalf of the Ngatiraukawa Tribe*, 10–11.

122. Claudia Orange, *Treaty of Waitangi*, 31.

123. These texts are taken from the appendices to Claudia Orange, *Treaty of Waitangi*, 258–66. The English rendering of the Māori version is from the official translation prepared by T. E. Young of the Native Department.

124. Lester and Dussart, *Colonization and the Origins of Humanitarian Governance*.

125. Porter, "Trusteeship, Anti-Slavery, and Humanitarianism," 209; Dalziel, "Southern Islands," 578.

126. British Parliament, *Report from the Select Committee on Aborigines (British Settlements)*, 425 (1837), 77–81.

127. Where contact was already established, the report emphasized that the "civilizing mission" should progress, but that the equal rights of indigenous peoples must be recognized and that their welfare must be guarded through good laws and an ethical justice system.

128. This interpretation echoes a key element of Lauren Benton's argument about the function of "modalities of protection" in the British empire in this period, but my approach places greater emphasis on the importance of humanitarianism and the culture of sensibility than does Benton's more narrowly legal reading. Benton, "Modalities of British Protection in the Early Nineteenth Century World." Lester and Dussart also provide a compelling case for the political weight of humanitarianism in *Colonization and the Origins of Humanitarian Governance*.

129. This formulation draws from Lata Mani's discussion of sati. Mani, *Contentious Traditions*.

Conclusion. Bodies and the Entanglements of Empire

1. Jolly and Tcherkézoff, "Oceanic Encounters," 3, 12.

2. For a similar argument about the Cape Colony, see Robert Ross, *Status and Respectability in the Cape Colony*, 112–13.

3. Dening, *Performances*, 34.

4. This reading reworks Ballantyne, "Print, Politics and Protestantism." It draws from some of the arguments about conversion in Viswanathan, *Outside the Fold*.

5. Sinclair, *The Origins of Maori Wars*, 13; Sinclair, *A History of New Zealand* (1988), 42.

6. Binney, "Introduction," in Yate, *An Account of New Zealand*, v.

7. Walker, *Ka Whawhai Tonu Matou*.

8. For a narrower version of this argument focused solely on language, see Jones and Jenkins, *He Kōrero*, 126. For an example of work that stresses the ability of missionaries and their wives to transform Māori culture, see Rountree, "Remaking the Maori Female Body."

9. Adams, *Fatal Necessity*, 46.

10. Robert Ross also emphasizes the highly selective and composed nature of texts published by metropolitan missionary societies, in *Status and Respectability in the Cape Colony*, 113.

11. Paul Landau has stressed this dynamic in central Botswana, highlighting the ability of Tswana speakers both to work within the conventions of introduced cultural forms and to bend them in innovative ways. For example, see his discussion of hymns, in Landau, *The Realm of the Word*, 187.

12. See, for example, Taiw[h]anga to Richard Davis, 23 October 1826; Coleman Davis Aoheke to Richard Davis, n.d.; Paratene to Richard Davis, 25 January 1834, in Coleman, *A Memoir of the Rev. Richard Davis*, 448–52.

13. Belich, "Imperial Myth and Colonial Actuality." I have also elaborated a similar line of critique with regard to the history of sealing and whaling. Ballantyne, *Webs of Empire*, 134–35.

14. Waitangi Tribunal, *Muriwhenua Land Report*, esp. 49–50.

15. Following Owens, "The Unexpected Impact."

16. On those marriage connections, see Puckey, "The Substance of the Shadow" (esp. 355–58, on the Davis, Puckey, and Matthews families).

GLOSSARY

atua	supernatural being or force; "god"
haehae	to cut or incise the flesh, typically as part of mourning rituals
haka	action dance, often performed as a challenge, as a prelude to conflict, or to mark a notable event or achievement
hākari	ritual feast
hapū	subtribe, clan
hara	offence, a violation of tapu, sin
hau	breath, life-force, vitality
hei tiki	amulet in human form worn around the neck
hui	meetings, ceremonial gatherings
iwi	tribe
kainga	village, settlement
Kākā	a large forest parrot (*Nestor meridionalis*)
karakia	ritual chants, prayers
kaumātua	elder
kō	digging stick
kokowai	ochre, used as a bodily adornment
kuki	"cook," slave
kūmara	Polynesian "sweet potatoes" (*Ipomoea batatas*)

kutu	lice
mana	status, power, authority
manākitanga	support or hospitality that enhances mana
Matariki	the rising of Pleiades
mate	sickness, death, "existential danger" (Anne Salmond)
muka	prepared fibers of flax
muru	plunder
ngārara	evil lizard, reptile, monster
noa	the antithesis of tapu
pā	fortified settlement
Pakepakehā	supernatural beings, "fairy folk"
pātaka	elevated storage house
pāuruhanga	lengths of timber used to define social space
pepeha	tribal saying, formulaic expression, proverb
pihanga	window
pounamu	"greenstone," nephrite or jade
puhi	a tapu young woman, a "high-ranking" virgin
pūkana	to dilate the eyes and stare intently, often while performing haka or waiata (songs)
puke	hill, mound
rangatira	chief, the state of being noble and well-born
rā tapu	"sacred day," Sunday
rauaruhe	fern
raupo	bulrush (*Typha angustifolia*)
ritenga	custom
rōpū	gang, group, party of people
taiaha	staff-like weapon
tā moko	tattooing
Tāne	god of the forests
Tāngaroa	god of the sea
tāngata	people
tangi, tangihanga	rites for the dead, funeral
taonga	treasured goods, anything highly valued
tapu	sacred, in conjunction with the supernatural, set apart
taua	war party

taurekareka	captive, scoundrel, slave
te ao Māori	the Māori world, Māori culture
te ao mārama	the "world of light," the human world
te reo Māori	the Māori language
tikanga	rules, protocols
tītī	"muttonbirds," sooty shearwater (*Puffinus griseus*)
tohu	markers, symbols, signs
tohunga	ritual expert
Tū-mata-uenga (Tū)	god of war
tupua	goblin, supernatural being
tūtūā	mean, low-born, slave
utu	revenge, reciprocation, restoring balance
waka	canoe
waka huia	treasure box
wakaau	tokens made out of flax
wairua	spirit
whakamā	shame, embarrassment
whakamomori	suicide
whakanoa	to render something noa; to remove tapu
whakatauki	aphorism, proverb, saying
whānau	family
whanaunga	relative
whare	house (traditionally, a one-room dwelling)
whāriki	large woven mats
whata	elevated storage platform

BIBLIOGRAPHY

Manuscripts

ALEXANDER TURNBULL LIBRARY, WELLINGTON (ATL)

Busby, James. "Despatches and Letters of James Busby 1833–1839," qMS-0345.

Busby, James. "Official Letters to Various People, 1833–1870," qMS-0352.

Church Missionary Society. General Committee minutes, CN/M9, 533, Micro-MS-Coll-04-08.

———. "Mission Books—Letters Received CN/M11, CN/M12," Micro-MS-Coll-04-33.

Clarke, George. Outward Correspondence, George Clarke Papers, MS-0250-5.

Colenso, William. Journal 1833–45, MS-0582.

Edwards, Bruce." A Bibliography of Material Relating to the Reverend William Woon, 1803–1858, Wesleyan Methodist Missionary to Tonga and New Zealand." Philip Granger Parkinson Papers, 2003-105-089.

Hall, William. Private Diary, 1816–1838, Micro-MS-0853.

Kendall, Thomas. "Thomas Kendall Journal 9 Mar 1814–13 Feb 1815," MS-Papers-0921.

London Missionary Society. "South Seas Letters 1812–1818: Minutes and Selected Records Relating to Australia and the South Pacific," Micro-MS-Coll-02-019.

Stack, James. Journal, MS-Papers-3306.

Taylor, Richard. Diary, MS-Papers-0254-12.

———. Journal, qMS-1987.

Tuai and Titere. Letters, MS-Papers-0288.

Turner, Nathaniel. Letterbook 1836–1849, qMS-2065.

Wade, William Richard. "John Alexander Wilson—Letters from William Richard Wade." Wilson Family: Papers, MS-Papers-5512-14.

Williams Family Collections, qMS-2225.

AUCKLAND CATHOLIC DIOCESAN ARCHIVES

Pompallier, Jean Baptiste François. "Instructions pour travaux de la mission," POM 14-3.

AUCKLAND PUBLIC LIBRARY

Baron de Thierry, Charles. "Historical Narrative of an Attempt to Form a Settlement in New Zealand," Grey Collection, MS 55, APL, 166.

Hadfield, Octavius. "System of Government among the New Zealand tribes," GNZ MS17.

AUCKLAND WAR MUSEUM AND LIBRARY (AWM)

Hobbs, John. Diary, MS 144.

Maunsell, Susan. Letters, MS 93/111.

Puckey, Williams. Papers, MS 250.

Taylor, Richard. Journals, 1833–1873, MS 302.

Wesleyan Missionary Society. Papers relating to early Wesleyan Missionaries in New Zealand. William White Papers, MS 329.

BRITISH LIBRARY

Napier, Macvey. Papers, ADD, MS 34620.

HOCKEN LIBRARY AND COLLECTIONS, DUNEDIN (HC)

Ashwell, Benjamin Yate. Letters and Journals, MS-0860/001.

Baker, Charles. Journal 1827–39, MS-0517/A.

Butler, John. "Journey from Whangaroa by Whaleboat Oct.–Nov. 1820," MS-0557.

Butler, John Gare. "Collected papers of and relating to Reverend John Gare Butler." Journal 1819–23, PC-0053.

Church Missionary Society. Archives Relating to the Australian and New Zealand Missions, 1808–1884. Home Letters to CMS Secretaries, Hocken Microfilm, CH/O 19.

——. Archives Relating to the Australian and New Zealand Missions, 1808–1884. Mission books containing correspondence to the CMS, Hocken Microfilm, CN/M1, CN/M2, CN/M9.

——. Archives Relating to the Australian and New Zealand Missions, 1808–1884. Original papers and correspondence relating to the CMS, Hocken Microfilm, CN/O 30, CN/O 54, CN/O 96, CN/O 61/28. Home Letters Out, 5 July 1833 to 14 February 1838, CH/L2, Hocken Microfilm, 121/66.

——. Records Relating to the New Zealand Mission. "General inwards letters, March 1808–November 1812," MS-0498/001.

——. Records Relating to the New Zealand Mission. "General inwards letters, February 1813–December 1817," MS-0498/002.

Clarke, George Sr. Collected papers of and relating to George Clarke senior and family. "George Clarke [senior]. Letter and Journals. 1822–1849. Vol 1. Documents 1–57," PC-0054.

———. Collected papers of and relating to George Clarke senior and family. "George Clarke [senior]. Letter and Journals. 1822–1849. Vol 1. Items 91–99," PC-0056.

Colenso, William. Letters 1834–1853, PC-0059.

Davis, Richard. Letters and Journals, MS-0066, PC-066-0068.

"Grant of land at Keddee Keddee by Shunghee Heeka to the Church Missionary Society, 4 November 1819," MS-0070/A.

Hall, William. Private Diary, 1819–1832, MS-0067.

Hamlin, James. Collected Papers. "Collected papers of and relating to Reverend James Hamlin," Journal 13 April 1830–22 October 1832, PC-0040.

Kemp, James. Letters and Journals, MS-0070.

Kendall, Thomas. Collected Papers. "Diary of Thomas Surfleet Kendall," MS-0071/072.

Kendall, Thomas. Letters etc. 1816–1827, PC-0151.

King, John. Letters and Journals, PC-0152.

Markham, Edward. "Transcript of New Zealand or recollections of it by Edward Markham," MS-0085.

Marsden, Samuel. Collected Papers. "Correspondence, 1813–1814," PC-0118.

———. Collected Papers. "Correspondence 1814–1815," PC-0119.

———. Collected Papers. "Correspondence July 1819–August 1821," PC-0134.

———. Collected Papers. "Correspondence July 1835–February 1838," PC-0139.

———. Collected Papers. "Correspondence June 1815–October 1815," PC-0128.

———. Collected Papers. "Correspondence March 1816–February 1817," PC-0130.

———. Collected Papers. "Correspondence March 1817–August 1818," PC-0131.

———. Collected Papers. "Correspondence March 1818–May 1819," PC-0132.

———. Collected Papers. "Correspondence October 1815–March 1816," PC-0129.

———. Collected Papers. "Observations on My Fourth Visit to New Zealand," PC-0034.

———. Collected Papers. "Observations on the introduction of the Gospels into the South Sea Islands: Being my first visit to New Zealand in Dec 1814," MS-0176/001, PC-0030.

———. Collected Papers. "Rev. Sam. Marsden's journal from Feb 13 to Nov 25 1820," MS-0177/002.

———. Collected Papers. "Rev. S. Marsden's journal from July 2 to Nov 1, 1823," MS-0177/003.

———. Collected Papers. "Rev. S. Marsden's journal of proceedings at New Zealand from July 29 to Oct 19, 1819," MS-0177/002, PC-0140.

———. Correspondence, 22 March 1813 to 13 June 1815, MS-0054.

"Missionary Letters etc., F Hall 1821, H. Williams 1864," MS-0053, PC-0306/001-006.

Shortland, Edward. "Notes on Maori language, customs and traditional history," MS-0096.

Wade, William R. Outwards Letters, Misc-MS-0323.
Yate, William. Correspondence, Microfilm: 10096:1.
Yate, William. Journal, Microfilm: 10096:2.

MITCHELL LIBRARY, STATE LIBRARY OF NEW SOUTH WALES, AUSTRALIA

King, Philip Gidley. Letterbook, c187.
"Tippahee a chief of New Zealand," Sv/Mao/Port/14.

NATIONAL ARCHIVES, KEW, LONDON

Clerke, Charles. "RESOLUTION: Log kept by Lieutenant Charles Clerke, towards the South Pole. Discovery and surveying, Pacific, Australia, west coast of North America," Adm 55/103.

Records of the Colonial Office (RCO). Correspondence, Original – Secretary of State. Norfolk Island. 1 January 1795 to 31 December 1800, RCO 201/18.

———. New South Wales Original Correspondence. Correspondence, Original – Secretary of State. 1 January 1783 to 31 December 1822, RCO 201/1.

———. New South Wales Original Correspondence. Correspondence, Original – Secretary of State. Individuals, etc. 1 January 1830 to 31 December 1830, RCO 201/215.

———. New South Wales Original Correspondence. Correspondence, Original – Secretary of State. Port Jackson. 1 January 1792 to 31 December 1792, RCO 201/7.

———. New Zealand Original Correspondence. Correspondence, Original – Secretary of State. Despatches and Individuals. 1 January 1830 to 31 December 1835, RCO 209/1.

———. New Zealand Original Correspondence. Correspondence, Original – Secretary of State. Despatches, and Miscelleneous. 1 January 1839 to 31 December 1839, RCO 209/4.

———. New Zealand Original Correspondence. Correspondence, Original – Secretary of State. Despatches, Offices and Individuals. 1 January 1836 to 31 December 1837, RCO 209/2.

NATIONAL ARCHIVES, WELLINGTON

"Bay of Islands Missions/Waimate—Register: marriages (1823–1835), baptisms (1815–1835), burials (1821–1835)," R21906666.

NATIONAL LIBRARY, AUSTRALIA

Marsden, Rev. Samuel. Letter to Captain Wilson, November 1800, G7753.

RHODES HOUSE LIBRARY, OXFORD

Buxton, Thomas Fowell. Papers, GB 162 Bodleian Library of Commonwealth and African Studies at Rhodes House MSS. Brit. Emp. s. 444.

STATE RECORDS OF NEW SOUTH WALES

Colonial Secretary. Letters Received, 1837, 36/10481 in 4/2357.1.

Periodicals and Official Publications

Annual Register, 1773–74
British Parliamentary Debates, 1833–40
British Parliamentary Papers, 1835–40
Church Missionary Quarterly Papers, 1826–36
Church Missionary Record, 1832
Colonist, 1836
Connecticut News, 1820
The Diary, or, Woodfall's Register, 1793
Evangelical Magazine, 1795
Evangelical Magazine and Gospel Advocate, 1837
Fisher's Colonial Magazine and Colonial Maritime Journal, 1843, 1845
Journal of the House of Commons, 1817
London Magazine, or, Gentlemen's Monthly Intelligencer, 1773
Missionary Notices, 1823–25, 1826–28, 1835–38
Missionary Papers, 1816, 1818, 1826
Missionary Register, 1813–38
Parliamentary History, 1783–85
Proceedings of the Church Missionary Society, 1810–12
Sydney Gazette, 1804–10
Sydney Gazette and New South Wales Advertiser, 1836
Tait's Magazine, 1850
Te Ao Hou, 1965

Maps

ALEXANDER TURNBULL LIBRARY, WELLINGTON (ATL)

"Bay of Islands." London: The Admiralty, 1836.
"The Islands of New Zealand." Engraved by J. and C. Walker. London: Society for the Diffusion of Useful Knowledge, 1838.
"New Zealand (Cook's Strait) Current Basin." Engraved by J. and C. Walker. London: The Admiralty, 1836.
"New Zealand." Drawn and engraved by W. and A. K. Johnston. Edinburgh: Fraser and Crawford, 1839.
"New Zealand." Engraved by James Wyld. London: Wyld, 1837.
"Wangeroa." London: The Admiralty, 1836.

Historical Books and Pamphlets

Anson, F. A., ed. *The Piraki Log (e Pirangi ahau koe): Or, Diary of Captain Hemple-man*. Oxford: Oxford University Press, 1910.

Australia Parliament Library Committee. *Historical Records of Australia: Series 1, Governors' Despatches to and from England.* 26 vols. Sydney: Library Committee of the Commonwealth Parliament, 1914–25.

Baker, Mary, ed. *Never the Faint Hearted: Charles Baker Pioneer Missionary, 1803–1875.* Waikanae: Heritage, 1986.

Banks, Joseph. *The Endeavour Journal of Joseph Banks, 1768–1771.* 2 vols. Edited by J. C. Beaglehole. Sydney: Angus and Robertson, 1962.

B[ennet], G[eorge], ed. *Letters to the Rev. William Yate, from Natives of New Zealand Converted to Christianity.* London: James Nisbet, 1836.

Bewick, Thomas. *A Memoir of Thomas Bewick.* London: Cresset, 1961 [1862].

Bladen, F. M., ed. *Hunter and King, 1800, 1801, 1802.* Vol. 4 of *Historical Records of New South Wales.* Sydney: Government Printer, 1896.

———. *King and Bligh, 1806, 1807, 1808.* Vol. 6 of *Historical Records of New South Wales.* Sydney: Government Printer, 1898.

Bridges, Charles. *The Christian Ministry: With an Inquiry into the Causes of Its Inefficiency.* 7th edn. London: Seeley, Burnside and Seeley, 1849 [1829].

The British Colonization of New Zealand: Being an Account of the Principles, Objects, and Plans of the New Zealand Association: Together with Particulars Concerning the Position, Extent, Soil and Climate, Natural Productions, and Native Inhabitants of New Zealand. London: John W. Parker, 1837.

British Parliament. *Report from the Select Committee of the House of Lords, Appointed to Inquire into the Present State of the Islands of New Zealand, and the Expediency of Regulating the Settlement of British Subjects Therein,* 680 (1837–38).

———. *Report from the Select Committee on Aborigines (British Settlements): Together with the Minutes of Evidence, Appendix and Index,* 538 (1836).

———. *Report from the Select Committee on Aborigines (British Settlements): With the Minutes of Evidence, Appendix and Index,* 425 (1837).

———. *Report from the Select Committee on Transportation,* 1838, House of Commons Papers, 374 (1838).

Burke, Edmund. *A Philosophical Enquiry into the Origins of Our Ideas of the Sublime and Beautiful.* Edited by J. T. Boulton. Notre Dame: 1958 [2d edn., 1759].

Burtner, Robert, and Robert Chiles, eds. *A Compendium of Wesley's Theology.* Nashville: Abingdon, 1954.

Busby, James. *A Brief Memoir Relative to the Islands of New Zealand.* Auckland: Pelorus Press, [1832?].

Butler, John. *Earliest New Zealand: Journals and Correspondence of John Butler.* Edited by R. J. Barton. Masterton: s.n., 1927.

Buxton, Charles, ed. *Memoirs of Sir Thomas Fowell Buxton.* London: Dent, 1900.

Buxton, Thomas Fowell. *The African Slave Trade.* 2d edn. London: John Murray, 1839.

———. *The Distresses of the People, the Blessed Effects of the Pitt System.* London: W. Hone, 1816.

———. *An Inquiry, Whether Crime and Misery Are Produced or Prevented by Our Present System of Prison Discipline.* 3d edn. London: J. and A. Arch, 1818.

———. *Severity of Punishment: Speech of Thomas Fowell Buxton, Esq., in the House of Commons, Wednesday, May 23rd, 1821.* London: Arch, 1821.Carey, Eustace. *Memoir of William Carey D.D.* London: Jackson and Walford, 1836.

Carey, William. *An Enquiry into the Obligations of Christians to Use Means for the Conversion of the Heathens.* Leicester: Ann Ireland, 1792.

Church Missionary Society. *Instructions of the Committee of the Church Missionary Society, Delivered August 6, 1822: To the Rev. Henry Williams, Proceeding as a Missionary to New Zealand: With Mr. Williams's Reply, and Address by the Rev. Edward Garrard Mask, M.A., Minister of Hampstead Chapel, and Late Fellow of Oriel College.* London: Richard Watts, 1822.

———. *Order of Consecration of a Burial-Ground.* Paihia: n.p., 1838.

Clarke, George, [Jr]. *Notes on Early Life in New Zealand.* Hobart: J. Walch and Sons, 1903.

Coates, Dandeson. *The Principles, Objects and Plans of the New Zealand Association Examined, in a Letter to the Right Hon. Lord Glenelg, Secretary of State for the Colonies.* London: n.p., 1837.

Coleman, John Noble. *A Memoir of the Rev. Richard Davis for Thirty-nine Years a Missionary in New Zealand.* London: James Nisbet, 1865.

Cruise, Richard A. *Journal of a Ten Months' Residence in New Zealand (1820).* Edited by A. G. Bagnall. Christchurch: Pegasus, 1957.

Darwin, Charles. *Charles Darwin's Diary of the Voyage of H.M.S. Beagle.* Edited by Nora Barlow. London: Cambridge University Press, 1933.

———. *Journal of Researches into the Natural History and Geology of the Countries Visited by the H.M.S. Beagle.* 2d edn. New York: Cambridge University Press, 2011 [1845].

David, Andrew, ed. *The Charts and Coastal Views of Captain Cook's Voyages.* 3 vols. London: Hakluyt Society, 1988–97.

Davies, John. *The History of the Tahitian Mission 1799–1830.* Edited by Colin Newbury. Cambridge: Hakluyt Society, 1961 [1831].

De Thierry, Charles Philip Hippolytus. *To the People of England: An Address on the Colonization of New Zealand.* London: Knight and Lacey, 1824.

Dieffenbach, Ernest. *Travels in New Zealand: With Contributions to the Geography, Geology, Botany and Natural History of that Country.* 2 vols. London: J. Murray, 1843.

Dillon, Peter. *Extract of a Letter from Chevalier Dillon to an Influential Character Here: On the Advantages to Be Derived from the Establishment of Well Conducted Commercial Settlements in New Zealand.* London: Geo. Nichols, [1839].

d'Urville, Jules Sébastien César Dumont. "Voyage de M. Duperry." *Duperrey's Visit to New Zealand in 1824,* ed. Andrew Sharp, 31–50. Wellington: Alexander Turnbull Library, 1971.

Edwards, Jonathon. *Practical Sermons, Never before Published: By the Late Reverend Mr. Jonathan Edwards, President of the College of New-Jersey.* Edinburgh: n.p., 1788.

Elder, J. R., ed. *Marsden's Lieutenants*. Dunedin: Coulls Somerville Wilkie and A. H. Reed for the Otago University Council, 1934.

Engels, Friedrich. *The Condition of the Working Class in England*. Translated and edited by W. O. Henderson and W. H. Chaloner. Oxford: Basil Blackwell, 1971 [1844].

Fitzgerald, Caroline, ed. *Te Wiremu/Henry Williams: Early Years in the North*. Wellington: Huia, 2011.

Forster, Johann Reinhold. *The Resolution Journal of Johann Reinhold Forster 1772–1775*. 3 vols. Edited by Michael E. Hoare. London: Hakluyt Society, 1982.

Franklin, Benjamin. *Political, Miscellaneous, and Philosophical Pieces*. London: J. Johnson, 1779.

Grey, George. *Proverbial and Popular Sayings*. London: Trubner, 1857.

Gunson, Niel, ed. *Australian Reminiscences and Papers of L. E. Threlkeld, Missionary to the Aborigines, 1824–1859*. 2 vols. Canberra: Australian Institute of Aboriginal Studies, 1974.

Hartley, John. *Researches in Greece and the Levant*. 2d edn. London: R. B. Seeley and W. Burnside, 1833.

Havard-Williams, P., ed. *Marsden and the New Zealand Mission: Sixteen Letters*. Dunedin: University of Otago Press, 1961.

Haweis, Thomas. *Carmina Christo: Or, Hymns to the Saviour: Designed for the Use and Comfort of Those Who Worship the Lamb that Was Slain*. Bath: S. Hayward, 1792.

———. *The Evangelical Expositor: Or, a Commentary on the Holy Bible*. 2 vols. London: n.p., 1765–66.

———. *Evangelical Principles and Practice: Being Fifteen Sermons, Preached in the Parish-Church of St. Mary Magdalen in Oxford*. 4th edn. London: C. Dilly, 1794 [1762].

———. "The Very Probable Success of a Proper Mission to the South Sea Islands." *Evangelical Magazine* 1 (1795): 261–70.

Hawkesworth, John. *An Account of the Voyages Undertaken by the Order of His Present Majesty for Making Discoveries in the Southern Hemisphere*. 3 vols. London: W. Strahan and T. Cadell, 1773.

Joppien, Rudiger, and Bernard Smith, eds. *The Art of Captain Cook's Voyages*. 4 vols. Melbourne: Oxford University Press, 1985–87.

———, eds. *The Art of Captain Cook's Voyages*. Vol. 2, *The Voyage of the* Resolution *and* Adventure, *1772–1775*. New Haven: Yale University Press, 1985.

Kendall, Thomas. *A Grammar and Vocabulary of the Language of New Zealand*. London: Church Missionary Society, 1820.

———. *A Korao no New Zealand: Or, the New Zealander's First Book: Being an Attempt to Compose Some Lessons for the Instruction of the Natives*. Sydney: n.p., 1815.

Lamb, W. Kaye, ed. *A Voyage of Discovery to the North Pacific Ocean and Round the World*. London: Hakluyt Society, 1984.

Letter of the Right Honorable Lord Viscount Goderich, and Address of James Busby, Esq. British Resident, to the Chiefs of New Zealand: Ko te pukapuka o te Tino

Rangatira o Waikauta Koreriha, me te koreo o Te Puhipi ki nga rangatira o Nu Tirani. Sydney: n.p., 1832.

Macbean, Alexander. *A Dictionary of the Bible: Historical and Geographical, Theological, Moral and Ritual, Philosophical and Philological.* London: n.p., 1779.

Mackaness, George, ed. *Some Private Correspondence of the Rev. Samuel Marsden and Family, 1794–1824.* Sydney: D. S. Ford, 1942.

Mackay, Alexander. *A Compendium of Official Documents Relative to Native Affairs in the South Island.* 2 vols. Wellington: Government Printer, 1873.

Macquarie, Lachlan. *A Letter to the Right Honourable Sidmouth.* London: Richard Rees, 1821.

Markham, Edward. *New Zealand or Recollections of It.* Edited by E. H. McCormick. Wellington: Government Printer, 1963 [1834].

Marsden, J. B. *Memoirs of the Life and Labours of the Rev. Samuel Marsden of Parramatta.* London: Religious Tract Society, 1858.

Marsden, Samuel. *Letters and Journals of Samuel Marsden.* Edited by J. R. Elder. Dunedin: Coulls Somerville Wilkie and A. H. Reed for the Otago University Council, 1932.

Marshall, William Barrett. *A Personal Narrative of Two Visits to New Zealand in His Majesty's Ship Alligator, A.D. 1834.* London: J. Nisbet, 1836.

Marx, Karl. *Capital.* Edited by Ernest Mandel. Translated by Ben Fowkes. London: Penguin, 1992 [1867].

Matthew, Patrick. *Emigration Fields: North America, the Cape, Australia and New Zealand: Describing These Countries and Giving a Comparative View of the Advantages They Present to British Settlers.* Edinburgh: Adam and Charles Black, 1839.

McCalman, Godfrey. *A Natural, Commercial and Medicinal Treatise on Tea: With a Concise Account of the East India Company.* Glasgow: David Niven, 1787.

McCrae, Alexander. *Journal Kept in New Zealand in 1820.* Edited by Sir Frederick Revans Chapman. Wellington: Alexander Turnbull Library, 1928.

McNab, Robert, ed. *Historical Records of New Zealand.* 2 vols. Wellington: John Mackay, Government Printer, 1908–14.

Mead, Hirini Moko, and Neil Grove, eds. *Ngā Pēpeha a ngā Tīpuna.* Wellington: Victoria University Press, 2001.

More, Hannah. "Sensibility: An Epistle to the Honourable Mrs. Boscawen." *Sacred Dramas: Chiefly Intended for Young Persons: The Subjects Taken from the Bible: To Which Is Added, Sensibility, a Poem,* 269–90. London: Printed for T. Cadell, 1793.

———. *Strictures on the Modern System of Female Education.* London: T. Cadell and W. Davies, 1799.

———. *The Works of Hannah More in Eight Volumes, Including Several Pieces Never before Published.* 8 vols. London: T. Cadell and W. Davies, 1801.

Nicholas, John Liddiard. *Narrative of a Voyage to New Zealand.* 2 vols. London: Black and Son, 1817.

Ollivier, Isabel, trans. and ed. *Extracts from New Zealand Journals Written on Ships under the Command of d'Entrecasteaux and Duperry (i.e., Duperrey) 1793 and 1824.* Wellington: Alexander Turnbull Library Endowment Trust, 1986.

Orange, James. *Life of the Late George Vason of Nottingham.* London: John Snow, 1840.

Parata, Hoani. *The Maori of New Zealand: Past, Present, and Future.* London: n.p., 1911.

Parkinson, Phil, and Penny Griffith. *Books in Māori, 1815–1900: An Annotated Bibliography.* Auckland: Reed, 2004.

Pilley, Henry Miles. *The New Zealand Missionary.* Cheltenham: William Wight, 1838.

Polack, J. S. *Manners and Customs of the New Zealanders: With Notes Corroborative of Their Habits, Usages etc. and Remarks to Intending Emigrants.* 2 vols. London: James Madden / Hatchard, 1840.

———. *New Zealand: Being a Narrative of Travels and Adventures during a Residence in that Country between the Years 1831 and 1837.* 2 vols. London: Richard Bentley, 1838.

Porter, Frances, ed. *The Turanga Journals, 1840–1850: Letters and Journals of William and Jane Williams, Missionaries to Poverty Bay.* Wellington: Victoria University Press, 1974.

Prospectus of the Scots New Zealand Land Company. Edinburgh: Adam and Charles Black, 1839.

Savage, John. *Some Account of New Zealand: Particularly the Bay of Islands, and Surrounding Country.* London: J. Murray, 1807.

A Sermon Preached at the Parish Church of St. Andrew by the Wardrobe and St. Anne Blackfriars on Tuesday, 3 May 1814. London: n.p., 1814.

A Sermon Preached at the Parish Church of St. Andrew by the Wardrobe and St. Anne Blackfriars on Tuesday, 2 May 1815. London: n.p., 1815.

Sharp, Andrew, ed. *Duperrey's Visit to New Zealand in 1824.* Wellington: Alexander Turnbull Library, 1971.

———, ed. *The Voyages of Abel Janszoon Tasman.* Oxford: Clarendon, 1968.

Smith, Adam. *The Theory of Moral Sentiments.* Edited by D. D. Raphael and A. L. Macfie. Oxford: Clarendon, 1976.

———. *The Wealth of Nations: Books I–III.* Edited by Andrew Skinner. London: Penguin, 1982 [1776].

Taylor, Ann, and Jane Taylor. *Hymns for Infant Minds.* 2d edn. London: T. Conder, 1810.

Turton, H. Hanson, ed. *Maori Deeds of Old Private Land Purchases in New Zealand, from the Year 1815 to 1840, with Pre-Emptive and Other Claims.* Wellington: Government Printer, 1882.

Tyerman, Daniel, and George Bennet. *Journal of Voyages and Travels: Deputed from the London Missionary Society, to Visit Their Various Stations in the South Sea Islands, China, India, etc., between the Years 1821 and 1829.* Comp. James Montgomery. 2 vols. London: F. Westley and A. H. Davis, 1831.

Vason, George. *An Authentic Narrative of Four Years' Residence at Tongataboo, One of the Friendly Islands, in the South-Sea.* London: Longman, Hurst, Rees and Orme, 1810.

Venn, Henry. *The Complete Duty of Man: Or A System of Doctrinal and Practical Christianity to which Are Added Forms of Prayer and Offices of Devotion for the Various Circumstances of Life.* London: S. Crowder and G. Robinson and Carnan and Newbery, 1779.

Wade, William Richard. *A Journey in the Northern Island of New Zealand: Interspersed with Various Information Relative to the Country and People.* Hobart Town: George Rolwegan, 1842.

Weber, Max. *The Protestant Ethic and the Spirit of Capitalism.* Translated by Talcott Parsons. London: Unwin Paperbacks, 1985.

Wesley, John. *The Letters of John Wesley.* Edited by John Telford. 8 vols. London: Epworth, 1931.

———. *The Works of John Wesley: Volume 2: Sermons 34–70.* Edited by Albert C. Outler. Nashville: Abingdon, 1985.

———. *The Works of John Wesley: Volume 4: Sermons 71–114.* Edited by Albert C. Outler. Nashville: Abingdon, 1985.

Whitcombe, John. *A Sermon Preached in the Parish-Church of Walesby, in Lincolnshire, on Sunday the 3d October 1779.* Lincoln, NZ: W. Wood, 1780.

White, John. *The Ancient History of the Maori: Volume 9.* Hamilton: Waikato Print, 2001.

White, William. *Important Information Relative to New Zealand: Intended to Be an Answer to All Inquiries Made by Those Interested in the Occupancy of that Country by British Subjects.* Sydney: Thomas Brennard, 1839.

Wilberforce, William. *A Practical View of Christianity.* Edited by Kevin Charles Belmonte. Peabody, MA: Henderickson, 1996 [1797].

Williams, Frederic Wanklyn. *Through Ninety Years, 1826–1916: Life and Work among the Maoris in New Zealand: Notes of the Lives of William and William Leonard Williams, First and Third Bishops of Waiapu.* Christchurch: Whitcombe and Tombs, 1940.

Williams, H. W. *He Whakatauki, He Titotito, He Pepeha.* Gisborne: Te Rau Kahikatea, 1908.

Williams, Henry. *The Early Journals of Henry Williams: Senior Missionary in New Zealand of the Church Missionary Society 1826–40.* Edited by Lawrence M. Rogers. Christchurch: Pegasus, 1961.

Williams, Marianne. *Letters from the Bay of Islands: The Story of Marianne Williams.* Edited by Caroline Fitzgerald. Auckland: Penguin, 2004.

Williams, T. C. *A Letter to the Right Hon. W. E. Gladstone Being an Appeal on Behalf of the Ngatiraukawa Tribe.* Wellington: J. Hughes, 1873.Yate, William. *An Account of New Zealand.* New edn. Wellington: Reed, 1970.

———. *An Account of New Zealand and of the Formation and Progress of the Church Missionary Society's Mission in the Northern Island.* London: Seeley and Burnside, 1835.

———. *A Letter to the Committee of the Church Missionary Society, to Which Is Added a Statement, by the Reverend William Yate.* Poole and Bournemouth: John Sydenham, 1843.

———. *To the Parishioners of St James' Church, Sydney.* Sydney: Stephens and Stokes, 1836.

Secondary Sources

Adams, Peter. *Fatal Necessity: British Intervention in New Zealand, 1930–1947.* Auckland: Auckland University Press, 1977.

Adshead, S. A. M. *Central Asia in World History.* Basingstoke: Macmillan, 1993.

Aldrich, Robert. *Colonialism and Homosexuality.* London: Routledge, 2003.

Ariès, Philippe. *The Hour of Our Death.* Translated by Helen Weaver. London: Allen Lane, 1981.

Atkins, Keletso E. "'Kaffir Time': Preindustrial Temporal Concepts and Labour Discipline in Nineteenth Century Colonial Natal." *Journal of African History* 29.2 (1988): 229–44.

Bach, John. *The Maritime History of Australia.* Melbourne: Thomas Nelson, 1976.

Ballantyne, Tony. *Between Colonialism and Diaspora: Sikh Cultural Formations in an Imperial World.* Durham: Duke University Press, 2006.

———. "The Changing Shape of the Modern British Empire and Its Historiography." *Historical Journal* 53 (2010): 429–52.

———. "Empire, Knowledge, Culture: From Proto-Globalization to Modern Globalization." *Globalization in World History,* ed. A. G. Hopkins, 115–40. London: Pimlico, 2002.

———. "On Place, Space and Mobility in Nineteenth-Century New Zealand." *New Zealand Journal of History* 45.1 (2011): 50–70.

———. *Orientalism and Race: Aryanism in the British Empire.* Basingstoke: Palgrave, 2002.

———. "Print, Politics and Protestantism: New Zealand, 1769–1860." *Information, Communications, Power through the Ages,* ed. Hiram Morgan, 152–79. Dublin: University College Dublin Press, 2001.

———. "Religion, Difference, and the Limits of British Imperial History." *Victorian Studies* 47.3 (2005): 427–55.

———. "Thinking Local: Knowledge, Sociability and Community in Gore's Intellectual Life, 1875–1914." *New Zealand Journal of History* 44.2 (2010): 138–56.

———. *Webs of Empire: Locating New Zealand's Colonial Past.* Wellington: Bridget Williams, 2012.

———. "Writing Out Asia: Race, Colonialism and Chinese Migration in New Zealand History." *East by South: China in the Australasian Imagination,* ed. Charles Ferall, Paul Millar, and Keren Smith, 87–109. Wellington: Victoria University Press, 2005.

Ballantyne, Tony, and Antoinette Burton, eds. *Bodies in Contact: Rethinking Colonial Encounters in World History.* Durham: Duke University Press, 2005.

Ballara, Angela. "Pana-kareao, Nopera ?–1856." Te Ara: The Encyclopedia of New Zealand, www.teara.govt.nz/en/biographies/1p3/pana-kareao-nopera, updated 30 October 2012. Originally published in Guy Scholefield, ed., *Dictionary of New Zealand Biography*, vol. 1 (Wellington: Allen and Unwin, 1990).

———. *Proud to Be White?: A Survey of Pakeha Prejudice in New Zealand*. Auckland: Heinemann, 1986.

———. "Ruatara ?–1815." Te Ara: The Encyclopedia of New Zealand, www.teara.govt .nz/en/biographies/1r19/ruatara, updated 30 October 2012. Originally published in Guy Scholefield, ed., *Dictionary of New Zealand Biography*, vol. 1 (Wellington: Allen and Unwin, 1990).

———. *Taua: "Musket Wars," "Land Wars" or Tikanga?: Warfare in Māori Society in the Early Nineteenth Century*. Auckland: Penguin, 2003.

———. "Te Pahi ?–1810." Te Ara: The Encyclopedia of New Zealand, www.teara.govt .nz/en/biographies/1t53/te-pahi, updated 30 October 2012. Originally published in Guy Scholefield, ed., *Dictionary of New Zealand Biography*, vol. 1 (Wellington: Allen and Unwin, 1990).

Barber, Ian. "Archaeology, Ethnography, and the Record of Maori Cannibalism before 1815: A Critical Review." *Journal of the Polynesian Society* 101.3 (1992): 241–92.

Barker-Benfield, G. J. *The Culture of Sensibility: Sex and Society in Eighteenth-Century Britain*. Chicago: Chicago University Press, 1992.

Barthes, Ronald. *Mythologies*. Translated by Annette Lavers. London: Vintage, 1993.

Bawden, Patricia. "The Mechanic Missionaries: Were They Effective?" *Mission and Moko: Aspects of the Work of the Church Missionary Society in New Zealand, 1814–1882*, ed. by Robert Glen, 38–55. Christchurch: Latimer Fellowship of New Zealand, 1992.

Bebbington, David. *Evangelicalism in Modern Britain: A History from the 1730s to 1980s*. London: Routledge, 1989.

Belich, James. "Imperial Myth and Colonial Actuality: Findings from a New Zealand Laboratory." *Melbourne Historical Journal* 20 (2002): 7–13.

———. *Making Peoples: A History of the New Zealanders: From Polynesian Settlement to the End of the Nineteenth Century*. Auckland: Penguin, 1996.

Benton, Lauren. "Modalities of British Protection in the Early Nineteenth Century World." Paper presented at the Australia New Zealand Law and History Society Conference, Dunedin, November 2013.

Best, Elsdon. *Forest Lore of the Maori*. Wellington: Polynesian Society, 1942.

———. *The Maori As He Was: A Brief Account of Life as It Was in Pre-European Days*. Wellington: Dominion Museum, 1924.

———. "Maori Eschatology: The Whare Potae (House of Mourning) and Its Lore." *Transactions and Proceedings of the Royal Society of New Zealand* 38 (1905): 148–239.

———. *Maori Religion and Mythology: Part 2*. Wellington: Government Printer, 1982 [1924].

Biggs, Bruce. *Maori Marriage: An Essay in Reconstruction*. Wellington: Polynesian Society, 1960.

Binney, Judith. "Christianity and the Maoris to 1840: A Comment." *New Zealand Journal of History* 3.2 (1969): 143–65.

———. "Introduction." *An Account of New Zealand*, by William Yate, new edn. Wellington: Reed, 1970, v–xxi.

———. "Introduction." *Te Kerikeri 1770–1850: The Meeting Pool*, ed. Judith Binney, 9–25. Wellington: Bridget Williams, 2007.

———. *The Legacy of Guilt: A Life of Thomas Kendall*. Auckland: Auckland University Press, 1968.

———. *The Legacy of Guilt: A Life of Thomas Kendall*. 2d edn. Wellington: Bridget Williams, 2005.

———. "Papahurihia: Some Thoughts on Interpretation." *Journal of the Polynesian Society* 75 (1966): 321–31.

———. "Tuki's Universe." *Tasman Relations: New Zealand and Australia, 1788–1988*, ed. Keith Sinclair, 15–33. Auckland: Auckland University Press, 1987.

———. "Whatever Happened to Poor Mr Yate?: An Exercise in Voyeurism." *New Zealand Journal of History* 9.2 (1975): 111–25.

Blain Biographical Directory of Anglican Clergy in the South Pacific. 2011 edn. Project Canterbury, http://anglicanhistory.org/nz/blain_directory/directory.pdf.

Blainey, Geoffrey. *The Tyranny of Distance: How Distance Shaped Australia's History*. Sydney: Macmillan, 2001 [1966].

Blake, Richard. *Evangelicals in the Royal Navy, 1775–1815: Blue Lights and Psalm-Singers*. Woodbridge: Boydell, 2008.

Bollen, J. D. "English Missionary Societies and the Australian Aborigine." *Journal of Religious History* 9.3 (1977): 263–90.

Bowerbank, Sylvia. "Taylor, Jane (1783–1824)." *Oxford Dictionary of National Biography*, Oxford University Press, 2004. www.oxforddnb.com/view/article/27039.

Bradshaw, David J., and Suzanne Ozment, eds. *The Voice of Toil: Nineteenth-Century British Writings about Work*. Athens: Ohio University Press, 2000.

Broadbent, James, Suzanne Rickard, and Margaret Steven. *India, China, Australia: Trade and Society 1788–1850*. Glebe, NSW: Historic Houses Trust of New South Wales, 2003.

Brock, Peggy. "New Christians as Evangelists." *Missions and Empire*, ed. Norman Etherington, 132–52. Oxford: Oxford University Press, 2005.

Brown, Vincent. *The Reaper's Garden: Death and Power in the World of Atlantic Slavery*. Cambridge: Harvard University Press, 2008.

Brown-Haysom, Ryan. "The Awful Fall of Mr Yate." Unpublished essay in author's possession.

Brubaker, Rogers. *The Limits of Rationality: An Essay on the Social and Moral Thought of Max Weber*. London: Allen and Unwin, 1984.

Canning, Kathleen. "The Body as Method?: Reflections on the Place of the Body in Gender History." *Gender and History* 11.3 (1999): 499–513.

Carson, Valerie. "Submitting to Great Inconveniences: Early Missionary Educa-
tion for Māori Women and Girls." *Mission and Moko: Aspects of the Work of the
Church Missionary Society in New Zealand, 1814–1882*, ed. Robert Glen, 56–72.
Christchurch: Latimer Fellowship of New Zealand, 1992.

Caunce, S. A. "Agriculture in North-Eastern England, 1750–1914: Relic, Parasite or
Key Part of Development?" *Northern Landscapes: Representations and Realities
of North-East England*, ed. Thomas Faulkner, Helen Berry, and Jeremy Gregory,
53–65. Woodbridge: Boydell, 2010.

Chandler, James. "Moving Accidents: The Emergence of Sentimental Probability."
The Age of Cultural Revolutions: Britain and France, 1750–1820, ed. Colin Jones and
Dror Wahrman, 137–70. Berkeley: University of California Press, 2002.

Chapman, Robert. "Fiction and the Social Pattern." *Landfall* 7.1 (1953): 26–58.

Chase, Karen, and Michael Levenson. *The Spectacle of Intimacy: A Public Life for the
Victorian Family*. Princeton: Princeton University Press, 2000.

Chisholm, Jocelyn. "Brind, William Darby." Te Ara: The Encyclopedia of New
Zealand, www.teara.govt.nz/en/biographies/1b32/brind-william-darby, updated
30 October 2012. Originally published in Guy Scholefield, ed., *Dictionary of New
Zealand Biography*, vol. 1 (Wellington: Allen and Unwin, 1990).

Church, R. A. "Nineteenth-Century Clock Technology in Britain, the United States,
and Switzerland." *Economic History Review* 28.4 new series (1975): 616–30.

Clark, Anna. *Scandal: The Sexual Politics of the British Constitution*. Princeton:
Princeton University Press, 2004.

Clark, Gregory, and Ysbrand Van Der Werf. "Work in Progress?: The Industrious
Revolution." *Journal of Economic History* 58.3 (1998): 830–43.

Cloher, Dorothy Urlich. *Hongi Hika: Warrior Chief*. Auckland: Viking, 2003.

Cocks, H. G. *Nameless Offences: Homosexual Desire in the Nineteenth Century*. London: I. B. Tauris, 2003.

Colgan, Aloma, and Judy McGregor. *Sexual Secrets: The New Zealand Report on Love
and Marriage*. Martinborough: Alister Taylor, 1981.

Comaroff, Jean. *Body of Power, Spirit of Resistance: The Culture and History of a
South African People*. Chicago: University of Chicago Press, 1985.

———. "Missionaries and Mechanical Clocks: An Essay on Religion and History in
South Africa." *Journal of Religion* 71.1 (1991): 1–17.

Comaroff, Jean, and John Comaroff. *Of Revelation and Revolution*. Vol. 1, *Christianity, Colonialism and Consciousness in South Africa*. Chicago: University of Chicago
Press, 1991.

Cook, James. *The Voyage of the Endeavour, 1768–1771*. Vol. 1 of *The Journals of Captain James Cook on His Voyages of Discovery*. Edited by J. C. Beaglehole. Cambridge: Hakluyt Society 1968.

Cooper, Frederick. "Work, Class and Empire: An African Historian's Retrospective
on E. P. Thompson." *Social History* 20.2 (1995): 235–41.

Cox, Jeffrey. *Imperial Fault Lines: Christianity and Colonial Power in India, 1818–
1940*. Stanford: Stanford University Press, 2002.

Dalziel, Raewyn. "Southern Islands: New Zealand and Polynesia." *The Oxford History of the British Empire: The Nineteenth Century*, ed. Andrew Porter, 573–96. Oxford: Oxford University Press, 1998.

De Vries, Jan. "Between Purchasing Power and the World of Goods: Understanding the Household Economy in Early Modern Europe." *Consumption and the World of Goods*, ed. John Brewer and Roy Porter, 85–132. London: Routledge, 1993.

———. "The Industrial Revolution and the Industrious Revolution." *Journal of Economic History* 54.2 (1994): 249–70.

Deed, Steven. "Unearthly Landscapes: The Development of the Cemetery in Nineteenth Century New Zealand." Master's thesis, University of Otago, 2004.

Dening, Greg. "The Comaroffs Out of Africa: A Reflection Out of Oceania." *American Historical Review* 108.2 (2003): 471–78.

———. *Performances*. Chicago: University of Chicago Press, 2006.

Ditchfield, G. M. *The Evangelical Revival*. London: University College London Press, 1998.

Dixon, Thomas. *From Passions to Emotions: The Creation of a Secular Psychological Category*. Cambridge: Cambridge University Press, 2003.

Dowbiggin, Ian. *A Concise History of Euthanasia: Life, Death, God, and Medicine*. Lanham, MD: Rowman and Littlefield, 2005.

Easdale, Nola. *Missionary and Maori: Kerikeri, 1819–1860*. Lincoln, NZ: Te Waihora, 1991.

Edmond, Rod. *Representing the South Pacific: Colonial Discourse from Cook to Gauguin*. New York: Cambridge University Press, 1997.

Elbourne, Elizabeth. *Blood Ground: Colonialism, Missions, and the Contest for Christianity in the Cape Colony and Britain, 1799–1853*. Montreal: McGill-Queen's University Press, 2002.

———. "The Sin of the Settler: The 1835–36 Select Committee on Aborigines and Debates over Virtue and Conquest in the Early Nineteenth-Century British White Settler Empire." *Journal of Colonialism and Colonial History* 4.3 (2003): unpaginated.

———. "Word Made Flesh: Christianity, Modernity, and Cultural Colonialism in the Work of Jean and John Comaroff." *American Historical Review* 108.2 (2003): 435–59.

Elias, Norbert. *The Civilizing Process: Sociogenetic and Psychogenetic Investigations*. Translated by Edmund Jephcott. Edited by Eric Dunning, Johan Goudsblom, and Stephen Mennell. Rev. edn. Oxford: Blackwell, 2000.

Ellis, M. H. *Lachlan Macquarie: His Life, Adventures and Times*. Sydney: Dymock, 1947.

Ellis, Markman. *The Politics of Sensibility: Race, Gender and Commerce in the Sentimental Novel*. New York: Cambridge University Press, 1996.

Etlin, Richard A. *The Architecture of Death: The Transformation of the Cemetery in Eighteenth Century Paris*. Cambridge: Massachusetts Institute of Technology Press, 1984.

Firth, Raymond. *Primitive Economics of the New Zealand Maori*. London: George Routledge, 1929.

Fischer, David Hackett. *Albion's Seed: Four British Folkways in America*. New York: Oxford University Press, 1989.

Fitzgerald, Tanya. "Creating a Disciplined Society: CMS Women and the Re-making of Nga Puhi Women 1823–1835." *History of Education Review* 32.1 (2003): 84–98.

———. "Fences, Boundaries and Imagined Communities: Re-thinking the Construction of Early Mission Schools and Communities in New Zealand 1823–1830." *History of Education Review* 30.2 (2001): 14–25.

———. "Jumping the Fences: Māori Women's Resistance to Missionary Schooling in Northern New Zealand 1823–1835." *Paedagogica Historica* 37.1 (2001): 175–92.

Foucault, Michel. *The History of Sexuality*. Vol. 1, *An Introduction*. Translated by Robert Hurley. London: Allen Lane, 1979.

Frost, Alan. *Botany Bay Mirages: Illusions of Australia's Convict Beginnings*. Melbourne: Melbourne University Press, 1994.

———. *The Global Reach of Empire*. Carlton, Victoria: Miegunyah Press, 2003.

Gallagher, Catherine. *The Body Economic: Life, Death, and Sensation in Political Economy and the Victorian Novel*. Princeton: Princeton University Press, 2006.

Gammage, Bill. "Early Boundaries of New South Wales." *Historical Studies* 19.77 (1981): 524–31.

Gardella, Peter. *Innocent Ecstasy: How Christianity Gave America an Ethic of Sexual Pleasure*. New York: Oxford University Press, 1985.

Gascoigne, John, *The Enlightenment and the origins of European Australia*. Cambridge: Cambridge University Press, 2002.

Gilbert, A. D. *Religion and Society in Industrial England: Church, Chapel, and Social Change 1740–1914*. London: Longman, 1976.

Gilbert, Arthur N. "Conceptions of Sodomy and Homosexuality in Western History." *Journal of Homosexuality* 6.1–2 (1980–81): 57–68.

Gilchrist, Catie. "The 'Crime' of Precocious Sexuality: Young Male Convicts and the Politics of Separation." *Journal of Australian Colonial History* 8 (2006): 43–66.

Glen, Robert. "Those Odious Evangelicals: The Origins and Background of CMS Missionaries in New Zealand." *Mission and Moko: Aspects of the Work of the Church Missionary Society in New Zealand, 1814–1882*, ed. Robert Glen, 14–37. Christchurch: Latimer Fellowship of New Zealand, 1992.

Goldsbury, S. J. "Behind the Picket Fence: The Lives of Missionary Wives in Precolonial New Zealand." Master's thesis, University of Auckland, 1986.

Graham, Mark W. "'The Enchanter's Wand': Charles Darwin, Foreign Missions, and the Voyage of H.M.S. Beagle." *Journal of Religious History* 31.2 (2007): 131–50.

Griffiths, Tom. "Boundaries of the Sacred: The Williams Family in New Zealand, 1823–30." *Journal of Religious History* 13.1 (1984): 35–45.

Grove, R. N. "Te Whatanui: Traditional Maori Leader." Master's thesis, Victoria University of Wellington, 1985.

Guha, Ranajit. *Elementary Aspects of Peasant Insurgency in Colonial India.* Delhi: Oxford University Press, 1983.

Gunson, Niel. *Messengers of Grace: Evangelical Missionaries in the South Seas 1797–1860.* Melbourne: Oxford University Press, 1978.

Hainsworth, D. R. *The Sydney Traders: Simeon Lord and His Contemporaries, 1788–1821.* Melbourne: Cassell Australia, 1972.

Hall, Catherine. *Civilising Subjects: Colony and Metropole in the English Imagination, 1830–1867.* Chicago: University of Chicago, 2002.

———. *White, Male and Middle Class: Explorations in Feminism and History.* Cambridge: Polity, 1992.

Halttunen, Karen. "Humanitarianism and the Pornography of Pain in Anglo-American Culture." *American Historical Review* 100.2 (1995): 303–34.

Hamilton, Carolyn. *Terrific Majesty: The Powers of Shaka Zulu and the Limits of Historical Invention.* Cambridge: Harvard University Press, 1998.

Hansen, Kath. *In the Wake of the Active: A Social History of the First European Settlers.* Auckland: self-published, 1994.

Hanson, F. Allan, and Louise Hanson. *Counterpoint in Maori Culture.* London: Routledge and Kegan Paul, 1983.

Hargreaves, R.P. "Waimate-Pioneer New Zealand Farm." *Agricultural History* 36.1 (1962): 38–45.

Heath, Kay. *Aging by the Book: The Emergence of Midlife in Victorian Britain.* Albany: State University of New York Press, 2009.

Hickford, Mark. *Lords of the Land: Indigenous Property Rights and the Jurisprudence of Empire.* Oxford: Oxford University Press, 2011.

Hilton, Boyd. *The Age of Atonement: The Influence of Evangelicalism on Social and Economic Thought, 1795–1865.* Oxford: Clarendon, 1988.

Hiroa, Te Rangi. *The Coming of the Maori.* Wellington: Whitcombe and Tombs, 1950.

Hoganson, Kristin L. *Fighting for American Manhood: How Gender Politics Provoked the Spanish-American and Philippine-American Wars.* New Haven: Yale University Press, 2000.

Hohepa, Patu. "My Musket, My Missionary, and My Mana." *Voyages and Beaches: Pacific Encounters, 1769–1840,* ed. Alex Calder, Jonathan Lamb, and Bridget Orr, 180–201. Honolulu: University of Hawai'i Press, 1999.

———. "Kerikeri, Tapu, Wāhi Tapu." *Te Kerikeri 1770–1850: The Meeting Pool,* ed. Judith Binney, 85–92. Wellington: Bridget Williams, 2007.

Hudson, Pat. "From Manor to Mill: The West Riding in Transition." *Manufacture in Town and Country before the Factory,* ed. Maxine Berg, Pat Hudson, and Michael Sonenscher, 124–44. Cambridge University Press: Cambridge, 1983.

Hylson-Smith, Kenneth. *Evangelicals in the Church of England, 1734–1984.* Edinburgh: T. and T. Clark, 1989.

Jacobsin-Widding, Anita. "Subjective Body, Objective Space." *Body and Space: Symbolic Models of Unity and Division in African Cosmology and Experience,* ed. Anita Jacobsin-Widding, 15–50. Uppsala: Acta Universitatis Upsaliensis, 1991.

Jalland, Patricia. *Australian Ways of Death: A Social and Cultural History, 1840–1918*. Melbourne: Oxford University Press, 2002.

———. *Death in the Victorian Family*. Oxford: Oxford University Press, 1996.

Johnston, Anna. *Missionary Writing and Empire, 1800–1860*. Cambridge: Cambridge University Press, 2003.

———. *The Paper War: Morality, Print Culture, and Power in Colonial New South Wales*. Crawley: UWA Publishing, 2011.

Jolly, Margaret, and Serge Tcherkézoff. "Oceanic Encounters: A Prelude." *Oceanic Encounters: Exchange, Desire, Violence*, ed. Margaret Jolly, Serge Tcherkézoff, and Darrell Tryon, 1–36. Canberra: Australian National University Press, 2009.

Jones, Alison, and Kuni Jenkins. *He Kōrero: Words between Us: First Māori-Pākehā Conversations on Paper*. Wellington: Huia, 2011.

Kane, Penny. *Victorian Families in Fact and Fiction*. New York: St Martin's, 1995.

Laidlaw, Zoe. " 'Aunt Anna's Report': The Buxton Women and the Aborigines Select Committee of 1835–7." *Journal of Imperial and Commonwealth History* 32.2 (2004): 1–28.

Landau, Paul. *The Realm of the Word: Language, Gender, and Christianity in a Southern African Kingdom*. Portsmouth, NH: Heinemann, 1995.

Laqueur, Thomas. "Bodies, Details, and the Humanitarian Narrative." *The New Cultural History*, ed. Lynn Hunt, 176–204. Berkeley: University of California Press, 1987.

Latour, Bruno. "Visualisation and Cognition: Drawing Things Together." *Knowledge and Society: Studies in the Sociology of Culture Past and Present*, ed. S. N. Eisenstadt and Ilana Friedrich Silber, 6:1–40. London: JAI Press, 1986.

Leach, B. F. "Four Centuries of Community Interaction and Trade in Cook Strait, New Zealand." *Trade and Exchange in Oceania and Australia*, ed. Jim Specht and J. Peter White, 391–405. Sydney: Sydney University Press, 1978.

———. "Prehistoric Communities in Palliser Bay, New Zealand." PhD diss., University of Otago, 1976.

Leach, Helen. "Horticulture in Prehistoric New Zealand: An Investigation of the Function of the Stone Walls of Palliser Bay." PhD diss., University of Otago, 1976.

Lester, Alan. *Imperial Networks: Creating Identities in Nineteenth-Century South Africa and Britain*. London: Routledge, 2001.

Lester, Alan and Fae Dussart. *Colonization and the Origins of Humanitarian Governance: Protecting Aborigines across the Nineteenth-Century British Empire*. Cambridge: Cambridge University Press, 2014.

Lineham, Peter. "This Is My Weapon: Maori Response to the Bible." *Mission and Moko: Aspects of the Work of the Church Missionary Society in New Zealand, 1814–1882*, ed. Robert Glen, 170–78. Christchurch: Latimer Fellowship of New Zealand, 1992.

Macey, Samuel L. *Clocks and the Cosmos: Time in Western Life and Thought*. Hamden, CT: Archon, 1980.

Makereti. *The Old-Time Maori*. Auckland: New Women's Press, 1986 [1938].

Mani, Lata. *Contentious Traditions: The Debate on Sati in Colonial India*. Berkeley: University of California, 1998.

Manihera, Te Uira, Ngoi Pewhairangi, and John Rangihau. "Foreword: Learning and Tapu." *Te Ao Hurihuri: Aspects of Maoritanga*, ed. Michael King, 9–14. Auckland: Reed, 1992.

Massey, Doreen. *For Space*. London: Sage, 2005.

Maude, H. E. *Of Islands and Men: Studies in Pacific History*. Melbourne: Oxford University Press, 1968.

McKenzie, Kirsten. *Scandal in the Colonies: Sydney and Cape Town, 1820–1850*. Carlton: Melbourne University Publishing, 2004.

McLachlan, N. D. "Bathurst at the Colonial Office, 1812–27: A Reconnaissance." *Historical Studies* 13.52 (1969): 477–502.

McLean, Gavin. "The Kerikeri Stone Store: A Backwater White Elephant." *Te Kerikeri 1770–1850: The Meeting Pool*, ed. Judith Binney, 99–104. Wellington: Bridget Williams, 2007.

McLintock, A. H., ed. *An Encyclopaedia of New Zealand*. 3 vols. Wellington: Government Printer, 1966.

McNab, Robert. *From Tasman to Marsden: A History of Northern New Zealand from 1642 to 1818*. Dunedin: J. Wilkie, 1914.

———. *Murihiku and the Southern Islands: A History of the West Coast Sounds, Foveaux Strait, Stewart Island, the Snares, Bounty, Antipodes, Auckland, Campbell and Macquarie Islands, from 1770 to 1829*. Invercargill: William Smith, 1907.

Mead, Hirini Moko. *Tikanga Maori: Living by Maori Values*. Wellington: Huia, 2003.

Meredith, Paul. "Who Was Nayti?" *Te Matahauariki: Laws and Institutions for Aotearoa/New Zealand: Newsletter* 8 (2004): 2.

Middleton, Angela. *The Archaeology of the Te Puna Mission Station: Report to New Zealand Historical Places Trust*. Wellington: New Zealand Historic Places Trust, 2005.

———. *Kerikeri Mission and Kororipo Pā: An Entwined History*. Dunedin: University of Otago Press, 2013.

———. "Potatoes and Muskets: Maori Gardening at Kerikeri." *Te Kerikeri 1770–1850: The Meeting Pool*, ed. Judith Binney, 33–39. Wellington: Bridget Williams, 2007.

———. "Silent Voices, Hidden Lives: Archaeology, Class and Gender in the CMS Missions, Bay of Islands, New Zealand, 1814–1845." *International Journal of Historical Archaeology* 11.1 (2007): 1–31.

———. *Te Puna: A New Zealand Mission Station: Historical Archaeology in New Zealand*. London: Springer, 2008.

Moon, Paul. *Te Ara Kī Te Tiriti: The Path to the Treaty of Waitangi*. Auckland: David Ling, 2002.

Morton, Harry. *The Whale's Wake*. Dunedin: University of Otago Press, 1982.

Nanni, Giordano. *The Colonisation of Time: Ritual, Routine, and Resistance in the British Empire*. Manchester: Manchester University Press, 2012.

Newell, Jennifer. *Trading Nature: Tahitians, Europeans, and Ecological Exchange*. Honolulu: University of Hawai'i Press, 2010.

Nuttall, Sarah. *Entanglement: Literary and Cultural Reflections on Post Apartheid*. Johannesburg: Wits University Press, 2009.

O'Malley, Vincent. *The Meeting Place: Māori and Pākehā Encounters, 1642–1840*. Auckland: Auckland University Press, 2012.

Oppenheim, R. S. *Maori Death Customs*. Wellington: A. H. and A. W. Reed, 1973.

Orange, Claudia. *Treaty of Waitangi*. Wellington: Allen and Unwin, 1988.

Outler, Albert C. "The Use of Money: An Introductory Comment." *The Works of John Wesley*, ed. Albert C. Outler, 2:263–65. Nashville: Abingdon, 1985.

Overton, Mark. *Agricultural Revolution in England: The Transformation of the Agrarian Economy, 1500–1850*. Cambridge: Cambridge University Press, 1996.

Owens, J. M. R. "Christianity and the Maoris to 1840." *New Zealand Journal of History* 2.1 (1968): 18–40.

———. *The Mediator: A Life of Richard Taylor, 1805–1873*. Wellington: Victoria University Press, 2004.

———. *Prophets in the Wilderness: The Wesleyan Mission to New Zealand, 1819–27*. Auckland: Auckland University Press, 1974.

———. "The Unexpected Impact: Wesleyan Missionaries and Maoris in the Early Nineteenth Century." *Wesley Historical Society, New Zealand Branch, Proceedings* 27.6 (1973).

Parkinson, Philip. "'A Most Depraved Young Man': Henry Miles Pilley." *Outlines: Lesbian and Gay Histories of Aotearoa*, ed. Alison J. Laurie and Alison Evans, 19–23. Wellington: Lesbian and Gay Archives of New Zealand, 2005.

Parkinson, Philip Granger. "Our Infant State: The Maori Language, the Mission Presses, the British Crown and the Maori, 1814–1838." PhD diss., Victoria University of Wellington, 2003.

Parsonson, Ann R. "The Expansion of a Competitive Society: A Study of Nineteenth-Century Māori Social History." *New Zealand Journal of History* 14.1 (1980): 45–60.

Peel, Dawn. "Death and Community in a Colonial Settlement." *Journal of the Royal Historical Society of Australia* 88.2 (2002): 137–46.

Petrie, Hazel. *Chiefs of Industry: Māori Tribal Enterprise in Early Colonial New Zealand*. Auckland: Auckland University Press, 2006.

Phillipson, Grant. "Religion and Land: The Church Missionary Society, 1819–50." *Te Kerikeri 1770–1850: The Meeting Pool*, ed. Judith Binney, 51–71. Wellington: Bridget Williams, 2007.

Pickmere, Nancy. *The Story of Paihia*. Kerikeri: self-published, 2000.

Pinch, Adela. *Strange Fits of Passion: Epistemologies of Emotion, Hume to Austen*. Stanford: Stanford University Press, 1996.

Pollock, Linda A. *Forgotten Children: Parent-Children Relations from 1500 to 1900.* Cambridge: Cambridge University Press, 1983.

Poovey, Mary. *Making a Social Body: British Cultural Formation, 1830–1864.* Chicago: University of Chicago Press, 1995.

Porter, Andrew. "'Commerce and Christianity': The Rise and Fall of a Nineteenth Century Missionary Slogan." *Historical Journal* 28.3 (1985): 597–621.

——. *Religion Versus Empire?: British Protestant Missionaries and Overseas Expansion, 1700–1914.* Manchester: Manchester University Press, 2004.

——. "Trusteeship, Anti-Slavery, and Humanitarianism." *The Oxford History of the British Empire: The Nineteenth Century*, ed. Andrew Porter, 198–221. Oxford: Oxford University Press, 1998.

Porter, Frances. "All that the Heart Does Bear: A Reflection on the Domestic Life of Missionary Wives." *Mission and Moko: Aspects of the Work of the Church Missionary Society in New Zealand, 1814–1882*, ed. Robert Glen, 134–51. Christchurch: Latimer Fellowship of New Zealand, 1992.

Price, Richard. *Making Empire: Colonial Encounters and the Creation of Imperial Rule in Nineteenth-Century Africa.* Cambridge: Cambridge University Press, 2008.

Prickett, Nigel. "An Archaeologist's Guide to the Maori Dwelling." *New Zealand Journal of Archaeology* 4 (1982): 111–47.

Puckey, Adrienne. "The Substance of the Shadow: Māori and Pākehā Political Economic Relationships, 1860–1940: A Far Northern Case Study." PhD diss., University of Auckland, 2006.

Purnell, Edward Kelly. *Magdalene College.* London: F. E. Robinson, 1904.

Reid, Kirsty. *Gender, Crime and Empire: Convicts, Settlers and the State in Early Colonial Australia.* Manchester: Manchester University Press, 2007.

Reynolds, Henry. *Frontier: Aborigines, Settlers and Land.* Sydney: Allen and Unwin, 1987.

——. *The Law of the Land.* Ringwood, Victoria: Penguin, 1987.

——. *With the White People.* Ringwood, Victoria: Penguin, 1990.

Roach, Joseph R. *Cities of the Dead: Circum-Atlantic Performance.* New York: Columbia University Press, 1996.

Roberts, M. J. D. "Making Victorian Morals?: The Society for the Suppression of Vice and Its Critics, 1802–1886." *Historical Studies* 21.83 (1984): 157–73.

Roediger, David R., and Philip S. Foner. *Our Own Time: A History of American Labor and the Working Day.* London: Verso, 1989.

Rosenberg, Emily. "Revisiting Dollar Diplomacy: Narratives of Money and Manliness." *Diplomatic History* 22.2 (spring 1998): 154–76.

Ross, Cathy. *Women with a Mission: Rediscovering Missionary Wives in Early New Zealand.* Auckland: Penguin, 2006.

Ross, Robert. *Status and Respectability in the Cape Colony, 1750–1870: A Tragedy of Manners.* Cambridge: Cambridge University Press, 1999.

Ross, Ruth. "Old Roses for Waimate." www.rosarosam.com/articles/waimate/roses_for_waimate.htm, accessed June 2005.

Rountree, Kathryn. "Re-making the Maori Female Body: Marianne Williams's Mission in the Bay of Islands." *Journal of Pacific History* 35.1 (2000): 49–66.

Rugg, Julie. "From Reason to Regulation: 1760–1850." *Death in England: An Illustrated History*, ed. Peter C. Jupp and Clare Gittings, 202–29. Manchester: Manchester University Press, 1999.

Ryan, Lyndall. "Was New Zealand part of New South Wales, 1788–1817?" Paper presented at Australia New Zealand Law and History Society Conference, University of Otago, November 2013.

Salesa, Damon Ieremia. "Afterword: Opposite Footers." *The Atlantic World in the Antipodes: Effects and Transformations since the Eighteenth Century*, ed. Kate Fullagar, 283–300. Cambridge: Cambridge Scholars Press, 2012.

———. *Racial Crossings: Race, Intermarriage, and the Victorian British Empire.* Oxford: Oxford University Press, 2011.

Salmond, Anne. *Between Worlds: Early Exchanges between Maori and Europeans, 1773–1815.* Auckland: Viking, 1997.

———. "Maori and Modernity: Ruatara's Dying." *Signifying Identities: Anthropological Perspectives on Boundaries and Contested Values*, ed. Anthony Cohen, 37–58. London: Routledge, 2000.

———. *Two Worlds: First Meetings between Maori and Europeans, 1642–1772.* Auckland: Viking, 1991.

Salmond, Jeremy. "The Mission House, Kerikeri." *Te Kerikeri 1770–1850: The Meeting Pool*, ed. Judith Binney, 93–98. Wellington: Bridget Williams, 2007.

Samson, Jane. "The 1834 Cruise of HMS Alligator: The Bible and the Flag." *Northern Mariner* 3.4 (1993): 37–47.

———. *Imperial Benevolence: Making British Authority in the Pacific Islands.* Honolulu: University of Hawai'i Press, 1998.

Sargeson, Frank. "An Imaginary Conversation: William Yate and Samuel Butler." *Landfall* 80 (1966): 349–57.

Schilder, Gunter. *Australia Unveiled: The Share of the Dutch Navigators in the Discovery of Australia.* Amsterdam: Theatrum Orbis Terrarum, 1976.

Seeman, Erik R. *Death in the New World: Cross-Cultural Encounters, 1492–1800.* Philadelphia: University of Pennsylvania, 2010.

Seidman, Steven. *Romantic Longings: Love in America, 1830–1980.* New York: Routledge, 1991.

Sewell, William H., Jr. *Logics of History: Social Theory and Social Transformation.* Chicago: University of Chicago Press, 2005.

Sinclair, Keith. *A History of New Zealand.* Rev. edn. Harmondsworth: Penguin, 1969.

———. *A History of New Zealand.* Rev. edn. Auckland: Pelican, 1988 [1959].

———, ed. *Laplace in New Zealand, 1831.* Waikanae, New Zealand: Heritage, 1998.

———. *The Origins of Maori Wars.* Wellington: New Zealand University Press, 1957.

Sinha, Mrinalini. *Colonial Masculinity: The "Manly Englishman" and the "Effeminate Bengali" in the Late Nineteenth Century.* Manchester: Manchester University Press, 1996.

Sissons, Jeffrey. "Hongi Hika." *Te Kerikeri 1770–1850: The Meeting Pool*, ed. Judith Binney, 47–50. Wellington: Bridget Williams, 2007.

Sissons, Jeffrey, Wiremu Wi Hongi, and Pat Hohepa. *The Pūriri Trees Are Laughing: A Political History of the Ngā Puhi in the Inland Bay of Islands*. Auckland: Polynesian Society, 1987.

Smith, Ian W. G. *The New Zealand Sealing Industry: History, Archaeology, and Heritage Management*. Wellington: Department of Conservation, 2002.

Smith, Ian, and Angela Middleton et al. *Archaeology of the Hohi Mission Station: Volume 1: The 2012 Excavations*. Otago Studies in Archaeology, no. 24 (2012).

Smith, Vanessa. "Joseph Banks's Intermediaries: Rethinking Global Cultural Exchange." *Global Intellectual History*, ed. Samuel Moyn and Ander Sartori, 81–109. New York: Columbia University Press, 2013.

Stafford, Barbara Maria. *Body Criticism: Imaging the Unseen in Enlightenment Art and Medicine*. Cambridge: Massachusetts Institute of Technology Press, 1993.

———. "Voyeur or Observer?: Enlightenment Thoughts on the Dilemmas of Display." *Configurations* 1.1 (1993): 95–128.

Stallybrass, Peter, and Allon White. *The Politics and Poetics of Transgression*. London: Methuen, 1986.

Standfield, Rachel. *Race and Identity in the Tasman World, 1769–1840*. London: Pickering and Chatto, 2012.

Standish, M. W. *The Waimate Mission Station*. Wellington: Government Printer, 1962.

Stanley, Brian. *The Bible and the Flag: Protestant Missions and British Imperialism in the Nineteenth and Twentieth Centuries*. Leicester: Apollos, 1990.

———. "'Commerce and Christianity': Providence Theory, the Missionary Movement, and the Imperialism of Free Trade, 1842–1860." *Historical Journal* 26.1 (1983): 71–94.

———. "Nineteenth-Century Liberation Theology: Non-Conformist Missionaries and Imperialism." *Baptist Quarterly* 32.1 (1987): 5–18.

Stapleton, Eugenie. *Elizabeth Marsden: The Parson's Wife*. Spotlight on History 3. St. Mary's, New South Wales: St. Mary's Historical Society, 1981.

Steven, Margaret. *Merchant Campbell, 1769–1846: A Study of Colonial Trade*. Melbourne: Oxford University Press, 1965.

Stock, Eugene. *The History of the Church Missionary Society: Its Environment, Its Men and Its Work*. 3 vols. London: Church Missionary Society, 1899.

Stocking, George, Jr. *Victorian Anthropology*. New York: Free Press, 1987.

Stoler, Ann Laura. *Race and the Education of Desire: Foucault's History of Sexuality and the Colonial Order of Things*. Durham: Duke University Press, 1995.

Stoler, Ann Laura, and Frederick Cooper. "Between Metropole and Colony: Rethinking a Research Agenda." *The Tensions of Empire: Colonial Cultures in a Bourgeois World*, ed. Frederick Cooper and Ann Laura Stoler, 1–56. Berkeley: University of California Press, 1997.

Stone, Lawrence. *The Family, Sex and Marriage in England, 1500–1800*. London: Weidenfeld and Nicolson, 1977.

———. *The Past and the Present*. Boston: Routledge and Kegan Paul, 1981.

Tarlow, Sarah. *The Archaeology of Improvement in Britain, 1750–1850*. Cambridge: Cambridge University Press, 2007.

Tave, Stuart M. *The Amiable Humorist*. Chicago: University of Chicago Press, 1960.

Taylor, E. G. R. *Tudor Geography 1485–1583*. London: Methuen, 1930.

Te Awekotuku, Ngahuia. *Mana Wahine Maori: Select Writings on Maori Women's Art, Culture and Politics*. Auckland: New Women's Press, 1991.

———. *Mau Moko: The World of Māori Tattoo*. Auckland: Penguin, 2007.

Te Kahu, Taare Wetere. "The Wars of Kai-Tahu with Kati-Toa." *Journal of the Polynesian Society* 10 (1901): 94–100.

Thomas, Lynn M. *Politics of the Womb: Women, Reproduction, and the State in Kenya*. Berkeley: University of California Press, 2003.

Thomas, Nicholas. *Entangled Objects: Exchange, Material Culture and Colonialism in the Pacific*. Cambridge: Harvard University Press, 1991.

Thompson, E. P. *The Making of the English Working Class*. London: Victor Gollancz, 1963.

———. "Time, Work-Discipline, and Industrial Capitalism." *Past and Present* 38 (1967): 56–97.

Thomson, Jane. "Some Reasons for the Failure of the Roman Catholic Mission to the Māoris, 1838–1860." *New Zealand Journal of History* 3.2 (1969): 166–74.

Thorne, Susan. *Congregational Missions and the Making of an Imperial Culture in Nineteenth-Century England*. Stanford: Stanford University Press, 1999.

Tolley, Christopher. *Domestic Biography: The Legacy of Evangelicalism in Four Nineteenth-Century Families*. Oxford: Oxford University Press, 1997.

Travers, Robert. "Death and the Nabob: Imperialism and Commemoration in Eighteenth-Century India." *Past and Present* 196 (2007): 83–124.

Tsing, Anna Lowenhaupt. *Friction: An Ethnography of Global Connection*. Princeton: Princeton University Press, 2005.

Turner, B. S. *For Weber: Essays on the Sociology of Fate*. Boston: Routledge and Kegan Paul, 1981.

Turner, J. G. *The Pioneer Missionary: Life of the Rev. Nathaniel Turner*. Melbourne: George Robertson, 1872.

Upchurch, Charles. *Before Wilde: Sex Between Men in Britain's Age of Reform*. Berkeley: University of California Press, 2009.

Viswanathan, Gauri. *Outside the Fold: Conversion, Modernity, and Belief*. Princeton: Princeton University Press, 1998.

Voth, Hans-Joachim. "Time and Work in Eighteenth-Century London." *Journal of Economic History* 58.1 (1998): 29–58.

———. *Time and Work in England 1750–1830*. Oxford: Oxford University Press, 2000.

———. "Time Use in Eighteenth-Century London: Some Evidence from the Old Bailey." *Journal of Economic History* 57.2 (1997): 497–99.

Wahrman, Dror. *The Making of the Modern Self*. London: Yale University Press, 2004.

Waitangi Tribunal. *Muriwhenua Land Report, Wai 45*. Wellington: Waitangi Tribunal, 1997.

Walker, Ranginui. *Ka Whawhai Tonu Matou: Struggle without End*. Auckland: Penguin, 1990.

Wallace, Lee. *Sexual Encounters: Pacific Texts, Modern Sexualities*. Cornell: Cornell University Press, 2003.

Wanhalla, Angela. "The 'Bickerings' of the 'Mangungu Brethren': Talk, Tales and Rumour in Early New Zealand." *Journal of New Zealand Studies* new series 12 (2011): 13–28.

——. *Matters of the Heart: A History of Interracial Marriage in New Zealand*. Auckland: University of Auckland Press, 2013.

——. "The 'Natives Uncivilize Me': Missionaries and Interracial Intimacy in Early New Zealand." *Missionaries, Indigenous Peoples, and Cultural Exchange*, ed. Patricia Grimshaw and Andrew May, 24–36. Brighton: Sussex Academic Press, 2010.

Welch, Edwin. "Haweis, Thomas (1734?–1820)." *Oxford Dictionary of National Biography*, Oxford University Press, Sept 2004; online edn, May 2006.

Wevers, Lydia. *Country of Writing: Travel Writing and New Zealand, 1809–1900*. Auckland: Auckland University Press, 2002.

Wheeler, Michael. *Heaven, Hell, and the Victorians*. Cambridge: Cambridge University Press, 1994.

Williams, Glyndwr, and Alan Frost. "*Terra Australis*: Theory and Speculation." *Terra Australis to Australia*, by Glyndwr Williams and Alan Frost, Melbourne: Oxford University Press, 1988, 1–38.

Williment, T. M. I. *John Hobbs, 1800–1883: Wesleyan Missionary to the Ngapuhi Tribe of Northern New Zealand*. Wellington: Government Printer, 1985.

Wilson, Kathleen. *The Island Race: Englishness, Empire, and Gender in the Eighteenth Century*. London: Routledge, 2003.

Winiata, Maharaia. "Leadership in pre-European Society." *Journal of the Polynesian Society*, 65 no. 3 (1956): 212–31.

Wood, Beatrice Anne. *Evangelical Balance Sheet: Character, Family, and Business in Mid-Victorian Nova Scotia*. Waterloo, Ont.: Wilfred Laurier University Press, 2006.

Woods, Gregory D. *A History of Criminal Law in New South Wales: The Colonial Period, 1788–1900*. Annandale: Federation, 2002.

Woods, Robert. *The Demography of Victorian England and Wales*. Cambridge: Cambridge University Press, 2000.

Yalom, Marilyn. *The American Resting Place: Four Hundred Years of History through Our Cemeteries and Burial Grounds*. Boston: Houghton Mifflin, 2008.

Yarwood, A. T. *Samuel Marsden: The Great Survivor*. Carlton: Melbourne University Press, 1977.

Young, D. M. *The Colonial Office in the Early Nineteenth Century*. London: Longmans, 1961.

INDEX

Baker, Charles, 80, 133, 169, 188
Baker, Hannah, 86
Banks, Joseph, 34, 36, 40, 41, 64
Bantam, 30
Baring, Francis, 240–41
Barker, Ralph, 171
Batavia, 31
Bay of Islands, 3, 14, 15, 21, 24, 73, 76, 100; British networks and, 134; Charles Darwin on, 65–67; labor in, 121; muskets in, 111; political geography of, 28–29, 62, 68, 71–73, 111, 131; prostitution in, 152; time-keeping in, 126; trading networks in, 118
Bay of Plenty, 118, 215
Bean, William, 79, 189
Bebbington, David, 105, 177, 220
Belich, James, 59, 216, 257
Bengal, 41
Best, Elsdon, 121, 175
Bewick, Thomas, 105–6
Bible, 4; Corinthians, 13, 170, 294n151; "corrupted" by missionaries, 133; and death, 188–89; Exodus, 127; Genesis, 104, 127, 133, 188–89; Luke, 48; Māori, 5–6, 144, 240, 254, 258; Mark, 44; and marriage, 170; Matthew, 208, 292n112; New Testament, 4, 6, 178; Old Testament, 4, 133, 134, 163, 188–89; Papahurihia and, 133–34; parable of the tares, 162; Romans, 153, 160, 170, 294n151; and sexuality, 153, 160, 161, 162, 170, 172–73; and transgression, 161–65
Bigge, John, 50, 231
Binney, Judith, 110, 111, 136, 154, 191, 254
Birth, 178–79
Blacksmiths, 74, 78, 90, 94, 96
Bligh, William, 55
Blood, 11, 95, 194, 208
Bobart, Henry Hodgkinson, 167, 168
Bodies, 5; arrangement of, 83; British, 7, 9; "brush of," 252–53; "in contact," 5, 6–14, 19, 25, 85, 87–88, 92, 139, 176, 216–17, 252–53; corruptibility of, 183; and cosmology, 10; and humanitarianism, 218–19; and labor, 101, 121; laceration of, 194, 200–201; materiality of, 9; "in question," 176; politics of, 216–17;

polysemic quality of, 23; reform of, 7; and sexuality, 9; on ships, 149; and the souls, 183; and travel, 85
Books, 68, 91, 163
Botany Bay, 40
Bounty Islands, 41
Bradshaw, Daniel, 105
Breasts, 208
Bridges, Charles, 177
Brind, William, 152
Britain, 19–20, 24; Anglican authorities in, 140; Benjamin Franklin on, 39; capitalism in, 116, 123; clocks in, 125; deathways in, 175, 178, 186, 187; empire's impact on, 215; grief in, 194; humanitarianism in, 218–19; military power of, 214; New Zealand resemblance, 65–66; providential role of, 44, 238; religious history of, 44; "savages" within, 105–6; scale of, 214; slavery and 116; time in, 123; William Yate in, 165
Britishness, 19, 27, 65–67, 184
Broomhall, Benjamin, 142
Broughton, W. G., 148, 149, 151, 159, 165, 188
Brown, Alfred, 117
Brown, Vincent, 176
Brown, William, 229–30
Burke, Edmund, 221
Busby, James, 154, 159, 231–34
Butler, John, 79; burials by, 186, 189; dismissal, 139; on domestic labor, 83–84; house at Kerikeri, 81; on intimacy of missionary work, 92; on labor, 114
Buxton, Thomas Fowell, 147, 234–39, 247, 248

Calcutta, 41, 53, 184
Calvinism, 138
Cambridge University, 45, 127
Campbell, Robert, 53
Cannibalism, 254; Charles Darwin on, 66–67; in *Elizabeth* affair, 229; John Butler on, 197; John Hobbs on, 197; John King on, 92; Samuel Marsden on, 227; and "savagery," 227; and social rank, 197–99; William Yate on, 147
Canning, Kathleen, 9

Cornwall, 165

Cosmology, 11, 15, 133–34, 136, 174, 190, 195–97, 202, 204, 212

Cover, J. F., 52

Creed, Charles, 171

Cross-cultural relationships, 1–2, 251–54; and death, 175–76, 179–80; as dialogues, 258–59; and discipline, 86; and empire, 1, 26; as "encounters," 17; as "entanglements," 17, 253–54, 257; and gender, 68; gifts and, 43, 70, 71, 88; and illness, 179–80; and indigenous politics, 28; and food, 85; and labor, 113–14; and literacy, 4; material aspects of, 1–2; as "meetings," 17; missionaries and, 6, 58–59; and mission stations, 70; and national histories, 16, 18; physicality of, 68, 92; religious dimensions of, 1–2; and sexuality, 107–8, 152, 171, 232; and slavery's expansion, 198–99; and trade, 3–4, 18, 111–12; and travel, 85, 87–88, 171–72; as "two worlds," 16; and violence, 31–32, 55, 64, 91–92, 107–8; and webs of empire, 24; and work, 21; written records of, 14–15

Crucifixion, 176, 177, 178, 180, 192, 193–94

Dalrymple, Alexander, 39

Darling, Ralph, 229, 236

Darwin, Charles, 64–68

Davis, Richard, 76, 80, 119–20, 153

Death, 9, 12, 16, 19, 22–23; Aboriginal practices relating to, 175; accounts of, 224–26; in Africa, 178; *Ars moriendi*, 178; atua and, 195–96, 199; in Australia, 175; "bad deaths," 178; Benjamin Yate Ashwell on, 180–82; in Britain, 175, 176, 186; in British North America, 175; and burials, 179, 185–89; in the Caribbean, 178; and childbirth, 178–79; of children, 179, 188, 189; and Christ crucified, 176, 177, 178; in colonial spaces, 175, 178; and conversion, 209–10; cross-cultural significance of, 175–76; debates over, 174; and empire, 183–84; ethnographic knowledge of, 174, 176, 189–202, 212; evangelical practices relating to, 183–89; evangelical under-standings of, 176–83; George Clarke on, 181–82; George Clarke Jr on, 183; "good deaths," 210–11, 212; and graveyards, 179, 185–88, 212, 224–25; and Hell, 178, 210; historiography of, 175–76; in India, 178; in Jamaica, 176, 186; John Wesley on, 176; killing of slaves to mark, 115; Māori deathways, 174, 175, 184–85, 189–202, 249; meaning of, 180; periodization of, 175; psychic toll of, 180; published accounts of, 207–11; of sailors, 179; and sin, 183; tapu and, 176, 184–85, 196; Thomas Haweis on, 176–77; and wāhi tapu, 184–85; William Yate on, 207–11

Deck, Dick, 149

Declaration of Independence, 232–33

Dell, Edgar Thomas, 42

De Mendaña, Alvaro, 29

Dening, Greg, 15, 16

Denison, Edward Henry, 148, 149–51, 156, 157, 159, 165–66

De Quirós, Pedro, 29

Depopulation, 218, 232

De Thierry, Baron Charles, 232

De Vries, Jan, 102–3

Dieffenbach, Ernst, 11

Disease, 9, 161, 172, 177, 178, 186

Domesticity, 84–90

Donagh, 165

Donegal, 165, 166

Donkin, Rufane Shaw, 235

Du Fresne, Marion, 57

Dundas, Henry, 38

Dusky Sound, 37–38

Earle, Augustus, 67

East India Company (British), 30, 40, 244; in Afghanistan, 215, 244; in China, 215, 244; and naval stores, 42; and the Pacific, 53; and sealing, 41; and whaling, 41–42

Economics, 98–102, 135–37; evangelicalism and, 103–6; links between agriculture and trade, 101; of mission, 106–8, 111–14; relationships shaped by indigenous mentalities, 100. *See also* Improvement; Industriousness; Labor; Trade

plundered, 91–93, 119, 185; and private trade, 110–11; precariousness of, 138; and rangatira, 14–15; as repressive, 8, 88, 138–39; responsibilities of, 22; and rumors, 139, 152; and shipping networks, 95–96; and travel, 85; vulnerability of, 57, 91–93, 107–8, 113, 119, 143, 185; and worship, 66–67, 126, 127

Missionary Notices, 223

Missionary Papers, 8, 223–27

Missionary Register, 142, 223, 227

Missionary Society. *See* London Missionary Society

Mission stations, 10, 16; as assemblages, 95–96; as culturally mixed, 21, 77–78, 85; economic base of, 77–78, 100, 108–9; as "enchanter's wands," 65–69; as "English," 67, 70; and families, 83; gendered divisions on, 85–87; graveyards, 185–86, 212; hygiene on, 87–88; as ideal communities, 69; as indexes of progress, 79; intimate quality of, 139; links between, 95; locations of, 68–77; as "meeting-up" places, 97; plans for, 69; produced by mobility, 68, 93–95; as products of cultural negotiation, 70; as symbols, 68; and tapu, 85, 132–33, 184, 212

Missionary wives, 81; anxieties of, 92; authority of, 85; and childbirth, 179–80; and gendering of mission, 85; labor of, 83–5; life expectancy of, 180; on Māori women, 89; as teachers, 81

Missionary writing, 255–56; audience for, 147; as "composed," 23, 207–11; on death, 207–11; as fundraising instruments, 15; growth of, 215–16; as hyperbolic, 147, 207; as "mobile inscriptions," 222; as propaganda, 69; publication of, 15, 146; range of, 222; strategies for reading, 14–15; stressing Europeanization, 69–70; templates for, 209, 211

Mobility, 24, 68, 97, 214, 253; and families, 143; in *A Grammar and Vocabulary of the Language of New Zealand*, 95; and intimacy, 171; of missionaries, 139, 171; and missionary stations, 93–5; of texts, 222, 251, 255–56

Moka, 132

Money, 103–4

Montefiore, Joseph Barrow, 229–30, 239–40

Moorea, 52

More, Hannah, 143, 221

Motatau, 204

Muka. See Flax

Muriwhenua, 203, 215

Murray, Sir George, 234

Muru, 57

Muskets, 4, 13, 185, 236; discharged to mark deaths, 207; Hongi Hika and 90, 111–12; and Ngāpuhi, 63, 90, 111; as payment for labor, 114; repair of, 74, 90; Samuel Marsden on, 111–12; southern iwi and, 118; trade in, 63, 74, 111–12, 118

Nākahi, 133

Naming, 53, 104, 162–63, 172, 279n24

Nanni, Giordano, 126, 134, 278n5

Natal, 244

Nesbit, Ben, 81–82

Newcastle upon Tyne, 105

New England, 175

New South Wales, 20, 27, 40–41, 45, 49, 217; Anglican authorities in 140, 157; anxieties over same-sex relationships in, 158–59; and Asia, 41, 53; and Colonial Office, 232; Crown Solicitor of, 157–60; indigenous people of, 50; Māori in, 51, 214; Māori colony in, 132; missionaries from the Pacific in, 142; and New Zealand, 41, 51, 236, 252, 257; "ocean-mindedness" in, 41; and the Pacific, 41, 53, 55, 142, 257; Samuel Marsden and, 101–2; William Yate on, 149–50; William Yate case in, 157–61

Newton, John, 45

New Zealand, annexation of, 19, 218, 233–34, 238–39, 244–49; British law in, 55, 231; as a convict colony, 38, 39; Cook "possesses," 36, 231; Dutch understandings of, 32; in evangelical imagination, 44–48, 53–58, 215–16; fertility of, 37; and

www.ingramcontent.com/pod-product-compliance
Lightning Source LLC
Chambersburg PA
CBHW051949270326
41929CB00015B/2591